THE CAMBRID
FO

M000283906

Football is the world's most popula.. .... phenomenon and a global media spectacle. For its billions of fans, it serves as a common language. But where does its enduring popularity come from? Featuring essays from prominent experts in the field, scholars and journalists, this *Companion* covers ground seldom attempted in a single volume about football. It examines the game's oft-disputed roots and traces its development through Europe, South America and Africa, analysing whether resistance to the game is finally beginning to erode in China, India and the United States. It dissects the cult of the manager and how David Beckham redefined sporting celebrity. It investigates the game's followers, reporters and writers, as well as its most zealous moneymakers and powerful administrators. A valuable resource for students, scholars and general readers, *The Cambridge Companion to Football* is a true and faithful companion for anyone fascinated by the people's game.

ROB STEEN is a journalist, sportswriter, author and Senior Lecturer in Sports Journalism at the University of Brighton.

JED NOVICK is a journalist, author and Senior Lecturer in Sports Journalism at the University of Brighton.

HUW RICHARDS is a freelance journalist, lecturer and sports historian. He is also an Honorary Visiting Research Fellow at the International Centre for Sports History and Culture, De Montfort University.

THE CAMBRIDGE COMPANION TO
FOOTBALL

EDITED BY

ROB STEEN
University of Brighton

JED NOVICK
University of Brighton

HUW RICHARDS
De Montfort University

CAMBRIDGE UNIVERSITY PRESS

CAMBRIDGE UNIVERSITY PRESS
Cambridge, New York, Melbourne, Madrid, Cape Town,
Singapore, São Paulo, Delhi, Mexico City

Cambridge University Press
32 Avenue of the Americas, New York, NY 10013-2473, USA

www.cambridge.org
Information on this title: www.cambridge.org/9781107613690

First published 2013

Printed and bound in the United Kingdom by the MPG Books Group

A catalogue record for this publication is available from the British Library.

Library of Congress Cataloguing in Publication data
The Cambridge companion to football / edited by Rob Steen, Jed Novick, Huw Richards.
pages   cm
Includes bibliographical references and index.
ISBN 978-1-107-01484-8 (hardback) – ISBN 978-1-107-61369-0 (paperback)
1. Soccer.   2. Soccer – History.   3. Soccer – Cross-cultural studies.   I. Steen, Rob,
editor of compilation.   II. Novick, Jed, editor of compilation.
III. Richards, Huw, editor of compilation.
GV943.C238   2013
796.334–dc23   2012033998

ISBN 978-1-107-01484-8 Hardback
ISBN 978-1-107-61369-0 Paperback

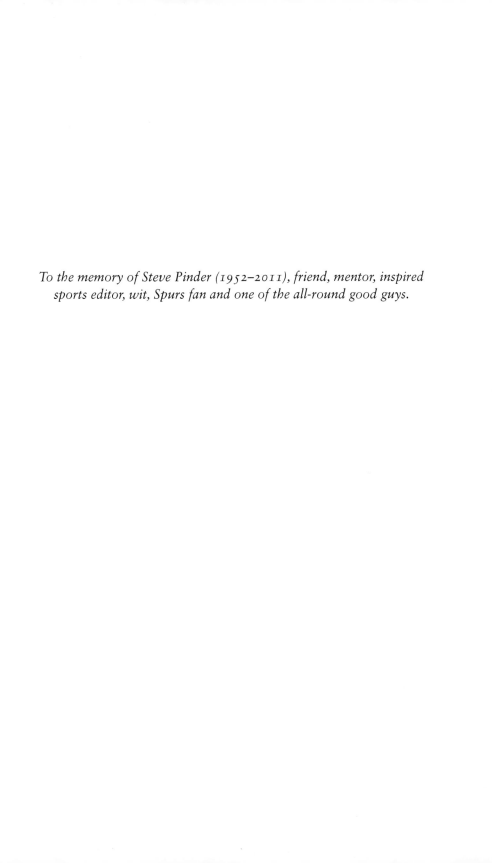

To the memory of Steve Pinder (1952–2011), friend, mentor, inspired sports editor, wit, Spurs fan and one of the all-round good guys.

CONTENTS

CONTENTS

CONTENTS

FIGURES AND TABLE

Figures

Table

CONTRIBUTORS

PADDY AGNEW is the Rome correspondent of the *Irish Times* and the Italy correspondent for *World Soccer*. Brought up in Kilrea, County Derry, Northern Ireland, he worked for the Dublin-based publications *Magill*, the *Sunday Independent* and the *Sunday Tribune* before moving to Italy, where he has lived and worked in Rome since 1986, covering news, politics, the Vatican and football, including three World Cups and five European Championship finals tournaments. He has contributed to a wide variety of news organisations including the BBC, ESPN, the *Guardian*, RAI, RTE and talkSPORT Radio. He is the author of *Forza Italia – A Journey in Search of Italy and Its Football* (2006), which was short-listed for the William Hill Irish Sports Book of the Year award.

PETER BERLIN studied politics and philosophy at the University College of Wales, Aberystwyth, and at the University of British Columbia. After freelancing at the *Daily Telegraph*, *Evening Standard*, *Evening News*, *Observer*, *Sunday Express* and BBC he settled at the *Financial Times* for seven years. For the last five he was, among other things, sports editor, then spent 15 years as sports editor of the *International Herald Tribune* before taking a buyout. He remains in Paris, blogging for *Sports Illustrated*, working on overly ambitious book projects and consulting for newspapers. He has covered four football World Cups, four European Championships, 15 seasons of the Champions League, four summer Olympics and four Rugby World Cups.

PAUL DARBY is a reader in the sociology of sport at the University of Ulster. His books include *Africa, Football and FIFA: Politics, Colonialism and Resistance* (2002) and *Gaelic Games, Nationalism and the Irish Diaspora in the United States* (2009), and he co-edited *Emigrant Players: Sport and the Irish Diaspora* (2008) with David Hassan and *Soccer and Disaster: International Perspectives* (2005) with Gavin Mellor and Martin Johnes. He sits on the editorial board of *Soccer and Society* and the advisory board of *Impumelelo: The Interdisciplinary Electronic Journal of African Sport*. He was born in Belfast, where he waits patiently and hopefully for his beloved Liverpool FC to end their league title drought.

TOBY MILLER has just returned to London from Mexico to teach at City University. His teaching and research cover the media, sport, gender, race, citizenship, politics and cultural policy, as well as Hollywood and electronic waste. His work has been translated into Chinese, Japanese, Swedish, German, Spanish and Portuguese. Among other posts, he has been Media Scholar in Residence at Sarai, the Centre for the Study of Developing Societies in India; Becker Lecturer at the University of Iowa and an international research collaborator at the Centre for Cultural Research in Australia. Author and editor of more than 30 books, he supports Leicester City and Fulham in that order, and has zero patience for Liverpool fans bleating and moaning about their pitiful history since the Cold War ended. You can follow his adventures at tobymiller.org and his podcast, 'cultural studies', on iTunes.

JED NOVICK is senior lecturer in sports journalism at the University of Brighton. He studied politics and sociology at Manchester, was trained at the BBC and has been a journalist for more years than he cares to remember. He has worked on the *Independent*, the *Times*, *Daily Express*, the *Guardian* and the *Observer*, and written 10 books, including two on football (one on the mighty Tottenham, voted the second best Spurs book ever by his mother). The finest player he ever saw was Alan Gilzean, though currently Gareth Bale is doing just fine. For more, see www.jednovick.com.

HUW RICHARDS is a London-based freelance journalist who has been a staff reporter for the *Times Higher Education Supplement*, rugby correspondent of the *Financial Times* and cricket correspondent for the *International Herald Tribune*. He has written or co-edited 10 books among which *Dragons and All Blacks* (2003) was short-listed for the William Hill Prize, *The Red and the White* (2009) for the Aberdare Prize for Sports History and the most recent was *The Swansea City Alphabet* (2009). He writes on Swansea and Wales for *When Saturday Comes* and was co-editor with Peter Stead of *For Club and Country: Welsh Footballing Greats*. He was the one contributor common to Nick Hornby's *My Favourite Year* and its rugby league counterpart *XIII Seasons*. He has a doctorate in history from the Open University, has lectured at London Metropolitan University and is an Honorary Visiting Research Fellow at the International Centre for Sports History and Culture, De Montfort University.

DAVE RUSSELL taught at schools in Bradford and Leeds, at the University of Central Lancashire and at Leeds Metropolitan University, from where he retired as professor of history and northern studies in 2010. He is a historian of popular culture with particular interest in sport, music and regional identity and has published extensively in these fields. His publications include *Popular Music in England, 1840–1914* (1997); *Football and the English* (1997) and *Looking North: Northern England and the National Imagination* (2004). He is now a freelance writer.

COLIN SHINDLER has enjoyed a wide-ranging career as a writer and producer in television, radio and motion pictures, and as an author of books and journalism for 30 years. He is best known as the screenwriter of the movie *Buster* starring Phil Collins and Julie Walters; the producer of *Lovejoy* and the author of the childhood memoir *Manchester United Ruined My Life* (1999). He has written three other books on football, including *George Best and 21 Others* (2004), and contributes regular articles on the game to the *Times* and the *Daily Mail*. In addition, he has written three novels and has been lecturing and teaching undergraduates at Cambridge University on films and American history since 1998.

PETER STEAD was born at Barry in South Wales and educated at Swansea University where he subsequently taught history for more than 30 years. He is currently a visiting professor at the University of Glamorgan and has been a Fulbright Fellow at Wellesley College, Massachusetts, and the University of North Carolina, Wilmington. He is the author of *Film and the Working Class* and *Acting Wales* as well as biographical studies of Richard Burton, Dennis Potter and Ivor Allchurch. With Huw Richards he edited *For Club and Country: Welsh Football Greats*. A writer and broadcaster, he chairs the Dylan Thomas Prize.

ROB STEEN is a sportswriter and senior lecturer in sports journalism at the University of Brighton. Formerly *Sunday Times* deputy sports editor and co-editor of *Full Time*, the last London Saturday classified newspaper, he has also written for, among others, the *Guardian*, *Financial Times*, the *Independent*, *India Today* and the *Melbourne Age*. Runner-up for the 1991 William Hill Prize and winner of the 1995 Cricket Society Literary Award, he won the UK section of the 2005 EU Journalism Award 'for diversity, against discrimination' and has written/edited 23 books, including *Sports Journalism: A Multimedia Primer* (2007) and *The Mavericks: English Football When Flair Wore Flares* (1994) – No. 39 in *FourFourTwo*'s '50 Football Books You Must Read'. Alone in contributing to both the *Cambridge Companion* to cricket and to football, he is currently writing a history of spectator sport, *Competitive Arts*. He supported Chelsea until the hooligans prompted a divorce. For more, see http://sites.google.com/site/bodaciouscom/.

CHRIS TAYLOR is a writer and journalist who has travelled extensively in Latin America since the 1970 Brazil team fired his imagination. After more than 20 years' experience at the *Guardian* in London he now lives and works in New York and is the author of the widely acclaimed *The Beautiful Game: A Journey through Latin American Football*. Translated into German and Japanese, it was described as 'superb' by the *Wall Street Journal* and 'the most convincing attempt yet at capturing the eclecticism and colour of South American football' by *FourFourTwo*. His latest book, *The Black Carib Wars: Freedom, Survival and the Making of the Garifuna*, was published in 2012 by Signal Books (UK) and by the University Press of Mississippi.

WILL TIDEY is the author of *Life with Sir Alex: A Fan's Story of Ferguson's 25 Years at Manchester United* (2011) and serves as world football editor/lead writer at the popular North American sports website Bleacher Report. A graduate in sports journalism from the University of Brighton, he is also a regular contributor to ESPNsoccernet and now lives in Wilmington, North Carolina, with his wife and their two children.

ALAN TOMLINSON is professor of leisure studies, and director of research and development (social sciences) at the University of Brighton as well as a qualified FA coach and referee. A pioneer of the critical social scientific study of sport, he is the author/editor of numerous books on sport, leisure and consumption, including *Consumption, Identity and Style* (1990); *Sport and Leisure Cultures* (2005); *A Dictionary of Sports Studies* (2010) and *The World Atlas of Sport* (2011). He has written for the *Financial Times, New Statesman, New York Times, When Saturday Comes, Gulf News* and *Der Taggesspiegel*, and contributed to BBC Radio, *Panorama*, BBC World Service, Radio Vienna, New York Public Radio and Canadian and Australian national radio. He was born in Burnley, Lancashire, and continues to follow Burnley FC.

JON VALE is a freelance sports journalist whose work has appeared in the *Guardian,* the *Express* and *thetimes.co.uk*. He reached the final four of the NCTJ Awards for Excellence in sports journalism in 2011 and has previously edited two student publications, *The Verse* and *overtimeonline.co.uk*, as well as contributing articles on all manner of subjects to the award-winning student blog *thestudentjournals.co.uk*. He also edits the training section of the Sports Journalists' Association website and offers advice to prospective sports journalists at *globalsportsjobs.com*. He graduated in sports journalism from the University of Brighton in 2012.

JIM WHITE is a columnist at the *Daily Telegraph*, writing mainly on sport. He is a regular participant on BBC Radio 5's *Fighting Talk* and Radio 4's *Saturday Review* and also wrote for the now-defunct *Word* magazine. The author of *Manchester United: The Biography* (2009), he has written and presented numerous television and radio documentaries, including two on José Mourinho and Sven-Göran Eriksson. He has also presented Scottish TV's Champions League coverage. Most weekends, he can be found on the touchline of council pitches, forlornly attempting to corral junior football teams into winning shape, a humiliation he describes in his memoir *You'll Win Nothing with Kids: Fathers, Sons and Football* (2008). Of the under-13 side he has recently been coaching he says this: 'It's not like watching Brazil.'

JEAN WILLIAMS is a senior research Fellow in the International Centre for Sports History and Culture, De Montfort University, Leicester. She has completed international projects funded by FIFA and UEFA, most recently an assessment of female player migration in *Women's Football, Europe and Professionalization 1971–2011* (2013), the first work to give an assessment of the women's game in each of UEFA's 53 member associations. The author of *A Game for Rough*

Girls: A History of Women's Football in England (2003) and *A Beautiful Game: International Perspectives on Women's Football* (2007), her latest projects include a research monograph called *A Contemporary History of Women's Sport* (2013) and a monograph on Britain's women Olympians (2014).

JOHN WILLIAMS is a senior lecturer in sociology at the University of Leicester. His most recent books include *Red Men: Liverpool Football Club, the Biography* (2010) and (with Andrew Ward) *Football Nation: Sixty Years of the Beautiful Game* (2009). His latest research projects include a socio-historical study of the Special Olympics movement in Britain and academic articles on football culture in Italy, football club ownership and fan activism, racism in football and (with Stacey Pope) on contemporary female sports fans. Born in Liverpool, he spends most of his winter Saturdays (and often – courtesy of Sky Sports – Sundays, Mondays, Thursdays, etc.) watching and analyzing the fortunes of Liverpool FC, where he continues to be a Kop season ticket-holder.

FOREWORD

My father first took me to Oakwell to watch Barnsley play when I was five. At half-time he asked me my opinion. I said: 'It's alright but I think I'd rather be at home.' Being a sensible and humorous man he interpreted my remark as an indication I possessed that sense of the ridiculous so necessary in a follower of football. We stayed and I was condemned to a life as a football fan, a condition so parlous it can lead to madness and for which there is no cure.

Once, in the days before instant communication, I read in the stop press of a Los Angeles paper the scoreline Barnsley 1 Stockport County 21 and spent a fortune before discovering the truth – we drew one-all – and throwing a party.

Since that day in 1940 I have followed the game to the most seductive of settings; I have travelled to and fro by private jet, limousine and a couple of times by gondola. I have met and talked with my heroes, become friendly with a few.

I have seen many wondrous things to justify my lifelong love but have also been dismayed by the manner in which the simple game of my youth has been transformed from a rough-and-tumble working-class pastime to a plaything for the very rich.

In 70 years of watching football, sometimes writing about it and now being required to analyse the evidence and make sense out of it all, I find it easier to explain its attraction to the child rather than define the growing doubts I nowadays have about a game I still love but not like I once did. The main reason is you can list the advances made in modern football – the fitness, the technical ability of the players, the improved stadia, the global presentation and glamourisation of the game as shown on TV – but what you can't claim is that the game is as much fun as it used to be.

In the 1950s, when Barnsley had been relegated to the Third Division North (and, even then, struggled), our manager Angus Seed was seen carrying a gramophone into the ground. A supporter looked enquiringly at the instrument. Noting his interest Mr Seed explained: 'I got it for the team.'

'Tha's been robbed,' said the fan.

As I write, it is calculated that Roman Abramovich's dream of Chelsea winning the European Cup cost him in excess of £1 billion. Manchester City's ambition to win the Premier League cost about the same to Sheikh Mansour, give or take a Balotelli or two.

Once you could touch your heroes, even after George Best transformed the footballer into a pop star. Best was made for the sixties, rock 'n' roll and Carnaby Street. He was a glorious footballer with the looks of a film star and a love of drink which finished him off before his time. But he was the template for footballers becoming showbiz stars in a celebrity culture. He was David Beckham's godfather.

Beckham, like most of them nowadays, is a multi-millionaire. Best, Bobby Charlton, Denis Law, Paddy Crerand and the rest of the team that won the European Cup were beggars by comparison. Nowadays there are mere unsung apprentices on the books of Manchester United earning more than they did.

What else has changed? I read the other day that during a Premier League game players run the equivalent of a half-marathon in 90 minutes' play. In the Barnsley side of my youth I doubt the accumulated work rate of the entire team would get them anywhere near that commitment. We had one player, Jimmy Baxter, who wouldn't have run the distance of a half-marathon in his entire career.

He was a wispy, pale man; a waif-like figure who looked like he lived on a diet of chips, cigs and Barnsley Bitter. He regarded running as a waste of time and concentrated on letting the ball do the work. He was a sublime artist with the ball, creating angles and openings with the geometric precision of a great snooker player on a maximum break. We sold him to Preston North End, where he played alongside Tom Finney and his talent was not diminished by comparison with one of the greatest players ever produced by these islands.

The England team of that time – I'm talking late 40s–early 50s – had one size kit so large that Sir Tom Finney told me his socks reached to the top of his thighs and his shirt and shorts were so baggy that when it rained he became waterlogged and unable to move. For his 76 internationals he was paid between £20 and £50 per match and a second-class rail ticket.

He still lives in Preston, where he was born. When I interviewed him and stopped a local to ask him where Tom Finney lived, he walked in front of my car for two streets like a chief mourner and brought me to the front door. 'A hero and a gentleman,' he said, by way of explanation. Tom Finney was a fine working-class product, a street footballer who learned his craft in a back alley. Nothing fancy. Certainly not glamorous.

I once turned out for a local team where our trainer did a deal to buy the T-shirts of a passing circus act fallen on hard times. Thus as an old-fashioned centre-forward I didn't have No. 9 on my back but 'Ramon The Dwarf'. My team-mates included 'Sheba and Her Pythons' and 'Carlos The Fire Eater'.

At the time I was writing for a local paper and reporting on my own performances. Headlines like 'Hot Shot Parkinson Strikes Again' or 'Hat-Trick Mike on the Goal Trail' began to attract scouts from local clubs. Coming off the field I heard one scout say to another: 'Well that was a wasted journey.' In that moment I decided I'd be better observing the game than playing it.

There was plenty of good material to write about at Barnsley. There was Johnny Kelly, our left-winger, who had pace, skill and a left foot capable of crossing the ball with the lace facing wherever the centre-forward desired it. He so diddled a Southampton full-back called Alf Ramsey that he changed the face of English football.

When he became the England manager Sir Alf produced his 'wingless wonders', based not so much on tactical inspiration as hatred of players like Johnny Kelly who had made his life a misery. Mr Kelly supplemented his £8-a-week wage by inventing a liquid bleach called 'Kelzone', which he was often seen delivering from the back of a lorry.

Similarly, Beaumont Asquith, another hero of my youth, had a milk round. Thus the player with a name more suitable for a Victorian novelist or an adventurer who climbed Everest in a Harris tweed jacket while smoking a pipe, became the first celebrity milkman. Statements like: 'I used to get my milk from the Co-Op but nowadays it's delivered by Beaumont Asquith' became commonplace on the terraces. Fans spoke of little else.

All else apart, Beaumont was a fine footballer and the best penalty taker I've ever seen. He always hit the bottom corner and with a flick of the hips would often send his goalkeeper the wrong way.

He once fooled Sam Bartram, the Charlton and England keeper, provoking Sam, a redhead of fiery disposition, to kick the ball over the stand and into the road. Whereupon our trainer shouted: 'Ayup Sam, tha's buggered it. That's only ball we've got.' And, being wartime, it was.

During my early apprenticeship as a journalist for the local paper I was much influenced by American writers like Ernest Hemingway, John Steinbeck and Scott Fitzgerald. Barnsley had a player called Roy Cooling, a blonde handsome lad, and I wrote in my report 'Roy Cooling, who bears a distinct resemblance to F. Scott Fitzgerald ...' This appeared in the paper as 'Roy Cooling, who bears a distinct resemblance to Scott of the Antarctic ...' When I asked why it had been changed, the editor pointed out that in Barnsley and environs more people were likely to have heard of the explorer than the writer.

The commentator who best captured those days when the link between football and the community was based on a shared experience was H.D. 'Donny' Davies of the *Guardian* and BBC Sports Report.

He began one report in the *Manchester Guardian* (as it was then): 'Happy is said to be the family which can eat onions together. They are for the time being separate from the world and have a harmony of aspiration. So it was with the scoring of goals at Old Trafford on Saturday.'

He told us of the man on the terraces at Bolton who, observing one player having a poor game, asked: 'Why doesn't he learn how to dribble? He's got nothing else to do.'

He reported a penalty-kick of such ferocity that when it struck the iron crossbar it made the metal frame 'hum like a tuning fork'.

Relating a bad day for Manchester City he said: 'City's defence are a fine statuesque lot. But what's the good of that? Albert Square is full of 'em.'

Of the great creative player Wilf Mannion he wrote: 'Mannion is Mozartian in his exquisite workmanship. His style is so graceful and so courtly that he wouldn't be out of place if he played in a lace ruffle and the Perruque.'

There are writers today who can match Mr Davies for style and humour. Indeed, some of the most memorable and perceptive writing in all of journalism is achieved by those who pursue a career once defined by an editor who knew no better as 'the toy department'.

Sadly, Mr Davies's demonstrations of the broadcaster's art appear not to have reached the TV commentary box where, with one or two exceptions, vocabulary is limited. There is another word for 'pressure' – strain, stress, tension, hassle all come to mind. There are alternatives for 'unbelievable'. Can I suggest astonishing, astounding, inconceivable, incredible? That oft-repeated phrase 'He's on fire' is simply banal and worthy of a red card.

There is an argument which says the commentators represent the speech and mores of the terraces. In which case, God help us all. It wasn't always thus. In the days when home and away fans were not kept in separate pens and were allowed to fraternise I watched Barnsley play Chesterfield standing next to a couple of away fans. In the closing minutes, with the scores level, Chesterfield had a penalty. Tommy Capel, the Chesterfield skipper, invited his brother to take the kick, which he missed by a fair distance, whereupon one Chesterfield fan turned to the other and said sorrowfully: 'Nepotism, bloody nepotism.'

Similarly, we had a centre-half at Barnsley who scored so many own goals our centre-forward was designated to mark him at corners in our own penalty area. He had a brief career and the end came when he was concussed during an attempt at another home goal and, as our trainer raced on to help, there came a cry from the terraces: 'Don't revive him, bury him.'

Nowadays no-one watching a game can be anything other than sickened at the way players disrespect each other, fake contact, dive, roll in agony to con the referee to get a fellow professional in trouble. It's called cheating and it is far and away the most unattractive aspect of modern football.

It was better when it was a game which allowed genuine physical contact and when every team had one known hard man. These were the pantomime villains of the game, hissed and booed as they went about their business. One of the best was Sydney Bycroft who, during a long career as a centre-half from the 30s to the 50s, put the frighteners on any team visiting Doncaster and thinking they would survive the encounter unscathed. He was also a special constable and often, when playing away and anticipating a rough reception from home fans after a game, would appear before the mob wearing his constable's uniform saying: 'Now lads, can I help you?'

I write of a lost world, one which gave me excitement, laughter and a lifetime of memories with which to bore my grandchildren. I take two of them – aged eight and nine – to watch Reading play and wonder what they make of it. I look at them and observe the way the game, for all its changes, still continues to enchant succeeding generations. The genius of football is its simplicity. All you need is something resembling a ball and a patch of spare ground and you have a game.

Is there a male spectator at a football game who has never kicked a ball? I doubt you can make the same claim of those attending other games.

There are, however, many other reasons that people go to football. Some go to fight, some to sing bawdy songs, some to abuse the opposition, some to make mischief, all of them to present the ugly face of our society.

Others – many more – go because the game gives them colour and humour and the joy which comes from watching athletes performing at their limits with grace and style. To observe Lionel Messi at play is to be both thrilled and baffled by genius, as it was with Best and Finney and John Charles and those great entertainers who succeeded them.

What do my grandchildren gain from the game, what memories will they carry through life? Will they, in 50 years' time, be as nostalgic as I? Will they perhaps share my disenchantment as they get older? I hope so. For all the frustrations I feel about some aspects of modern football, for all I mourn the passing of fun and humour in the name of 'commercial progress', I'm glad that all those many years ago my father didn't take me home at half-time.

Looking back at our long and loving relationship, I think it might have been one of the best decisions a wise father made on my behalf. A real and lasting legacy.

Sir Michael Parkinson, in his capacity as talk show host par excellence, has interviewed two footballing knights, Matt Busby and Bobby Charlton, as well as David Beckham, George Best and Brian Clough. He wrote acclaimed sports columns for the **Sunday Times** *and the* **Daily Telegraph** *and his books include* **Football Daft** *and* **Best: An Intimate Biography***. He still supports Barnsley.*

CHRONOLOGY

Of necessity, this is a selective guide. The intention is not to list every significant development in the entire history of football but to attempt to cover important or revealing ones not addressed in the ensuing chapters (though occasionally, honourable exceptions are made, such as the Bosman case and the Hillsborough disaster). We have endeavoured to trace and note the formation of a nation's first major club *only*.

Second and Third Centuries BC: Earliest form of football for which there is scientific evidence – an exercise from a military manual found in China.

1848	First rules drawn up at Cambridge University.
1855	Formation of Sheffield, oldest club still in existence.
1862	Formation of purported first club outside England – Oneida FC, Boston, USA.
1863	Formation, in London, of the Football Association, the first governing body; Cambridge Rules rewritten to provide the first uniform regulations.
1865	Tape stretched across the goals 8 ft (2.4 m) from the ground.
1866	Offside law changed to allow players to be onside provided there are three players between ball and goal.
1869	Goal-kicks introduced; handling outlawed.
1871	Inaugural FA Cup; goalkeepers first mentioned in the Laws.
1872	First international match – Scotland v England at Hampden Park, Glasgow; size of ball fixed; corner kick introduced.
1873	Rangers FC and Scottish FA formed; Scottish Cup begins.

1874	Shinguards introduced.
1875	Crossbar replaces tape at top of goalposts.
1876	Formation of Denmark's Kjøbenhavns Boldklub, Continental Europe's first club.
1877	The London Association and the Sheffield Association agree on rules; player allowed to charge an opponent if facing his own goal; Welsh Cup begins.
1878	Manchester United founded as Newton Heath; umpires use a whistle for the first time.
1882	Associations in Great Britain unify their rules and form the International Football Association Board (IFAB) to control them; two-handed throw-in introduced.
1883	First British International Championship.
1885	Professionalism legalized in England; first international not involving British teams – USA v Canada.
1887	Hamburg FC founded.
1888	Football League formed; Celtic FC founded.
1889	Barcelona CF, Koninklijke Nederland Voetbalbond (Dutch FA) and Dansk Boldspil-Union (Danish FA) formed.
1891	Introduction of the penalty-kick; referees and linesmen replace umpires; Penarol (Uruguay) founded.
1892	South African FA founded.
1893	Sparta Prague, FC Porto and Asociacion del Futbol Argentino (Argentine FA) founded; Scotland adopts professionalism.
1895	Federacion de Futbol de Chile (Chilean FA), Union Royale Belge des Societes de Football-Association (Belgian FA) and Schweizerischer Fussballverband (Swiss FA) formed; maximum width of goalposts and crossbar set at 5 in.
1897	Juventus founded.
1898	English Players' Union formed; Federazione Italiana-Giuoco Calcio (Italian FA) founded.

1899	L'Olympique de Marseille and Rapid Vienna founded.
1900	Ajax Amsterdam, Asociación Uruguaya de Futbol (Uruguayan FA) and Deutscher Fussball-Bund (German FA) formed; Jack Hillman, the Burnley goalkeeper, is banned for a year after attempting to bribe Nottingham Forest.
1901	First international in South America: Uruguay 2 Argentina 3; River Plate and Magyar Labdarugo Szovetseg (Hungarian FA) founded.
1902	Real Madrid founded; terracing collapses during Scotland-England match at Ibrox Park, Glasgow, killing 25.
1904	FIFA founded in Paris by Belgium, Denmark, France, The Netherlands, Spain, Sweden and Switzerland; Osterreicher Fussball-Bund (Austrian FA) and Svensk Fotbollförbundet (Swedish FA) founded; Glossop, from the English Second Division, fined £250 for wholesale mismanagement and deception, with four directors and six players suspended.
1905	Goalkeepers instructed to remain on goal-line for penalty-kicks.
1906	Asociación Paraguaya de Futbol (Paraguayan FA) founded.
1907	Philippine Football Federation founded.
1908	London stages inaugural Olympic tournament.
1909	George Parsonage of Fulham banned sine die for requesting a £50 signing-on fee from Chesterfield.
1912	Goalkeepers prohibited from handling outside the penalty area.
1913	FIFA joins IFAB; Real Federation Espanola de Futbol (Spanish FA) and United States Soccer Federation formed; defenders instructed not to encroach within 10 yards at free-kicks.
1914	Brazilian Football Confederation founded.
1916	South American Confederation (CONMEBOL) and Football Association of Thailand founded.

1918   Fédération Française de Football (French FA) founded.

1919   Leeds City expelled from Football League for making illegal payments; Fudbalski Savez Jugoslavije (Yugoslav FA) and Federation Zaireoise de Football-Association (Zaire FA) formed.

1920   Football Federation of the Islamic Republic of Iran founded; players no longer liable to be given offside at throw-in.

1921   All Ettihad el Masri Li Korat el Kadam (Egyptian FA) founded.

1922   Moscow Spartak, Russian Football Federation, the Football Federation of the National Olympic Committee (Afghanistan FA) and Federacion Peruana de Futbol (Peruvian FA) founded.

1923   First Wembley FA Cup final watched by 123,000 with as many again locked out; inception of Football Pools, inviting public to predict results for prize money.

1924   Football Association of the People's Republic of China and Federation of Uganda Football Association founded; scoring permitted direct from a corner.

1925   Offside rule amended – two rather than three players to be between attacker and goal; throw-ins to be taken with both feet on the touchline.

1927   Sparta Prague win inaugural Mitropa Cup; Kiev Dynamo and Federacion Mexicana de Futbol Asociacion (Mexican FA) founded; first FA Cup final broadcast on radio.

1928   British Associations leave FIFA over payments to 'amateurs'; Arsenal make Bolton's David Jack subject of the first £10,000 transfer fee.

1929   Football Association of Zambia founded; goalkeepers to stay still until penalty-kick taken.

1930   Uruguay hosts first FIFA World Cup.

1932   Soccer removed from the Olympic programme in Los Angeles after FIFA and the IOC squabble over definition of amateurism.

1934   Expanded to 16 nations (from a 32-strong qualification series), World Cup finals restructured as a straight knockout.

1937   All India Football Federation founded; ball increased from 13–15 oz (368–425 g) to 14–16 oz (397–454 g); arc added outside penalty area.

1938   Laws redrafted by FA secretary Stanley Rous.

1939   Compulsory numbering of players' shirts for English League matches.

1945   Nigeria Football Association and Football Association of the Democratic People's Republic of Korea founded.

1946   British associations rejoin FIFA.

1947   Santiago Bernabeu stadium opens in Madrid; Steaua Bucharest founded.

1949   Air disaster near Turin kills Torino's Italian championship-winning team.

1950   United States beat England 1–0 at the World Cup finals, restored to a pool/group format.

1951   Obstruction punishable by an indirect free-kick; studs to project 3/4 in. (19 mm) instead of 1/2 in. (13 mm).

1954   Union des Associations Européennes de Football (UEFA) founded in Basle; Estadio Da Luz (Stadium of Light) opens in Lisbon.

1955   European Cup of Champions and Inter-Cities Fairs Cup (later UEFA Cup) begin.

1956   Real Madrid win inaugural European Cup, South Korea the first Asia Cup; first floodlit match in England (Portsmouth v Newcastle); Stanley Matthews voted first European Footballer of the Year (Ballon D'Or).

1957   Nou Camp opens in Barcelona; Egypt win first African Nations Cup in Khartoum; Ghana Football Association founded.

1958   Munich air disaster kills eight Manchester United players flying home from a European Cup tie; in Sweden, Brazil become the first to win a World Cup outside their own continent; Barcelona win the first Inter-Cities Fairs Cup; substitutes permitted for injured goalkeeper and one other injured player; Everton introduce undersoil heating.

1960   Russia win first European Nations Cup final, the Henri Delaunay Trophy; Penarol win inaugural Copa Libertadores; Real Madrid beat Penarol to win the first World Club Cup; Federation Camerounaise de Football (Cameroon FA) founded.

1961   Fiorentina win inaugural European Cup–Winners' Cup; maximum wage abolished in England, where Johnny Haynes becomes the first £100-per-week player; Australian Soccer Federation founded.

1963   Football League's retain and transfer system declared illegal.

1964   More than 300 killed and 500 injured in rioting during Olympic qualifying game in Lima between Peru and Argentina; *Match of the Day* debuts on British TV.

1965   Stanley Matthews becomes the first player to be knighted; 10 League players jailed and banned for life by the FA for match-fixing in relation to the Treble Chance, a competition instituted by pools companies.

1966   English football's finest two hours: Bobby Moore receives the Jules Rimet Trophy at Wembley after Geoff Hurst scores the first hat-trick in a World Cup final.

1967   Football League authorizes player loans.

1970   Red and yellow cards introduced at the 1970 World Cup finals in Mexico, where Brazil take the Jules Rimet Trophy for the third time, and hence keep it.

1971   Arminia Bielefeld officials found guilty of putting up £90,000 to fix four West German League games; 66 fans die during Rangers-Celtic game at Ibrox Park.

1972   Spanish FA ends 10-year ban on imported players.

1973   Johan Cruyff (Ajax to Barcelona) becomes the first £1 million signing.

1974   Joao Havelange replaces Sir Stanley Rous as FIFA president; Polish players accuse Italian opponents of offering money to lose a World Cup match in Stuttgart; FA Amateur Cup abolished.

1975   Leeds United banned from European competition for two years after fans riot during European Cup final in Paris.

1976   Czechoslovakia beat West Germany on penalties to win the European Championship – first major final to be so decided.

1978   Argentina beat Holland in Buenos Aires to win the World Cup amid allegations over the credibility of a crucial 6–0 victory over Peru; English FA lifts ban on foreign players; Football League recognizes freedom of contract and introduces transfer tribunal.

1980   Paolo Rossi, the world's best-paid player, is among more than 30 Italians banned for match-fixing.

1982   World Cup finals in Spain feature 24 nations; 340 Russian supporters crushed to death in Moscow's Lenin Stadium during UEFA Cup tie.

1985   Liverpool supporters riot before the European Cup final against Juventus at the Heysel Stadium, Brussels, causing 39 deaths (31 Italian), 437 injuries and English clubs to be banned from European competition for five years; 56 fans die as a wooden stand burns down at Bradford City's Valley Parade.

1986   Roma banned from European competitions for a season after president Dino Viola tries to bribe a referee in a European Cup semi-final.

1988   More than 40 Hungarian players and officials arrested following match-fixing allegations.

1989   Ninety-five fans crushed to death at Hillsborough during FA Cup semi-final between Liverpool and Nottingham Forest.

1990   Offside law changed: attacker now *onside* if level with penultimate defender; 'professional' fouls to be punished by dismissal.

1991	Inaugural Women's World Cup in China; Lothar Matthäus (Germany) voted first FIFA World Footballer of the Year.
1992	Goalkeepers forbidden from handling back-passes; England and Germany play first indoor international at the Pontiac Silverdome near Detroit, Michigan, United States.
1993	Marseille banned from defending the European Cup for bribery; Zambian national team die in a plane crash.
1994	World Cup held in the United States, where the final, between Brazil and Italy, is settled by a penalty shootout for the first time; 'technical area' incorporated into the Laws.
1995	European Court of Justice upholds Bosman ruling, halting transfer fees for out-of-contract players; 'fourth official' introduced.
1996	Linesmen become 'assistant referees'; United States win first Olympic women's soccer gold medal.
1997	Laws revised.
2002	First World Cup in Asia (Japan and South Korea).
2010	First World Cup in Africa (South Africa); Russia (2018) and Qatar (2022) awarded World Cup hosting rights. Bribery allegations and plans to stage the latter tournament in winter horrify everyone from Arsène Wenger to Barack Obama.
2012	Former Peruvian senator Genaro Ledesma claims during an extradition hearing in Buenos Aires that Argentina's 6–0 controversial victory over Peru, which earned them a place in the 1978 World Cup final and had long been the subject of match-fixing allegations, resulted from a deal struck between General Jorge Videla and Peru's military ruler, General Francisco Morales Bermúdez. Mr Ledesma alleged that the latter had agreed to throw the match as part of 'Operation Condor', a clandestine plan cooked up by the leaders to help each other dispose of troublesome activists … The Hampshire Senior Cup final, first played in 1888, the year of the Football League's inception, becomes the first match to deploy goal-line technology.
2014	World Cup finals return to Brazil.

ALAN TOMLINSON

'And did those feet…': Introduction

The Adaptable Game

Football attracts some of the biggest media audiences in the world, for quadrennial spectaculars such as the men's FIFA World Cup, and annual showpieces such as the UEFA Champions League. The accumulative global audience, including the most casual and passing of viewers, for the South Africa 2010 World Cup was reported by FIFA to be 3.2 billion, 46.4 per cent of the world population; those catching longer chunks of action (20 minutes or more) numbered 2.2 billion, 530.9 million of whom watched the final, with those catching a minute or more of the final numbering 909.6 million (FIFA, 2011). The Champions League final between Barcelona and Manchester United in Rome in 2009 attracted a bigger global audience, 206 million, than that year's Super Bowl. This global football business has spawned superstars and millionaires, and created a nouveau riche class of celebrity sportsmen willing to travel the world in response to the lucrative contract.

But however global the apex of the game has gone, football still preserves its local identity, fostering tribal loyalties and community attachments. One of the underlying appeals of sport is that it can prosper in local, regional, national, international and global contexts; and football, the world's most popular sport, thrives at all of these levels. You can play for the local parks team, watch your city's professional outfit, cheer on the national side, admire teams from across the world, and revel in the simplicity and accessibility of the game. There are many dimensions to football at all of these levels, but when you see Zinedine Zidane volley the winning goal in a European final, he does not appear as some form of special species. You could be him, if only you'd had that inspirational teacher, that patient coach, the time and the opening in life and on the pitch. Many sports offer the opportunity for this mix of 'if only' vicariousness and wish-fulfilment. Arguably, football allows this more than most other sports, and the secret to this is the game's fundamental simplicity, in conception and execution. Sport draws us into a form of what Hans-Ulrich Gumbrecht (2006) has called a state of being lost in 'focused intensity', as we are at one with the performer or competitor, willing him/her on, being him/her. The Zidane volley was not just the sublime skill of the supreme player producing the perfect response at a critical moment; it was a shared experience of the collection of individuals lucky enough to be there and so able to say 'I was there', each time with a smile of privileged contentment, as long as the memory lasts.

The Unjust Game

Football is a form of culture, made in and by the collective watching of the event, the follow-up argument and analysis, the folklore that is passed down from generations. It is soap opera on grass, providing main narratives, sidelines, unlikely diversions, wonderful arrays of character. And it can defy logic and all attempts at rational analysis, a great sporting arena for the David and Goliath giant-killing trope. The most admired and feared team might lose its nerve, superstition and fatalism outweighing resources and talent. More and more, in a time of instantly available statistical breakdowns of performance, match analysis on the spot, technological assistance and psychological preparation, top football professionals make excuses for defeat, blaming referees and officials, fixture schedules and international commitments.

But it is one of the glories in football to see 11 versus 11 in a sport rooted in low-scoring. When the World Cup went to the United States in 1994, some seriously suggested that the goals should be made bigger, to provide higher scores for the U.S. public in particular. Even FIFA, or more accurately the International Football Association Board established in 1885 to harmonize interpretation of rules for 'Home Nations' international games within the United Kingdom, and to this day still the institutional body in charge of the laws of the game, resisted this crass proposal. The magnificence of a 0–0 draw might bypass those indifferent to the game or concerned only with high-scoring high-five achievers; but the epic defence against opponents of clearly superior technical skill, the match-of-a-lifetime performance by the underdog's goalkeeper, can provide rivetingly tense spectacle. The best teams can lose on the day, and two such losses are etched in World Cup history: Hungary's defeat by West Germany at the Miracle of Berne in 1954 and Holland's defeat by West Germany in Munich 20 years later.

The Simplest Game

A fundamental simplicity has fostered the transmission of the game across cultures and through time, so whatever style of play has been adopted or tactical innovation put in place, football has remained recognizable and familiar to its massive and culturally varied fan base. Go anywhere in the world with a ball and you won't be alone. Go into any bar with an opinion about football and you'll find a friend. On the streets, on the beach, anything will do. You don't need a pitch or any fancy kit. Two jumpers for goalposts and a pair of rolled-up gloves or an old coke can – anything will do. And that's the point.

The continuing attraction of football lies in the core features of what the pioneer John Charles Thring called 'the simplest game': football can be played at its highest level of excellence by a short and stocky figure such as Argentinean Diego Maradona, or by physically deformed Brazilian Garrincha, as well as by mercurial bad boys such as George Best. Its principles are simple, its equipment minimal, its dramas flowing and focused. We all know what it is: and yet we can all argue over Brazilian or Argentinean style, German pragmatics or French hubris, Italian ruthlessness or Dutch prima-donnism, Cameroonian indiscipline or English doggedness. It brings players of varied cultural backgrounds together in teams of global appeal, a metaphor for cosmopolitanism and cross-cultural harmony, yet it can still be a catalyst for local club loyalties and national passions. The simple game, the beautiful game, the bountiful game, feeds the diet of the fan worldwide. In international media markets, football may look to have reached peak after peak, yet still, 'final' frontiers are exceeded, and the saturation point that some commentators and analysts believe to have been reached continues to be stretched to new limits (Hamil and Chadwick, 2010).

The International Game

Football's first international match was a goalless Scotland-England encounter in 1872. It was in 1904, though, with the formation of the world governing body La Fédération Internationale de Football Association (FIFA), that a framework for truly international competition began to emerge (Sugden and Tomlinson 1998), though domestic football satisfied many national associations and it was not until 1930 that the first men's football World Cup was held, in Uruguay. The first international staged outside the British Isles was the United States–Canada match in 1885; the first in South America in 1901, between Uruguay and Argentina; South America also staged the first official international tournament, the inaugural Copa America, in 1916, the year which also saw the formation of the continent's confederation, CONMEBOL (Mason 1995; Miller and Crolley 2007). It was mid-Europe's Mitropa Cup, from 1927, that provided organized international competition for clubs; in the same year, Austria, Czechoslovakia, Hungary, Italy and Switzerland played for the Dr Gero Cup, in a tournament conceived as a Europe, International and/or Nations Cup.

British associations had withdrawn from both the Amsterdam Olympics and FIFA in 1928, in relation to issues of Olympic eligibility and principles of amateurism. In the absence of the self-isolating British, the growth of world football assumed an increasingly all-embracing international profile. The European association, UEFA (Union Européennes de Football Association), was established in 1954, followed by other continental federations for Africa, Asia, the Central Americas/Caribbean and Oceania. The growth of the game worldwide – imported into many countries initially by military personnel, migrant international workers, educators and colonial elites from Britain – has been phenomenal, and football is widely recognised as the world's most popular game, in terms of both participation and the fan-base for the professional game. Conservative authorities and associations have held back the development of women's football at different historical points, and effective levels of sponsorship prove difficult to secure and sustain for the professional women's game. The dominant men's form, though, has become increasingly visible in the international spotlight.

The Ugly Game

Football needs fans and clearly many fans need football. At its best, sport spectatorship is a positive affirmation of community or of the collective passion of a population. At its worst, football provides a front for anti-social sentiment and prejudice (Merkel and Tokarski 1996), as in the case of football hooliganism involving fans of clubs and national sides. This emerged in British professional football crowds or groups of supporters in the late 1960s and became a serious social problem in the 1980s. It exploited the collective passion of the game and stimulated group-based forms of aggressive and sometimes violent behaviour, widely but by no means exclusively associated with young-adult, white working-class males.

Social psychological studies have stressed the ritualistic dimensions of football hooliganism and the career stages through which young hooligans pass in becoming inducted into the culture (Marsh et al. 1978). Sociological studies have emphasised the socio-economic context out of which hooligans emerge – the displaced generations, for instance, of de-industrializing areas and regions, for whom identification with the team in the aggressive hooligan fashion becomes an alternative source for the expression of manhood and a traditional tough form of masculinity. Eric Dunning and his colleagues in the Leicester School and researchers at the University of Birmingham's Centre for Contemporary Cultural Studies were the most prominent among these researchers (Dunning 1999; Dunning et al. 1986; Clarke 1973). Football hooliganism has been a genuinely threatening social issue, but it has also been the focus of moral panics in the media and the wider society, and, when its incidence and nature have been exaggerated, has fuelled deviance amplification. The image of a dart in a fan's eye can be reported by a tabloid newspaper with disgust; the following week, posed photographs of a copycat case are cynically generated by journalists.

Some of the most interesting more recent research on football hooliganism has focused on international hooligan groups of 'Ultras', for whom the badge of the extreme hooligan – whether at Accrington or in Rome – appears to accrue a sense of self-esteem not elsewhere available. There is a playful irony in the idea of the Accrington ultras, a few hundred diehards in a parochial corner of north-east Lancashire, in comparison to the proven violent and often politically motivated intents of their Italian counterparts (Magee et al., 2005; Martin 2011: 217–18). At its peak, the hooligan phenomenon combined sport with politics; in the late 1970s, right-wing activist Martin Webster of the National Front targeted hooligan thugs for recruitment, marking them out as patriotic robust Englishmen. And football supporting has provided an outlet for collective aggression that has drawn in the least likely of adherents: *Granta* editor Bill Buford wrote of the worryingly seductive nature of crowd membership when spending time *Among the Thugs*: 'I know of no excitement greater ... Being in a crowd. And – greater still – being in a crowd in an act of violence. Nothingness is what you find there. Nothingness in its beauty, its simplicity, its nihilistic purity' (Buford 1991: 195).

The Bountiful Game

Football's epithet 'The Beautiful Game' emerged as a response to the dazzling skills of the all-conquering Brazilian sides of the 1950s and 1960s, and the country's World Cup winners of 1994 and 2002. From 1992 a combination of the reformatting of the European Cup into the Champions League, the formation in England of the Premier League and a post–Cold War expanded UEFA provided a set of interrelated economic, political and cultural influences that reshaped the structure and the media profile of the game; beautiful the game might be, but bountiful it was, for many, becoming (Giulianotti 1999: chapter 5).

In Europe, the Bosman case opened up Europe's football labour market and accelerated international recruitment, and Rupert Murdoch's BSkyB and competing broadcast providers invested unprecedentedly high levels of money into the sport: in 1996, Murdoch recognised that sport was News International's 'battering ram' for the expansion of global pay television networks; and what he wanted he usually got, including increasing slices of the Champions League action. In turn, this enriched product has attracted investors from Russia, the Gulf States and North America to invest in football, though with uneven results.

The Commodified Game

In this complex and unpredictable intermingling of the local and the global, the indispensable sense of belonging that is pivotal to football supporting and fan culture can be threatened by the extreme commodification of the game: English film director Ken Loach raised this theme in his 2009 film *Looking for Eric*, which starred the Manchester United idol of the first half of the 1990s Eric Cantona, but also captured the disillusionment of United fans marginalized by the increasing cost of following the game: Loach observed that the 'idea of a group of people who club together is lost. The sense of identity is split between people who treat it as a club and those who treat it as an investment and a brand'.

This Football Companion takes the reader from the origins of the formal, organised modern form of football within the privileged educational institutions of the English elite, to a highly developed and globally marketed commodity for worldwide media audiences. It shows how South American prowess challenged English claims to be the masters of the game, and how mid-European football emerged from the Austro-Hungarian empire as a less remote challenge to western European pioneers. The ruthless use to which politics has been put in football is laid bare in an overview of the fascist politics of Mussolini that secured two World Cup triumphs for Italy in the 1930s, and the political populism of Silvio Berlusconi that blurred the boundaries between football leadership and political power. The long-standing Uruguayan and Brazilian contributions to the international growth of the game are traced here, and the continent of Africa provides a further example of the cultural and political significance of sport in the making or masking of national identity.

The Companion then takes the reader into the different elements of the contemporary game, looking at the emergence of the football manager or coach, women's football, fans and fan cultures, celebrity players and the extraordinary story of economic boom in the English Premier League and the current ascendancy of the Spanish style of play. And how have writers and commentators tracked, documented, made sense of these trends? The Companion reflects on the changing relationship between the football reporter and his – very definitely, this has been for the most part 'his'– subject and sources, and also the ways in which players' and fans' lives and experiences have generated a sub-genre of popular literature.

The critique in *Looking for Eric* of the changing ownership in and precarious financing of top-level football gave prominence to the voices of the fans. In a way, in celebrating the collective experience of generations of supporters, Loach's critique is located in the tradition of the English novelist J.B. Priestley, whose opening pages of the 1929 novel *The Good Companions* captured the community significance and expressive base of professional football in the north of England in the 1920s: your shilling for the match at Bruddersford United Association Football Club 'turned you into a critic … a partisan … a member of a new community' (Priestley, 1976).While such cultural commentators could be accused of slipping into nostalgic romanticization of the sport, if top-level professional football does lose its community base then its historical and cultural legacies will be seriously jeopardised.

Of course football cannot go back to the days of maximum wages for players and intimate neighbourly relations between players and their public, as in, say, Barnsley in the 1950s (Alister and Ward 1997). But the dramatic explosion of the game as marketed cultural product has changed things beyond the imagination of the middle of the last century. And if that community base is wholly eroded, the game will be handed over to the billionaires and speculators to whom club ownership or football events are a form of global marketing and branding, an experiment in asset-stripping, or a vainglorious self-aggrandizing ego trip.

In 1959, the then secretary of the Football Association, Sir Stanley Rous, wrote that 'unlike cricket or, say, golf, which are more leisurely sports, football has perhaps not lent itself particularly well to reflective writing' (Rous 1959: v). Sir Stanley would be astonished, and in equal part delighted, to see how football writing, research, commentary and analysis have developed during the intervening 60 years, facilitating the informed evaluation of the social, financial and political influences and forces that have reshaped the game both in his native country and in the international context that Rous went on to influence in his 13 years as president of FIFA.

We need a Football Companion like this to remind us where the game has come from and to provide informed examples of where it might be going. As the Qatar Foundation buys its way onto the front of the shirts of Barcelona

FC, relegating UNICEF to players' sleeves; as Qatar enters its decade-long preparation to host the 2022 World Cup; and as £15-million-a-year-man Samuel Eto'o commutes thousands of miles from Moscow for home games for Anzhi Makhachkala (Dagestan), it is not mere nostalgia to talk of the collective walk to the match. My most recent spectator experiences bear this out.

In May 2011 my journey to Wembley Stadium was in a luxury coach from the Grosvenor House Hotel in Park Lane by Hyde Park to the red carpet of the VIP entrance at Wembley; I sat in front of cosmopolitan groups in hospitality boxes, their eyes on the menu as much as on Lionel Messi. In December 2011 I took 19 stops on London underground's District Line to Upton Park and walked past nail parlours and beauty salons, street markets and eyesore 1960s pubs, to West Ham United's Boleyn Ground, where I sat among away fans who baulked at the cost of a half-time pie. Barcelona dominated possession and showboated to an imperious European title. West Ham dominated possession, had 10 corners to visiting Burnley's one, and lost to two late headed goals. It was cold walking back along the high street to the Tube station, but the game had cost just £19, and so the spare change was there for a welcome in the Queen's Arms, and a chorus of 'I'm Forever Blowing Bubbles'; it was warmer inside Wembley back in May, but the sponsors' banquet halls were well policed and inaccessible to the grade 2 punter who'd paid only £250 for the ticket, and nobody was singing in the leather-seated luxury vehicle.

VIP coach or a walk among modern-day football companions? It's not mere nostalgia to talk about the walk to and from the match. It is a necessary prelude to debate about the core values of an extraordinarily resilient cultural phenomenon.

BIBLIOGRAPHY

Alister, I. and Ward, A. 1997. *Barnsley: A Study in Football 1953–59*. 2nd edn. Oxford. Crowberry.

Buford, B. 1991. *Among the Thugs*. London. Secker & Warburg.

Clarke, J. 1973. *Football Hooliganism and the Skinheads*. Birmingham. Stencilled Occasional Paper, Centre for Contemporary Cultural Studies, University of Birmingham.

Dunning, E. 1999. *Sport Matters: Sociological Studies of Sport, Violence and Civilization*. London. Routledge.

Dunning, E., Murphy, P. and Williams, J. 1986. 'Spectator Violence at Football Matches: Towards a Sociological Explanation', in N. Elias and E. Dunning (eds.), *Quest for Excitement: Sport and Leisure in the Civilizing Process*. Oxford. Basil Blackwell.

Fabian, A.H. and Green, G. (eds.). 1959. *Association Football Volume One*. London. Caxton Publishing.

FIFA. 2011. 'Almost Half the World Tuned In at Home to Watch FIFA World Cup South Africa™', www.fifa.com/worldcup/archive/southafrica2010/organisation/media/newsid=1473143/index.htm, accessed 6 December 2011.

Giulianotti, R. 1999. *Football: A Sociology of the Global Game*. Cambridge. Polity Press.

Gumbrecht, H. 2006. *In Praise of Athletic Beauty*. Cambridge, MA. Belknap Press of Harvard University Press.

Hamil, S. and Chadwick, S. (eds.). 2010. *Managing Football: An International Perspective*. London: Elsevier/Butterworth-Heinemann.

Initiative, futures sport + entertainment 2010. *ViewerTrack: The Most Watched TV Sporting Events of 2009*. London: Initiative, futures sport and entertainment.

Magee, J., Bairner, A. and Tomlinson, A. (eds.). 2005. *The Bountiful Game? Football Identities and Finances*. Aachen. Meyer & Meyer.

Marsh, P., Rosser, E. and Harré, R. 1978. *The Rules of Disorder*. London. Routledge & Kegan Paul.

Martin, S. 2011. *Sport Italia: The Italian Love Affair with Sport*. London. I.B. Tauris.

Mason, T. 1995. *Passion of the People? Football in South America*. London. Verso.

Merkel, U. and Tokarski, W. (eds.). 1996. *Racism and Xenophobia in European Football*. Aachen: Meyer & Meyer Verlag.

Miller, R. and Crolley, L. (eds.). 2007. *Football in the Americas: Fútbol, Futebol, Soccer*. London. Institute for the Study of the Americas.

Priestley, J.B. 1976 [1929]. *The Good Companions*. Harmondsworth. Penguin.

Rous, S. 1959. 'Foreword', in Fabian and Green (eds.), p. v.

Sugden, J. and Tomlinson, A. 1998. *FIFA and the Contest for World Football: Who Rules the Peoples' Game?* Cambridge. Polity Press.

Tomlinson, A. 1991. 'North and South: The Rivalry of the Football League and the Football Association', in J. Williams and S. Wagg (eds.), *British Football and Social Change: Getting into Europe*. Leicester. Leicester University Press.

PART ONE

Foundations

I

DAVE RUSSELL

Kicking Off: The Origins of Association Football

The desire to kick, throw or run with a ball, whether the inflated pig's bladder that gave its name to the Irish game *Caird* or the stuffed leather skin of the Chinese Han dynasty's *Cuju*, has long proved irresistible. Ball games were central to the Mayan civilisations of Mesoamerica for at least 3,000 years until the arrival of the Spanish in the sixteenth century; Aboriginal Australians, the Pacific islanders of Polynesia and Micronesia and Native Americans all enjoyed games with perhaps even longer histories and folk football existed in many parts of Europe from the medieval period.[1] Modern football therefore has an abundant pre-history of enormous importance in its own right, providing, as sports history so frequently does, rich insights into the social and cultural mechanisms of particular societies. The subsequent use (and abuse) of these traditions can also be revealing, as when, in a nationalist flourish, Benito Mussolini's regime not only re-introduced the medieval Florentine game of *Calcio* but identified it as the root of the modern game.[2]

For all its significance, however, 'folk', 'festival', 'mob', 'traditional', 'pre-codified' or whatever label is attached, had only marginal impact on the sport that emerged in the Victorian period. In a purely English context, both the relatively structured, rule- and space-bound variants such as the East Anglian Camp-ball and the large-scale, annual set-piece matches setting sections of local communities against each other, must certainly have left some legacy; indeed, some of the latter continue to this day.[3] They entrenched some potentially useable collective memory of the game and stimulated the civic and geographical rivalries that later sport fed upon. Nevertheless, they were precursors of association football rather than true ancestors, valuable above all else as evidence of that propensity of young men for ball games. Modern football was a distinctly British, especially English and Scottish, phenomenon, and the product of a particular conjunction of historical forces which generated previously unimagined opportunity for play.

The history of its development, once a relatively settled matter, has become a site of combative but fertile debate.[4] An increasingly influential body of work now challenges established narratives placing public school football and ex–public schoolboys at the heart of the game's codification and dissemination.[5] These schools, whose pupils adopted football in the mid-eighteenth century, have hitherto been seen as the sport's key refuge as popular folk forms withered in the face of industrialisation and urbanisation. They have also been regarded as critical to both the formal codification of individual school games, a process beginning at Rugby in 1845–46, and the search for a common, codified version that culminated in the foundation of the London-based Football Association (FA [1863]) and Rugby Football Union (RFU [1871]). Ex-pupils, influenced by the growing 'cult of games' and 'Muscular Christianity', have also been seen as key to football's introduction into wider society. Although not completely rejecting this picture, various recent revisionist texts prefer to emphasise the existence of a vibrant, proto-modern game in mid-century, beyond the public school; suggest a far greater role for Sheffield than allowed by London-centric interpretations and argue that public schools' insularity and status-consciousness may have actually retarded football's diffusion as much as facilitated it.

Beyond the Public Schools

Historians have long acknowledged the existence of organised, formal variants of the game with properly constituted teams playing on defined spaces and operating within agreed rules, but had tended to imply or assume they effectively disappeared by the 1830s. Adrian Harvey, however, has recorded the existence of 'at least ninety-three teams' playing games of this type between 1828 and 1859, which were involved in at least 58 matches.[6] He designates some 40 of these as 'local', essentially community-based, while locating the rest in schools, formal sporting clubs, military institutions and occupational groups. Collectively, it is argued, they supply the missing link connecting the traditional and modern football worlds.

The existence of this activity certainly demonstrates that organised mid-century football was not exclusive to public schools. However, while Harvey and other revisionist writers have added enormously to our understanding of football's early development, the case made for these games fails fully to convince. For example, closer scrutiny of Harvey's argument that 'during the 1840s Yorkshire had been one of the most active regions for football in Britain', shows that he lists only 12 Yorkshire teams in that decade, at least 10 of which came from a sub-region of just 30 square miles bounded by Holmfirth, Denby Dale and Penistone.[7] Although future research will undeniably identify more teams, their number, geographical spread and levels of activity are likely to have been modest and to have provided only the most limited basis for future development.

Much interest in these extra–public school games between 1830 and 1860 results from their appearing to resolve the conundrum as to why, if the game was indeed 'effectively extinct previous to the 1860s and 1870s … the working-class assimilated football so rapidly' in the later nineteenth century.[8] However, recent experience or folk memory of football may not have been a necessary prerequisite for the embrace of the association (or rugby) game. The working classes drew on a rich culture of cricket, pugilism, athletics and various local and regional pastimes and presumably turned to the new sport on the not unrealistic assumption that it offered similar pleasures and benefits. If socialisation into the game was actually required, then the informal football played by boys and young men on streets and open spaces is as likely a candidate for a central role.[9] Although the Highways Act of 1835 and a raft of similarly restrictive local bylaws had theoretically rendered it illegal, the street game proved impossible to eradicate. The *Morning Chronicle*'s 1849 survey of popular recreation in Birmingham noted that while football had declined among adults, it continued to exist in this way 'among young boys and lads'.[10] Continuity is perhaps to be found at this micro-level.

Arguments about the significance of Sheffield's role rest on much firmer ground.[11] Sheffield Foot Ball Club, founded in 1857, is certainly the longest-established club in Britain, boasting continuous existence to the present day, and the Sheffield area was home to 11 clubs by as early as 1862. It is unclear why the city developed a football culture so early and adopted a kicking game devoid of hacking and tripping: attempts to demonstrate formative links between Sheffield football and the games of the Holmfirth-Denby-Penistone region (some parts of which became rugby strongholds) remain highly speculative.[12] The city's influence, however, cannot be denied. Sheffield FC was an early member of the FA and exerted considerable influence on the parent body into the 1870s; 5 of the 12 major rule changes passed by the FA between 1863 and 1871 were originally proposed from Sheffield.[13] A local football association was founded in 1867 and its rules rather than those of the London-based FA were operative across a large swathe of provincial England, with adherents stretching from Middlesbrough in the north to Birmingham in the midlands and Grimsby to the east.[14]

Young men from the city's professional and industrial elite – albeit non–public school educated – typified Sheffield's early football fraternity, although the establishment of the Youdan Cup (1867) and Cromwell Cup

(1868), both founded by theatrical entrepreneurs, suggest both a gradual downward social diffusion and the beginnings of a commercial culture; 3,000 attended the 1867 Youdan Cup final. Again, the arrival in Sheffield in 1876 of Scottish players, J.J. Lang and Peter Andrews, almost certainly heralds the birth of the professional footballer in England.[15] However, the rigorously amateur stance of the local FA severely restrained commercial trends until the late 1880s, with neither Sheffield United nor The Wednesday joining the Football League until four years after its foundation. Pioneer status was not continued and modern commercial football had its deepest roots in Lancashire.

'Muscular Christianity'

This, however, is to run ahead. What of the public schools and their influence? For this writer at least, they must remain central to any account of football's early modernisation. Attempts to identify clear lineages between particular school games and later national codes are admittedly problematic. The former have often been broadly categorised as either 'kicking' or 'handling' games and, adopting this strategy (and outlining other rule differences), Dunning and Sheard posit the Eton Field Game and Rugby School football as the key antecedents for the association and rugby codes respectively. Kicking has also been seen as important in the Harrow game and Old Harrovians undoubtedly made an important contribution to the growth of London club football from the late 1850s. The fact that half the participants in the inaugural FA Cup final were educated at either Eton or Harrow and that 48 of the 154 players engaged in the first dozen finals were educated at Eton alone underlines the schools' roles in the establishment of the association game.[16]

Nevertheless, Tony Collins is surely correct to argue that 'the similarities between the various codes of football in the mid-nineteenth century were far greater than their differences', with kicking, handling and scrimmaging found in virtually every public school game, albeit with the exact balance varying.[17] Connections between school games and later codes are probably clearer in hindsight than they were to contemporaries and, as will be seen, individuals frequently swapped and shared codes. What mattered most was the fact that public schools were playing games at all. These provided much of the raw material for national codes and, most importantly, via the 'cult of games' and notions of 'Muscular Christianity', legitimised the act of playing football. In a society that debated the appropriate use of leisure so intensely, the upper-class embrace of football, broadly defined, was critical to its eventual success. It is undeniable that the public school game was largely hidden from wider view, with little sustained attempt to take the game to other social classes before the 1870s. However, active dissemination was hardly necessary when social emulation served so well.

Public school football was also crucial in generating a supply of players anxious to continue into adulthood, a collective desire inevitably leading toward the creation of codes that could be shared irrespective of school background. That rules needed to be 'agreed' upon at Cambridge University in 1837, 1846, 1848, 1856, 1862 and 1863 is indicative of how little was initially settled; handling and hacking proved especial points of dispute. Sporting patterns remained complex, with many old boys preferring to play under their school rules, while innumerable hybrids undoubtedly existed.[18] By the early 1860s, however, calls for unification were growing and, on 26 October 1863, 12 London-based clubs met to discuss the issue, terming themselves the Football Association. Over the course of a series of meetings lasting until December 1863, advocates of limited handling and the abolition of hacking established their writ, although only considerable chicanery on their part prevented the adoption of a rugby-style game.[19]

Towards a Common Code

The new body's immediate achievements and impact were extremely limited. The rules of 1863 went only a modest way towards the production of a genuinely new game. It was only the addition of further regulations that saw 'Association Football' ('association' soon became 'socker' in old boy slang) begin to exhibit a recognisably modern shape and define itself in clear contradistinction to handling games. Noteworthy here was the further limiting and then, in 1870, outlawing of handling by any player except the goalkeeper; the introduction of an offside rule in 1866 (drawn from Westminster and Charterhouse School rules) stipulating that an attacking player required three opponents in front of him to remain onside; the introduction of a tape under which the ball had to pass in order to register a goal (1866); the abolition of touchdowns (1867) and the introduction of free-kicks and corners (1872).

As already implied, the FA was initially in no sense a national body let alone a ruling one. It had only 10 members in 1867 and although this grew to 30 by the next year, its influence remained almost exclusively restricted to London and the Home Counties. Even there, the majority of clubs remained outside its jurisdiction and even some within it often played under other rules. This was not surprising for the period to about 1875 was one of experimentation and hybridisation as players sought fixtures of any sort while ascertaining their preferences. In 1863–64 Richmond played four matches in 10 weeks under three different codes. Beyond the capital, Stoke Ramblers initially adopted Sheffield rules but played two of their first games under rugby regulations, while Burton played under either Sheffield or rugby rules according to the opposition. Games were also frequently played with different rules in either half. Individuals consequently became skilled in more than one game, as exemplified by Arthur Guillemard, rugby player and a president of the RFU but also an early member of the Wanderers proto-association side in the 1860s; Henry Renny-Tailyour, both an FA Cup finalist with the Royal Engineers and a Scottish rugby international in 1872, and A.W. Hornby, Lancashire rugby (and cricket) stalwart but also a useful player with Blackburn Rovers in the 1870s.[20] This cross-fertilisation is illustrative of a strain of compromise easily obscured by the various narratives of conflict that sometimes govern our view. While the broad similarities between games made the level of self-denial often quite modest, old school loyalties and personal preferences could clearly be set aside.

For all the FA's initial weakness, its birth nevertheless remains, in Taylor's words, 'a major landmark in the development of the game'.[21] Although leading clubs held individual membership, it became essentially a confederation of county and district associations through which teams connected to the parent body. While eight years elapsed between the foundation of the Sheffield FA and that of its Birmingham counterpart in 1875, 6 more associations followed by 1879 and by 1884, 28 were affiliated.[22] By the late 1870s the FA was undisputedly the governing body of the English game, with the Sheffield Football Association's full adoption of its rules in 1877 symbolic in this regard. This marked, too, the inevitable end of any remote possibility of the game being governed from the provinces. Although London's centripetal pull was yet to reach its twentieth-century levels, the contemporary geographies of power demanded that football acknowledge the capital's growing reputation as the 'headquarters of everything'.[23] The FA's growth was a catalyst for the foundation of similar bodies in Scotland (1873), Wales (1876) and Ireland (1880). Harmonisation of rules by the four home nations in 1882 meant that a game far from unified only a decade earlier was now an agreed form across the British Isles.

Birth of the FA Cup

The organisation's rise to prominence resulted from its achieving significant degrees of administrative competence and energy at the moment when socio-economic changes made possible the wider dissemination of the game. Although the FA's executive was never entirely the preserve of ex–public schoolboys, it was another site of influence for them, with the most influential being the Old Harrovian Charles W. Alcock, secretary from 1870 to 1895. A footballer with Wanderers and England, a sports journalist[24] and, from 1872, secretary of Surrey County Cricket Club, his grasp of the evolving sporting landscape and instinct for compromise made him an ideal leader at such a critical juncture.[25] One of his central contributions was the introduction of the FA Cup, arguably the single most important mechanism for the establishment of FA hegemony.

It began in 1871–72 with just 15 entrants and by 1876 that number had risen to only 37, with just 4 from the provinces. Inevitably, public school old boy sides dominated but the tournament gave a focus to the more ambitious among the more popularly rooted clubs that had mushroomed in the 1870s and 1880s. Blackburn Rovers reached the final in 1882 and the following year, by when a clear majority of the 100 entrants were drawn from the north and midlands, Blackburn Olympic defeated the Old Etonians and ended the era of elite amateur dominance on the pitch. The scorer of the first FA Cup final goal in 1872 was Morton Peto Betts, an Old Harrovian and civil engineer. The winning goal in 1883 was scored by Jimmy Costley, a Lancashire cotton operative.[26] Association football, once the preserve of local and/or national elites, was democratising.

The tournament spawned numerous imitators with competitions commencing, for example, in Scotland (1873), Wales (1877), Lancashire (1879) and Cleveland (1881), often organised by the newly formed associations. Such tournaments stimulated football as a spectator sport, with an estimated 15,000 watching the 1876–77 Scottish Cup final replay in Glasgow, the city with perhaps Britain's most developed spectator culture. The FA Cup final itself also saw significant growth from the 4,500 watching in 1878 (when the game had a referee blessed by the name of E.R. Bastard) to 12,500 in 1885.[27] Moreover, cup competition was central to the continuing process by which footballing codes became distinct, the need for clear, agreed rules never more clearly required than when football started to become a key vehicle for the expression of powerful local and regional identities.

In absolute terms, late-nineteenth-century association football was still a modest creature in comparison with what it would become. While 1,000 clubs were affiliated to the FA by 1888, that figure had grown to 12,000 by 1910 (and 37,000 by 1937). Nevertheless, its growth in the 1870s and 1880s was striking. The Lancashire FA, founded in 1878 with 28 members, had 114 by 1886, while its Birmingham counterpart grew from 17 to 63 in roughly the same period. Beneath these formal structures lay numerous, often short-lived sides, playing on any available space and helping cement the game at neighbourhood level. Neil Tranter has traced the existence of 68 clubs in Stirling between 1876 and 1895.[28]

Rise of 'The People's Game'

Wider socio-economic changes were fundamental in facilitating this process and none more so than the emergence of the Saturday half-holiday. The closing of workplaces on Saturday afternoons had begun in the late 1840s but it was the dramatic increase in the early 1870s – partly the result of legislation, partly of trade union pressure – that made the half-holiday sufficiently common to allow for the potential emergence of new, shared leisure habits on a grand scale. This potential was realised by a rise in real wage rates of approximately one third between 1875 and 1890. The existence of a national railway network, rising literacy levels, an expanding press and a cheap postal service were further critical factors underpinning football's rapid popularisation.[29]

The actual mechanisms by which the working (and lower-middle) classes adopted the game were complex and varied. There is certainly evidence of direct dissemination from higher to lower social classes. Two of the best-known examples occurred in the Lancashire communities of Turton and Darwen, where returning Old Harrovians formed teams among local workers in the early 1870s. The role of old boys from leading public schools in this process should not be exaggerated – there simply were not enough to go round – but young men from a rather more generously defined elite are frequently encountered in the game's early spread. Football in Liverpool, for example, owed much to some half-a-dozen Cambridge University–educated curates, themselves the products of minor private establishments and local grammar schools, who introduced the game to their urban congregations from the late 1870s. Local grammar school boys were also responsible for establishing a number of sides including Blackburn Rovers, Chester City and Leicester.[30]

Too much emphasis, however, should not be placed on downward diffusion. While teams originating within church, chapel or workplace were always numerous, clubs that formed within communities, often working-class communities, always represented the largest single category. Again, religious and works teams were often the result of initiatives at the grass roots rather than from higher up the social scale. The history of association football, as with that of popular recreation more widely, also offers powerful evidence of working-class resistance to attempts at middle- or upper-class cultural domination. Christ Church FC, Bolton, eventually Bolton Wanderers, split from the parent body in 1877 when the vicar proposed compulsory church attendance as the price of his continued support.[31] While the working class never exerted significant levels of control over the football world – the 'people's game' epithet captures an emotional rather than a formal relationship – it entered it very much on its own terms.

Association football was initially highly regionalised in its spread. By about 1880, east and central Lancashire, Sheffield and district, much of the midlands and London were particular English strongholds, while the industrial belt of the Scottish central lowlands was establishing itself as a key crucible. The largely middle-class amateur Queens Park, founded in Glasgow in 1867 and enormously influential on and off the pitch, was Scotland's first club. Soccer, never a patrician game north of the border, spread rapidly down the social scale, however, and it was sides such as Renton, Vale of Leven and St Bernards that developed the 'Scotch professors', so many of whom were rapidly lured south.[32] The game was played in other areas but in many it remained under-developed and sometimes, as in the West Riding of Yorkshire beyond Sheffield and most of Wales outside the north-east, virtually non-existent. Elsewhere, rugby predominated, although, in much of Ireland, the game also met fierce competition from the sports of the nationalist Gaelic Athletic Association.[33] A quantitative analysis of leading clubs from 1868 to 1873 shows a more or less equal balance between rugby and soccer-style games, although the *Times* claimed as late as 1880 that 'the players of the Rugby Union game are probably twice as numerous as those of the Association'.[34]

During the 1880s, soccer began to pierce rugby's territories. Differing attitudes to cup (and, later, league) tournaments were crucial here, the FA encouraging them, the RFU hostile lest the game's social tone and sense of class exclusivity be compromised. Interestingly, where rugby enthusiasts ignored the centre and encouraged cup football, the game often became a part of popular culture. Where they did not, it remained a middle-class pursuit and left the field open to its rival. When the Lancashire FA was founded in 1878, all 28 member-clubs came from just 6 neighbouring towns in and between Bolton, Darwen and Blackburn. Stimulated by the FA and Lancashire Cups, soccer began to expand beyond this limited territory with sides including Preston North End and Burnley exchanging rugby for football. In 1888, while 5 of the 12 founder members of the Football League came from this expanded heartland, the Lancashire RFU, hostile to 'pot-hunting', saw rugby become almost moribund within it.[35]

Discussion of association football's emergence as a global game must await subsequent chapters, but it is essential at least to acknowledge that its reach soon spread beyond the British Isles.[36] As the dominant world power in the third quarter of the nineteenth century, Britain's political, commercial and industrial strength allowed the game to surface almost anywhere in the globe. Many of the earliest accounts relate to what were probably informal kickabouts involving sailors, soldiers and migrant workers. British school and technical college students, both those based abroad and those moving there, were playing football of a type by the 1860s. A noted centre of such activity was Switzerland, whose nationals were to play an important role in the diffusion of the game within Europe.[37] Although the really significant growth of soccer as the world's game began in earnest from about 1890, its potential was apparent long before.

Victory for Professionalism

The biggest potential problem facing the domestic game in the early 1880s was the growth of professionalism. Its resolution in 1885 (in England at least), with all the possibilities that legalisation raised for the game's future commercial evolution, makes the 1880s one of the most critical decades in football history. There was never a 'pure' amateur game in which the extrinsic pleasures of 'playing the game' overrode financial considerations; public school old boy sides expected and received substantial 'expenses' on their provincial tours. However, if amateurism was an aspiration sometimes muddied in practice, its supporters unfailingly recognised challenges to the ideal. Hostility toward emergent professionalism (not actually illegal until 1882) took many forms, with practical concerns that wealthier clubs might upset the game's competitive balance mixing with fears about the example set by the existence of men paid only to play and the status anxieties experienced as 'gentlemen' saw mere 'players' encroach upon their exclusive social space.

Although the importation of players and use of financial and other inducements were probably reasonably widespread, it was east and central Lancashire that formed 'the centre of innovation for professional football'.[38] Coming to the game at the very moment of its emergence as a popular, competitive sport, the towns and villages of the region embraced the practices of nascent professionalism far more readily than was possible in earlier amateur-dominated centres such as Sheffield and Birmingham. When, in 1884, the vehemently anti-professional Scottish FA named more than fifty emigré players requiring special dispensation to play in Scotland, a clear accusation of professionalism, all but Aston Villa's Archie Hunter were playing with Lancashire clubs. Although there were those within the FA, most notably Alcock, who long assumed that properly managed professionalism was inevitable and desirable, such views were outweighed by voices calling for ever more punitive measures against this 'evil'.[39]

Their campaign reached a climax in October 1884 when the FA introduced a body of draconian regulations that included a ban on affiliated clubs playing any other club 'whether belonging to the [Football] Association or not' that paid or imported players. Unsurprisingly, it was Lancashire that led the response. It provided, for example, all of the twenty-five or so formally affiliated members of the grandiosely named British Football Association (BFA). This was hardly the potential source of a Northern Union–style break-away it is sometimes presumed to have been, but it was a pressure group blessed with the wit to obtain legal advice deeming unlawful the FA's attempt to legislate on the affairs of clubs beyond its jurisdiction. Although the FA denied it, this counsel was critical to its executive committee's decision, in November 1884, to reverse previous policy and recommend legalisation. Similarly galvanised by the BFA, Lancashire FA representatives were key advocates for professionalism at the three General Meetings called to debate the issue in 1885. At the last of these, on 20 July, professionalism with strict controls over players' residence qualifications, movement between clubs and wider role within administration of the game was finally conceded.

That outcome resulted from, at first sight, an unlikely alliance between the industrial and commercial middle class of Lancashire and the largely public-school–educated upper and upper-middle classes of London and district. For a brief moment the extra-sporting tensions that so clearly existed between these different fractions of the propertied classes and between north and south and province and metropolis did not operate according to type. Lancashire had passed too far in the direction of professionalism to consider a change of direction, but in much of provincial England a strong investment in amateur ideology and a considerable mistrust of upstart Lancashire (a magnet for players from other regions) led to strong resistance. The leaders of London football had neither direct experience of professionalism nor expected to have any, making their acceptance of compromise much easier. Tired by the impasse and realising how little progress had been made by repression, some of the most unlikely individuals now accepted the inevitable.[40]

Thus, in January 1885, Nicholas 'Pa' Jackson, bitter critic of proto-professionalism, founder of the Corinthians and quintessential amateur, seconded, as assistant secretary of the FA, its motion stating that 'it was now expedient to legalise professionalism under stringent conditions'. Within a short period Jackson and many other London-based amateurs who had shared his logic bitterly regretted their actions. The foundation of the Football League in September 1888, designed in part to guarantee a pool of fixtures viable and attractive enough to meet the rising labour costs generated by legalised professionalism, typified what they saw as foot-ball's inexorable transformation into merely a 'business'. Nevertheless, as so often in football's early history, compromise had been possible at the defining moment. Crucially, those who had initially remained in opposition demonstrated similar propensities. Professionalism became a certainty at the General Meeting on 23 March 1885 when its antagonists acknowledged the growing shift against them and called for the establishment of a sub-committee dedicated to finding a compromise. Again, many of them accepted the changed situation after July 1885 and remained loyal to the FA; Charles Crump of the Birmingham FA and Sheffield's Charles Clegg, eventually an FA president, both once bitter opponents of professionalism, are striking examples. (The Scottish and Irish FAs, faced with the continued migration of leading players, followed the English example in 1893 and 1894 respectively.) Rugby's 'great split' in 1895 stands in stark contrast.[41]

Association football had made remarkable progress in Britain between about 1870 and 1885. In many ways, its growth and structures mirrored larger shifts in British society. The urban working class was trusted (mainly) to gather in large numbers to watch sport just as, since 1867, it could be trusted with the vote. The middle class's recreational life widened just as its larger economic, civic and political role had done from the 1830s, while, as ever, the upper class made concessions when necessary and often on its own terms. The game was also, however, developing an autonomous dynamic, providing a new and powerful mechanism, at least within male life, for the expression of collective and personal identities rooted in place, class and gender. Although the 'footballisation' of society, the penetration of its every level by discourses from and about the game, was still a hundred years away, a sport that had a formal existence of barely twenty years was playing a far greater role in daily life than its founders can have ever imagined.

NOTES

1 D. Goldblatt, *The Ball Is Round. A Global History of Football* (London: Penguin, 2006), pp. 4–18; P. Lanfranchi and M. Taylor, *Moving with the Ball* (Oxford: Berg, 2001), pp. 16–19; H. Hornby, *Uppies and Downies: The Extraordinary Football Games of Britain* (Swindon: English Heritage, 2008).

2 J. Foot, *Calcio. A History of Italian Football* (London: Harper Perennial, 2007), p. 2

3 D. Dymond, 'A Lost Institution: The Camping Close', *Rural History*, 1 (1990), 165–92; Hornby, *Uppies and Downies*, pp. 18–35.

4 For a fine historiographical account, M. Taylor, *The Association Game: A History of British Football* (Harlow: Pearson Education, 2008).

5 J. Goulstone, *Football's Secret History* (Upminster, Essex: 3–2 Books, 2001); A. Harvey, *Football. The First Hundred Years. The Untold Story* (Abingdon: Routledge, 2005); P. Swain, 'Cultural Continuity and Football in Nineteenth Century Lancashire', *Sport in History* 28, 4 (2008), 566–82.

6 Harvey, *First Hundred*, pp. 58–61, 64; N. Tranter, 'The First Football Club?', *International Journal of the History of Sport*, 10 (1993), 104–06.

7 Harvey, *First Hundred*, Table 3.1, p. 60.

8 Harvey, *First Hundred*, p. 58.

9 R. Holt, 'Football and the Urban Way of Life in Nineteenth-century Britain' in J.A. Mangan (ed.), *Pleasure, Profit and Proselytism* (London: Frank Cass, 1988), pp. 71–2.

10 D.A. Read, 'Folk-football, the Aristocracy and Cultural Change: A Critique of Dunning and Sheard', *International Journal of the History of Sport*, 5, 1 (1988), 227.

11 S. Hilton, G. Curry and P. Goodman, *Sheffield Football Club. 150 Years of Football* (Altrincham: At Heart Publications, 2007), pp. 5–41; Harvey, *First Hundred*, pp. 92–125; A. Harvey, 'A Curate's Egg Pursued by Red Herrings: A Reply to Eric Dunning and Graham Curry', *International Journal of the History of Sport*, 21, 1 (2004), 127–31.

12 Hilton et al., *Sheffield*, p. 18.

13 Goulstone, *Secret History*, p. 50.

14 I. Nannestad, 'From Sabbath Breakers to Respectable Sportsmen: The Development of Football in Lincolnshire', unpublished MA thesis, De Montfort University, 2003, 98.

15 G. Curry, 'Playing for Money: James J. Lang and Emergent Soccer Professionalism in Sheffield', *Soccer and Society*, 5, 3 (2004), 336–55.

16 E. Dunning and K. Sheard, *Barbarians, Gentlemen and Players; A Sociological Study of the Development of Rugby Union* (London: Routledge, 2nd edn., 2005), pp. 65–99; G. Williams, *The Code War* (Harefield, Middlesex: Yore Publications, 1994), p. 67; R. Sanders, *Beastly Fury. The Strange Birth of British Football* (London: Bantam Press, 2009), p. 68.

17 T. Collins, 'History, Theory and the "Civilising Process"', *Sport in History*, 25, 2 (2005), 294–5; G. Curry, E. Dunning and K. Sheard, 'Sociological versus Empirical History: Some Comments on Tony Collins' "History, Theory and the Civilising Process"', *Sport in History*, 26, 1 (2006), 110–23.

18 G. Curry, 'The Trinity Connection: An Analysis of the Role of Members of Cambridge University in the Development of Football in the Mid-nineteenth Century', *Sport in History*, 22, 2, (2002), 46–74.

19 Harvey, *First Hundred*, pp. 141–45.

20 Harvey, *First Hundred*, p. 148; Williams, *Code War*, pp. 32–33, 23; J. Blythe Smart, *The Wow Factor* (Blythe Smart, England, 2003), pp. 238–41; H. Berry, *Blackburn Rovers Football Club: A Century of Soccer* (Blackburn: Blackburn Rovers FC, 1975), p. 11.

21 Taylor, *Association Game*, p. 30.

22 *The Football Annual* (London: Wright, 1884), pp. 148–51, 152.

23 D. Read, *The English Provinces c.1760–1960. A Study in Power* (London: Edwin Arnold, 1964), p. 224.

24 For more on Alcock's contribution to football journalism, see Chapter 12 by Rob Steen in this volume, 'Sheepskin Coats and Nannygoats: The View from the Pressbox'.

25 K. Booth, *The Father of Modern Sport. The Life and Times of Charles W. Alcock* (Manchester: Parrs Wood Press, 2002).

26 T. Mason, *Association Football and English Society, 1863–1915* (Brighton: Harvester Press, 1980), pp. 60–62; Blythe Smart, England, *Wow Factor*, p. 161.

27 Mason, *Association Football*, pp. 138–39; M. Tyler, *Cup Final Extra* (London: Hamlyn, 1981), pp. 21, 27, 29.

28 Taylor, *Association Game*, pp. 37, 39.

29 D. Russell, *Football and the English* (Preston: Carnegie, 1997), pp. 13–14.

30 T.J. Preston, 'The Origins and Development of Association Football in the Liverpool District, *c*1879 until *c*1915', unpublished PhD thesis, University of Central Lancashire, 2006, 37–45; Taylor, *Association Game*, p. 34.

31 Anon, *Bolton Wanderers F.C.* (Bolton: Blackshaw: 1925), p. 2.

32 B. Crampsey, *The Scottish Footballer* (Edinburgh: William Blackwood, 1978).

33 D. Russell, '"Sporadic and Curious". The Emergence of Rugby and Soccer Zones in Yorkshire and Lancashire, c. 1860–1914', *International Journal of the History of Sport*, 5, 2 (1988), 185–205; Williams, *Code War*; 28–87; M. Johnes and I. Garland, '"The New Craze": Football and Society in North-east Wales, c.1870–90', *Welsh History Review* 22, 2 (2004), 278–304; N. Garnham, *Association Football and Society in Pre-partition Ireland* (Belfast: Ulster Historical Foundation, 2004).

34 Harvey, *Hundred Years,* p. 176; *Times*, 12 November 1880.

35 T. Collins, *A Social History of English Rugby Union* (London: Routledge, 2009), pp. 42–46; Russell, 'Sporadic', 189.

36 B. Murray, *The World's Game. A History of Soccer* (Urbana: University of Illinois Press, 1996), p. 23.

37 Lanfranchi and Taylor, *Moving,* p. 19, pp. 23–31.

38 R.W. Lewis, 'The Genesis of Professional Football: Bolton-Blackburn-Darwen, the Centre of Innovation, 1878–1885', *International Journal of the History of Sport*, 14, 1 (1997), 45, 54.

39 D. Russell, 'From Evil to Expedient: The Legalization of Professionalism in English Football, 1884–5', in S. Wagg, (ed.), *Myths and Milestones in the History of Sport* (London: Macmillan, 2012), pp. 32–56.

40 N.L. Jackson, *Association Football* (London: George Newnes, 1900), pp. 108–41.

41 T. Collins, *Rugby's Great Split: Class, Culture and the Origins of Rugby League Football* (London: Frank Cass, 1998).

Figure 1.1. Wales's Billy Meredith (a Manchester United player at this time), pictured in the team group before the game against Ireland in Wrexham on 19/1/1914. Credit: Colorsport/Wilkes.

HUW RICHARDS

The Game-Changers: Billy Meredith

Tony Mason, both pioneer and master of serious football history in Britain, has argued convincingly that Stanley Matthews was the first British footballer accorded the full national hero status previously attained by cricketers such as W.G. Grace and Jack Hobbs.[1] Billy Meredith (Figure 1.1) represents the strongest, perhaps the only, challenge to that view and exists more vividly in the game's collective memory than contemporaries such as Steve Bloomer or predecessors like Billy Bassett.

One reason is sheer longevity. Meredith made his league debut for Northwich Victoria in 1892 and, like Matthews, long outlasted contemporaries, appearing for Manchester City in an FA Cup semi-final in 1924, when he was 50. Another is that his significance extended beyond on-pitch exploits. Meredith was among the pioneers of football trade unionism, proudly acknowledged as a founder by the Professional Footballers Association. It does no harm to have played, as he did from 1907 to 1921, for Manchester United.

But above all – and one reason for his huge value to the early Players Union – he was the great hero of his day. James Catton argued before the First World War that Meredith was 'just as much a household name as W.G. Grace'.[2] In a poll conducted in 1904 to find the most popular current footballer – extending that definition to include rugby league players – by the Manchester-based *Umpire* newspaper, Meredith headed the list ahead of Bloomer and Blackburn and England full-back Bob Crompton.[3]

British football traditionally loves good wingers and Meredith is among the first and best of a line that includes Matthews, Tom Finney, Cliff Jones, George Best, Jimmy Johnstone and – even since Alf Ramsey's highly effective full-back's revenge on the breed – Ryan Giggs.

'Supreme Entertainer'

Meredith described his role in simple terms: 'Once I had the ball, I knew what was expected of me – to beat the wing-half and the full-back, take the ball to the corner-flag and centre. The other forwards knew my intention and kept up with me.'[4] He was, though, as his biographer John Harding has argued, 'More than just a winger. He was a forward in the broadest sense, a creator and a scorer as well as a supreme entertainer.'[5] Totals of 186 goals from 681 league games plus a further 10 in 48 for Wales underline that argument.

Sticking around for more than 30 years is a useful aid to getting noticed, but Meredith clearly had enough idiosyncrasies to be memorable at first sight. He was 'a colossus with bandy legs', who ran with jutting elbows and a crab-like style, with both his moustache and the toothpick adopted in the mines in preference to chewing tobacco offering further aids to identification. There was a gift for deception – *Athletic News* in 1907 recorded that 'a back expects the flying Welshman to travel one way and he finds himself left in the rear by a rapid veering circle made in just the opposite direction' – and a dexterity which, in Percy Young's description, foreshadows the prehensile footwork of Zinedine Zidane: 'It often seemed that his feet were endowed with the sensitivity and suppleness in manipulation of another man's hands.'[6]

Greatness does not arise in a vacuum. Meredith occasionally bemoaned being born – like Ian Rush, but not Michael Owen – just on the Welsh side of the Anglo-Welsh frontier, not from any lack of national feeling but because it so often condemned him to play in losing teams or to be refused release for international duties by his English clubs. But his native village of Chirk was a nest of footballing talent matched in Welsh history only by 1950s Swansea, under the tuition of T.E. Thomas producing a succession of fine players and teams capable of playing in six Welsh Cup finals (winning five) between 1887 and 1894. Meredith played in the last two, losing in 1893 and winning a year later.

It may not be a coincidence that his years in the mines – he finally left in 1895, after his first season with Manchester City – were those when North Wales's pitmen began to organise. Meredith appears to have been neither a radical like Jimmy Guthrie nor a natural member of the awkward squad like cricketing contemporary Sydney Barnes. What is not in doubt is that being suspended for a year for allegedly trying to bribe an Aston Villa player had an immense impact. 'It turned a taciturn but essentially contented man,' writes Harding, 'into a bitterly aggressive critic.'[7] It is also true, as the sympathetic but fair-minded Harding points out, that he never provided a convincing explanation for his actions and was probably fortunate not to be *sine died*.[8] But he undoubtedly felt both betrayed by his employers and belittled 'as though he were a little boy' by the Football Association.

Beyond this was a 'labourer worthy of his hire' outlook that would take more than half a century to prevail with the abolition of the maximum wage in 1961: 'What is more reasonable than our plea that the footballer, with his uncertain career, should have the best money he can earn? If I can earn £7 per week, should I be debarred from receiving it?'[9] Star quality and an eye for opportunity made him a pioneer of endorsements. Grand Central Railway posters before the 1904 FA Cup final carried a marketing message purportedly from Meredith, plus a picture of him firing the winning goal into the top left-hand corner of Bolton's net.[10] Matching life to art, he scored the only goal at Crystal Palace by doing precisely that.

Meredith was also a trenchant critic of the training methods of the time, telling the *Sunday Chronicle* that they involved 'too much running and too little of the ball'.[11]

If his own longevity owed something to the agility that steered him away from heavy challenges, other contributing factors included an obsessive daily personal training regime, a knowledge of massage that came from having two sisters and a wife in nursing and being a non-smoking teetotaller – not that this prevented his becoming a publican late in life. In addition, just as another hugely durable wingman Tommy Hutchison was wont to rub butter into his legs, Meredith's daughter remembered his applying 'a vile-smelling jelly used in the gears of coal-mining machinery'.[12]

Later life was tough, with the Players Union paying off Meredith's debts in the 1930s. He died in Manchester in April 1958, his place among the giants of the game – on and off the pitch – long secured.

NOTES

1 T. Mason, *Sport in Britain* (London: Faber and Faber, 1988), p. 51.
2 J. Harding, *Football Wizard: The Story of Billy Meredith* (Derby: Breedon Books, 1985), p. 171.
3 Ibid., p. 79.
4 J. Harding, *Billy Meredith* in P. Stead and H. Richards (eds.), *For Club and Country* (Cardiff: University of Wales Press, 2000), p. 15.
5 Harding, *Football Wizard*, p. 227.
6 Ibid; P. Young, *Billy Meredith* in Brian Glanville (ed.), *The Footballer's Companion* (London: Eyre and Spottiswoode, 1962), p. 231.
7 J. Harding, *For the Good of the Game* (London: Robson Books, 1991), p. 37.
8 Ibid, p. 113; *For Club and Country*, p. 14.
9 Harding, *Football Wizard*, p. 119.
10 ESPN soccernet, http://soccernet.espn.go.com/columns/story/_/id/969222/the-mavericks:-billy-meredith?cc=5739.
11 Ibid., p. 214.
12 Harding, *For Club and Country*, p. 18.

2

CHRIS TAYLOR

Uruguay: The First World Power

Had Diego Forlán's injury-time free-kick against Germany in Port Elizabeth been a few inches lower instead of thumping the crossbar, not only would it have taken the Uruguayan striker to the top of the World Cup goal-scoring charts, but it might also have helped the South Americans to third place in the tournament, their highest finish for 60 years. As it was, the Germans won a thrilling third-place play-off 3–2, although Forlán's second-half strike was named goal of the tournament. More importantly, though, Uruguay had left behind an exhilarating image of their football. As the defender Jorge Fucile said after the match, 'We've put Uruguay back where she belongs again.'

Most of the global television audience in 2010 probably had little idea that one of the smallest countries at the World Cup – with a population today of barely 3.5 million – had been the game's pre-eminent power in the first half of the twentieth century and that the four stars on the Uruguay badge represented four world titles won: two World Cups and two Olympic golds in the days when the Games were the pinnacle of international football. Before Brazil and more successfully than Argentina, it was the Uruguayans who adopted the British game and adapted it to their own Latin American culture, developing a unique style that was to sweep all before it. The smallest nation (by far) to win a World Cup, what they achieved, by any standards, was a small miracle.

As elsewhere in South America, football arrived in Uruguay with the British in the nineteenth century, when the country was an important part of Britain's 'informal empire'. The first games were casual affairs involving sailors ashore at the port of Montevideo. For the sport to get on to a more organised footing it took the intervention of the British schools which sprang up to serve the primarily expatriate elite. As with much else in the development of Uruguayan football, events in Montevideo largely paralleled those in Buenos Aires, the Argentinian capital 230 kilometres west across the wide mouth of the River Plate.

The first great rivalry in Uruguayan football was between Montevideo Cricket Club (founded 1861) and Montevideo Rowing Club (founded 1874), organisations that had added the increasingly popular sport to their repertoire. 'Cricket' allowed only English speakers as members, while 'Rowing', based in the port area, was more cosmopolitan. The first match between the two was played on 6 June 1881 and was refereed by the British ambassador. Cricket prevailed in a rain-lashed affair and also won the rematch three weeks later.

Both Cricket and Rowing decided to give up football in the mid-1890s but new clubs and new rivalries were already taking over. The football team of the Central Uruguay Railway Cricket Club (the forerunner of Peñarol) had its origins in a British company and 72 of the club's 118 founders were British. When members of the existing Montevideo Football Club and Uruguay Athletic Club met in 1899 to form Club Nacional de Football the new entity was conceived of as a *criollo* – local, Latin – reaction to the existing British-dominated clubs. The club drew on a growing pool of students for players and support. Football was taking hold in higher education. In a speech before a match between Defensa and Universitario in 1893, Alfredo Vázquez Acevedo, rector of University of the Republic, predicted that football would displace other sports and 'demonstrate that the Latin race can in the future compete with the Saxon race which today is more powerful than our own'.[1] Britain was the model, but it would ultimately be surpassed.

Uruguay's population in 1890 was about 700,000, of whom half were foreigners, with those of Italian origin outnumbering those from Spain. In Montevideo there were only about 1,000 British people. In 1891 Henry Lichtenberger founded Football Association, the country's first football-only club. Within months it had changed its name to Albion and proceeded to dominate local football for the next decade. Although the surnames of many of its founder members were English, most were locally born. The creolisation of Uruguayan football reached a symbolic point in 1905 when the league, which had been founded five years earlier on Lichtenberger's initiative as the Uruguayan Football Association League, changed its name to the Liga Uruguaya de Football (although not yet Fútbol).

Scottish Influence

But although Uruguayans were making the game their own they were in for a rude awakening. They were competitive against their larger neighbours in Argentina, but a series of tours by British sides, including Tottenham, Swindon and Nottingham Forest, showed they still lagged behind the traditional masters of the game, struggling to cope with their forceful style. It was into this situation that a Scot arrived with a tactical innovation. Most teams played a 2–3-5 formation adopted from the English. But when CURCC poached John Harley, a Glaswegian railway engineer, from the Argentinian team Ferro Carril del Oeste, he brought with him the W-M formation, with a fan-shaped forward line and, crucially, the new Scottish style –'*a la escosesa*'– emphasised short passing and combination play instead of English kick and rush.

Local players adapted readily and the new approach had its international baptism of fire in 1912 against Argentina. The two teams played four times in August and September with Uruguay winning three and drawing the fourth. So revelatory was this style that it became known as 'Fútbol del 12'. Uruguay's leading striker in that team, José Piendibene, believed the roots of its success lay in a combination of the 'effective' with the 'elegant'.[2]

Uruguay's economy, based on agricultural exports, was booming and the country was undergoing major changes under the modernising presidency of José Batlle y Ordóñez. Football was becoming ever more central to Uruguayan life. When Dr José María Delgado, president of Nacional, officially opened the club's new ground on 2 June 1911, he could boast that football now represented 'the greatest, if not the only, of our national sports' – a pre-eminence it has maintained, with basketball trailing in its wake and rugby a distant third. A British visitor to Montevideo in 1910 was struck by a scene in the working-class neighbourhood of Cerro: 'At one point in the midst of these primitive stone dwellings a small group of scantily clothed boys are playing football, the implement of their game being an old sheepskin rolled into the nearest imitation to a globe to which it will consent and held together roughly – one more instance of the spreading triumph of football, that wonderful game that seems to conquer its surroundings and to implant itself firmly throughout the world entire.'[3] It was boys just like these who formed the team that would claim the Olympic title in the Stade Colombes 14 years later.

Olympian Heights

The seventh modern Games in Paris saw the first Olympic football tournament to feature a team from South America. Uruguay's participation had stemmed directly from the previous year's South American championship, held in Uruguay itself. The president of the Uruguayan football association (AUF), Atilio Narancio, had promised the team that if they won on home soil he would send them to the Olympics. A 2–0 victory over Argentina in the final meant he was obliged to make good on his word. In the end

Narancio had to use his own money, mortgaging a property to fund 23 transatlantic berths on the steamer *Desirade*. (Five boxers and six fencers made up the rest of the Olympic contingent.)

The ship docked in Vigo and the Uruguayans made an immediate impression in a series of friendly matches against local Spanish teams. A record of played nine, won nine told its own story. A journalist who watched them defeat Celta Vigo wrote: 'We have now seen the South Americans play. And how they play!'[4]

The Olympic football tournament was wildly popular, generating a third of the Games' income, due in no small part to the startling impression made by the Uruguayans. In their first three matches, Yugoslavia were thrashed 7–0, the United States fared only marginally better in a 3–0 defeat, while the hosts could at least console themselves that they managed to score in a 5–1 beating. The semi-final, against the Dutch, was closer, the Uruguayans going behind for the first time in the competition. But Pedro Cea equalised early in the second half and Uruguay ran out 2–1 winners. In the final a crowd of 41,000 saw Switzerland swept aside 3–0 and Uruguay crowned world champions.

Uruguay's football was a revelation to European observers. Gabriel Hanot, the journalist who dreamt up the European Cup, wrote: 'The principal quality of the victors was a marvellous virtuosity in receiving the ball, controlling it and using it. They have such a complete technique that they also have the necessary leisure to note the position of partners and team-mates. They do not stand still waiting for a pass. They are on the move, away from markers, to make it easy for their team-mates ... The Uruguayans are supple disciples of the spirit of fitness rather than geometry. They have pushed towards perfection the art of the feint and swerve and the dodge, but they also know how to play directly and quickly. They are not only ball jugglers. They created a beautiful football, elegant but at the same time varied, rapid, powerful, effective. Before these fine athletes, who are to the English professionals like Arab thoroughbreds next to farm horses, the Swiss were disconcerted.'[5]

The players were fêted in Paris, particularly the cultured right-half José Leandro Andrade, who earned the nickname 'Le Merveille Noir'. A leader on and off the pitch, and a fine tango dancer, he was also one of the most notable in a long line of Afro-Uruguayans (who form some 5–6 per cent of the population) to grace the national side; his nephew Víctor Andrade helped win the decisive match of the 1950 World Cup. The team, which included a meat packer and a grocer, was led by 'The Marshal', José Nasazzi, who had worked as a marble-cutter for Montevideo's new Legislative Palace and played as a defender for Bella Vista. Remarkably, though, the winning squad was not the strongest possible. Domestic football had been split by the formation of a rival to the Uruguayan football association. Peñarol, half of the domestic duopoly, supported the rival 'Federation' and thus its players were overlooked when the 'Association' selected the squad for the Olympics.

In the wake of the Olympic triumph Uruguayan football acquired an international cachet. In 1925, Nacional, including numerous Olympic champions, embarked on a successful tour of Europe. They played 38 games in 159 days, winning 26, drawing seven and losing five, while scoring 130 goals and conceding only 30. Nacional could afford to be away for such a lengthy tour because domestic football was still divided and the championship was not played. Uruguay did not even send a team to the 1925 South American championship in Argentina.

However, by the time of the 1928 Olympics in Amsterdam, Uruguay's domestic schism was resolved and the national team approached the tournament with confidence even though they had not measured themselves against European opposition since the final in Colombes. This time, though, their old adversaries Argentina would be vying for supremacy.

Argentina's passage through the competition had been fearsome. In three matches to the final they had racked up 23 goals. Uruguay had found it more difficult, particularly in a hard-fought semi-final against Italy in which they had gone behind to an early goal before equalising – once again through Cea – and going on to win 3–2. The final was even tougher: the first attempt ended 1–1. The replay was also tied at 1–1 until the 73rd minute when the Wanderers forward Roberto Figueroa combined with his clubmate René Borjas who, with his back to goal, headed the ball down with a cry of 'Yours, Héctor' for Scarone, who volleyed home the winner for Uruguay.

World Champions

Uruguay were confirmed as the best in the world, but perhaps the most telling effect of their victory came the following year in Barcelona when Fifa delegates decided who should host the inaugural World Cup competition. Despite the rival candidacies of Hungary, Holland, Sweden, Italy and Spain, the honour was awarded to Uruguay by acclamation, no doubt aided by the country's promise to build a new stadium worthy of the event and to pay the passage of the participating teams.

The stadium they built, named the Centenario in honour of the centenary of Uruguay's democratic constitution, could hold more than 90,000 spectators, making it the biggest ground in Latin America at the time, and was crowned by a futuristic 'Tower of Homages'. The foundation stone had been laid on 21 July 1929, and even though the stadium was constructed simultaneously by two separate contractors who each worked on two stands, there was still scaffolding in place for Uruguay's first match, against Peru. The lift planned for the tower was only installed in 2004.

The tournament was marred by no-shows from a number of European countries, including all the defeated host candidates and the British associations, and no little cajolery was needed to ensure that France, Yugoslavia, Romania and Belgium made the transatlantic voyage. Nevertheless, the presence of Uruguay and Argentina among the 13 participating teams guaranteed the competition's credibility and it can have been to no one's surprise that these two antagonists met in the final after having won their respective semi-finals 6–1. The local championship had been suspended to aid the preparations of Alberto Suppici's team, while Argentina had shown impressive form and boasted the tournament's top scorer in Guillermo Stábile, although they had benefited from erratic refereeing in their group match against France when the official inexplicably blew for time six minutes early as the French were poised to equalise.

Some 30,000 Argentinians made the journey across the River Plate for the final, but fog meant that some missed the match. At the Centenario, Uruguay took an early lead through Pablo Dorado but within eight minutes Carlos Peucelle had equalised and, with Argentina dominating, Stábile put them ahead eight minutes before the interval. The home crowd was palpably worried but Cea, as he had done in the Olympic semi-finals in Paris and Amsterdam, scored a crucial equaliser and the tide turned. Santos Iriarte and Héctor Castro, who had lost a hand at work as a 13-year-old, added two more goals to ensure that Uruguay would be the first winners of the World Cup.

The result was greeted with dismay and some disorder in Buenos Aires, where the Uruguayan consulate was stoned. In part because of the bad feeling engendered, no South American championship (normally an annual or biennial event) was staged until 1935. Reflecting on the final, the Argentina inside-forward Francisco Varallo said: 'There were problems with everything, even including the ball. We wanted to play with ours and they wanted to play with theirs ... In the end we played the first half with our ball and we won it 2–1. In the second half we played with theirs and they turned the score around ... Every time I remember it I feel bitterness. They won by being craftier and more cunning. Not by being better players.'[6]

Others were more complimentary. The FIFA president, Jules Rimet, felt the 'victory was deserved' and praised the Uruguayans' 'robust' style ('without at any time resorting to roughness that might endanger the physical integrity of the players').[7] A number of observers commented that while the Argentinians perhaps had the better ballplayers, Uruguay combined better as a team.

Mindful of the European stayaways from their own tournament, Uruguay did not attend the second World Cup, staged in Italy, and the team, who had won only twice in four years, approached the reconvened South American championship in Peru in 1935 with expectations low. La Celeste narrowly prevailed in their first two matches, whereas Argentina, their opponents in the deciding game, had won both theirs 4–1. Los Albicelestes were strong favourites, but Uruguay, captained again by Nasazzi and wearing unfamiliar red shirts and white shorts, pulled off a shock 3–0 victory. It was this performance more than any other which sealed the national myth of *la garra charrúa*. *Garra* (literally 'claw') means 'guts' or 'fighting spirit', while *charrúa* refers to the indigenous inhabitants of Uruguay (exterminated as a people in the nineteenth century). It is a never-say-die attitude on which Uruguayan footballers to this day pride themselves.

Uruguay again stayed away from the 1938 World Cup in France so the question of how *la garra charrúa* would have fared against Europe's best at this time remains moot. But Uruguay were not entirely unrepresented. Miguel Andreolo, a South American champion in 1935, subsequently transferred from Nacional to Bologna, took Italian nationality and became a world champion in the same Colombes stadium where Uruguay had first dazzled the world.

The Maracanazo

When the World Cup resumed after the second world war it did so in neighbouring Brazil. For Uruguay, the off-field build-up had been less than ideal. In 1948, the new players' union had gone on strike for seven months in pursuit of freedom of contract and a percentage of transfer fees. Although a qualified success for the players, who enjoyed widespread popular support, it left a legacy of bitterness on both sides. Management of the national side was chaotic. They began the year with the fitness trainer as de facto coach, and went through a further three managers as Nacional and Peñarol battled to get their man in place. Finally, a neutral candidate in the form of Juan López, the young coach of Central, was appointed just two weeks before the squad set off for Brazil.

The team incorporated three of the devastating forward line who had won the 1949 championship for Peñarol: Juan Schiaffino, Oscar Míguez and Alcides Ghiggia. They also had that side's colossus of a centre-half, Obdulio Varela, as captain. Known to some as 'The Black Boss' and to his friends by his middle name of Jacinto, Varela had made his international debut back in 1939 and was the team's on-field organiser. Schiaffino maintained that: 'Peñarol ... was no less than the foundation for the '50 world champions. An extremely rare coming together of technique, strength, power, speed, goal scoring, temperament and character. Because it's not enough to have technique and know how to play; football is a game and also a struggle, so that character and personality are fundamental.'[8]

However, a bad atmosphere hung around the squad and relations between players and officials and the press were tense. Varela had been reluctant to travel because of his dissatisfaction with off-field disorganisation. One of the team, Matías González, had worked through the 1948 strike and was being shunned by his team-mates. Although he had been one of the strike's leaders, Varela took action when he found González alone in the hotel bar. 'We Orientales [Uruguayans] never drink alone,' declared Varela – himself a prodigious drinker – and team unity was restored.

Uruguay were lucky in that withdrawals meant their first-round group amounted to just themselves and Bolivia, whom they duly dispatched 8–0. But in the final round robin (uniquely, the champions were to be decided by a league system) they had to rely on a last-minute thunderbolt from Varela to salvage a 2–2 draw against Spain and needed two late goals from Míguez to beat Sweden 3–2, having trailed 2–1. In the deciding game awaited the hosts, Brazil, who needed only a draw to be world champions.

The Brazilians had been in scintillating form, destroying Sweden and Spain 7–1 and 6–1 respectively. Before the final match in the magnificent new Maracanã stadium – twice the size of the ground Uruguay had built 20 years earlier – newspapers had already been printed proclaiming Brazil as the world's best. One Uruguayan official told Míguez in the changing room immediately before the match that keeping the score down to four would save face.

The teams entered the field to the deafening sound of more than 170,000 watching Brazilians as streamers cascaded and doves were released. Undeterred, the Uruguayans began the game well and got to half-time with the match scoreless. Two minutes after the break, however, Friaça put Brazil ahead. As the crowd went wild, Varela marched up to the English referee, the ball under his arm, to protest that the goal had been offside. The Uruguayan captain, though, was under no illusion that he would overturn the decision. 'While the whole stadium was insulting me, I stopped the game for a couple of minutes,' he recalled. 'Their enthusiasm had been transformed into rage, into anger against me, who was going around in the middle of the pitch, holding the ball as if I owned it, putting a stop to the party. That rage got into the soul of the Brazilian players. When we restarted, they were blind, they were no longer thinking clearly, calmly. And we took advantage of that.'[9]

Instead of the Brazilians capitalising on their breakthrough, Schiaffino, the inside-left known for his 'cold rationalism' on the pitch, scored an equaliser in the 77th minute (he later said it was a mis-hit). The balance had swung. Ghiggia on the right wing had the beating of his full-back Bigode, who was perhaps intimidated by a blow in the face from Varela earlier in the game, and seized the moment, beating Barbosa at the near post. At the final whistle the crowd was stunned. Jules Rimet, on hand to present the trophy that bore his name, recalled: 'There was no longer any guard of honour, national anthem, speech, nor solemn presentation of the trophy ... I found myself alone, in the middle of the multitude, shoved in the ribs, with the Cup in my arms, not knowing what to do. Eventually I found the Uruguayan captain and handed the Cup over, almost furtively, offering my hand and unable to say a single word. Then, confusion descended. The crowd left as if from a cemetery.'[10]

In Uruguay the victory was taken as the apotheosis of *la garra charrúa*, a breathtaking triumph against the odds, commemorated as the Maracanazo. But for some, this ignored the qualities of the Uruguay team. A month before the World Cup, despite the off-field chaos, they had defeated Brazil in São Paulo 4–3 (although they lost and drew two further games in Rio de Janeiro). Varela felt the press had talked up the 'miraculous' nature of the victory to justify their previous lack of belief in the team. The night of the final he left the team hotel, where the Uruguayan delegation worried about their safety in a city in mourning, and toured the bars of Rio downing caipirinhas with the locals. 'They recognised our worth, better than ourselves,' Varela would remember. 'Brazil are an example. From their defeat, so crushing, they drew the lessons, they didn't stay put, they rescued the good, threw away the bad ... look at them now!'[11] Varela complained that the heroes of 1950 had not been valued, that instead of building on their success there was no continuity in the transmission of football culture as there had been from the 1930 generation. Certainly, the goal-scoring heroes that day in the Maracanã were not around long to pass on their experiences: Schiaffino and Ghiggia moved to Italy and eventually became Italian internationals.

Swiss Watershed

Like the England team that went to Mexico to defend their world title in 1970, the 1954 Uruguay side is sometimes spoken of as better than the vintage of four years previously. But according to their captain, preparations for the Swiss tournament again left much to be desired. 'The disorganisation was astounding,' recalled Varela. To the dismay of his team-mates, Uruguay went into the key quarter-final against the mighty Hungary without their all-time top scorer in the World Cup, Míguez, after a team official objected to him for reasons rumoured to involve the official's wife. Varela too was absent, having picked up an injury after scoring with a characteristic long-range shot in the 4–2 quarter-final victory over England.

Hungary, without their own injured star Ferenc Puskas, went into a 2–0 lead shortly after half-time but, in driving rain, the Uruguayans dug in and pulled level through two goals from Peñarol's Juan Hohberg. In extra-time Schiaffino hit the post and Uruguay had to play with 10 men after Víctor Andrade was injured. The Hungarians, though, proved too strong, and two headed goals from Sandor Kocsis meant they emerged as 4–2 winners. Hungary's coach, Gyula Mandi, said afterwards: 'We beat the best team we have ever met.' It was Uruguay's first World Cup defeat.

It was not evident at the time, but that rainy evening in Lausanne marked the end of the heroic age of Uruguayan football. The fall was rapid and precipitous. Uruguay missed qualifying for the World Cup in Sweden four years later when, needing a draw against Paraguay, they crashed to a 5–0 defeat. Instead it was Brazil who unleashed a new, devastating and beautiful incarnation of Latin American football upon the world. In Chile in 1962 Uruguay registered a solitary win before an early exit. Four years later Uruguay and Argentina were left muttering darkly of a European fix after, in the quarter-finals, a German referee sent off the Argentina captain against England and an English referee dismissed two Uruguayans against West Germany. Uruguay did make it to the 1970 semi-finals but little of the élan of earlier generations was on show: in six matches they scored only four goals.

At club level Uruguayan sides could still hold their own. The country's big two were major players in the Copa Libertadores, with Peñarol winning the trophy three times in the competition's first decade. Even in the 1980s, Nacional claimed the continental title twice to Peñarol's once. Away from the peak of the professional game, though, football was showing signs of strain. In the booming 1910s, nearly 2,000 new players were registered each year. By the 1960s, the figure was barely half that as the population aged. In the 1950s and 1960s, cumulative weekly attendances at professional football rarely exceeded 40,000, except when Nacional met Peñarol. In contrast to the early part of the century, as one Uruguayan writer observed in the late 1960s, 'For the average Uruguayan, professional football is neither a passion nor a spectacle: it's just a habit.'[12]

The proud democratic republic of 1930 was also a thing of the past: between 1973 and 1985, Uruguay endured repressive military rule. On the field, Uruguay departed the 1974 World Cup with just a single goal to their name and failed to qualify in 1978 and 1982. It was Argentina, the eventual winners, who knocked Uruguay out in the second round in 1986, but their participation was remembered more for recording the fastest-ever sending-off at the tournament, José Batista seeing red in the first minute of an unpleasant, foul-strewn match against Scotland. The secretary of the Scottish FA, Ernie Walker, memorably complained: 'There was no game of football here today. We found ourselves on the field with cheats and cowards and we were associated with the scum of world football.' La Celeste had also had a man sent off early in their 6–1 drubbing by Denmark and the abiding image of the team was of a niggly, mean-spirited and, for many, plain dirty side. It seemed that Uruguayan football had looked at the Maracanazo and taken the wrong lesson. Instead of Varela, the ball under his arm, embodying *la garra charrúa* through his calm, indomitable spirit, some appeared to have taken his example as one of gamesmanship, dissent and foul play. In the 1990s it was a Uruguayan, Paolo Montero, who held the record for most red cards in Italy's Serie A, and indiscipline was a factor in a dismal 1998 World Cup qualification campaign.

In the late 1980s and 1990s, about 100 Uruguayan footballers plied their trade at top clubs in Europe – many moving abroad at a very young age. The most important man in Uruguayan football by now was an agent, Paco Casal, who was responsible for brokering the passage of most of those players to Europe. But although Uruguayan players remained sought after, there was a growing feeling that traditional virtues alone might not be enough to restore national fortunes. Daniel Passarella, the Argentinian World Cup–winning captain who had a largely unhappy spell in charge of Uruguay around the turn of the millennium, observed: 'The stuff about *la garra charrúa* is true. Uruguayan players have a very marked personality. They don't bottle out wherever they play and have no fear on any field in the world. You've also got to be aware [though] that he who fouls gets sent off, especially in international competitions. We have to think carefully that these days you win by playing, not by fighting and kicking. But, also, the days of sneaking free-kicks, putting pressure on the referee and getting in his ear, are over. That doesn't work any more. These days, you have to play, pass and move, be quick and mentally prepared, all plugged in, because any national team can show you up.'[13]

Víctor Púa, Passarella's successor, also felt the national style needed to adapt. 'The key is to understand that it's a game, but a serious game. It's important to maintain our identity, go in fully committed to each challenge, but adding what's most lacking: technique, tactics and speed.'[14] Púa led the Under-20 team to second- and fourth-place finishes in the world tournaments of 1997 and 1999, supported by players such as Forlán and Diego Pérez, who would become mainstays of the senior team.

Uruguay had not been to a senior World Cup since 1990 when a Celeste team containing the great striker Enzo Francescoli failed to win a single match. After a 12-year absence, they returned in Korea and took part in one of the tournament's most thrilling matches, but their recovery from 3–0 down against Senegal to draw 3–3 only confirmed their exit, winless, at the group stage.

Perhaps it should have come as no surprise that Uruguay had been relegated to one of the also-rans of world football, occasionally making undistinguished appearances on the global stage. The country has, after all, a smaller population than Costa Rica's, or just slightly bigger than that of Wales. When Uruguay won the first World Cup in 1930 its population was a little over 1.7 million; today it is roughly 3.5 million. Historically, professional football in both Uruguay and Argentina was concentrated in the respective capitals, and when it was essentially a case of Montevideo competing against Buenos Aires the Uruguayans did so on a more or less equal footing. Now there are more than 40 million Argentinians from whom to pick a team.

Resurrection in South Africa

But then, in 2010, something wonderful happened. Uruguay were back at the World Cup, although only just – thanks to a solitary goal in San José in a play-off against Costa Rica. They arrived in South Africa having won only five World Cup finals matches since their first defeat in Switzerland 56 years earlier.

They began with a 0–0 draw against France, then defeated the hosts and Mexico to set up a second-round clash with South Korea, who in turn were overcome 2–1. It was already Uruguay's best showing in 40 years, but more than that the team's performances were stylish, displaying not just discipline and teamwork, but exciting forward play, particularly from Forlán and Luis Suárez.

The quarter-final against Ghana was the most dramatic game of the tournament. A Forlán goal early in the second half meant the scores were tied at 1–1 as the game entered the final seconds of extra-time. Then, in a desperate scramble in the Uruguayan goalmouth, Suárez kept out Matthew Amoah's goal-bound header with his hands, preventing almost certain elimination. Suárez was sent off but Ghana missed the resultant penalty and Uruguay progressed to the semi-final via a shoot-out. Some observers denounced Suárez's handball as a despicable act for which a red card was insufficient punishment, especially as it had denied Africa a representative in the semi-finals of the first African World Cup.

The Uruguayan writer Eduardo Galeano, though, maintained Suárez's intervention had been 'a sacrifice for his country, an act of love'. He argued that the striker's action had been instinctive and blatant – he had not tried to con the referee – and that he 'got himself sent off so that his team would not be sent home'. He might have added that Suárez had only been the culprit because Fucile, standing directly in front of him, had failed in his own attempt to stop the ball with his hand. While abroad the handball was the abiding memory of the match, for Uruguayans it was another side of native *viveza* (cunning) that stood out: the final penalty in the shoot-out, audaciously chipped, Panenka-style, down the middle of the goal by Sebastián Abreu. Uruguay went on to lose by the odd goal in five in their semi-final against the Dutch.

Much of the credit for Uruguay's best World Cup showing since 1950 was due to long-term, patient work. In particular, Oscar Washington Tabárez, who had presided over the mediocre campaign at Italia 90, had on this occasion been given time and allowed to get on with his job, creating a good team spirit and a well-drilled side. In Galeano's words, it had created 'a climate which favours miracles'.

Uruguay's gilded 2010 may not herald a return to the greatness of the early twentieth century. After all, recent World Cup semi-finalists such as Bulgaria, Croatia, Turkey and South Korea have struggled to build on their performances. However, a year on from their success in South Africa, Uruguay made the short trip across the River Plate to take part in the Copa América in Argentina. They performed consistently well and in the best match of the tournament knocked out the hosts in the quarter-finals. In the final at the Monumental stadium, the Uruguayans demolished Paraguay 3–0 with a goal from Suárez and two from Forlán. Their success was largely down to their team spirit, fostered by Tabárez, augmented by the fine finishing of their striking duo. Suárez, 24, was named player of the tournament and the defender Sebastián Coates the best young player, giving some grounds for optimism for the future. Uruguay, once a byword for on-field cynicism, even won the fair play trophy, though Suarez would earn notoriety in a Liverpool shirt.

In the wake of their Copa América victory, tiny Uruguay were officially ranked as the world's fifth-best team. They were South American champions for the 15th time, more than any other country. While the victory owed much to the consistent work of recent years, it also drew on tradition. Forlán's father had won the trophy as a player, as had his grandfather, twice, as coach, and Tabárez dedicated the title to those who had won the previous 14. The triumphs of the past can never be taken away from Uruguay, but in the early twenty-first century that tradition seems more like an inspiration and less of the burden it had perhaps become.

BIBLIOGRAPHY

Castro, R., *Garrincha: The Triumph and Tragedy of Brazil's Forgotten Football Hero* (London: Yellow Jersey, 2004).

Davies, P., *All Played Out: The Full Story of Italia '90* (London: Heinemann, 1990).

Galeano, E., *Football in Sun and Shadow* (London: Fourth Estate, 1997).

Goldblatt, D., *The Ball Is Round: A Global History of Football* (London: Viking, 2006).

Taylor, C., *The Beautiful Game: A Journey through Latin American Football* (London: Orion, 1998).

NOTES

1 A. Giménez Rodríguez, *La Pasión Laica: Una breve historia del fútbol uruguayo* (Montevideo: Rumbo, 2007), p. 23.

2 Ibid., p. 60.

3 W. H. Koebel, *Uruguay* (London and Leipsic: T Fisher Unwin, 1911), pp. 169–70.

4 Giménez Rodríguez, *La Pasión Laica*, p. 81.

5 D. Goldblatt, *The Ball Is Round: A Global History of Football* (London: Penguin, 2006), p. 245.

6 Giménez Rodríguez, *La Pasión Laica*, p. 100.

7 Ibid.

8 F. Morales, *Reyes, Príncipes y Escuderos: Del fútbol nuestro desde los años '40, vol 1* (Montevideo: Tradinco, 2004), p. 32.

9 A. Pippo, *Obdulio: Desde el Alma* (Montevideo: Fin de Siglo, 1993), p. 108.

10 Ibid., p. 118.

11 Ibid., p. 110.

12 F. Morales, *Fútbol: Mito y Realidad* (Montevideo: Nuestra Tierra, 1969).

13 A. Etchandy, *12 Años de Ausencia: de Italia a Corea* (Montevideo: Caballo Perdido, 2003), p. 125.

14 Ibid., p. 55.

The Game-Changers: Henri Delaunay

Great double acts work precisely because they are complementary, synthesising a whole that is greater than the sum of two parts. As Brian Clough, in a moment of acute self-knowledge, said of assistant Peter Taylor: 'I'm the shop front, he's the goods at the back.'[1]

Yet rewards and recognition are rarely distributed equally, and not only in sport. That vice-chancellors are likelier than registrars to be remembered when campus buildings are named reflects the shop window/goods in the back dynamic as much as the manner in which football names trophies and grandstands or chooses the subjects of statues.

Just as Taylor's daughter Wendy Dickinson remains aggrieved at Nottingham Forest's failure to recognise her father's contribution to a league title and two European Cups, Paul Dietschy records that Henri Delaunay felt that his own contribution to football at national, regional and international level during the first half of the twentieth century was unfairly overshadowed by Jules Rimet.[2] It was Rimet who got to be president of the French Football Federation (FFF) and of FIFA, and to have his name on the World Cup trophy. Delaunay's son Pierre showed a filial concern anticipating Ms Dickinson's when he wrote to FIFA to express concern that his father's role, in particular in creating the World Cup, was being forgotten.[3]

While, as Bill Murray notes, 'at times stormy', the Rimet-Delaunay double act was perhaps the supreme expression of France's contribution to the internationalisation of sport.[4] As Dietschy points out, 'In the 1920s the majority of international sports federations were based in Paris and, like FIFA, were headed by a Frenchman.'[5] Most of these sports were British-devised and it would easy to depict the French assumption of international leadership as a shot in the age-old *trans-manche* rivalry. Easy, but wrong. The Frenchmen wanted to work with Britain, and were even prepared to defer to it – Robert Guerin only finally going ahead with the foundation of FIFA in 1904 after finding that trying to get the Football Association interested was 'like slicing water with a knife'.[6]

They were products of a French middle class which turned to British examples and pastimes as a reaction to the decadence apparently revealed by the Franco-Prussian war of 1870. None was more dedicatedly Anglophile than Delaunay, a fluent English speaker known, as Murray records, 'as Sir Henry for his British airs, his pipe and his cocker spaniel, as well as his predilection for British names'.[7]

It was men like this who, as Geoff Hare has written of Rimet and Delaunay, 'helped move football beyond the national context to internationalise the playing and governance of the game, at times when its English inventors, with an insularity that went beyond the sporting domain, were reticent about the internationalisation of football and reluctant to be involved at the heart of European or world football until there was no alternative and most decisions were irreversible.'[8]

Born in 1883, Delaunay played football in the Paris suburbs from the age of 12. This kindled a passion that survived even the trauma of, as a referee, being struck full in the face by the ball, swallowing the whistle and losing two teeth. That he progressed rapidly through the roles of player, referee and administrator – becoming president of the Entre deux Lacs club in 1907 and founder secretary-general of the Comite Francais Interfederale (CFI), forerunner of the FFF, a year later when only 25 – was characteristic of young sports. Inevitably, lacking experienced elders, they also have young leadership. Because they arrive young, some of those leaders, like Delaunay, go on to have immensely long careers. The risk this carries, as with the remarkably durable early leaders of rugby union, is of ossification as the pioneers grow old. This does not appear to have happened to Delaunay, who was in his late 60s when he pressed for the creation of UEFA, Europe's own regional federation, and past 70 when he took office in 1954 as its first secretary-general.

As CFI chief he was among the progenitors of France's first national competition, the Coupe Charles Simon, founded in 1917 after years of campaigning along the lines of the FA Cup – a competition that had entranced him ever since he attended the 1902 final at Crystal Palace. He was a natural choice as the founding secretary-general of the FFF in 1919, presiding as chief 'technician of football matters' alongside Rimet over the rapid expansion of French football in the interwar years and its acceptance of professionalism in 1930.

It is, though, the World Cup that stands as his lasting achievement. Appointed to the four-man committee, chaired by Gabriel Bonnot of Switzerland, set up in February 1927 to discuss a possible competition, it was his proposal for a worldwide cup held every four years that carried the committee against rival suggestions of a Europe-only or amateur-only tournament, and his resolution to stage it for the first time in 1930 that was carried by 23 votes to 5 at the 1928 FIFA Congress in Amsterdam.[9] He was also a member of the organising committee for the 1930 tournament, and a photograph from the period shows him alongside Bonnot and Hugo Meisl, taller than both, slightly ascetic in appearance, bespectacled and clad in a long overcoat and clearly the focus of the conversation.[10]

He was also a key member of FIFA's Rules and Regulations committee, not least for his language skills. Fellow member Stanley Rous recalled that Dr Mauro, the Italian chairman, would explain his views in 'pidgin French' to Delaunay, who would then relay them in excellent English.[11]

He died in November 1955, still in office as secretary-general of UEFA, a post in which he was succeeded by his son Pierre, already also secretary-general of the FFF. His fatal illness meant that he missed, in March of that year, the first meeting held to discuss his long-cherished ambition to create a European Nations Cup. When that aspiration came to pass in 1958, there was only one possible name to attach to the trophy. It also, in the longer term, gave him the last laugh over Rimet. The Jules Rimet Trophy was retired after Brazil's third victory in 1970, and lost in 1983. The Henri Delaunay Cup remains to this day, his name recalled again in 2012 when it was competed for in Ukraine and Poland.

NOTES

1 P. Shaw, *The Book of Football Quotations* (London: Ebury Press, 2003), p. 190.
2 P. Dietschy, *Henri Delaunay*, www.wearefootball.com (accessed 15 January 2012).
3 Ibid.
4 B. Murray, *Football: A History of the World Game* (Aldershot: Scholar Press, 1994), p. 73.
5 P. Dietschy, *France and the Internationalisation of Sports,* Sport-in-europe.group. cam.ac.uk/symposium2summariesdietschy.htm (accessed 10 January 2012).
6 P. Lanfranchi, C. Eisenberg, T. Mason and A. Wahl, *100 Years of Football* (London: Weidenfeld and Nicholson 2004).
7 B. Murray, *The World's Game: A History of Soccer* (Urbana and Chicago: University of Illinois Press 1998), p. 61.
8 G. Hare, *Football in France: A Cultural History* (London: Berg, 2003), p. 34.
9 Lanfranchi et al., *100 Years of Football*, pp. 102–3.
10 Ibid., p. 103.
11 S. Rous, *Football Worlds, A Lifetime in Sport* (London: Faber and Faber 1978), p. 127.

3

HUW RICHARDS

Austria and Hungary: The Danubian School

When former England manager Steve McClaren discovered that an opponent was planning a tactical change against his Dutch club Twente Enschede, he asked a 21- year-old midfielder how he could counter the shift. McClaren recalled: 'He proceeded to talk for 20 minutes on the tactical aspects of our game plan, in terms of how we defended and attacked. After 20 minutes I said, "Very good, that's exactly what we were going to do – and by the way, where did you learn that?" He said, "We've been doing this since we were eight or nine".'[1]

That vignette helps explain how the Netherlands, with fewer than 17 million people, have over the past 40 years appeared in three World Cup finals and one semi-final, won one European Championship and been a semi-finalist in four more. As McClaren asked: 'Could I have that conversation in England?'[2]

Size does matter in football. Until the Dutch and Spain broke the pattern in 2010, every World Cup final had been contested by at least one of Italy, Germany, Argentina and Brazil, since 1930 usually the largest nations in Western Europe and South America. But size is not everything. As the Dutch show, one way to contest sheer weight of numbers is to not merely play football, but to think about it. Nor is this new. England's unquestioned lead as the codifier of football lasted only until the far less numerous Scots devised their passing game in the 1880s. It was a first, close-to-home example of a historic tendency in football and other British-codified sports. British traders, settlers and soldiers may have been missionaries taking their sports to new territories, but the converts were rarely passive recipients. They rapidly transformed them into something of their own.

Hogan's Heroes

McClaren and his tactically literate Dutch tyro echoed Jimmy Hogan's experiences in Vienna a century earlier. Hogan was a key figure in the development of football in Central Europe. When Hungary beat England 6–3 at Wembley in 1953, their coach Gustav Sebes said that they 'played football as Jimmy Hogan taught us' while Sandor Barcs, an official, said: 'He taught us everything we know about football.'[3]

Yet the teacher learnt as much from his pupils as they from him. In 1912 Hogan was invited to coach the Austrian Olympic squad but made a poor initial impression. His biographer Norman Fox writes that the Austrians 'found it difficult to understand him while his coaching seemed too concerned with basic premises'.[4] He took his problem to Hugo Meisl – nominally a banker, but in truth a full-time worker for football who drove the development of the game in Austria, a polymathic Jewish Anglophile polyglot and the promoter of Hogan's appointment. As Meisl's brother Willi recalled, 'With Hugo he worked out a more satisfactory scheme, probably the first modern training schedule in soccer.'[5]

Yet even that scheme was insufficient to satisfy the Austrian squad brought together to plan for the 1916 Olympics. Hogan offered a standard session and, as Fox writes: 'Afterwards the captain, looking disappointed, approached him and asked if that had been a typical session in England. Hogan again had to accept that the demands of continental players were going to be much different to those at home ... Now he realised they wanted everything he could give, and quickly.' Club demand for his services was so great that he had to schedule coaching sessions with Vienna FC between 5.30 and 7.30 A.M.[6]

Intellectual and Economic Vigour

What made the great cities of the late Austro-Hungarian empire – Vienna, Budapest and Prague – so receptive to football is as much a matter for anthropologists as historians of sport. While a stream of British teams visited from the 1890s onward, these would-be missionaries were not heading into a vacuum. They needed aspirant natives to issue invitations and provide opposition.

The Empire might have looked a palsied relic, but its great cities were places of intellectual and economic vigour. Vienna was host to the talents of Arnold Schoenberg and Sigmund Freud and a political culture that would generate the interwar phenomenon of Red Vienna. Budapest, one of the fastest-growing cities of the second half of the nineteenth century, was home to the continent's first underground railway, Béla Bartók and, in 1919, a short-lived experiment with Communist government. Prague had two satirical literary giants, Franz Kafka and Jaroslav Hasek, both born in the same year.

Football in these cities reflected and fed off this vigour. From the start, players wanted not only to play but also to think about the game, debating it and seeking out fresh nuances and layers of tactical sophistication. This 'Danubian school' of football would generate two of the most memorable teams in the sport's history.

The first recorded match in Vienna was in 1894. Within two years a city team was playing Budapest, where organised football began as an adjunct to gymnasia in the 1880s. The first working-class club, Wiener Arbeiter FK (rapidly renamed Rapid Vienna), was formed in 1898; growth down the social scale was paralleled in Budapest by the foundation of Ferencvaros in 1899.[7] In 1902, Austria played Hungary in continental Europe's first international match on the European continent, launching a series that, as Bill Murray writes, was 'fought with all the drama of a local derby'.[8]

Austria won 5–0, but this was essentially a false dawn. As Willi Meisl wrote, 'the Hungarians were usually a short step ahead of the rest',[9] winning 12 to Austria's 8 of 24 meetings before the First World War, including the only competitive clash, the Consolation Final at the 1912 Olympics.

The first Hungarian *aranycsapat* (Golden Team) emerged after 1906, a practical expression of what the Zionist intellectual Max Nordau memorably labelled 'muscular Judaism'.[10] Alfred Hajos-Guttmann, a fencer who won one of Hungary's first two Olympic gold medals in 1896 and inside-left in the team beaten 5–0 in Vienna in 1902, was by 1906 selector-manager. When Hungary broke the rivalry's pattern of home-team dominance by winning 4–3 in Vienna in 1909, a majority of its team – including Gyula Biro, reckoned by historian Andrew Handler to have 'the qualities ahead of time of a midfielder' – were Jews.[11]

Austria and Hungary were not the first European nations to take up football. But as David Goldblatt has written, they achieved 'what neither the Swiss nor the Low Countries could manage before the First World War. They created an entrenched popular football culture in which the game was played by a broad spread of the social scale and which could draw on growing and passionate crowds.'[12] The consequence was, as Murray has observed, that before 1914 they led the football world outside the United Kingdom 'and into the 1930s they continued to do so'.[13] Notable absentees as yet from this discussion were their neighbours Italy and Germany.

The First World War ended traumatically for Austria and Hungary. Dual imperial partners since 1867, they were summarily diminished in power, status, population and territory. Vienna and Budapest, capitals of empire, now loomed disproportionately over small nations. The defeated states were diplomatically isolated, and only determined resistance from internationalists such as Henri Delaunay stopped this extending to football as they thwarted attempts to expel defeated powers from FIFA. Neither Austria nor Hungary attended the 1920 Olympics in Antwerp.[14] The freshly minted third corner of the Danubian triangle, Czechoslovakia, established in 1918, showed on debut a gift for performing well in major tournaments that became a constant thread, reaching the final before being denied a medal because their team, 2–0 down after 30 minutes to Belgium, walked off complaining about biased refereeing.

Losing an Empire, Gaining a Role

As Pierre Lanfranchi has suggested, postwar trauma may have enhanced the importance of football in Vienna and Budapest: 'More than a pastime for boys, football became an export product for these capitals without hinterlands. The endemic economic crises which characterised the nations of Central Europe in the twenties, the weakness of the markets and the difficulties which these "new little nations" encountered on the international scene, further accentuated the importance to them of football. Since they were masters of their craft at continental level, their teams sought to achieve real gains from the hitherto symbolic gains achieved on the field of play.'[15]

In 1914 there were 14,000 registered footballers in Austria; by 1921 there were 37,000, the majority in Vienna. Crowds showed a similar trend. In 1914 Austria met Hungary and attracted 24,000 spectators; the 1921 match pulled in 45,000, rising a year later to 65,000 and remaining above 40,000 until the late 1930s.[16]

Football in all three of these successor states was metropolitan, concentrated in capital cities to the extent that only Vienna teams played in the Austrian national league until 1949. Vienna's football culture was so vibrant that the *Neues Wiener Journal* proclaimed it the 'football capital of the European continent' in November 1924. Its description is an unmistakeable foretaste of the most vital of modern city-state sporting cultures, Australian football in Melbourne: 'Where else can you see at least 40–50,000 spectators gather Sunday after Sunday at all the sports stadiums, rain or shine? Where else are the majority of the population so interested in the results of games that in the evening you can hear almost every other person talking about the result of the league matches and the clubs prospects in the coming games?'[17]

Among the fabled coffee houses, the Ring Café became 'a kind of revolutionary parliament of the friends and fanatics of football ... one-sided club interests could not prevail because just about every Viennese club was present'.[18] Even the physical layout of Vienna favoured the game, according to Horak and Maderthaner, who record that large open spaces between industrial and residential areas on the fringe of the city became 'a focus for sub-cultural learning and leisure. It was here that football grew and it was from the suburbs that the majority of the spectators and protagonists came.'[19]

Sophistication did not preclude physicality. The first authentic folk-hero was Rapid's bulldozing Josef Uridil, forerunner of British archetypes like Trevor Ford. Celebrated in the music hall song 'Heute Spielt Uridil', his charges on goal were wont to end with 'Uridil and three or four of his opponents lying on the ground and the ball in the other side's net'.[20] Hugo Meisl, as ever ahead of the game, imported a German athletics coach in the 1920s to advise on fitness training.[21] But as Hogan had already discovered, 'their players understood that it took no special skill to get fit. They did that automatically. They demanded much more.'[22]

From this concatenation of forces emerged a distinctive footballing aesthetic. When Austria drew 2–2 with Scotland in Glasgow in 1930, one Scottish club director recognised 'the game we used to play 20 years ago'.[23] It was, though, as Jonathan Wilson has written, 'a radicalised extension of the Scottish game'.[24] In Brian Glanville's memorable characterisation it was 'a sort of competitive ballet in which scoring goals was no more than the excuse for the weaving of a hundred intricate patterns'.[25]

Hugo Meisl's faith in this approach, which evolved from the 'pass and move' style he and Hogan developed before the First World War, was shaken in the early 1920s when Austria were slaughtered 5–1 on a frozen pitch by South Germany. It was reaffirmed only after spending the 15-and-a-half-hour rail journey back from Nuremberg discussing with his players whether a more direct style should be adopted.[26]

The Symbolism of Sindelar

It was incarnated in the style and personality of Matthias Sindelar, a centre-forward who, as the writer Frederick Torberg once attested, differed from Uridil 'as a tank from a wafer'.[27] Basing his style of play on that of a Hungarian, Kalman Konrad, Sindelar became, in Horak and Maderthaner's words, 'a figure of the literary imagination, a metaphor and symbol of the Viennese character'.[28]

While Hugo Meisl is often labelled autocratic, the way Sindelar, an immigrant from Moravia and former brickworker first capped in 1926, was recalled after a four-year international exile in 1931 epitomises both the player's literary resonance and Meisl's willingness to listen to others. Meisl was cornered, and ultimately persuaded, in the Ring Café by a coterie of the resident pro-Sindelar footballing intelligentsia.[29]

There is no film of Sindelar in action, while his resistance to Nazism following the Anschluss takeover of Austria in 1938 and mysterious early death a year later have cast a retrospective glamour, but as Goldblatt points out there is a striking consistency to written descriptions.[30] The theatre critic Alfred Polgar remembered that Sindelar 'would play football as a grandmaster plays chess'; for Torberg he was 'endowed with such an unbelievable wealth of variations and ideas that we could never really be sure which manner of play was to be expected'.[31]

To Willi Meisl he was 'truly symbolical of Austrian soccer at its peak period; no brawn, but any amount of brain. Technique bordering on virtuosity, precision work and an inexhaustible repertoire of tricks and ideas. He had a boyish delight in soccer exploits, above all in unexpected twists and moves which were quickly understood and shared by his partners brought up on the same wavelength, but was baffling to an opposition mentally a fraction of a second slower.'[32]

Mitropa and Beyond

Sindelar also played in a context a little ahead of most European contemporaries. That mass following drove early professionalization. Hungary and Austria accepted payment for players in 1924 and Czechoslovakia a year later.[33] But clubs could rarely survive on domestic income alone. Tours and friendlies proliferated against attractive foreign opposition, often from other parts of the Danubian triangle. The visionary Hugo Meisl saw, and persuaded neighbouring nations, of the potential for giving these matches a meaningful competitive framework. So in 1927 the annual Mitropa Cup, for leading club sides from the Danubian trio, Italy and Switzerland, was created alongside the International Cup – a parallel three-year competition for their national teams. Clubs from Vienna, Prague and Budapest were between them to win the Mitropa Cup in 11 out of 13 years as well as providing 10 out of 13 runners-up. Still more significant, as Willi Meisl wrote, was that this proto-European Cup 'did much to popularise football on the continent and enhance its qualities. The most gifted ball-playing people – Hungarians, Austrians, Czechs and Italians – exchanged styles and ideas on club as well as international level.'[34]

It may have postponed a pan-European tournament by two decades. When French journalist Gabriel Hanot raised the idea in 1934 he was rebuffed by the Mitropa nations, content with their own competition.[35] It also underpinned the competitive advantage enjoyed by those countries, who provided all four finalists at the two European-staged World Cups in the 1930s. The first European non-Mitropa finalist was neighbouring Germany in 1954; the exploits of Sweden in 1958 and England in 1966 were one-offs based on home advantage, and it was not until the emergence of the Netherlands in 1974 that Europe produced a wholly non-Mitropa world power.

In one sense the most successful Danubian teams of the 1930s were Czechoslovakia and Hungary, World Cup runners-up in 1934 and 1938 respectively. Both lost to Italy, which as recently as 1924 had gone down 7–1 to a Hungary team featuring an all-Jewish forward line.[36] Italy's coach, Vittorio Pozzo, recognised the Czechoslovakia of 1934 as a fine team with 'a unity and cohesion guaranteed by the fact that the players which form it come from only two clubs' and high-quality teamwork based on 'intricate movement and short passes', but diagnosed a potentially fatal weakness in the Danubian style, where 'movements develop largely in a line, in a uniform and even a monotonous way'. Czechoslovakia were still, he acknowledged, superior for long periods in that final. They took the lead after 70 minutes, then hit a post and missed another chance before a weirdly dipping shot by Raimundo Orsi– one of three imported Italian-descended Argentinians who gave Pozzo's team yet another dimension – rescued Italy with eight minutes left.[37]

The Wunderteam

Yet the most memorable team of this period lost in the semi-finals. Austria, still recovering from a brawling quarter-final against Hungary, fell to an Italian team reaping every benefit of home advantage. Like many fine teams who have disappointed in World Cups, they had peaked a couple of years too early. The Austrian team built by Hugo Meisl around Sindelar earned its enduring Wunderteam label in a spectacular 18-match unbeaten run spanning 1931 and 1932, including a 5–0 demolition of Scotland hailed by *Arbeiterzeitung* as 'a tribute to Viennese aesthetic sense, imagination and passion', an 8–2 win over Hungary highlighted by a Sindelar hat-trick and 6–0 away and 5–0 home defeats of Germany.[38] Yet, as Horak and Maderthaner dryly note, the Wunderteam 'would not have been a uniquely Austrian, or to be more precise, uniquely Viennese phenomenon, if its greatest triumph had not been a defeat'.[39]

England beat Austria 4–3 at Chelsea in December 1932 but it was, recorded the *Daily Herald*, 'A most disturbing victory – the kind that leaves one wondering how it happened ... definitely and beyond all shadow of doubt, Austria played football better than England did.'[40] Two down early on, Austria dominated most of the subsequent play, with Sindelar scoring a solo goal in which he befuddled two would-be tacklers before beating goal-keeper Harry Hibbs: referee John Langenus reckoned it 'a masterpiece such as no-one ever before accomplished against such opponents as England'.[41] Veteran former international Ivan Sharpe thought Austria better than Scotland's 'Wembley Wizards', who had flattened England 5–1 four years earlier.[42]

There was only one more defeat, against Czechoslovakia, before the 1934 tournament, which they entered as favourites. But they were an ageing team, tired and, as Goldblatt suggests, disturbed by events at home, where only a few weeks earlier Engelbert Dollfuss's right-wing government had violently suppressed 'Red Vienna' and with it Austrian democracy. Playing the fired-up hosts on a mudheap calculated to defuse the Danubian style was the final blow.[43] Horak and Maderthaner argue that the Wunderteam label applies truly only to 1931 and 1932.[44]

By 1938 Hugo Meisl was dead and so in effect was Austria, swallowed by Hitler's Greater Germany. Sindelar wrote the final lines in his legend by insisting that Austria play in national colours and inspiring a 2–0 victory over the invaders in the match played to mark the Anschluss, refusing either to play for Germany or display Nazi posters in his café and dying in unexplained circumstances in early 1939.[45]

Austrian football's return from war had a tentativeness befitting a nation unsure whether its relationship with Nazism was as early victim (the official line) or all-too-complaisant collaborator. In 1950, a lively team was deemed too young to take to the World Cup in Brazil. As Glanville notes acidly, 'By 1954 it would be too old.'[46] In Ernst Ocwirk, 'tall, muscular and dark, the possessor of a wonderfully strong and accurate left foot and impeccable technique', last of the great attacking centre-halves, they had a player worthy in style and quality of the Wunderteam.[47]

But confidence in their own methods was flagging. National coach and former Wunderteam centre-half Walter Nausch evidently concurred with Glanville's view that his team was 'delightfully artistic and maddeningly inconclusive', saying even after beating Scotland at Hampden Park in 1950 that the Vienna school 'is good to watch, but it is not effective. We like to play with the ball too much.' By 1953 Ocwirk had been converted into a wing-half.[48]

The Mighty Magyars

By then the baton of the Danubian style had passed down-river to Budapest. Hungary lost to Italy in the 1938 World Cup final, having inflicted a majestic semi-final beating on Sweden. Pozzo, hardly neutral but invariably acute, reckoned them less impressive than the Czechs of 1934, 'always inferior, by and large, to the potential of an Italian team functioning and playing its normal game'. But their achievement marked a rising generation. Ferenc Puskas, who would define postwar Hungary much as Sindelar symbolised interwar Austria, recalled that the 1938 team 'inspired a lot of players as well as us youngsters'.[49]

Less wracked by the war than its neighbours, Hungary instead had the postwar trauma of a progressive communist takeover culminating in the declaration of a People's Republic in 1949. Its football has been seen as both expression of, and respite from, communism. Sebes argued that 'the fierce style between capitalism and socialism took place as much on the football field as anywhere else', but his free-thinking goalkeeper Gyula Grosics recalled that 'our victories made it possible for ten million Hungarians to regain and celebrate their "Hungarian-ness" in a way the state could hardly disapprove of'.[50] Historian Andrew Handler votes with Grosics: 'In the highly and forcibly politicised Hungarian society of the 1950s, no area of public entertainment offered more satisfying moments of respite and refuge from reality than sport.'[51]

That team also lends itself to football's variation on the nature versus nurture debate – players or tactics? Walter Winterbottom, England's coach of the time, was a footballing intellectual and the last man to undervalue imaginative tactics. But he argued that the indispensable foundation of any great team is great players, and reckoned that the Hungarians who so devastated his sides in 1953 and 1954 had no fewer than five – Puskas, Nandor Hidegkuti, Jozsef Boszik, Zoltan Czibor and Sandor Kocsis.[52] As Glanville put it, 'when Kocsis and company were present, every man looked like a giant'.[53]

All, though, were the products of a culture, as Rogan Taylor points out, 'used to thinking about the game and how it could or should be played'.[54] Jeno Buszansky, one of the 'other men' of Glanville's formulation, recalled of Hungary's victories over England: 'It was because of tactics that Hungary won. The match showed the clash of two formations and, as so often happens, the newer, more developed formation prevailed.'[55] Though a functionary of Stalinism, Sebes did not practise it with his team. Buszansky recalled that 'tactics were very much up for discussion' in what Goldblatt has characterised as 'a protected enclave of trust, dialogue and spontaneity'.[56]

Nor did the control of leading clubs MTK and Honved by the secret police and army respectively act as a brake on creativity. MTK were coached by Marton Bukovi, whom Grosics and journalist Georgi Szepesi credit with the creation of the 4–2–4 playing formation – using Hidegkuti as a 'deep-lying centre-forward' – later adopted with such success by the national team.[57] Honved briefly employed the peripatetic polyglot Bela Guttmann, described by Jonathan Wilson as the 'last of the coffee house coaches'.[58]

The pattern fell fully into place at the 1952 Olympics, creating a system that as Glanville recalled combined 'the craft and artistry of the older school of football with the speed and power of modern play'. With both Hidegkuti and Boszik, the wing-half who had been Puskas's next-door neighbour in childhood, playing in modern parlance 'between the lines', opponents were utterly bemused. As Grosics recalled: 'No one else seemed to know about it in advance and consequently, all found it very difficult to defend against.'[59] England defender Billy Wright, flummoxed, as Geoffrey Green famously observed in the *Times*, 'like a fire-engine going to the wrong fire' by the Puskas drag-back that preceded the most famous of Hungary's six goals at Wembley in 1953, recalled 'marking the spaces they had just left'.[60]

Tommy Docherty, who played against Hungary for Scotland, left a vivid picture of the problems they set: 'They would lull you into a false sense of security with a procession of quick, short passes that took them nowhere and then suddenly unleash a paralysing long pass that would arrive in space a split second ahead of one of their "turned-on" team-mates. They more than any team I have ever seen realised the importance of supporting runs. Every time a player was in possession he would have a minimum of two and sometimes as many as five team-mates getting into positions where they could receive the ball. It made it a nightmare for we defenders trying to work out who to pick up'.[61]

And then there was Puskas, of whom Buzansky recalled: 'If a good player has the ball he should have the vision to spot three options. Puskas could always see at least five'.[62] Allied with lieutenants of such quality and innovative tactics, he was irresistible. Sweden were beaten 6–0 in the Olympic semi-final, England demolished by an aggregate of 13–4 in home and away matches in 1953 and 1954 that Syd Owen remembered as 'like playing men from outer space', and – perhaps just as importantly for Hungarian self-belief – historic bête noire Italy beaten for the first time in a quarter of a century, 3–0 in Rome in 1953.[63]

Between 1950 and 1956, Hungary scored 219 goals in 50 matches, an average of nearly 4.4 per match. Victory over holders Uruguay in the 1954 World Cup semi-final gave them what still remains the highest rating ever under the Elo system, a formula designed by Arpad Elo, a Hungarian physics professor, for rating chess players but since adapted to football.[64] They won 42 of those 50 matches, lost only one and are kept off the top of 'greatest-ever' lists usually headed by the 1970 Brazilians by that single defeat, against West Germany in the 1954 World Cup final, the 'Miracle of Berne' of German legend.

Numerous explanations have been advanced for West Germany's 3–2 win. They include indiscipline, Puskas playing when not fully fit, complacency after taking an early 2–0 lead, plain ill-luck, having an apparently legitimate late equaliser disallowed and a miraculous display by German goalkeeper Anton Turek. The emergence of the Germans, retarded by resistance to professionalism and the lack of a national league, was long overdue. Both teams were playing their third match in a week, but while the Germans had enjoyed a comparatively comfortable route, including a 6–0 semi-final demolition of the fading Austrians, Hungary had an epic quarter-final brawl with Brazil and a classic semi-final, extending to extra-time, against Uruguay.

Brazilians might argue that their loss as hosts to Uruguay in 1950 was still more shocking and traumatic. But Brazil, with its huge population and insights into the 4–2–4 formation taken there by Guttman in 1957, did not take long to recover, winning three of the four tournaments from 1958. Hungary never has recovered. As Tibor Nyilasi told Jonathan Wilson, 'It is as though Hungarian football is frozen at that moment, as though we have never quite moved on from there.'[65]

Hungary's players continued to debate tactics, and win matches, after 1954 but the sense of glad, confident morning was gone for good and signs of decline evident even before the Soviet invasion of 1956 and its aftermath decapitated the team. Broadcast reports of the death of Puskas in the fighting in Budapest proved happily unfounded, but he was just as surely lost to Hungarian football. Honved, MTK and the national under-21 squad were all out of the country when the Russians invaded. Some returned, but the bulk of these three outstanding teams were among the 12,000 players the Hungarian FA reckoned to have lost following the invasion.[66]

Decline and Fall

All great teams eventually decline, but the two emblematic Danubian teams were cut off abruptly by external events. The Russians in 1956 did for the greatest *aranyscapat* what the crushing of Red Vienna did in 1934 to the Wunderteam. Hungary still qualified for World Cups, but their eliminations told a story of decline. In 1958 in Sweden it was Wales's Ivor Allchurch, with a stunning play-off volley from a cross by John Charles, who summoned up the brilliance once associated with Hungarians. In 1962 in Chile they dominated a quarter-final against Czechoslovakia, but French writer Thierry Roland might have been talking about those artistic but inconclusive Austrians of a decade earlier when he observed: 'The quality of play, attacks and possession, territory and chances to score were all in favour of Hungary, but once more verified the dictum that to dominate is not the same as winning.' Roland said much the same of the group stage defeat by

Portugal in 1966. That sent Hungary into a quarter-final against the Soviet Union, who with all-too-obvious symbolism simply overpowered them.[67]

Occasional reminders of a better past were offered for the benefit of British audiences – the defeat of England in Chile in 1962, Florian Albert's Goodison Park masterclass and Janos Farkas's spectacular goal in a 1966 World Cup defeat of Brazil that Roland saw as 'at the level of their distinguished predecessors of 1954' and a marathon solo goal by Janos Mate at Liverpool in 1975 as Ferencvaros progressed towards the UEFA Cup final, the last Hungarian club to get that far in Europe.[68]

Subsequent World Cup appearances have been few, and disappointing. They scared hosts Argentina in the opening match of the 1978 tournament before falling 2–1 and having their best players, Tibor Nyilasi and Andras Toroscik, sent off in the closing stages. Arriving with high hopes after topping their qualifying group in 1986, they were crushed 6–0 by the Soviet Union. Not only have they not been back but they have rarely looked like doing so. Reaching 27th in the world rankings in September 2011 was hailed, admittedly by FIFA's official website, as 'historic' – and compared to 62nd four years earlier at least represented some sort of revival.[69]

Austria too have disappeared from the top level of the game, with no World Cup finals appearance since 1990. Their most memorable contribution to the three tournaments for which they qualified post-1954 was the unpleasant aroma hanging around a 1–0 defeat by West Germany in 1982 that enabled both to progress at the expense of Algeria. While there were players of distinction such as Hans Krankl, good enough in a Spanish league containing such luminaries as Mario Kempes to win the 1978–79 Pichichi trophy for leading scorer with 29 goals (more than half of Barcelona's total) in 30 games, most teams were markedly short of *wunder.* Horak dates the end of 'the weekly ritual of masses of spectators at the Viennese football grounds' to the late 1960s. In the 1940s four league matches on the same day in Vienna were likely to attract 60,000 spectators; by the late 1980s it would be 10,000–15,000 and the admission of the provinces, which joined the league in 1949 and provided their first champion, Linzer ASK, in 1965, could not compensate for the demise of the Vienna school.[70]

Nor did the thawing of the Cold War bring relief. Hungarian living standards declined heavily in the 1990s, with the gross domestic product not returning to 1989 levels until 2002.[71] Social anthropologist Janos Bali diagnosed his compatriots as suffering 'an inferiority complex and a sense of peripheral status nationally', unsure quite where they belonged in a reshaped Europe.[72] For Austria the thaw ended a role as a trading post uniquely well connected to the East. Residual Austro-Hungarian influence was seen most elsewhere. After taking 4–2–4 to Brazil, Bela Guttmann coached Benfica to two European Cups.

Czechoslovakia proved more capable of sustained success, reaching the World Cup final in 1962 then winning the European Championship in 1976 with Antonin Panenka's chipped winning penalty-kick both a reminder of traditions of audacious technical virtuosity and the completion of a rare shoot-out defeat of Germany. After the post-Communist schism, the Czech Republic made it to a Euro final in 1996 and a semi-final in 2004. But the Czechs have not produced a team as memorable or influential as the Wunderteam or the postwar Hungarians.

The football of Austria and, in particular, Hungary ranks alongside French cycling, Australian men's tennis and American heavyweight boxing as once-hegemonic sporting cultures that have fallen to a point where redemption can seem impossible. What goes down can of course rise up again. Their fall, if not the extent of it, is grounded, however, in the logic that says that once small nations lose competitive advantage – in this case tactical sophistica-tion – over larger neighbours, adversity will become the norm. The wonder is not that they now struggle, but that they were once so good.

NOTES

1 Guardian.co.uk, 5 August 2011.

2 Ibid.

3 N. Fox, *Prophet or Traitor? The Jimmy Hogan Story* (Manchester: Parrs Wood Press, 2003), pp. 11–12.

4 Ibid., p. 57.

5 W. Meisl, *Soccer Revolution* (London: Phoenix, 1955), p. 58.

6 Fox, *Prophet or Traitor?* p. 64.

7 Ibid., p. 61; D. Goldblatt, *The Ball Is Round: A Global History of Football* (London: Pegasus, 2007), pp. 139–40.

8 B. Murray, *Football: A History of the World Game* (Aldershot: Scholar Press, 1994), p. 60.

9 Meisl, *Soccer Revolution*, p. 59.

10 Goldblatt, *The Ball Is Round*, p. 198.

11 A. Handler, *From the Ghetto to the Games: Jewish Athletes in Hungary* (New York: Columbia University Press, 1985), pp. 52–61.

12 Goldblatt, *The Ball Is Round*, p. 139.

13 Murray, *Football: A History of the World Game*, p. 60.

14 P. Lanfranchi, C. Ehrenberg, T. Mason and A. Wahl (eds.), *100 Years of Football* (London: Weidenfeld and Nicholson, 2004), p. 66.

15 P. Lanfranchi, 'Notes on the Development of Football in Europe' in R. Guilianotti and J. Williams (eds.), *Game without Frontiers: Football, Identities and Modernity* (Aldershot: Arena, 1994), p. 35.

16 R. Horak, 'Austrification as Modernisation: Changes in Viennese Football Culture' in Guilianotti and Williams, *Game without Frontiers*, pp. 47–48.

17 *Neues Wiener Journal*, 15 November 1924, quoted in R. Horak and W. Maderthaner, 'A Culture of Urban Cosmopolitanism: Uridil and Sindelar as Viennese Coffee-House Heroes' in R. Holt, J.A. Mangan and P. Lanfranchi (eds.), *European Heroes, Myth, Identities, Sport* (London: Frank Cass, 1996), p. 139.

18 *Welt am Montag*, 22 March 1948, quoted in Horak and Maderthaner, *European Heroes, Myth, Identities, Sport*, p. 141.

19 Ibid., p. 143.

20 Ibid., p. 146.

21 Meisl, *Football Revolution*, p. 109.

22 Fox, *Prophet or Traitor? The Jimmy Hogan Story*, p. 67.

23 Meisl, *Football Revolution*, p. 26.

24 J. Wilson, *Inverting the Pyramid: A History of Football Tactics* (London: Orion Books, 2008), p. 33.

25 B. Glanville, *Soccer Nemesis* (London: Secker and Warburg, 1955), p. 50.

26 Ibid., p. 52.

27 Quoted in Horak and Maderthaner, *European Heroes, Myth, Identities, Sport*, pp. 146–47.

28 Ibid., p. 147.

29 Goldblatt, *The Ball Is Round*, p. 257.

30 Ibid., pp. 257–58.

31 Polgar quote from *Pariser Tagezeitung*, 25 January 1939, quoted in Horak and Maderthaner, *European Heroes, Myth, Identities, Sport*, pp. 147–48; Torberg quoted in Wilson, *Inverting the Pyramid*, p. 61.

32 Meisl, *Football Revolution*, p. 59.

33 Murray, *Football: A History of the World Game*, p. 90.

34 Meisl, *Football Revolution*, p. 60.

35 Murray, *Football: A History of the World Game*, pp. 164–65.

36 Handler, *From the Ghetto*, p. 72.

37 Ibid., pp. 145–46; B. Glanville, *The Story of the World Cup* (London: Faber and Faber, 1997 edn.), p. 28.

38 *Arbeiterzeitung*, 14 May 1931, quoted in Horak and Maderthaner, *European Heroes, Myth, Identities, Sport*, p. 150; Goldblatt, *The Ball Is Round*, p. 257.

39 Horak and Maderthaner, *European Heroes, Myth, Identities, Sport*, p. 152.

40 Fox, *Prophet or Traitor? The Jimmy Hogan Story*, p. 119.

41 Ibid., p. 117.

42 Meisl, *Soccer Revolution*, p. 61.

43 Goldblatt, *The Ball Is Round*, pp. 258–59.

44 Horak and Maderthaner, *European Heroes, Myth, Identities, Sport*, p. 152.

45 Goldblatt, *The Ball Is Round*, p. 310.

46 Glanville, *The Story of the World Cup*, p. 45.

47 Ibid., p. 64.

48 Glanville, *Soccer Nemesis*, pp. 167–73.

49 Pozzo quote from *La Stampa*, 20 June 1938, reprinted in B. Glanville (ed.), *The Footballer's Companion* (London: Eyre & Spottiswoode, 1967), p. 154; Puskas quote from R. Taylor and K. Jamrich (eds.), *Puskas on Puskas* (London: Robson Books, 1997), p. 20.

50 Ibid., p. 105; Goldblatt, *The Ball Is Round*, p. 343.

51 A. Handler, *From Goals to Guns: The Golden Age of Soccer in Hungary 1950–56* (New York: Columbia University Press, 1994), p. 124.

52 Taylor and Jamrich (eds.), *Puskas on Puskas*, p. 99; Glanville, *The Story of the World Cup*, p. 67.

53 Ibid., p. 67.

54 Taylor and Jamrich (eds.), *Puskas on Puskas*, p. 67.

55 J. Wilson, *Behind the Curtain* (London: Orion Books, 2006), p. 71.

56 Ibid., p. 73; Goldblatt, *The Ball Is Round*, p. 343.

57 Taylor and Jamrich (eds.), *Puskas on Puskas*, p. 36.

58 Wilson, *Inverting the Pyramid*, p. 95; Taylor and Jamrich (eds.), *Puskas on Puskas*, pp. 67–69.

59 Ibid., p. 69.

60 Fox, *Prophet or Traitor? The Jimmy Hogan Story*, p. 195.

61 Ibid., p. 208.

62 Wilson, *Behind the Curtain*, p. 75.

63 Wilson, *Inverting the Pyramid*, p. 90.

64 World Football Elo ratings: Hungary, http://eloratings.net/hungary.htm (accessed on 4 January 2012).

65 Wilson, *Behind the Curtain*, p. 84.

66 Taylor and Jamrich (eds.), *Puskas on Puskas*, p. 160.

67 T. Roland, *La Fabuleuse Histoire de la Coupe du Monde* (Geneva: Minerva, 2002), pp. 80, 97, 104.

68 Ibid., p. 98.

69 'Hungary's historic rise', FIFA.com, 29 September 2011.

70 Horak, 'Austrification as Modernisation', pp. 53–59.

71 Wilson, *Behind the Curtain*, p. 90.

72 Ibid., p. 93.

Figure 3.1. Del Sol, Alfredo Di Stéfano, Ferenc Puskas, Gento – Real Madrid 1950s.
Credit: Colorsport.

ROB STEEN

The Game-Changers: Alfredo Di Stéfano

Of all the fields of sporting endeavour, footballing excellence is perhaps the hardest to measure – and not simply because the game's relentless pace can impair full appreciation. Unlike most other team pursuits, it has traditionally used statistics to convey the quality of the collective, all but shunning the individual. Until the recent growth of companies such as Opta, cruncher of all manner of illuminating numbers about tackles completed and passes executed in the Premier League, scoring goals was the only solo act that captured imaginations and penetrated memories. But how can a prolific striker be fairly proclaimed a better player than a redoubtable centre-half, a perceptive playmaker or a tireless wing-back?

Pelé and Diego Maradona, of course, are the names most commonly fêted as the apogee of footballing wonder – not solely by dint of their capacity to bulge nets but that uncanny ability to outwit opponents and persuade a spherical object to indulge their every whim. But does this accepted wisdom do an injustice to those with a broader palette? You don't have to be Welsh, for example, to prefer John Charles, a giant equally at home in Serie A or the Football League, at the heart of defence or attack. Nor are Mancunians alone in contending that, but for the Munich air disaster, Duncan Edwards's potent blend of bone-rattling tackle, spatial awareness, incisive passing and iron-clad shot might have set unimaginable standards of all-round accomplishment. The difficulty with Alfredo Di Stéfano (Figure 3.1) is that he never took the field in a single World Cup finals match. In his artful labours for a Real Madrid at the zenith of their powers, there remains every reason to cite him as the greatest player famed exclusively for his deeds for club rather than country. Or, in his case, countries.

Unlike Pelé and Maradona, 'La Saeta Rubia' – the blond arrow – was born too soon to be garlanded on the televisual stage. Politics, injury and qualification failures prevented him from gracing the final phase of a single World Cup, further reducing his visibility. As it is, and welcome as they unquestionably are, those YouTube clips of his hat-trick for Real Madrid in the 1960 European Cup final, even of that apparently telepathic partnership with Ferenc Puskas, merely skim the surface. Has any player done more to bridge that clichéd divide between South American flair and European work-rate? Even Pelé is disinclined to disagree: 'People argue between Pelé or Maradona. For me, Di Stéfano is the best. He was much more complete.'[1]

Controversy, initially, was a constant companion. A farmer's son whose grandfather had migrated from Capri, Di Stéfano, the eldest of three brothers, was brought up just outside Buenos Aires; some have suggested that his dutiful toiling on the family farm was the source of that seemingly inexhaustible stamina, though he himself attributed it to cross-country running. Emerging at River Plate, for whom his father had played, he scored six goals in as many games at the 1947 Copa America but two years later a general strike ravaged professional football in Argentina, whereupon Di Stéfano, doubtless impelled in part by his country's isolation under Peron, joined the Latin American exodus to Colombia, a nation engulfed by civil war.[2] The Colombian FA had severed ties with FIFA, which in turn suspended the national team from international competition following the launch, in 1948, of Dimayor, a renegade league whose members had no need to pay transfer fees.

Joining Millonarios for the so-called El Dorado era, it was in 1952 that Di Stéfano helped win a tournament celebrating Real's 50th anniversary, alerting Spanish scouts. When Colombia and FIFA kissed and made up, Real and Barcelona were equally determined to sign him, prompting the Spanish FA to play Solomon: he would spend alternate seasons with each. The ensuing uproar in Catalonia culminated in the Barcelona board resigning en masse and Real being sold the full transfer rights. Granted, Di Stéfano had done little in his first six weeks in Madrid, but the very day after Barcelona sold their share, he scored four times against them. Timing always was an asset.

He may not have been the first Argentinian to use Italian ancestry as their route to Europe (Luisito Monti, a member of the side that finished runners-up at the 1930 World Cup, helped Italy go one better four years later). Nor was he the first deep-lying centre-forward – Nandor Hidegkuti is widely cited as the prototype – but Di Stéfano did broaden perceptions of what was possible, pioneering 'Total Football' (though others would reap the credit). To him, the logic was inescapable: 'I am always on the move: up, back and across, trying not to be fixed in one position and so allowing the defender to see too much of me. Or I may be trying to avoid "bunching" with other forwards. Or I may be reading what is to come, and be moving to help the next man on the ball … For forwards should accept it as part of their job that they should help the defence … We are all footballers, and as such should be able to perform competently in all eleven positions.'[3]

If his international loyalties were flexible – he represented Argentina, Colombia and, after naturalization, Spain – Di Stéfano left his heart in Madrid, with Real, whom he inspired to victory in the first five European Cup finals, twice being anointed the continent's player of the year. Geoffrey Green, the first football correspondent sent overseas by the *Times*, hailed him as 'the most complete, all-round player' he ever saw: 'He had a swift short stride with a high-stepping knee action and he moved lightly with bouts of timed acceleration like someone stepping over burning coals or broken glass. He possessed peripheral vision; his eyes darted here and there hungrily as his mind measured and calculated every situation.'[4] To Brian Glanville, never shy of musical metaphors, he was not only 'an absolute perfectionist' but 'a Toscanini of his time'.[5]

'The less you have the ball at your feet [the] better.' Thus did Di Stéfano, now Real's honorary president, expound his philosophy in 2010.[6] The following year, after a draw with Barcelona, he publicly chastised José Mourinho for his tactics, his very ethos. Castigating his players for running 'back and forth constantly, tiring themselves out', he lionised Lionel Messi and drew an unflattering comparison with opponents who treated the ball 'with adoration and respect'.[7] A refreshing case of 'do as I do *and* as I say'.

NOTES

1   A. Comas, 'Real Madrid great Di Stéfano turns 85', Reuters.com, 4 July 2011, http://blogs.reuters.com/soccer/2011/07/04/real-madrid-great-di-Stéfano-turns-85.

2   T. Mason, 'The Bogota Affair' in J. Bale and J.A. Maguire (eds.), *The Global Sports Arena: Athletic Talent Migration in an Interdependent World* (London: Frank Cass, 2003), pp. 39–41, http://books.google.co.uk/books?hl=en&lr=&id=OT4sCZOJOCkC&oi=fnd&pg=PA39&dq=%22Alfredo+Di+Stéfano%22+&ots=ueqmItGplU&sig=LUpN7MnOtjoECP7f-wHTHYYp5pI#v=onepage&q=%22Alfredo%20Di%20Stéfano%22&f=false.

3   B. Glanville, *Champions of Europe – The history, romance and intrigue of the European Cup* (London: Guinness 1991), p. 14.

4   G. Green, *Pardon me for Living* (London: George Allen & Unwin, 1985), p. 157.

5   Glanville, *Champions of Europe*, p. 15.

6   'Di Stéfano, 'Now, the best of all is Messi', Donbalon.com, 26 October 2010.

7   'Alfredo Di Stéfano criticises Real Madrid's style under Jose Mourinho', *Guardian*, 18 April 2011, www.guardian.co.uk/football/2011/apr/18/alfredo-di-Stéfano-real-madrid-jose-mourinho.

4

PADDY AGNEW

Italy: Football as Politics – Mussolini to Berlusconi

It is simply no coincidence that two of the most powerful figures of the last 100 years of Italian public life – namely, Fascist dictator Benito Mussolini and media tycoon-cum-prime minister Silvio Berlusconi – made no bones about attaching themselves to the bandwagon of football. In their different ways and, albeit, with links to very different teams – Mussolini to the Italian national team of the 1930s, Berlusconi to the modern outstanding club side, AC Milan – both men had an intuitive understanding of the groundbreaking role that football could and does play in modern Italy.

If football is often the looking glass through which we observe reflections of the socio-economic concerns of the society in which it is played, then both Mussolini and Berlusconi illustrate the extent to which, as John Foot put it, 'football history and Italian history simply cannot be separated'.[1] This was one big wave that both men were more than able to surf.

This is not to say that both men owed and owe their political success to football. That would be much too simplistic. Mussolini's ruthless political ambition and drive had led to the creation of his Fascist state long before his 'Italia' won the 1934 and 1938 World Cups. Berlusconi's entrepreneurial success and his huge media empire were clearly more important to the realisation of his political aims than AC Milan.

Yet, along the road to government house, both men sensed very clearly that, in Italy, football could prove itself a vital, cutting-edge weapon in the national political debate. Clearly, they had different uses for football – Mussolini used it to help create a national identity whereas Berlusconi found it useful in the creation of a Peronist-style populism.

Struggles and Scandal

It is, of course, patently reductive to assess Italian football exclusively in relation to Mussolini and Berlusconi, however revealing that analysis might be. In so many other ways, Italian football has mirrored the society in which it has been played.

If much of postwar Italian public life was rocked by a mix of violent political struggle and recurring public scandals – the 1978 Red Brigade killing of Aldo Moro, the 1980 Bologna train station bombing, the 1992–94 Tangentopoli scandal, not to mention the succession of vicissitudes that have touched Berlusconi – then the same observation might be made of Italian football.[2]

For a start, there was the sense of nationwide grief prompted by the 1949 'Superga' tragedy in which almost the entire Torino team (18 players), then by far the strongest in Italian football, was wiped out when the team plane crashed into the Superga Basilica, high in the hills above Turin, on the way back from a friendly game in Portugal. For Italian football, this tragedy was as traumatic as that which hit English football when a Manchester United plane crashed in Munich in 1958. Torino had won the previous five league titles, whilst the Italian national team of the day sometimes fielded nine or even ten Torino players.[3]

In more recent times, there have been scandals aplenty. From the match-fixing scandal of 1979–80 which almost cost Paolo Rossi his place in Italy's 1982 World Cup-winning team through to the 2006 'Calciopoli' scandal which unwittingly acted as motivation for that year's Germany World Cup victory by the Marcello Lippi-coached Italy,[4] modern Italian football has been besmirched by a bewildering series of outrages as well as violent and racist episodes.

Allegedly false passports for talented non–European Union (EU) players such as Argentine Juan Sebastian Veron and Uruguayan Alvaro Recoba have abounded.[5] Rome derbies and Champions League encounters have been abandoned because of fan intimidation or violence.[6] Serie A has habitually seemed on the brink of economic meltdown[7] whilst Serie A clubs such as Lazio and Parma have been almost liquidated by the financial collapse of their owners, namely, Sergio Cragnotti of Cirio and Calisto Tanzi of Parmalat.[8]

Racism, too, has regularly raised its ugly head. Incidents involving black players such as Arsenal's Frenchman Patrick Viera and Messina's Ivory Coast defender Mark Zoro[9] were just the tip of the iceberg. In more recent times, black Italian Mario Balotelli was the persistent focus of racist chants.[10] Then, too, there was the unsavoury incident in January 2000 at the Olympic Stadium in Rome when some Lazio fans unfurled a 70-foot-long, hand-painted banner reading 'Honor to the Tiger Arkan', the recently assassinated Serbian paramilitary leader and warlord, indicted for crimes against humanity.[11] It has also come as a huge shock to find Juventus of Turin, arguably the most famous of all Italian clubs and one which in the eyes of many represents the best traditions of Italian football, involved in not one but two major scandals. Not only was the 'Old Lady', as Juventus is called, a major protagonist in the 2006 'Calciopoli' match-fixing scandal but it also featured in the unedifying spectacle of the five-year-long 'Processo Juve' (2002–07).

In the end, Juventus paid a heavy price for the role played by their director, Luciano Moggi, in 'Calciopoli'; the club was punished by being relegated to Serie B for the first time in its history, whilst Moggi was subsequently banned for life from football by the Italian Federation.[12] As for the 'Processo Juve', a trial in which the club stood accused of systematic doping practices, it concluded with the Cassazione Appeals Court ruling in 2007 that club doctor, Ricardo Agricola, was guilty of 'sporting fraud' but that the crime came within the statute of limitations and therefore the charges were dropped.

Nor has another scourge of modern Italy, namely, organised crime, left the national game untouched. The links between Napoli's great Argentine ace, Diego Maradona, and the camorra, the Neapolitan mafia, have long since been documented.[13] What is perhaps less well known is the extent to which another of Italy's mafias, namely the Calabrian 'N'drangheta', has sought to win influence and consensus by controlling lower-division sides in its region.[14] Furthermore, as we write, the role of organised crime in Italy's most recent football scandal, namely a betting scam entitled 'Last Bet', remains unclear.[15]

Setting the European Standard

Despite the problems of the society around it, however, Italian football has long been highly competitive. Italy has won four World Cups (1934, 1938, 1982 and 2006), and such was the dominance of Italian clubs in the period between 1989 and 1999 that they played in nine out of the ten Champions Cup/League finals, winning the trophy four times and being the losing finalist on the other five occasions. Even in the twenty-first century, which has seen Italy's Serie A completely overtaken in terms of both results and economic power by the English Premiership, Italian clubs have still managed to pick up three Champions League trophies (AC Milan in 2003, 2007 and Inter Milan in 2010), while Lippi's team picked up the 2006 World Cup.

For the last 20 years of the twentieth century, Italian football had set the European standard. Not for nothing, Italian know-how, in the shape of coaches such as Fabio Capello (England), Roberto Mancini (Manchester City), Carlo Ancelotti (ex-Chelsea) and Giovanni Trapattoni (Ireland), has been much sought-after. From Giuseppe Meazza through Gianni Rivera and onto such as Roberto Baggio and Francesco Totti, Italian football, too, has consistently thrown up prodigious talents. Known to football fans worldwide for its ultra-defensive 'catenaccio' mentality (a tactical system that first won trophies in the 1950s and 1960s), Italian teams at both club and national level often remain true to a defensive and cautious mindset, complementing the talents of such as Baggio and Totti with the skill of defenders like the peerless Paolo Maldini. It often seems that, for Italian teams, the first tactical concern is not how to score but rather how not to concede a goal.

In that, too, Italian football merely reflects the cautious, pragmatic nature of many Italians. This is, after all, the land of Machiavelli. The successful coach Nereo Rocco, winner of two Italian titles with AC Milan (1962 and 1968) and a man closely identified with defensive Italian play, has passed into popular legend for a revealing exchange. When a reporter once said to him, 'May the best team win', his immediate reply was 'Goodness, I hope not'.[16]

Unity through Football

As already stated, Mussolini and Berlusconi clearly had very different uses for football. For Mussolini the idea was to promote the 'ideal of an organic, patriotic, nationalist and united nation through football'.[17] To be fair, Mussolini was happy to use other sporting disciplines to achieve this end but, as Italy developed, it became clear to him that no sport could rival football in the Italian mind.

For Berlusconi, on the other hand, the 'ideal' was to promote Silvio Berlusconi through the creation of a vast media empire in which AC Milan was at first merely an addendum.[18] His 1986 purchase of the club was initially about the creation of a potent loss leader for his Fininvest empire, one that would help promote a 'synergy' of winning images. Only later, when circumstances changed, did the 'Great Communicator' realise that Milan could be part of the message.[19]

It would, of course, be naïve to imagine that one could sum up the first hundred-plus years of football in Italy merely by addressing its links to Mussolini and Berlusconi. There have been other powerful players on the Italian football scene – the automobile giant FIAT at Juventus, the shipbuilder Achille Lauro at Napoli and the petrol millionaires, Moratti father and son, at Inter Milan (Internazionale), to name but the very most obvious. For all that they were (are) clearly big time 'fans' of their clubs, the interest of the Agnellis at Juventus, Lauro at Napoli and the Morattis at Inter clearly had (has) a socio-economic dimension to it, linked to the creation of a broad consensus among their fellow fans, be they FIAT car workers, Naples mayoral election voters or (half of) the citizens of Italy's industrial capital. All three cases are worthy of study – in particular, Lauro tends to look like a Berlusconi before his time in that he served as mayor of Naples for much of the 1950s and 1960s.

Yet the nexus between power, politics and football in Italy is nowhere better illustrated than in the persons of Mussolini and Berlusconi because, after all, they both ended up running the country and not without the help of football. If this seems overstated, then just consider the following statement from Mussolini:

> Sport represents the exaltation of the moral and physical force of youth and enhances a country's prestige. Sport will become the trademark of fascist Italy.[20]

The point about this statement is that 'Il Duce' made it in a private conversation in January 1923, just three months after the de facto coup of his infamous 'March on Rome'. Mussolini had summoned Giorgio Vaccaro, an ambitious young Fascist militant and First World War veteran who had boldly introduced himself to Il Duce at a Fascist Congress in Rome in November 1921. Vaccaro had declared a major interest in sport so Mussolini, always on the lookout for trusted lieutenants who could help establish his dictatorship, had plans for him.

Mussolini's own interest in sport was twofold. Firstly, he was convinced that his totalitarian regime would have to stake out a moral dominion over every sphere of the individual citizen's life, including sport and recreation. Secondly, he was equally convinced that sport, in particular football, could have a hugely important unifying role in the new Fascist Italy. In those early meetings with the young Vaccaro, Il Duce stressed that sport could in no way be allowed to remain the preserve of a privileged minority.

To put it another way, from very early on Mussolini perceived the potential of sport in helping to enhance and consolidate national identity. In a foreword for a book by the Olympic athlete Ugo Frigiero in 1933, Il Duce wrote:

> Sporting achievements enhance the nation's prestige and they also prepare men for combat in the open field and in that way they testify to both the physical well being and moral vigour of the people.[21]

The Viareggio Charter

A 1926 referees' strike, itself prompted by a series of bitterly contested incidents of the familiar 'goal-non-goal' variety in previous seasons (in particular a Genoa v Bologna 1925 play-off and a Casale v Torino 1926 encounter), offered the Fascist regime the opportunity to intervene and reorganize Italian football. Mussolini had tried (and failed) to convince Italians that football was not in fact an importation from the dreaded 'Inglesi' but rather the logical development of the old Florentine 'calcio'. The heavy involvement of Englishmen in the foundation of Italy's earliest clubs such as Genoa, Milan and Juventus suggested otherwise.

The 1926 crisis prompted the Viareggio Charter, which oversaw a serious reorganization of Italian football. Not only were the leagues reshaped but the Charter also de facto established both professionalism and the transfer market. More importantly, though, the Charter placed the governing body of Italian football, the FIGC (Federazione Italiana Giuoco Calcio), under the wing of CONI, the Italian Olympic Committee which by that time was a 'virtual arm of the party'.[22] Thus it was a Fascist-controlled FIGC which in the 1929 season instigated the first truly national league championship (until then, there had been Northern and Southern leagues). In a sense, then, it was Mussolini who invented Serie A.

The preparations, too, for that new Serie A indicated clearly just what role Mussolini attributed to sport. Under the original rules, the new Serie A would have had to start off without Triestina (the side from Trieste on the border with Slovenia) and without either Napoli or Lazio. The new Serie A was to combine the first eight in the Northern and Southern leagues; the problem was, Triestina had finished ninth in the north and Lazio and Napoli had tied on eighth in the south.

Vaccaro, knowing all too well what Mussolini required of him, was having none of it. With splendid 'flexibility', he simply changed the rules and decided that the new Serie A would have 18 rather than 16 teams, thus making way for all three sides. Shortly afterwards, Mussolini summoned Vaccaro to government house to congratulate him on his handling of the problem and in particular on how he had overcome the resistance of senior Fascist figure and under-secretary at the Ministry of the Interior, Leandro Arpinati:

> The single league championship represents the unity of Italy and that would have been a deformed unity without Trieste. I don't understand Arpinati... Football is a sport of the 'popolo', we must never forget that. This new national championship will improve our best players and generate great enthusiasm for the national team. And now we have a new horizon to conquer, the World Cup.[23]

And indeed, that 'new horizon' was duly conquered. Quick to recognize the value of the then fledgling World Cup, Mussolini lobbied hard to have the second edition in 1934 staged in Italy. Il Duce saw the tournament as an obvious promotional opportunity for his Fascist regime, 'as much for the technical value of its game as its organizational knowledge'.[24]

'Team, Be Ready, Salute …'

Football historians have long argued that Mussolini then worked even harder to make sure that Italy would have a team capable of winning the tournament. With pragmatic cynicism, legislation banning foreign players was reversed and suddenly the Italian national team was able to field a number of Argentine stars of Italian origin, with three of them, Raimundo Orsi, Luis Monti and Enrique Guaita, playing a key role in the 1934 World Cup triumph. (All three had played for Argentina before switching allegiance to Italy.)

That Italian team, coached by Vittorio Pozzo, then went on to stage a repeat World Cup win four years later in France. By this stage, however, the 'Azzurri' came with a very clear Fascist tag. When Italy lined out to meet Norway in their opening match of that tournament, they met with a very hostile reception inspired above all by an estimated 10,000 political exiles on the terraces.[25] Things got so rough that police had to be called in to restrain the anti-Fascist protestors.

Those exiles who argued that the team had become closely identified with the Mussolini regime seemed to have their point proved for them that day in Marseilles when coach Pozzo ordered his players to give not one but two Fascist salutes to the crowd. Pozzo himself described the incident thus:

> 'At the salute, as predicted, we were greeted by a solemn and deafening barrage of whistles and insults … We had just put down our hands when the violent demonstration started again. Straight away. 'Team, Be Ready, Salute'. And we raised our hands again to confirm we had no fear … Having won the battle of intimidation, we played.'[26]

If Mussolini could be dubbed 'the man who invented Serie A', he was also arguably the man who invented the 'stadio comunale', the local authority–run stadium intended for football and often for other sports such as athletics. State funding was pumped into the building of stadiums in towns all over Italy, including major cities such as Milan (the original San Siro), Bologna, Florence, Genoa, Pisa, Palermo, Roma, Trieste and Turin. Ironically, today's top Italian clubs suffer economically from this Fascist investment because they continue to use increasingly outdated, local authority–run stadia, thus missing out on the valuable revenue that could be generated by having their own modern stadiums. It was only in the autumn of 2011 that Juventus became the first current Serie A side to own their own stadium when they unveiled a spanking new 42,000-seater on the site of the 1990 World Cup Stadio Delle Alpi. Prior to Juventus, Reggiana, a lower-division club, had been the only Italian professional club to own its own stadium.

Mussolini's stadium-building programme, of course, led to a significant moment in Italian life when he travelled to Bologna in October 1926 to preside over the inauguration of the city's new 'Littoriale' stadium, very much the brainchild of the local Fascist leader, Leandro Arpinati. On an occasion that was intended to mark the fourth anniversary of the Fascist rise to power, Il Duce entered the stadium on a white horse to an ecstatic reception. The Fascist newspaper, *L'Assalto*, described the event thus:

> When ... we saw the mighty Duce enter like a conductor of people, bathed in the light of the sun that had finally driven away the clouds, greeted by a mass that only Eternal Rome will have seen paying tribute to a 'triumph' and to a victorious consul, we truly thought the hearts of all Italians must have been beating with his.[27]

The idyllic climate, however, turned ugly when shots were fired at Mussolini as he was being driven to the train station. In the ensuing chaos, a 13-year-old boy, Anteo Zamboni, son of a well-known local anarchist, was brutally beaten to death by the crowd, which had identified him as the would-be assassin.[28] The dynamics of this ugly incident remain unclear. What is sure, however, is that the alleged assassination attempt gave the green light for a whole range of highly repressive measures. By the end of 1926, new legislation had re-introduced the death penalty, had banned all political parties other than the Fascist Party and had set up a special Fascist police service. Clearly, the Fascist dictator was always going to ride roughshod over free speech and fundamental democratic principles, but the Bologna stadium incident provided a perfect excuse.

Despite such moments, however, it was clear that Italian Fascism, by and large, was good for football and football was good for Italian Fascism. Above all, the Italian national team had made significant progress, winning two World Cups and the gold medal at the 1936 Berlin Olympics. Even if those victories must be qualified by the consideration that several important football powers – above all, England– did not deign to play in World Cups in those days, Italy seemed to have progressed. Remember that in 1913, in the space of a few days on an Italian tour, the then minor English club Reading FC drubbed Milan 5–0, beat the reigning Italian champions, Pro Vercelli, 6–0 and concluded by beating the Italian national team 2–0.

In the meantime, Il Duce had clearly used football to great effect in the process not just of empire building but also in the consolidation of a national identity. Sixty years after Il Duce, another powerful Italian with autocratic tendencies, namely, media mogul and three times centre-right Prime Minister Silvio Berlusconi, also piggy-backed on that same sporting identity.

Football as Showbiz

When Berlusconi paid out approximately $11 million for AC Milan in February 1986, he clearly was not thinking in terms of political ambition. By 1986, Berlusconi was already one of the wealthiest men in the land, someone who had moved from property development in the 1960s to the creation of a huge commercial television empire, all controlled by his Fininvest holding company.

As a self-confessed AC Milan fan, it seemed only logical that he should step in to rescue his favourite club, then struggling in mid-Serie A, burdened by debt and run by a president, Giuseppe Farina, who would eventually depart for South Africa under a cloud.[29] The Milan fans certainly saw him as the saviour of the day with banners appearing at the Meazza (San Siro) stadium urging him to purchase the club.

Obviously, Berlusconi's media empire, his wealth and, above all, his political alliances with such as the late, disgraced Socialist prime minister Bettino Craxi were fundamental to preparing the way for his entry into politics in 1994. Yet, the AC Milan factor weighed in too. As the silverware piled up on the AC Milan sideboard, Berlusconi began to enjoy the populist experience.

This is hardly surprising – just try walking out into the San Siro stadium to be greeted by wild applause from 70,000 fans at the mere mention of your name and not be moved by the experience. In those early Milan days, Berlusconi was often present for stadium celebrations of a Champions Cup[30] or Serie A title success. Like Mussolini before him, he could never resist a good photo op with his winning team.

The Art of Synergy

It is at least arguable that nothing quite plugged Berlusconi into the psyche of the 'popolo' as effectively as regular spectacular success at the nation's favourite game. Long before he had entered the political arena, the popolo was only too familiar with the name Berlusconi – he was a winner not just via the creation of his multi-billion Fininvest empire but also via a football team that he had rescued from imminent financial collapse and then led on to stylish Italian, European and World club tournament success. (Under Berlusconi, Milan, to the end of 2011, had won eight Serie A titles, four Champions Cup/League trophies and two World club tournaments.)

In those early Milan days, too, Berlusconi was very much a hands-on owner. Not only did he himself make the call to buy important players such as Dutchmen Marco van Basten and Ruud Gullit but he also oversaw a complete overhaul of the club, with much emphasis placed on the creation of a stylish, winning image:

> Our teams have always been given the mission of going out there not just to win but above all to be spectacular and impressive.[31]

Italian football had never seen anything like it. At his first pre-season presentation of the new team in July 1986, Berlusconi had the players flown into Milan's old 'Arena' stadium in a helicopter to the accompaniment of Wagner's 'The Ride of the Valkyries'. Ten thousand fans, too, were on hand for this *Apocalypse Now*–style fanfare.

Later that summer, speaking to the players in the private of his San Martino villa, he told them that he was 'not accustomed to finishing second'. Berlusconi could see only too clearly the potential gains to be had from creating a winning 'synergy' (one of his favourite words at the time) of football success, consumer advertising and national television audiences. Not for nothing was AC Milan listed under the 'Cinema and Showbiz' arm of Fininvest.

When his own TV channels were covering games played by Milan, Berlusconi would tell his producers to focus on pretty, usually female faces in the crowd so as to encourage the concept of the football match as a family occasion.[32]

The Berlusconi-owned Milan also got quickly into the merchandising act, opening a 'Milan Point' shop close to the city's celebrated Duomo (Cathedral) and printing a magazine called *Forza Milan*, which sold over 100,000 copies. It all sounds like old hat now, but it was vibrantly new for Italy at the time.

Berlusconi also set new standards when it came to levels of pay. By 1989, tax declarations showed that striker van Basten and captain Franco Baresi were receiving an estimated annual wage of $1.5 million; attacking midfielder Roberto Donadoni, $1.1 million; and players such as Carlo Ancelotti (later to become club coach), Paolo Maldini and Mauro Tassotti, $1 million.[33] Furthermore, these high wage levels had been stimulated by a 'productivity' bonus system (then unknown in Italy) whereby the more the club won, the more wages its star players earned.

As the AC Milan juggernaut began to roll and the club established itself as arguably the best in the world, its wealthy owner was never shy about underlining his own role in the success story:

> I've been a football coach myself, you know, and not of the firm's kick-around team but of regular teams that played in the Football Federation's youth and

junior team championships, teams that won every competition they took part in. I never interfere in the work of our coaches (at AC Milan) but if you are the President of a club, above all if you are someone with the sort of experience that I have had as an entrepreneur in the handling of people and of normal business activity, then you simply have to try and stimulate people, make suggestions and express your opinions in your relations with your managers, even your football manager.[34]

So then, how much of his political success does Berlusconi owe to football? Over lunch at Palazzo Chigi, government house, in December 2005, I once asked Berlusconi precisely that question. Even if he tended to play down the impact of football, the prime minister's answer was nonetheless revealing:

> Certainly, no one has ever won as much as I have, not only with AC Milan but also with other sports teams (rugby, ice skating etc.) … but the reality is that I owe my political success to the historical context of 1994 …

What is undeniable is that when Berlusconi did eventually decide to enter politics, his carefully prepared entrance was heavily underlined with populist, football language. In an American-style presidential TV address from his study in his San Martino villa at Arcore, outside Milan, on 26 January 1994, Berlusconi solemnly announced:

> I have chosen to take to the field and involve myself in public life because I don't want to live in an illiberal country governed by immature forces and by men (the ex-Communists) who are still closely linked to a past that proved both a political and economic disaster …[35]

The key phrase was 'take to the field'. His new party was to be called 'Forza Italia' or 'Up Italy', a cry which until then had applied only to an Italian national team, and his party deputies were to be referred to as 'Azzurri', a term previously used for national team players. As he campaigned in the Rome 1 constituency for the 1994 election, he even taunted his opponent, economist Luigi Spaventa, saying to him: 'Before running against me, go win yourself two Champions Cups.'[36]

Changing Italian Politics

In an article published in the geo-political review, *Limes*, in 2005, political analyst Ilvo Diamanti argued that Berlusconi's synergy of football and politics has completely changed the face of Italian politics:

> Today, in the wake of Silvio Berlusconi's 'taking to the field' (a term that was certainly not used by accident by Berlusconi) it is hard to differentiate between football, the media and politics. That taking to the field transferred

from football to politics organisational models, symbols and a sense of identity which pre-1994 politics had lost ...[37]

Obviously, during his near-two decades in politics, 9 in government house, Berlusconi's links to football and his day-to-day involvement in the running of AC Milan have all been hugely reduced. The running of the club is now very firmly in the hands of longtime Berlusconi aide, Adriano Galliani. Yet Berlusconi still often availed himself of football to distract attention from weightier matters of state. Take the July day in the summer of 2010 when AC Milan held a news conference to officially 'present' their new squad for the forthcoming season. Not only new players such as reserve goalkeeper Marco Amelia, Colombian defender Mario Yepes and Greek defender Sokratis Papastathopoulos were to attend but, arguably more importantly, this was to be the first 'Milan' outing for the new coach, Massimiliano Allegri.

Berlusconi, however, had other ideas. Helicoptered into the Milan training ground of Milanello, close to the Italo-Swiss border, he presided over the 'presentation' so completely that the unfortunate Allegri never got a word in, edgeways or anyways. The veteran football commentator Marco Ansaldo, of *La Stampa*, speaking of the 'uncontrollable protagonism' of the prime minister, described the scene thus:

> We witnessed a surreal show, we've never seen a 'presentation' where those 'presented' remained totally silent. OK, Amelia, Papastathopoulous and Yepes, we can pass on them but it would have been nice to know more about Allegri. To know more than the Berlusconi observation about him, namely that he looks like a handsome fashion model.[38]

On those regular occasions when he attended a Milan game at the San Siro, Berlusconi was often happy to give a post-match interview, glad no doubt not to be answering questions about either Italian public debt or his alleged involvement in yet another sex scandal. Thus in August 2011, with Italy caught in the grip of market speculation, Berlusconi had time to watch his club win the annual friendly trophy, 'Trofeo Luigi Berlusconi' (named after his father).

Furthermore, after the game he gave an impromptu press conference in which he analysed his team. He spoke of the 'quality, but also the clouds' that hung over the star striker Antonio Cassano, while he admitted that Milan were interested in the Italian international Alberto Aquilani (who subsequently joined Milan on a season-long loan from Liverpool). He went on to state that it was 'unlikely' that Milan would buy either Mario Balotelli from Manchester City or Kaka from Real Madrid. As always, when speaking of football, Berlusconi sounded like he knew his onions.

On occasions, too, Berlusconi has availed himself of football diplomacy. When the Brazilian president Lula da Silva met him during an official visit in November 2008, Berlusconi surprised his guest of honour by introducing him to the Brazilian clan then at AC Milan – players Dida, Emerson, Kaka, Pato, Ronaldhino and the future coach, Leonardo. Rather than be annoyed by this distraction, President Lula, according to members of the Brazilian press corps, was delighted with this 'photo op' alongside some of Brazil's most famous sons.

The Berlusconi relationship to AC Milan is far from finished. In future, his daughter Barbara may well play a leading role in the administration of the club. Obviously, AC Milan is a very expensive toy – for example, the club recorded losses of €69.7 million in the financial year 2009–10.[39] Berlusconi picks up the tab but he could argue that investment in this particular loss leader has yielded some very impressive returns.

As indeed sociologists could argue that the excellence, professionalism and success of Italian football have yielded very impressive returns. In a country that often distinguishes itself for all the wrong, scandal- and corruption-related reasons, Italian football has regularly been a world leader. Italian teams may not always have been the best, but they have indeed won a lot. In the process, of course, certain powerful figures have gone along for the ride.

NOTES

1   J. Foot, *Calcio: The History of Italian Football* (London: Fourth Estate, 2006), p. 27.
2   P. Ginsborg, *Italy and Its Discontents: Family, Civil Society, State, 1980–2001* (London: Palgrave MacMillan, 2003); P. Ginsborg, *Silvio Berlusconi: Television, Power and Patrimony* (London: Verso, 2004); and D.M. Smith, *Modern Italy: A Political History* (New Haven, CT: Yale University Press, 1997).
3   Italy v Hungary, May 1947, Austria v Italy, November 1947.
4   P. Agnew, *Forza Italia: A Journey in Search of Italy and Its Football* (London: Ebury Press, 2006), p. 311.
5   'Veron Assolto, Un Anno A Recoba', *La Repubblica*, 27 June 2001.
6   Agnew, *Forza Italia*, ch. 11.
7   See *World Soccer*, P. Agnew, March 2004.
8   See *World Soccer*, P. Agnew, February 2004.
9   Agnew, *Forza Italia*, p. 295.
10 P. Agnew, 'Balotelli and Italy's Racism Debate', CBC FIFA World Cup Blog, November 2009.
11 *World Soccer* news, 31 January 2000.
12 The Federation ban was subsequently upheld by a Lazio Regional Appeals Court (Tar) on 3 August, 2012.

13 Agnew, *Forza Italia*, ch. 3; J. Burns, *Hand of God* (London: Bloomsbury, 1996); 'Quelle Feste Con I Boss', *La Repubblica*, 15 February 1991.

14 Agnew, *Forza Italia*, pp. 195–98.

15 See 'Matchfixing: A Worldwide Problem', *World Soccer*, July 2011.

16 See 'Inferno Rossonero' at www.infernorossonero.forumfree.it.

17 S. Martin, *Football and Fascism* (Oxford: Berg, 2004), p. 3.

18 Agnew, *Forza Italia*, ch. 4.

19 Ibid.

20 Mario Pennachia, *Generale Vaccaro* (Rome: Nuove Idee, 2008), p. 11.

21 Ugo Frigerio, *Marciendo Nel Nome dell' Italia* (Walking in the Name of Italy), Preface by Il Duce Mussolina (Rome: UTEP, 1934).

22 Martin, *Football and Fascism*, p. 42.

23 Pennachia, *Generale Vaccaio*, p. 30.

24 G. Zanetti and G. Tornabuoni, *Il giuoco del calcio*, p. 43, quoted in Martin, *Football and Fascism*.

25 Martin, *Football and Fascism*, p. 183.

26 Ibid., p. 182.

27 Ibid., p. 130.

28 Foot, *Calcio*, p. 39.

29 Agnew, *Forza Italia*, p. 110.

30 See photos of Berlusconi on pitch at Camp Nou with AC Milan team, after it had won the 1989 Champions Cup.

31 *Gazzetta Dello Sport*, interview with Berlusconi, 17 September 1991.

32 *La Repubblica*, 'I Soldi Del Diavolo', 10 July 1992.

33 Agnew, *Forza Italia*, p. 107.

34 *Gazz etta Dello Sport*, interview with Berlusconi, 17 September 1991.

35 Agnew, *Forza Italia*, p. 120.

36 Ibid.

37 I. Diamanti, 'Foot Politics: Tifo Dunque Voto', *Limes*, Summer 2005.

38 M. Ansaldo, 'Surreale, Un Tecnico Senza Parole', *La Stampa*, 21 July 2010.

39 See 'Bilancio Milan', Tuttomercatoweb, www.tuttomercatoweb.com, 20 April 2011, accessed 1 October 2011.

Figure 4.1. Pelé of Santos during the game at Craven Cottage, 1972–73 season.
Credit: Colorsport/Mike Wall.

The Game-Changers: Pelé

Donald Bradman, Gareth Edwards and Wayne Gretzky are among the sporting equivalents of *Citizen Kane*, *War and Peace* and *Hamlet* – usually no. 1 when 'greatest' lists are composed. Football's consensus answer is voiced by Hugh McIlvanney: 'If all the qualities that make football irresistible to countless millions have ever been embodied in one supreme player, that man is Pelé.'[1] He never bestrode a World Cup as completely as his Brazilian compatriot Garrincha in 1962, Johan Cruyff in 1974 or Diego Maradona in 1986, but he was integral to the two most compelling winning teams, as teenager in 1958 and veteran in 1970. He never, as a modern equivalent would, played in Europe. But the imperatives driving modern talent flows did not then exist – and nobody downgrades Cruyff for never playing in South America. Manuel Vazquez Montalban's analysis of his 'Gods of Football' places Pelé (Figure 4.1) neatly in relation to his immediate predecessor among the immortals: 'If Di Stéfano was the complete footballer, Pelé appeared the footballer of genius in whom technique and creativity found an exceptional synthesis.'[2]

That genius, born Edson Arantes do Nascimiento in October 1940, was sufficient to earn a first football pay-cheque at 13. By 16 he was playing not only in the big leagues with Santos, but for Brazil – characteristically scoring minutes into his debut. Scoring goals at a Gerd Muller–like rate while being more playmaker than striker was merely the most spectacular of an awe-inspiring range of skills. Tarcisco Burgnich, a 1970 World Cup final adversary, recalled that 'I told myself "he's flesh and blood just like me". I was wrong.'[3]

Talent, though, will only take you so far without temperament. Brazil's psychologist famously argued before the 1958 World Cup that the team prodigy was 'obviously infantile … lacks the necessary fighting spirit … does not possess the sense of responsibility necessary for a team game'.[4] It is football's equivalent of John Lennon (also born in October 1940) being told that 'you'll never make a living with that bloody guitar'. It is so utterly wrong that it would be funny but for the ugly underlying assumptions about black Brazilians.

Fortunately, coach Vicente Feola ignored the advice. Pelé's first World Cup match, against the Soviet Union, was, as Alex Bellos has pointed out, 'the moment that Brazil darkened'.[5] It was also, perhaps uncoincidentally, the point at which a magical team coalesced.

Lula, his coach at Santos, showed clearer understanding than the psychologist when he enumerated the qualities he thought made Pelé the ideal player: 'He is fast on the ground and in the air, he has the physique, the tricks, the ball control, the ability to dictate play, a feeling for the manoeuvre, he is unselfish, good-natured and modest.'[6]

He was also, as career totals of 1,324 games and 1,283 goals testify, remarkably durable, and relentlessly competitive. The world remembers three moments from the 1970 World Cup – the lob from half-way against Czechoslovakia, the sumptuous dummy that dumbfounded Uruguayan goalkeeper Ladislao Mazurkiewicz and the cobra-strike header somehow saved by England's Gordon Banks – as moments of supreme artistry; their author's recall is that none led to a goal and the lob 'would have been much more beautiful had it gone in'.[7]

While not lacking ego – no great athlete does – he was always prepared to sink his genius into a team pattern, enabling the hugely effective combinations with Didi in 1958, Gerson and Tostao in 1970 and, most of all, with the elemental force of nature Garrincha. They were, as David Goldblatt has observed, a temperamental yin-and-yang: 'Pele planned for the future, Garrincha lived for the moment. Pele trained. Garrincha slept.'[8]

Detachment

One clue to the calm self-awareness that enabled him to find an accommodation with celebrity that eluded Maradona and George Best, and that Garrincha appears never to have sought, can perhaps be found in his relationship with his famous *nom de football*.

To himself he remained Edson, to his mother Dico. His frequent third-person references to Pelé were not the vainglory evident in some sportsmen, but an expression of detachment. Pelé was, as Bellos wrote, 'the name of the myth, not of the man', even if, as the man himself wrote, 'Pele had taken on a life of its own'.[9]

The name itself, attributable to a childish mispronunciation of Bile, an idolised goalkeeper, was serendipitously perfect for purpose.[10] It was short, memorable, unique and meant nothing beyond itself, so ideal for trademarking. In the 1970s it was the second most recognised brand name in Europe, trailing only Coca-Cola.

When the United Nations proclaimed him a 'Citizen of the World' in 1977, there was some substance to the title, earned not only at World Cups but through the years of relentless touring that earned Santos – a middle-sized club he helped turn into two-time World Club Champions – the funds to retain him for nearly two decades, and the happy coda to his career with New York Cosmos. While by 1975 the United States was 'the one place in the world I could go without being mobbed', his was also the only football name sufficiently resonant to register with a self-sufficient and insular sporting culture.[11]

Another tangible consequence of his time in the United States was the phrase 'The Beautiful Game', a literal translation of the Jogo Bonito of his native Portuguese. It is hardly his fault that it has deadened through relentless repetition into one of the most irksomely tedious of football clichés. He is perhaps more to be criticised for complaisance with Brazil's ugly military regimes of the 1960s, but his one venture into active politics, as sports minister under President Cardoso, was marked by a positive attempt to bring logic and legality to Brazil's shambolic footballing structures. His intended law was passed, but in unrecognisably diluted form, after obstruction by ruthless and well-connected vested interests. Even the greatest lose sometimes.

NOTES

1 H. McIlvanney, *McIlvanney on Football* (Edinburgh: Mainstream, 2007), p. 73.

2 M.V. Montalban, *Futbol: Una Religion en Busca de un Dios* (Barcelona: Edicions de Bolsillo, 2006), p. 33.

3 Pele, with O. Duarte and A. Bellos, *Pele: The Autobiography* (London: Pocket Books, 2007), p. 155.

4 D. Goldblatt, *The Ball Is Round* (London: Penguin Books, 2007), p. 371.

5 A. Bellos, *Futebol, the Brazilian Way of Life* (London: Bloomsbury, 2003), p. 102.

6 Goldblatt, *The Ball Is Round*, p. 376.

7 Pele et al., *Pele: The Autobiography*, p. 185.

8 Goldblatt, *The Ball Is Round*, p. 376.

9 Bellos, *Futebol, The Brazilian Way of Life*, p. 229; Pele with O. Duarte and A. Bellos, *Pele, the Autobiography*, p. 285.

10 Ibid., p. 42.

11 Ibid., p. 220.

5

JIM WHITE

Brazil: Rhythm and Grooves

It is a September evening in west London and the streets around Craven Cottage football ground are filling up with supporters. Not the usual quiet, undemonstrative folk who turn up to watch the home club Fulham, this clapping, dancing, chanting bunch are excited enough to disturb the peace as far away as the London Borough of Ealing. Over there is a bloke in a totteringly tall yellow hat whacking a samba beat out of a bass drum. He is leading a wobbly looking band, a collective of instrumentalists who, judging by the trumpeter's off-key squawking, have clearly spent much of their warm-up time in the pub. Keeping pace with them a trio of young women strut about exhorting the rest of the crowd to join the atonal jamboree. Their every exaggerated wiggle asks the important question: do their mothers know they're out in jeans quite that spray-on tight?

Brazil are in London to play a friendly against Ghana and the area around the Cottage, a discreetly monied quarter of London where the action generally takes place behind closed terra-cotta–toned front doors, has been temporarily colonised by the exuberant and the uninhibited. So much so, the easily confused might take in the scene and think they had been transported to Rio during carnival time. But for the rain sheeting in from the North Sea, that is. And the increasingly fractious scrum growing around an under-manned ticket office whose occupants seem to have been taken by surprise by the numbers gathering here.

A handy proportion of the expatriate Brazilian population resident in Britain – which stood between 180,0000 and 200,000 according to the British embassy – has headed down the Fulham Palace Road to gee along their national side. As is the way of Brazilian football there are almost as many women present as men. Mingling with curious neutrals and cheerful Ghanaian supporters, they shout, sing and snap each other draped around the comically inept statue of Michael Jackson, recently installed at the ground by the Fulham chairman in homage to his moon-walking acquaintance. A police spokesman estimates there are as many as 20,000

Brazil supporters here. You can't fail to notice them. It's not just the noise. It's the costume. Most – whether they hail from Brasilia or Brixton, Belo Horizonte or Balham – are wearing the canary-toned football shirt that is the world's most instantly recognisable sporting brand. Graced by Pelé, Didi and Garrincha, popularised by Socrates, Dunga and Zico, worn by Romario, Rivaldo and Ronaldo, the shirt is the vibrant symbol of extravagant footballing prowess. Not simply yellow, this is the garment that offers the promise of sporting gold.

It is a sizeable following the Brazilians have here, given that this is a home game being played some 5,750 miles from the Maracana, the concrete bowl of a stadium in Rio that was once the national team base. Yet, boisterous as it is, this crowd is less than half the number that showed up when their heroes played Scotland at Arsenal's Emirates stadium the previous February. But then this is the seventh time in five years that the increasingly peripatetic Brazil team have organised a friendly in London. And the 'Brazil World Tour', as the circuit encompassing such diverse venues as Dortmund, Derby and Doha is known, is beginning to give vivid demonstration of the law of diminishing returns.

It began, this footballing equivalent of the Harlem Globetrotters' perpetual caravan, in 2006. The CBF, the governing body of the game in Brazil, signed a deal with the sporting agency Kentaro to exploit the yellow shirt on a global scale; every game overseas would be a selling opportunity to buff up the finances of an organisation trying to generate the necessary readies to host the World Cup in 2014. Give the rest of the planet a chance to join the carnival, was the idea – the spirit of Brazilian generosity made manifest at £45 a ticket.

'Very much at the start, the CBF saw that their players were playing in Europe anyway, and they saw from a logistical and practical objective this was a way to manage that,' Kentaro's chief executive officer, Jonathan Hill, told Four Four Two magazine. 'The CBF also understand, as we understand, that there is a demand for seeing Brazil play. We've had over one and a half million paying spectators since we had that first game. We get global TV audiences of over 200 million for the games. All are shown live on Globo TV in Brazil.'

Cynics in Rio, however, suggest that, with a succession of stuttering players failing over the decade since they won their fifth World Cup in 2002 to live up to the traditions of the golden shirt, it was probably wise to extend the invitation to outsiders: better to play in front of naïve new markets than the jeers which had recently soundtracked internationals in Brazil.

There could be something in that. After all, there are no boos inside Craven Cottage. As Ronaldinho and Neymar, Lucio and Danny Alves, the current generation of idiosyncratically coiffed Brazilian brand ambassadors, pass the ball around in the pouring rain the noise is overwhelmingly positive. This is Brazil in action, and the crowd knows what that means. Or at least what it should mean. No other sporting operation has quite the historic connotations of those yellow shirts dampening in the autumnal squall. No other country's reputation and character is as intimately woven into sporting fabric. Never mind that this game produces nothing more than a laboured, pedestrian 1–0 victory (and this only after Ghana have a man sent off in the first half), the expectation is still everything. And, whatever the missed passes and the scuffed chances littering the Craven Cottage turf, the proposition remains the same: when Brazil play in those yellow shirts, it should be like no other team on earth.

O pais do futebol

Part dance, part carnival, all celebration, Brazilian football promises a unique cocktail, one which not only holds the entire nation in its thrall, but defines it. Sure, New Zealanders love their rugby, Indians are obsessed by cricket, Kenyans can run rather well. But Brazilians associate themselves with football in way no-one else can match. O pais do futebol is what they call their homeland: the country of football.

A stroll along the seafront in Rio confirms all stereotypes. Everywhere the tourist looks, across the miles of Copacabana and Ipanema beach, sun-smothered youths in micro Speedos play games of foot volley. This is the sight that will greet fans arriving for the 2014 World Cup: both beaches are peppered with football pitches marked in the sand, filled with games going on all day long. And night-time too. Many are floodlit and on those that aren't matches take place just about illuminated by the halogen haze from the streetlights. On the concrete promenade, jet-lagged visitors can watch buskers playing keepy-uppy for a few tourist dollars at three in the morning.

Farther inland, in the favelas running down the mountains that fringe the city, every rare patch of open space is colonised by the game. Here, on scuffy stretches of gravelly earth, generally flanked by rusting steel fencing, locals play endless rounds of *futebol de salao*, the small-sided kickabout with a heavy ball designed by a South American academic to exploit the least prepossessing of venues.

Rio is not unusual. Everywhere in the country, people play football. The skills developed in the seemingly continuous pick-up games are highly marketable. Here the 10,000 hours of youth development thought to be necessary to hone excellence are being played out on every stretch of open space in the land. These days the country of football exports its practitioners across the world. From the Faroe Islands to Cape Town, from Vancouver to Vladivostok, there are currently more than 10,000 Brazilians employed to play football professionally. Which means there are a greater number of the sons of the samba stroking the ball around for money than any other nationality.

And if they aren't playing, Brazilians are watching football. In Brazil there is an interminable round of matches going on all the time; here the annual season seems to last 13 months. Local leagues, inter-state leagues, national leagues, South American championships – at any moment there will be a match going on somewhere to take in. If you can't get there, then it's on television. And if you haven't got a telly, there's always someone willing to find their extension cable and perch their set on a chair out on the pavement for the neighbours to gather round.

Ignore the manifestly mad decision to grant the 2022 World Cup to the desert kingdom of Qatar, or the enormous economic and social risk that is Russia 2018; of this there can be no doubt: when the 2014 competition kicks off in Rio, football will have come to its spiritual home. As the oft-heard local aphorism puts it: 'Osingleses o inventaram, osbrasileiros o aperfeiçoaram' (The English invented it, the Brazilians perfected it).

This is the country where the game matters, where playing stars are more trusted than priests, where ex-footballers become politicians, where the assumption is widespread that Planet Earth is ball-shaped. To the extent, some commentators wearily argue, that football has become all that matters: if Brazil win, everything is good in the world. Crime, corruption and inequality are all forgotten. But when they lose …

And the trouble is, even as the national economy booms, even as Brazil's growth rate outstrips the developed world five- or sixfold, even as democratic advances mean the fruits of development slowly begin to be shared, all too often these days, the Brazilian team are failing to deliver on the stifling sense of national expectation. As the country prepares to play host to the world, the game at home is locked into one of the periodic eras of gloom that act as counterpoint to the cheery carnival of success, the seemingly inevitable hangover of a footballing culture that has so often scaled the peaks of a good time.

Magnificent Obsession

All this from an obsession planted little more than a century ago. Nothing, not the internal combustion engine, not television, not social networking, has had quite the profound effect the arrival of football had on Brazil.

In just over 100 years it colonised the country absolutely, gripping it round the throat and overwhelming its consciousness. In many ways it was the social glue that bound a sprawling, disparate society, the one focal point of communality in a new country riven by racial, class and economic divide.

An expat called Charles Miller, the son of a pioneering Scottish railway engineer father and a Brazilian mother, who grew up in a British enclave in São Paolo, is credited with bringing the game to this part of South America. He was sent to board at Bannister Court in Hampshire, picked up the game's recently codified rules on the school playing fields and became a stalwart for the aristocratic by-invitation-only touring side Corinthians. He returned home in 1894 with two leather balls in his luggage and persuaded members of the São Paulo athletic club, where he already played cricket, to start a team.

From there, like a raging contagion in a sci-fi movie, the game spread, its virus beetling along the railway tracks, through the growing urban conurbations, into the countryside; the founding Scot's part in fuelling the fire is memorialised in downtown São Paolo where a street – Praca Charles Miller – bears his name. By 1902 the import was so well established, an extensive league programme and city championship could be staged; 'some 2,000 footballs have been sold here within the last 12 months. Nearly every village has a club,' Miller wrote in his diary that year. In 1910, Miller invited his old mates from Corinthians over for a tour. After they played in São Paolo, a new club was formed in their name, adopting their colours of white shirt and black shorts. One hundred years on, Corinthians are now the most widely supported, wealthiest club in Brazil.

Four years later, as Europe was poised on the lip of self-destruction, a combined side made up of the best players from Rio and São Paolo played for the first time as Brazil. Their opponents were a visiting team from Exeter City, then of the Southern League. The Brazilians won 2–0. Or possibly the score was 3–3. The records are inconsistent on the matter. What we do know from a photograph is that the Brazil selection wore those yellow shirts.

In its earliest days, Brazilian football was the game of the moneyed classes. As it was in Britain, where the product of public schools dominated, the people's game was initially played by amateurs in exclusive membership clubs. And in Brazil, that meant it was the white population of European settlers who had first access to its pleasures. The game they played on their neatly trimmed lawns would have borne very little comparison with what visitors see today on Rio's beaches: football was then reckoned a game of physicality, of structure, of lines of players advancing together. Individuality, ball control and instinct were valued far less than head-down kick-and-rush. Elegant it wasn't; think Stoke City, but without the swaggering exhibitionism.

But the game was persuasive, its rules simple and logical. And soon its attraction spread downward through society, taking it into the lives of the country's black and mixed-race people. Slavery had been abolished in the mid-nineteenth century, and the freed slaves upped sticks from the plantations to the cities; rapid urbanisation driven by migration saw the population of São Paolo swell from 40,000 in 1880 to 800,000 in 1920. Managers and technicians at British-owned factories on the industrialised edge of the cities were isolated from the main concentrations of upper-class footballers in the affluent centre. Often unable to muster two full elevens of their own kind, the boss classes were organising informal games with their Brazilian workers by the turn of the century. And the workers liked what they were being made to play.

The descendants of African slaves quickly began to impose their own way on the Brazilian game. The clichéd assumption has long held that, with the beat of the *samba* and *capoeira* in their veins, the black and so-called mulatto populations approached the game like a dance and, with their languid physicality, imposed on it an entirely new rhythm. But geography and urbanisation had more influence on the way they approached a ball than genetics: in the cramped shantytowns of the new cities, there was not enough space to play the long ball game. On the few yards of open ground available in the densely populated *favelas*, the bare-footed converts brought a new way of thinking to football, one of tight control, of short-passing, in which tricks and flicks and individualism were cherished, the spiritual opposite of the straight-lined inflexibility of the European-style rush for goal. It is from here that the Brazilian way of football developed, the compelling mix of the street game and the organised structures of the establishment. It became known as jogo bonito: the beautiful game.

A Question of Colour

Not that those who ran Brazilian football were initially keen to embrace the flamboyant approach of the masses. It was all very well for the blacks and mulattos to play on the street, but they weren't going to play at the top. And certainly they weren't going to represent the country. A colour bar operated at the leading clubs for the first couple of decades of the twentieth century. Rio's most elitist outfit, Fluminense, held out longest against the acceptance of black players. Yet, even before it abandoned its prejudicial recruitment policy, the pressure for results meant that skilled mixed-race players were taken on, particularly those who might pass for white. In 1916 Fluminense signed Carlos Alberto, a mulatto. Before each game he would lighten his appearance by daubing rice powder over his face. It was not a disguise that generally survived longer than the first ten minutes: as he sweated, the rice powder would smear and wash away. The opposition fans began chanting 'poz de arros' (rice powder) at him as he played, mocking the attempt to cover up his skin tone. Its derogatory genesis now lost in the haze of tradition, Poz de Arros remains the club nickname.

Fluminense's big rivals are Flamengo, the club that recently persuaded the prodigal Ronaldinho to return home from Europe. The Fla-Flu counterpoint goes right back to the two clubs' origins. In 1911, after winning the Carioca championship, the inter-Rio league competition, the whole Fluminense first team – mainly made up of medical students – walked out in a dispute with the club's directors. The team without a club sought a new home across town and were given a billet by the Flamingo Rowing Club on the shores of Rio's circular lagoon. The rebel players called the club they formed there Flamengo. In the first years of the club matches were often temporarily halted as the balls would often end up in the river. At one early Fla-Flu derby match Fluminense used this to their advantage while losing and spent much of the latter stages of the game petulantly kicking the ball into the water.

Flamengo's mascot was the *urubu,* a type of vulture which can be seen circling over the hillside favelas of Rio, from where the bedrock of the club's support soon came to be drawn. The *urubu*'s key characteristic is that it is black. And so, its rivals sneeringly maintained, were most of its supporters. Race was at the heart of football from the start in Brazil.

Any attempt, however, by the Brazilian football organisers to maintain a colour bar was doomed to demographic failure. The skills of the *favela* masses were too compelling to ignore. Wholesale change was precipitated in 1923 when Vasco de Gama came from nowhere to win the Carioca with a team dominated by black and mixed-race players. Mind, some of the bureaucrats tried to preserve the game for the elite. The reaction to Vasco's triumph was immediate: the other big Rio clubs formed a strictly amateur organisation, the Associação Metropolitan para o esporte Amador (AMEA), which not only banned any player who had no other job than football, but also issued edicts against those who worked in low-paid jobs, such as waiters, drivers and factory workers, by insisting that all footballers had to be literate.

By now prepared to do whatever was necessary to win, clubs circumvented the new regulations by employing tutors whose sole job was to teach players how to form the letters of their own name, AMEA's preferred test for literacy. Some players had their names changed for them to make the strange patterns easier to copy. Thus Pascol Cinelli became Pascol Silva. Others simply used their nicknames. And thus was a grand tradition born. From Pelé to

Hulk, this is a country which has long produced the most evocatively named cast of characters in the game.

Still, the old ways of bureaucracy persisted. Disputes over professionalism kept many of the better players out of the national side, even as Brazil entered the first World Cup. The country's pre-war performances were slowed by the anchor drag of snobbery, a semi-final in 1938 the best showing. It was not until 1950, when the tournament was staged in Brazil, that a properly representative side – mixed in race, fully professional – was fielded. And what an effect they had on the national psyche.

From Maracanazo to jogo bonito

This was the competition the hosts not only expected to win but assumed they would. And things went well as the last game of a round robin competition approached on 16 July 1950. Effectively the final, Brazil had merely to earn a draw against Uruguay to lift the trophy; the Uruguayans had to win to take it. A reported 199,854, a world-record crowd that still stands (albeit subsequently rounded down to 174,000), crammed into the newly built Maracana stadium. They were overwhelmingly white. But the black and mixed-race urban poor had many role models in a team whose balance reflected the nation's demographics. Everyone was behind them: in shanties and swanky apartment blocks, in farms and in mines, on factory floor and on the beach, football was the one point of commonality in the nation. Everyone thought Brazil – the most populous footballing nation on earth – was destined to win, certain to overcome their tiny southern neighbours. But, after leading 1–0, they lost the match 2–1. The trauma was so extensive it held almost religious significance, as if the world order had been disturbed. The match became known as the Maracanazo (or the Maracana blow). In Brazil it is still called the Final Fatídica (the fateful final).

Immediately after the game, Brazilian football entered the first of its subsequently regular periods of introspection and depression. Borrowing a characteristic from their erstwhile colonial masters the Portuguese, a fatalism manifest in the national musical form of fado, the game entered a downward spiral. Gloom encompassed all, an assumption that their best efforts were perpetually doomed to disappointment. There are those who maintain the psychological hangover was still there in the 1954 World Cup in Switzerland, when Brazil lost 4–2 to Hungary in a brutal quarter-final that became known as the Battle of Berne. And that the assumption of inferiority was only cleared eight years after the Maracanazo, in Stockholm.

So convinced was Brazil's coach Vicente Feola of his players' capacity for mental frailty, he took a psychologist with his squad to Sweden to compete in the 1958 finals. The intrusion of a shrink had the desired effect (possibly more than Feola's own; the coach was prone to nodding off during training sessions): Brazil won the trophy they felt was theirs by right. More to the point, they did so by demonstrating the jogo bonito.

At their core were two players Feola initially felt too fragile for the competition: the bow-legged winger Garrincha and a 17-year-old forward named simply Pelé. Persuaded to put them in the side by a deputation of senior players ahead of an early group game against the physically demanding Soviet Union, Feola was rewarded for his adventure. Pelé, an astonishingly strong youth, scored twice in the semi-final and once in the final. As he was lifted high by colleagues, so an institution was born. Two years before Cassius Clay won a gold medal at the Rome Olympics, here was the first black global sporting superstar. His good grace, his winning smile and his ability with both feet, made him celebrated not just in the favelas from which he came, but across the globe, the perfect embodiment of the Brazilian way.

It also made him a marked man. In the 1962 finals in Chile he was kicked out of the tournament early (it was Garrincha who propelled Brazil to their second title). And in England in 1966 he was subject to the savage attention of neanderthal tactics, his competition ending with him being tearfully carried from the pitch at Goodison Park after the Portuguese used his legs as target practice for their studs. Brazil limped home early with him, eliminated at the group stages, like it was the 1930s all over again. So distraught was their talisman at his treatment, he declared he was finished with the World Cup: without protection this was not a tournament in which the representatives of jogo bonito had a prayer. Gloom encircled once again.

But in Mexico in 1970 Pelé had his revenge on the hackers. Leading a team including Carlos Alberto, Jairzinho, Tostao, Gerson and Roberto Rivelino, a side long accepted as the greatest ever assembled, Pelé embraced a tournament which had sought to humiliate him. As they beat the champions England in the group stage, beat their nemesis Uruguay in the semis, beat the crafty, cynical Italians in the final, Brazil established a new level of aspiration for the game.

Transmitted on colour television across the globe, the yellow shirts became the gold standard. In every schoolyard in every nation, everyone wanted to play like these Brazilians. The fourth goal in their final rout of Italy, the one in which Pelé completed a lengthy passing movement by slipping the ball into the path of his captain (another) Carlos Alberto, advancing from a position way outside the frame of the television camera, is still considered the best team build-up of all time.

With that performance, Brazil had won the World Cup three times. To mark their achievement, FIFA gave them the Jules Rimet trophy to hold on to in perpetuity. And with it, Pelé and Carlos Alberto led the way to new footballing wealth. Both picked up contracts to play in the fledgling U.S. market, Pelé's with the New York Cosmos worth an eye-watering $3 million a year, making him easily the world's highest paid sportsman. Soon the world's leading clubs came shopping in Brazil. Though it was the year 1995, which simultaneously saw the Bosman ruling and the signing of the Schengen Agreement on the free movement of labour within the EU (which gave Brazilians with colonial heritage in Portugal a passport into the northern markets), that turned a trickle of exports into a torrent. From then on, Brazilians could play anywhere. And they did.

Failure and Renewal

It was as well the nation had the Jules Rimet to look at after 1970. It would help sustain their passion over the next 24 years as they watched the tournament they had believed to be their sinecure being dominated by Europeans. Or worse, the Argentines, the South Americans who were more European than the Europeans. Indeed, failure in five successive World Cups from 1974 to 1990 made the Brazilian football system turn once again to introversion. A conviction gripped that the game in Brazil was not sufficiently European to win, that defence needed tightening, that midfielders needed to learn to tackle, that the jogo bonito was no longer enough. Sure, they remained the only country to appear in every World Cup finals, sure the team of 1982 rivalled the Dutch of 1974 and the Hungarians of 1954 as the greatest not to win the cup, but something had to be done to restore their dominance.

In 1994, pragmatism prevailed. Played in the United States not for reasons of heritage but finance, the Brazilians were every neutral's favourite, whether they understood the game or not. In a rerun of the 1970 final, played this time in Los Angeles, Brazil defeated Italy once again. But they did so not by coruscating patterns of passing, but by tight defence, cagey attacks and the Italian talisman Roberto Baggio missing the decisive kick in the penalty shoot-out.

The next tournament was almost as successful, with Brazil losing in the final to France, an engagement overshadowed by Ronaldo, their new star striker, suffering an epileptic seizure in the build-up. He played, but was barely noticed as France won 3–0. In the aftermath, the rumour circulated that Nike, who pumped millions into the CBF in return for the right to sell the golden shirt, had compromised the Brazilian effort by insisting Ronaldo, their most visible brand ambassador, play though he was visibly not up to it. Nike denied all such culpability.

The nation's record fifth title, the stunning achievement that entitled the CBF to decorate those yellow shirts with a unique collection of five stars above the crest, was gained in 2002 in Japan and South Korea. The team of the three Rs – Rivaldo, Ronaldo and Ronaldinho – if not quite in the class of the boys of '70, re-established the primacy of jogo bonito. This was the World Cup in which commercialism reached its zenith, in which the boys from Brazil were exploited as Rio's answer to Hollywood, as the Asian market opened itself up to the lure of the yellow shirt. It was also the competition in which television achieved its final dominance, a tournament of mega slo-mo and action replay. The Brazilians perfectly suited the new frame of the game. With its emphasis on moments of showy individualism they became the focus of attention. And not just for their goals. Rivaldo was punished by FIFA after it became clear on slo-mo that he had not been struck in the face by a Turkish opponent during a group game as his exaggerated fall suggested, but on the shin. His fine of $5,000 for simulation was the biggest yet meted out by the organisers.

Thereafter, the first decade of the new century saw Brazilian football sunk once more into one of its regular periods of despair and self-analysis. The World Cups of 2006 and 2010 were both huge disappointments; the Copa America offered little consolation: in 2011 Brazil were defeated in the quarter-finals by Paraguay. And back in the pais do futebol the explanations are many and varied for decline: the defensive mindset of the national coach, Dunga; too many players earning their keep abroad or too many players staying at home and not completing their education abroad. If it's not that it's too many defenders coming through the ranks or the way the domestic calendar furs up with pointless inter-state competitions. And most of all, the blame was said to lie with the corrupt national organising body, the widely loathed CBF, made up as it is by the representatives of the 27 states, whose self-interest ensures the continuation of the pointless inter-state competitions that cause such irritation to the major clubs. In particular its relationship with Nike, who are reckoned by many to have hijacked the golden shirt in a 1996 deal worth £100 million, is said to sum up the manner in which the soul of the game has been sold to the commercial devil.

The fans vented their disappointment on the national side, howling their dismay during friendly fixtures. The CBF responded by exporting matches on the Brazil World Tour. That they trousered a handy fee in the process was perhaps not the best way to gainsay charges of venality.

Carnival 2014

Which is why hosting the 2014 World Cup has come to represent so much. When Ricardo Texeira's successful bid was announced in 2006, the celebrations in Rio were epic, as if the trophy itself had once again been secured. With the economy booming, driven by the country's vast mineral wealth, here was the opportunity to demonstrate to the rest of the world that Brazil is brisk, efficient, modern, a place with which to do business. Or at least that is the theory. So far the preparations have been dogged by cost overruns and labour disputes, the refurbishment and rebuilding of stadiums slowed at times to a drag by wildcat strikes among construction workers cheerfully flexing industrial muscles strengthened in the country's building boom.

But never mind the apparently relaxed approach to timetable and deadline. Never mind the bickering over tactics and existential angst over direction. Never mind the endless accusations of corruption. When the home nation kicks off the competition, a month-long carnival will commence. In the land of the yellow jersey, the football party will be like no other before it. In Fulham, they are already practising for the main event.

BIBLIOGRAPHY

Bellos, A., *Futebol: The Brazilian Way of Life* (London: Bloomsbury, 2003).
Goldblatt, D., *The Ball Is Round: A Global History of Football* (London: Penguin, 2007).
Castro, R., *Garrincha: The Triumph and Tragedy of Brazil's Forgotten Footballing Hero* (London: Yellow Jersey, 2005).
Pele, *Pele: The Autobiography* (New York: Simon & Shuster, 2006).
Taylor, C., *The Beautiful Game: A Journey Through Latin American Football* (London: Orion, 1998).

Figure 5.1. Diego Maradona (Argentina), Argentina v Brazil, World Cup Finals, 1982, Spain.
Credit: Colorsport/Andrew Cowie.

HUW RICHARDS

The Game-Changers: Diego Maradona

Somehow, as 2011 gave way to 2012, he was still standing. True, he was doing so in Dubai – that epitome of all that is flashily meretricious – and apparently as much a rich man's trophy as the al-Maktoum family's race-horses. The job did not last, but that he was not only still alive, but working, at 51 was a better outcome than many had forecast for Diego Maradona (Figure 5.1).

The first obituaries were drafted after a heart attack in 2000. Newer versions must include a further near-death in 2004, a spell as Argentinian national coach and that recent role with Al-Wasl in Dubai. That a man so famously self-destructive should also be apparently indestructible is the latest paradox in a lifetime of them.

Athletes of genius – and few more fully justify the description – are sui generis. Yet Maradona in action combined unique talents with echoes of others, both individual and collective. He was a super-charged, raised to the nth, incarnation of the archetypal Latin American street urchin, the *Pibe de Oro*.

In play there were hints of giants from other sports. The low centre of gravity, a gymnast's balance, fearsome power, pace and exceptional delicacy of touch brought to mind rugby union's Gareth Edwards while the squat build, timing and sheer gamin shamelessness smacked irresistibly of the Pakistani cricketer Javed Miandad. The trajectory of his career, from poverty to almost inconceivable fame and success, followed by a hideous self-fuelled crash, reminded Hugh McIlvanney more of boxers than footballers.[1]

It was a progress so compelling as to fascinate the finest writers on the game. Brian Glanville rejoiced that 'in an era when individual talent was at a premium, defensive football more prevalent than ever, Maradona – squat, muscular, explosive, endlessly adroit – showed that a footballer of genius could still prevail'.[2] Eduardo Galeano felt that 'in the icy football of the end of the century, which demanded victory and prohibited pleasure, he was one of the few to show that fantasy can also prevail'.[3]

Galeano also argued for Maradona as a radical countervailing force: 'Every goal was a desecration of the established order and a revenge on history.'⁴ His incongruous friendship with Fidel Castro and support for Hugo Chavez have been well advertised, but as Jimmy Burns pointed out, the reality was 'little more than a crude but fervent nationalism' salted with admiration for the traditional strong man.⁵

Genius, though, makes its own rules. Maradona, the fifth of eight children who grew up in a two-room shanty in the Buenos Aires barrio of Villa Florito, was juggling a football for television before he was 10, a First Division player at 15 and an international four months later. A late and often lamented exclusion from Argentina's World Cup-winning squad in 1978 when he was 17, he comprehensively dominated the youth version staged in Japan in 1979.

Apotheosis came in 1986. Sheer weight of lifetime achievement, plus having been invariably an asset to *every* team he ever played for, give Pelé the edge in the 'all-time greatest' debate – with Di Stéfano taking the 'Greatest Club Player' prize. But if individual peaks could be isolated and quantified in the manner of cricket ratings Maradona's 1986 World Cup would surely represent the all-time high. As Jonathan Wilson has pointed out, his pairing with Carlos Bilardo, 'presenting one of the most system-driven managers of all time with arguably the greatest individual player of all could have been one of football's great jokes'.⁶ The joke was entirely on Argentina's rivals.

Maradona was a system in himself. As his cerebral team-mate Jorge Valdano said: 'He is the soul of our team. He is our great offensive key. Diego can make a balanced team into world champions. Without him we would have to change our whole tactical scheme, perhaps have to find new players.'⁷

England remembers the piquant juxtaposition of the shameless Hand of God goal with a second score that really did suggest divine inspiration. The second of his two goals in the semi-final against Belgium may have been even better, the angled pass which opened up Germany for Jorge Burruchaga's first goal the decisive moment of the final. It truly was, as Galeano wrote, 'El Mundial de Maradona'.⁸

That his club career should peak – taking Napoli to their first Serie A championship – but also crash in Naples, a city both made for him and, with its pervasive drug-funded gangsterism, designed to destroy him, was sadly inevitable. He dragged a much-diminished Argentinian team almost single-handedly to the 1990 World Cup final, but the significant dates thereafter are 1991 and 1994, the years of his failed drug tests.

'Poor Old Diego'

Burns points to 'a vicious cycle of pain, recovery and more pain' as a body more vulnerable than it appeared was subjected to incessant battering by humiliated and outmatched defenders, then patched via cortisone injections.[9] Valdano empathised: 'Poor old Diego. For so many years, we have told him repeatedly "you're a god" ... that we forgot to tell him the most important thing – "you're a man".'[10] While few would query the decision, the subsequently-discredited names on the FIFA committee that banned him in 1994 show that football has ills other than drug-taking geniuses.

Since vastly better-adjusted athletes with a fraction of his talent struggle with the mid-life necessity to find something else they can do remotely as well, the post-retirement odds were always against Maradona. As he said himself, during an unsuccessful spell coaching Deportivo Mandiyu, 'I can't teach players things that only I can do.'[11]

No more vivid tribute to his hold on the Argentinian psyche could have been imagined than ignoring questions over his mental, never mind physical, competence and making him national coach. That Argentina qualified for the 2010 World Cup finals and reached the last eight before being dismantled by Germany was down to the underlying quality of a squad subjected to capricious scatter-shot selection.

But with all that he's still here, and still an unmatched hero to his countrymen. If Buenos Aires is, as Andre Malraux reckoned, 'The capital of an empire that never existed', there is no doubt who is its emperor.[12]

NOTES

1 H. McIlvanney, *McIlvanney on Football* (Edinburgh: Mainstream, 2007), p. 283.
2 B. Glanville, *The Story of the World Cup* (London: Faber and Faber, 1997), p. 271.
3 E. Galeano, *Futbol a Sol y Sombra* (Madrid: Siglo XXI, 2006), p. 347.
4 Ibid., p. 350.
5 J. Burns, *Hand of God: The Life of Diego Maradona* (London: Bloomsbury, 2002), p. 6.
6 J. Wilson, *Inverting the Pyramid: A History of Football Tactics* (London: Orion, 2008), p. 268.
7 McIlvanney, *McIlvanney on Football*, p. 257.
8 Galeano, *Futbol a Sol y Sombra*, p. 293.
9 Burns, *Hand of God: The Life of Diego Maradona*, p. 152.
10 D. Goldblatt, *The Ball Is Round* (London: Penguin, 2007), p. 809.
11 Burns, *Hand of God: The Life of Diego Maradona*, p. 234.
12 M.V. Montalban, *Futbol, Una Religion en Busca de un Dios* (Barcelona: Ediciones de Bolsillo, 2006), p. 35.

6

PAUL DARBY

Africa: Towards Global Football Citizenship?

The hosting of the 2010 World Cup in South Africa represented a coming of age for African football and, for a short period at least, placed it at the epicentre of the world game. This represented a culmination of events. For more than a century Africa had had an engagement with and passion for football characterised by imposition and transformation, marginalisation and resistance, exclusion and democratisation, pain and triumph and a slow march towards global football citizenship. This essay tells the story of this engagement.

Colonial History

Football in Africa is a legacy of European colonialism. The game was transported to the continent on the wings of empire in the late nineteenth century. Colonial administrators, educators, missionaries, soldiers, traders and settlers brought football to major port cities and coastal towns before the construction of railways allowed it to spread to the interior. The game was originally played mainly by Europeans but it was gradually diffused downwards to indigenous elites and then on to the African labouring classes. Western-style schools were instrumental in the popularisation of the game among elite groups while the emergence of large urban centres, massive population transfers and informal contact with Europeans provided ample opportunity for the working class to become acquainted with the game. More structured exposure in missionary schools was crucial and these further facilitated Africans' passionate embrace of the round ball (Darby, 2000a).

While football developed in a relatively haphazard fashion in more remote towns and villages, in the larger industrial centres, it represented one ingredient in a broader cultural stew that was served by colonial authorities to socialise indigenous populations into accepting colonial rule as the norm, and in the process, facilitate continued economic penetration (Darby,

2002). However, from the 1920s control of football was incrementally wrested from European hands and Africans began to imbue it with local flavour. African civil servants such as Hyder Kindy in Mombasa, Kenya; graduates of elite schools such as those from Gordon Memorial College in Sudan; employees of government agencies and departments in Nigeria including the Nigeria Police Force, Public Works Department and Nigerian Railway; and workers in Zambia's copper mines and South Africa's gold mines were all important in this process (Alegi, 2010). Rapid urbanisation also lay at the heart of the growth of African teams, and some of the continent's oldest clubs were established in expanding urban centres such as Accra (Hearts of Oak, 1911), Tunis (Espérance, 1919), Dakar (Jeanne d'Arc, 1921), and Yaoundé (Canon, 1930). This transition of football from a colonial institution to an African one was particularly marked in South Africa. British civil servants and soldiers in the Cape and Natal colonies and South African whites had been playing football since the early 1860s, and their promotion of the game gave rise to the continent's first football federation, the whites-only South African Football Association (SAFA) in 1892. By the 1920s, the game had become the game of the black working class while cricket and rugby were favoured by the white middle classes (Alegi, 2004; Nauright, 1997).

The pace of the Africanisation of the game quickened in the 1940s, and football soon developed as a site for anti-colonial protest. Alongside offering opportunities for young African men to exercise their bodies, their masculinity and their ethnic, neighbourhood and familial loyalties, football increasingly allowed them to express a growing desire to break free from the colonial yoke. The game could function this way because of its simplicity, the sheer enjoyment that it offered and the lack of expense it required, but also because it was one of the few meaningful institutions over which African labouring classes could realistically secure ownership and control. In an environment where most socio-political and cultural organisations were either proscribed or under colonial control, the establishment of teams, leagues and governing bodies by Africans was symbolically important. This symbolism was duly noted by a number of leading African nationalists in the late colonial period, and figures such as Nnamdi Azikiwe in Nigeria, Kwame Nkrumah in the Gold Coast and Ferhat Abbas in Algeria sought to harness it as a weapon in the anti-colonial armoury. The game was particularly effective in this regard in Algeria where the Front de Libération National (FLN) established what was essentially a proxy national team, playing a series of international matches in the late 1950s and early 1960s in order to help generate anti-French feeling and Algerian pride (Hawkey, 2009).

Post-Colonial Politics

By the mid-1960s more than 30 African nations had cast aside the shackles of colonialism. These newly independent nations wanted to register their presence on the international stage and they quickly joined organisations such as the Organisation of African Unity (OAU) and the United Nations. Given the popularity and political pedigree of football, it is unsurprising that these nations also viewed the world game as a platform on which to announce their new-found freedom, their confidence as members of the international community and their aspirations for the future. Emboldened by the establishment of the Confédération Africaine de Football (CAF) in 1957, they joined the FIFA 'family' confident that this would provide opportunities to participate on an equal footing with football powerhouses in Europe and South America. It soon become patently obvious that FIFA's established constituencies were not about to buy into this vision and they sought to protect their privileged position in the game's corridors of power. The world body's European members adopted a particularly entrenched position. Under the stewardship of a succession of European presidents, FIFA regarded Africa largely as an irrelevance and until the late 1950s the world body simply refused to countenance Africa's lobby for democratisation in the international game. For example, attempts to secure a place on FIFA's Executive Committee and organise a continental confederation for the African game in the first half of the 1950s were routinely frustrated by the world body's European constituents. Africa's calls for a more equitable distribution of World Cup places was met with similar intransigence and it took an African boycott of the qualifying rounds of the 1966 competition to secure a guaranteed berth for future tournaments (Darby, 2002).

Despite this victory, the marginalisation of Africa in the world game continued into the late 1960s and early 1970s. As CAF saw it, for as long as the Englishman Sir Stanley Rous remained president of FIFA, their hopes and ambitions would remain frustrated. Africa's difficulty, though, was that acting alone, it could not have hoped to effect change at the top of the world body. FIFA's franchise arrangements at their annual congress operated on the principle of one-nation-one-vote and it was clear that the continent needed to align itself with other national football federations. João Havelange, a Brazilian business magnate, emerged as the fulcrum around which these swirling political dynamics revolved. In 1971, Havelange launched his campaign to unseat Rous and become the first non-European FIFA president. His election manifesto was built unashamedly around appealing to the aspirations of the disenfranchised. For example, he promised underdeveloped football regions financial and technical support, opportunities to play a central role in new international youth championships and, crucially, more places at the World Cup. African football federations, alongside those from Asia, rallied around Havelange's manifesto and the Brazilian was duly elected at the world body's congress in 1974 (Darby, 2003).

Africa on the World Stage

Havelange's election victory marked a watershed in Africa's relationship with the world game, and with increased opportunities, the continent quickly made its mark. Prior to the enlarged World Cup in 1982 which saw two African nations compete in the tournament for the first time, African performances were mixed. Morocco began North Africa's World Cup tradition by going out in the group stages of the 1970 tournament with a single point following a draw with Bulgaria, a narrow 2–1 defeat by West Germany and a comprehensive loss to Peru. Zaire, heavily backed by General Joseph Désiré Mobutu, who saw football as a platform for personal aggrandisement and a vehicle for engendering patriotism, performed dismally in 1974, suffering a nine-goal defeat at the hands of Yugoslavia in one group game. While Tunisia secured Africa's first victory in World Cup competition in 1978 following a win over Mexico, they also went out at the group stages.

At Spain' 82, Africa's footballers began to demonstrate that they could compete with the world's best. Although both Cameroon and Algeria failed to progress beyond the opening round, the former exited undefeated following three draws, one of which was against the eventual champions, Italy. Algeria defeated West Germany in their opening game before being put out following a notoriously uncompetitive 0–0 draw between Austria and West Germany, a match dubbed the 'great Gijon swindle' that saw both European teams progress to the next round. At the next tournament in Mexico, Morocco topped a group containing England, Poland and Portugal before losing by a last-minute goal to West Germany in the second round. Italia '90 will long be associated with Cameroon's 'Indomitable Lions', who defeated Argentina in the opening game before losing narrowly to England in the quarter-finals. Since then Nigeria have twice reached the second round of the finals while both Senegal and Ghana matched Cameroon's feats in making it through to the quarter-finals in 2002 and 2010 respectively. Beyond the World Cup, Africa has placed its stamp on the Olympic football tournament in recent years with gold medals for Nigeria and Cameroon in 1996 and 2000. At the under-age level, the continent has also made its mark, not least Ghana and Nigeria, who have each won the under-17 World Cup twice and finished as runners-up on two occasions.

The rise of African football has extended beyond the field of play. Within FIFA's corridors of power Africa has been able to secure important administrative positions. Given that it holds around one quarter of the votes at the FIFA congress, the continent has also become a key constituency around which recent struggles for the world body's highest office have revolved (Darby, 2003). This has allowed the needs and aspirations of the continent's football federations to feature prominently on the election manifestos of presidential contenders such as the current incumbent Sepp Blatter and recent challengers including Lennart Johannson, Issa Hayatou and Mohammed Bin Hammam. All of this has meant that Africa has become less marginal in international football than it was in previous decades and is increasingly viewed as a football region deserving of respect and support. The clearest example of this was the FIFA executive committee's decision in 2004 to grant South Africa the hosting rights for the 2010 World Cup. This was not a straightforward process though. While USA '94 and Japan/South Korea 2002 indicated a willingness to bring the tournament to new constituencies, it was clear that up until 2004, FIFA's executive did not see the African continent as a realistic host for its most prized competition. However, following the failure of Morocco's bids for the 1994 and 1998 tournaments, the exclusion of Africa was becoming increasingly untenable and indeed, when South Africa launched its bid to host the 2006 World Cup, it did so on the simple but compelling premise that 'it was Africa's turn' (cited in Alegi, 2001).

Buoyed by comments from Blatter that Africa represented the 'logical choice' for 2006, the South African bid committee were confident about their chances (Harris, 1998). Unfortunately, narrow regional interests and some quite bizarre last-minute politicking undid South Africa's bid. After the first round of voting, it looked likely that the ballot would be tied between South Africa and Germany, and this would have given Blatter the casting vote. He had clearly indicated that this would go to South Africa, thus gifting the country hosting rights. However, Jack Dempsey, head of the Oceania Football Confederation, decided to abstain from voting at the last minute despite being mandated by his confederation to vote for South Africa. This effectively handed the World Cup to Germany. There was considerable speculation about the circumstances surrounding Dempsey's decision. The media spoke about bribery, personal feuds and even death threats. While none of these were ever confirmed, what is clear is that the exclusionary practices on the part of FIFA towards the African continent had reached a tipping point. Immediately after the vote, Danny Jordaan, the chief executive officer of the South African bid, encapsulated this perfectly: 'Africa is a member of the FIFA family and a family can't keep feeding one child while leaving the others to starve, which is what they have done today' (cited in

Perlman, 2000). FIFA's executive went some way towards remedying what happened in 2000 when in 2004 it voted to award the 2010 tournament to South Africa. While there are considerable question marks around the legacy and impact of the tournament (Pillay, Tomlinson and Bass, 2009; Alegi and Bolsman, 2010; Maguire, 2011), the success of South African 2010 commercially, organisationally and as a football spectacle marked another milestone in Africa's engagement with the world game and its quest for global citizenship.

The Domestic Front

While African football has taken significant strides forward in the international scene in the last 30 years, the trajectory of the domestic game across the continent in recent years has been decidedly mixed. As noted earlier, football acquired massive popularity during the colonial era and this gave rise to a whole series of colonial leagues and competitions. Once a country won independence, newly established sovereign football federations were quick to replace these structures with national competitions. For example, in North Africa, league championships were established in Egypt in 1948, in Tunisia in 1956 and in Morocco in the same year. In West Africa, Ghana organized a nationwide league in 1958. Francophone countries in the region were somewhat slower in setting up national competition, although by the close of the 1960s Ivory Coast and Senegal had both established leagues. In East Africa, national championships were established in Kenya in 1963 and Tanzania in 1965 (Alegi, 2010).

These leagues were initially successful. Local clubs became important markers of identity, matches provided great drama and spectacle and in a number of African countries the game attracted the support and patronage of newly installed heads of state. This was evident in a range of countries including Ghana, Nigeria and Zambia, where the local game benefited from the financial and moral support of Nkrumah, Azikiwe and Kaunda. However, as the quest for economic prosperity was stalled by a combination of civil war, economic mismanagement, corruption and global recession, state funding for football dried up and local teams and leagues began to struggle. By the late 1980s and early 1990s, it became clear to CAF and the national federations that steps were needed to halt the decline.

The succession of Ydnekatchew Tessema by Issa Hayatou as CAF president in 1987 saw the African game embrace commercialisation much more tightly than it had previously. During the 1990s, leagues and clubs south of the Sahara sought to catch up with their northern counterparts by professionalising their activities and adopting a more commercial outlook. The introduction of pseudo-professional leagues across the continent in the 1990s and the inception of the CAF Champions League in 1997 were clear examples of this. The South African Professional Soccer League, established in 1996, has emerged as the most financially robust African domestic championship. The corporatization of the game there and the role of television has allowed many clubs to be transformed from haphazardly run institutions based in poor communities into professional commercial enterprises. While there are examples of healthy, well-run clubs, particularly in North Africa, and signs of recovery in Kenya and Ghana, the domestic game on the continent remains in a precarious position. Indeed, to a large extent, the development of the game in the international context has served to mask the continued struggles of local clubs and leagues (Sugden and Tomlinson, 1998).

Persisting Problems and Future Challenges

It is clear then that African football faces many challenges at the outset of the twenty-first century. These challenges are multifarious, complex and difficult. The broader economic context that the continent operates in has a debilitating effect on the game at local and national levels. Finances have been at a premium. However, state investment and sustained interest from the private sector have been largely absent, and the finances necessary to put the game on a sound footing have simply not been available. While Africa's largely subordinate place in the global economy and the concomitant inability of the game to secure adequate funding have been major barriers to growth, they are not the only factors. The administration and management of the game in Africa has long been beset with problems. As Faouzi Mahjoub (1992), the respected Moroccan sports journalist, notes: 'Whichever African competition you look at, national or international, the fact remains: imperfection is a fact of life in African soccer. It is accepted to the point of institutionalisation, and nobody takes up cudgels to fight it.'

This imperfection manifests itself in a range of ways. There has been a tendency for those who own or who are involved in the management of domestic clubs to see the game as a vehicle for pursuing narrow self-interest and a medium to acquiring social, symbolic and economic capital (Pannenborg, 2012). Government interference in the running of football, particularly at the level of the national team, has been a long-standing problem. As highlighted earlier, in the post-colonial period, African governments and political leaders have sought to associate themselves with the mobilising power of football and they have invested in national teams in order to enhance their reputation and profile. While the financial subsidies that they provide are welcome, the influence of government ministers and politicians often creates havoc for African football. For example, in the aftermath of three defeats at the 1994 World Cup in the United States the entire leadership of the Moroccan football federation was dismissed on the orders of King Hassan II. These actions led to an unprecedented wave of turmoil which swept through many of Africa's national federations, and serious disputes have since ensued between football authorities and their national governments in Cameroon, Nigeria, Sierra Leone, Algeria, Tanzania, Niger, Gabon, Ghana and Egypt.

The destabilising influence of government interference in the affairs of football federations was recognised by FIFA, and at its 1994 congress, it decided to recognise only those member associations with properly elected ruling bodies. FIFA's stance has become increasingly hard-line, and since the mid-1990s, it has temporarily suspended numerous African member associations on account of government interference. Since 2004, the federations of Chad, Ethiopia and Madagascar have faced this fate while others, including Zambia, have been threatened. These sorts of actions on the part of FIFA may be motivated by a genuine desire to protect football administrators from politicians or they may be part of a strategy aimed at maintaining the sorts of patronage networks that allow FIFA's high-ranking elected officials to remain in positions of power. Irrespective of the reasons behind it, the suspension of national federations is both debilitating and destabilising.

While interference in football by government ministers and officials is often motivated by self-interest and a desire to curry populist support, there are occasions when mismanagement, particularly financial, warrants governmental and judicial scrutiny. In 1998, Sugden and Tomlinson highlighted endemic corruption on the part of football administrators, suggesting that 'we could present material in support of this claim from almost every sub-Saharan African country'. If anything, the problem has worsened since then. A recent dossier published by the Forum for African Investigative Reporters (2010) entitled 'Killing Soccer in Africa' highlighted numerous incidents of serious financial impropriety perpetrated by football officials across a range of African countries. The involvement of senior African football officials in the bribery scandals that engulfed FIFA's process for deciding the hosts of the 2018 and 2022 World Cups in late 2010 has done little to challenge the view that corruption blights the highest echelons of the African game. Indeed, of the six FIFA officials who received suspensions of between one and three years from all football-related activity by the world body's ethics committee, the involvement of four Africans – the Malian Amadou Diakite, the Botswanian Ismael Bhamjee, Tunisian Slim Aloulou and the Nigerian FIFA vice-president Amos Adamu – highlights that corruption represents a major challenge across all levels of the African game.

Beyond economics, government interference and corruption, increasing satellite television coverage of top-level European football across the continent seriously threatens the future health and prosperity of the African game. Deregulation and technological advances in TV broadcasting during the 1990s created a surge in audience figures across Africa. Satellite TV providers looked eagerly at the potential of the African market and, well aware of the popularity of football on the continent, they used it to sell subscriptions. The English Premiership, La Liga in Spain, Serie A in Italy, the German Bundesliga and Ligue 1 in France as well as the UEFA Champions League were aggressively marketed, and channels such as Supersport and Canal Horizon were happy to pay for the rights to satisfy an increasingly insatiable appetite for European football among African consumers (Alegi, 2010).

While the sale of rights packages to those seeking to broadcast European football across the continent helped to enrich European clubs, it has had the opposite effect on those in Africa. Wall-to-wall coverage of exciting, skilful football played in gleaming, modern stadia quickly reinforced the gulf between local leagues and their European counterparts. This process, described by Gerard Akindes (2008) as 'electronic colonialism', has had a debilitating impact on local leagues and clubs. As local fans have developed passionate affinities for Manchester United, Barcelona, Marseille, Milan and Bayern Munich, they have turned away from the domestic game in increasing numbers. This has significantly decreased attendances at matches, depriving clubs of an important source of revenue. Without a sufficient audience at games and a poor product offering, investment from the private sector and interest from national and satellite broadcasters has been slow in materialising, leaving the local game in a precarious position.

Player Exodus

The domestic game in Africa has not only struggled to compete with Europe's biggest brands for the affections and loyalties of local football fans but has also lost out to European clubs in terms of playing resources. Almost every aspiring local footballer seeks to leave home for the glitz and glamour of the Premiership, La Liga or the Bundesliga, creating a steady exodus of Africa's best talent to Europe. This migratory flow has a long history that reaches far back into the colonial period. France and Portugal were particular beneficiaries, but since the early 1990s the trade has accelerated exponentially with Africans gracing arenas right across Europe. The success of African 'stars', improving performances by African teams on the global stage and the Bosman ruling of 1995 – which permitted free movement of European Union nationals in European football and ended restrictive quotas of non-EU nationals – have been the main contributors to the outflow of African talent. Economics have also been key, with the wealth of the European game and the fragility of Africa's local clubs and leagues driving the process. Put simply, with limited opportunities to carve out a professional career at home, talented young players have fixed their sights firmly on the fame and fortune enjoyed by players such as Weah, Essien, Drogba, Eto'o and Adebayor. While these sorts of players are highly successful and have been lavishly rewarded, there is a much darker side to the trade.

In 2003, Blatter described European clubs who recruit African players as 'neo-colonialists who don't give a damn about heritage and culture, but engage in social and economic rape by robbing the developing world of its best players' and went on to lament that their recruitment of young Africans as 'unhealthy if not despicable' (cited in Bradley, 2003). In an era of free movement, it might appear that Blatter was seeking to grab the headlines with another broadside at the growing financial dominance of Europe's top leagues. However, what underpinned his outburst were deep-rooted concerns about the trafficking of young African players. Disquiet over this issue was first expressed in the early 1990s when it became clear that African minors as young as 14 or 15 were being brought to Europe on temporary visas by agents and scouts only to be abandoned and left to fend for themselves as illegal immigrants if unsuccessful during trials. The United Nations Commission on Human Rights got involved in a growing debate about this practice, and in 1999 it published a report that concluded by referring to the 'danger of effectively creating a modern day "slave trade" in young African footballers' (cited in Bale, 2004: 240).

Other aspects of the trade were equally nefarious and saw young talent being treated as commodities and exploited by European agents, scouts and clubs as well as by African football officials and team owners. By the start of the new millennium, FIFA decided to intervene, introducing a set of transfer regulations that effectively prevented clubs from signing players under the age of 18. These regulations have helped to curb, although not completely eradicate, the most exploitative aspects of the international transfer market, particularly the maltreatment of minors. This is not to say that the trade in African football talent has slowed – quite the opposite in fact. As competition for cheap, highly skilled playing resources has deepened, European clubs are increasingly setting up a presence on the continent, either through establishing an academy or feeder clubs, thus emulating their American baseball counterparts who have set up similar outposts in Central America and the Caribbean. Under these circumstances, the exodus looks set to continue for some time yet. While a small minority of players will continue to benefit from opportunities to earn the sort of salaries that they could only have dreamed of, the majority will have their dreams dashed and will simply be discarded in what is an unforgiving industry.

Beyond its impact on individuals, the migration of Africa's finest talent to foreign fields brings mixed blessings to the continent. The opportunity to play in Europe's elite professional leagues clearly improves the technical and tactical capabilities of players. Countless commentators, coaches and players have acknowledged that this in turn benefits national teams and improves performance in international competition. Indeed, for some, it is an absolute article of faith that the surge of African teams over the last 20 years or so is a consequence of increased exposure to European football. It is also suggested that the involvement of European teams in developing young players in the continent via academies or feeder clubs provides varying levels of financial and technical capital for the game, although this investment is squarely focused on uncovering the next Drogba or Eto'o. Successful migrant players, like ordinary African economic migrants, send remittances back home to support their families and local communities while some will establish charitable or philanthropic foundations in their country of origin. This provides an economic stimulus in the African context, albeit one that is small scale and often temporary.

Ultimately, though, the trade is oriented around talent extraction, and this de-skills and impoverishes the domestic game across Africa. The fact that Africa's most talented players typically play outside the continent reduces standards of play. This has had a negative effect on the economics of the domestic game because the player drain has made it much less attractive to local fans, most of whom watch the English Premier League on satellite television rather than support their local team. Thus, attendances and gate receipts have tailed off, depriving local clubs of a vital source of income. This reduction in the quality of the local product also makes the domestic game a less enticing proposition for sponsors and television, and further undermines the possibility of initiating the sort of financially viable leagues that might slow the talent exodus and significantly improve the level of the local game.

Ghana's Heartbreak

On a trip to Zimbabwe in July 2011, Sepp Blatter suggested that African teams can one day rank among the best in the world. Blatter's comments echoed the views of a whole host of football luminaries including Pelé, Sir Walter Winterbottom and Liberia's George Weah who, over the last 25 years, have predicted that the name of an African nation will soon be inscribed on the World Cup trophy. The African game has taken considerable strides towards reaching that objective. Ghana were desperately unlucky not to become the first African team to qualify for the World Cup semi-finals, and had it not been for a penalty miss by Asamoah Gyan with the last kick of their quarter-final against Uruguay, the Black Stars might well have gone all the way. Gyan's dramatic miss and Ghana's heartbreaking departure from the tournament encapsulated all that keeps millions around the world so enthralled and enraptured by football.

The unrivalled drama that the game often delivers simply shows that while it is possible to prepare meticulously for success, the final outcome can be totally unpredictable. The success or otherwise of African football in the years ahead is likely to be determined by a range of variables over which administrators, government officials, coaches or players have little control. That said, if those issues over which they have some control, such as weak governance, financial investment, the exodus of the highly skilled, the deep penetration of European football in the African psyche and the slow decline of domestic football, can be properly managed, then the future for African football is likely to be one of progress. The alternative is stagnation and decline.

BIBLIOGRAPHY

Akindes, G. 2008. 'Football in Sub-Saharan Africa, New Technologies and Broadcasting Deregulation: Football Development or Electronic Colonialism?', paper presented at the African Studies Association annual meeting, Chicago.

Alegi, P. 2001. '"Feel the Pull in Your Soul": Local Agency and Global Trends in South Africa's 2006 World Cup Bid', *Soccer and Society*, 2, 3: 1–21.

2004. *Laduma! Soccer, Politics and Society in South Africa*. University of Kwa-Zulu-Natal Press.

2010. *African Soccerscapes: How a Continent Changed the World's Game*. Hurst.

Alegi, P. and Bolsman, C. (eds.). 2010. *South Africa and the Global Game: Football, Apartheid and Beyond*. Routledge.

Bale, J. 2004. 'Three Geographies of Africa Footballer Migration: Patterns, Problems and Postcoloniality' in Armstrong, Gary and Giulianotti, Richard (eds.), *Football in Africa: Conflict, Conciliation and Community*. Palgrave Macmillan, pp. 229–246.

Bradley, M. 'Blatter Takes Swipe at G-14 "Colonialists"', *Guardian*, 18 December 2003.

Darby, P. 2000a. 'Football, Colonial Doctrine and Indigenous Resistance: Mapping the Political Persona of FIFA's African Constituency', *Culture, Sport, Society*, 3, 2: 61–87.

2000b. 'The New Scramble for Africa: African Football Labour Migration to Europe', *European Sports History Review* 3: 217–244.

2002. *Africa, Football and FIFA: Politics, Colonialism and Resistance*. Frank Cass.

2003. 'Africa, the FIFA Presidency and the Governance of World Football: 1974, 1998 and 2002', *Africa Today*, 50, 1: 3–24.

Harris, N. 1998. 'Double Blow to England's 2006 Bid', *Independent*, 27 October 1998.

Hawkey, I. 2009. *Feet of the Chameleon: The Story of African Football*. Portico.

Maguire, J. 2011. '*Invictus* or Evict-us? Media Images of South Africa through the Lens of the FIFA World Cup', *Social Identities*, 15, 5: 681–694.

Mahjoub, F. 1992. 'Culture of Mediocrity', *African Soccer*, 1: 38.

Nauright, J. 1997. *Sport, Cultures and Identities in South Africa*. Leicester University Press.

Pannenborg, A. 2012. *Big Men Playing Football: Money, Politics and Foul Play in the African Game*. African Studies Centre.

Perlman, J. 'Favourites South Africa Left Out in the Cold', *Guardian*, 7 July 2000.

Pillay, U., Tomlinson, R. and Bass, O. (eds.). 2009. *Development and Dreams: The Urban Legacy of the 2010 Football World Cup*. HSRC Press.

Rukini, C. and Groenink, E. (eds). 2010. Killing Soccer in Africa. FAIR Transnational Investigation.

Sugden, J. and Tomlinson, A. 1998. *FIFA and the Contest for World Football: Who Owns the Peoples' Game?* Polity Press.

ROB STEEN

The Game-Changers: Eusébio

My first football book was the English translation of *My Name Is Eusébio*. Published in the wake of the 1966 World Cup, the intoxicating subtitle of the Portuguese edition was 'the autobiography of the greatest footballer in the world'. At nearly half a century's distance, this may sound somewhat hubristic; Brazil, after all, could still claim the services of Pelé and Garrincha. To deny the publisher's right to make such a claim, nevertheless, would be to grossly underestimate the impact and import of Africa's first globally renowned footballer – though even that claim is far from invulnerable to contradiction. To tout this as purely a rags-to-riches tale, however, would be to ignore football's all-too-willing role in the murky world of migrant labour.

Shortly before Africa hosted its first World Cup in 2010, Eusébio was asked whether he regarded himself as a 'figurehead' for the event, as widely portrayed. 'I do,' came the reply, 'I feel very proud.'[1] As well he might. The son of an Angolan railway mechanic, he grew up kicking makeshift balls in the streets of a shantytown in Mozambique (then Portuguese East Africa), just outside what is now Maputo, and was rejected by Desportivo for lacking the appropriate footwear. His idol was Benfica's celebrated midfield general Mario Coluna, a Mozambican émigré who would lend financial support to the quest for independence.[2] Yet, as Ayo Akinfe argued, it is not strictly accurate to call Eusébio African. He was born in 1942, in the 'native quarter' of what was then Lourenço Marques, 'the finest city' in the region[3]; independence did not come to Mozambique until 1975, by which time he was already a Portuguese icon. Indeed, characterising himself as anything other than Portuguese could have earned him a death sentence for treason. 'Eusébio has only known one flag throughout his lifetime,' observed Akinfe, 'and it is certainly not an African one.'[4]

'The world Eusébio left,' noted Paul Hayward, 'was one of European colonies and lasting exploitation.'[5] Moreover, as Paul Darby[1] emphasizes, his

---

[1] For an analysis of the impact of migration on African football, see Chapter 6 in this volume, 'Africa: Towards Global Football Citizenship?' by Paul Darby.

'naturalization' under the 'Indigenous People's Rule' 'can also be read as a process that functioned to reinforce Portuguese colonial hegemony'; a naturalization that 'can be described in terms of enrichment of the developed world at the expense or impoverishment of the developing world'.[6]

But enough of semantics and moral deficiency. Let us celebrate the man whose athleticism, skill and power enriched the game (the International Federation of Football History & Statistics voted him the ninth-best player of the twentieth century), a man possessed, as Brian Glanville rejoiced, of an 'almost spiritual face ... [a] lithe, flexible body [and] long legs, so expert at conjuring the ball past tackles, so explosive both in movement and in the enormous power of his right-footed shot'.[7]

A saga of serendipity and intrigue, Eusébio da Silva Ferreira's flight to Portugal, in late 1960, stemmed from a chance encounter in a Lisbon barbershop between Bela Guttman, Benfica's shrewd Hungarian coach, always eager to exploit colonial resources, and Carlos Bauer, Brazil's right-half at the 1950 World Cup and now a coach with São Paulo (where he had played under Guttman) about to embark on a trip to Portuguese East Africa; the next month, at the same barbershop, Bauer rhapsodised about a remarkable inside-left with ties to Sporting Lisbon who could run 100 metres in 11 seconds. A few days later Guttman flew to Lourenço Marques and signed the teenager for £7,500, infuriating Benfica's city rivals.[8] Fearing a kidnap attempt by Sporting, Benfica sent him to the Algarve for 12 days, under the codename Ruth Malosso, The wait was worthwhile. After just 25 club games Eusébio, having qualified under the Indigenous People's Rule introduced by the dictator Antonio Salazar, was playing for Portugal and scoring on debut against Luxembourg – the first of 41 goals he would collect for the national team in 64 appearances.

When Eusébio arrived in Lisbon, Benfica were already en route to becoming the first club other than Real Madrid to win the European Cup; any doubts about what the newcomer offered were roundly and loudly dispelled in the epic 1962 final against Real in Amsterdam. Despite a Ferenc Puskas hat-trick, Benfica were only a goal behind at the break, whereupon Guttman instructed one of his goalscorers, Cavem, to mark Alfredo di Stéfano, blocking Puskas's supply. Now it was Eusébio's turn. Having seen Coluna equalize, he outpaced Di Stéfano and won a penalty, converting it himself with aplomb; five minutes later, he lashed in Coluna's pass. At the final whistle, he sprinted 30 yards to swap shirts with Puskas, the trade richly symbolic.

Guttman left for Uruguay but Benfica carried on regardless, reaching three of the next half-dozen European Cup finals, albeit fruitlessly. European Footballer of the Year in 1965, Eusébio won the continent's inaugural Golden Boot award in 1968 and a return to his unhappiest hunting-ground,

Wembley, where Alex Stepney's courageous late block of a point-blank drive denied him the winner and Manchester United romped home in extra-time. Missing, nonetheless, was assuredly no habit: 614 outings for Benfica brought an astonishing 638 goals.

Joybringer

He is best remembered, though, for his contribution to that 1966 World Cup. In a tournament scarred by cynicism and hatchet-men, his finishing – nine goals, easily the most – was no less ruthless, especially against North Korea, who piled up an improbable 3–0 quarter-final lead before the 'Black Pearl' restored order with four goals. Even more endearing, and enduring, was the face-splitting smile and the courtliness towards opponents. Has any player conveyed more infectiously the sheer joy – innocent, childlike, wholly unconfined – of football?

Even so, his greatest assets were a thick skin and a long temper. In 2011, after Alan, a black winger playing for Braga, alleged that Javier Garcia, a white Benfica midfielder, had called him a 'black piece of s***', Eusébio chided Alan for going public: 'So what is he [if not black]? I was called that and a lot more. If I had reacted, I wouldn't have finished many games.'[9]

He wound down his career in North America and Mexico, a walking billboard for the flexible lot of the modern footballer, unfettered by the apron-strings of nation-state, a black man free to maximize his talent – and campaign against racism. Joseph Maguire and Mark Falcous rightly contend that sports migration today 'is bound up in a sports industrial complex that is itself embedded in a series of power struggles that characterize the global sports system',[10] but that should not blind us to what seems, on balance, to be a sign of progress.

NOTES

1 P. Hayward, 'From Africa to posterity: How Eusébio lit up the World Cup', *Guardian*, 6 June 2010, www.guardian.co.uk/football/2010/jun/06/Eusébio-africa-world-cup (accessed 24 December 2011).

2 P. Alegi, *African Soccerscapes: How a Continent Changed the World's Game* (Columbus: Ohio University Press, 2010), p. 88.

3 Eusébio da Silva Ferreira, *My Name Is Eusébio* (London: Routledge & Kegan Paul, 1967), pp. 5–6.

4 A. Akinfe, 'Eusébio is not African', *Guardian*, 20 January 2008, www.guardian.co.uk/football/2008/jan/20/sport.comment5.

5 Hayward, 'From Africa to posterity'.

6 P. Darby, 'African Football Labour Migration to Portugal: Colonial and Neo-Colonial Resource', *Soccer & Society*, 8, 4 (2007), 495–509.

7　B. Glanville, *Champions of Europe – The history, romance and intrigue of the European Cup* (London: Guinness, 1991), p. 32.

8　J. Wilson, *Inverting the Pyramid – A History of Football Tactics* (London: Orion, 2008), p. 99.

9　G. Marcotti, 'Patronising Blatter off the hook as Fifa family turn a blind eye', *Times*, 18 November 2011, p. 111.

10　J. Maguire and Falcous, M. (eds.), *Sport Migration: Borders, boundaries and crossings* (Oxford: Routledge, 2011), p. 5.

PART TWO

Development

7

PETER BERLIN

Money, Money, Money: The English Premier League

This is a story about money. In just over two decades English soccer has raised itself from the ashes of Bradford, the ruins of Heysel and the wreckage of Hillsborough. It has climbed from the financial mire to become a global 'brand' with support at unprecedented levels at home and abroad. It rakes in the cash for television rights, sponsorship and advertising. Its teams are stuffed with international stars playing in packed modern stadia. Money has transformed the top division of English football and that, in turn, has made it more attractive to fans, investors, broadcasters, sponsors and advertisers, which, in turn, brings in more income. Since its birth in 1992, the Premier League has become a money magnet. Yet wealth has not brought happiness. The more they have the more, it seems, the clubs need. Many traditional fans, meanwhile, are disillusioned that finances seem to dominate the sports pages and by the way the tidal wave of cash has reshaped the football landscape.

The Premier League was an expression of an existing desire by the largest clubs to take a bigger share of English football's revenue. Football has always had financial disparities, but in the Premier League those inequalities grew in such a way that, for a while, they seemed to create a permanent elite. Between them, Manchester United, Arsenal and Chelsea won every league title from 1995 up to the end of the 2010–11 season. One measure of this domination is the precious league and cup double. It was achieved just three times in the twentieth century before the birth of the Premier League. Since then, those three clubs have done it six times. With Liverpool they make up the Premier League's Big Four, or 'Sky Four'. The Big Four seemed able to insulate themselves from the usual cyclical dips in fortune caused by poor management, mistakes in the transfer market or bad luck with injuries.

Two external developments helped the Big Four capitalise on, and increase, their advantage: the development of the Champions League, which increasingly gave an added financial advantage to the top-finishing clubs, and the Bosman ruling in 1995, which created free agency and thus lowered one of the barriers that prevented teams from translating financial wealth into playing strength.

One consequence of the amount of money flowing into football and of the success in the United States of Michael Lewis's *Moneyball*,[1] a book about baseball, is that the game has suddenly become interesting to economists. Much of what happens on the football field has proved resistant to the sort of revelations that *Moneyball* claims statistical analysis has produced for baseball, but the economists are well equipped to look at competition between businesses and have applied a host of measures to football. Every one of them suggests that the Premier League became steadily less competitive, dominated by a small oligopoly of three or four companies or clubs. The statistics suggest that trend started in the late 1980s and peaked in 2008, the last season in which the Big Four filled the top four places.

The question is whether the more confused picture at the top of the Premier League after 2008 presaged a new period of domination by a slightly different Big Four or was a structural change produced by changes in the Premier League rules on squad composition and proposed UEFA rules on club finances.

The Golden Triangle

Long before the Premier League was born, many in sport were beginning to grasp the potential of the 'Golden Triangle' of television, advertising and sponsorship. Joao Havelange, president of FIFA from 1974 to 1998, was an exponent of the concept and applied it to the World Cup. FIFA was not alone. The International Olympic Committee lost its distaste for money. The first Games after the Berlin Wall fell, in 1992 in Barcelona, fully embraced professionalism, thus ensuring that it could offer broadcasters, sponsors and spectators the best athletes for their money. The pattern was repeated in other sports.

English football also shed its distaste for overt commercialism. In the 1980s, teams began to display advertising on their shirts. Broadcasting revenue began to rise and, in the late 1980s, that market suddenly grew more competitive with the arrival of satellite television. By 1992 'the pressure was irresistible', said Michael Payne, who as the International Olympics Committee's (IOC's) first director for Marketing and Broadcast Rights had helped shape the Olympic movement's commercial strategy. The money was there, largely untapped but seeking a way in. The clubs desperately needed it.

Football League attendance had been as high as 41 million in 1948–49, with the 22 clubs in the top division drawing 17.9 million. By 1985–86, the season after the Bradford fire and the Heysel disaster, it had dropped to 16.5 million, of which 9 million were for Division One games.[2] Business was bad.

Chasing the Money

When American economists started to study sports in the 1950s, they found they could treat U.S. franchises as 'profit maximising' businesses. The one slight problem was that the natural urge of successful businesses to establish themselves as monopolies is self-defeating in sport. If there is only one competitor, there can be no competition. When economists started to look beyond the United States at football, they found another problem. Peter J. Sloane, a British economist, concluded that club owners were not profit-maximisers but 'utility-maximisers'. They were in it for something other than money. That could be status, competitiveness, love for a team or a sense of responsibility to the community. Utility maximisation, wrote Sloane, in a phrase that will resonate with many fans frustrated by their club's board, is 'consistent with almost any type of behaviour'.

The fact that teams need healthy opponents has never stopped clubs trying to crush their rivals both on and off the field. The Football League and the Football Association had rules limiting economic competition, enforcing revenue-sharing and restricting what directors and shareholders could take out of clubs.

In the changing political and economic climate of the 1970s and 1980s, the rules were allowed to wither. Martin Edwards at Manchester United started to exploit ways round the rule limiting dividends and a director's salary. Irving Scholar floated Tottenham in 1983.

The principle of shared revenue was also compromised, as big clubs sought to increase revenue by taking money from other clubs. During the 1981–82 season, Philip Carter of Everton hosted a meeting of chairmen. The big clubs started muttering about a breakaway. 'Smaller clubs are bleeding the game dry,' said Edwards. 'For the sake of the game they should be put to sleep.'[3] In 1983, the smaller clubs gave ground. They agreed to end the 20 per cent of the declared take for each league match the home team shared with the away club. The battle lines were drawn. The war was to be fought over television revenue.

In 1984, the BBC and ITV jointly bought the rights to 10 live games for £2.2 million per season. That money was divided equally between the 92 clubs, which worked out at £23,000 each.[4] In 1986, the First Division clubs forced a change, which meant they got 50 per cent of the revenue. The launch of satellite television in 1988 transformed the market for broadcasting rights. Rupert Murdoch was already making live sport a cornerstone of his global gamble on television. Sky bid for the Football League rights in 1988 even though it was not yet on-air.

In that auction, ITV broke with the BBC, creating a three-way competition, and paid a sharply higher price, £11 million a year.[5] Of this, 75 per cent went to the First Division, and the 'Big Five' of Tottenham, Everton, Liverpool, Manchester United and Arsenal between them took 40 per cent.

The Breakaway

Greg Dyke, the managing director of London Weekend Television, anticipated competition from Sky in the next auction in 1992. In November 1990, he met with the men who ran the Big Five and promised that if ITV won the next contract, it would focus on their teams and they would obtain the lion's share of the revenue. The clubs also knew that if they could end sharing with the Football League that would mean even more money for their clubs. But breaking with the Football Association risked putting the clubs, and their players, outside the official structure of football not just in Britain but the world as a whole.

When the top clubs approached the FA, Graham Kelly, the chief executive, saw the proposed breakaway as a chance to protect his employer from pressure from the Football League and regain momentum in the FA's long-running battle to shrink the top division. It does not seem to have occurred to Kelly that the FA should actually run the country's top professional division, even though that is what the football associations in other countries do, or to ask for a cut of the revenue. He did not make 18 clubs a condition of starting the league. He was content with a reduction to 20 teams and a promise that at some point in the future the new league would get around to dropping two more teams.

Sky TV

On 18 May 1992, a week before they formally broke away from the Football League, the 22 First Division clubs met in a London hotel to vote on the next television contract. LWT bid £262 million for five years. Sky responded with a bid of £305 million over five years, which also included money from the BBC for highlights. The number of live matches would jump to 60 a season.[6] The clubs voted for the Sky bid.

The Premier League contract, wonderfully generous as it seemed to the clubs who voted for it, paid off for Sky, which had made losses every year up to 1992. Sam Chisholm, the BSkyB chief executive at the time, has said that the company would have paid twice as much. Sky has never adopted pay-per-view, a phrase it whispered seductively in the ears of chairmen in 1992. It never needed to. The Premier League attracted subscribers prepared to pay a premium for sport from the start. In 1993, the first full year in which it broadcast the Premier League, Sky made a profit for the first time.

In 1992, it seemed to be a risk to remove the league from a free-to-air channel and put it on a satellite station with only 2.87 million subscribers.[7] Even though live league football was only a fairly recent innovation, the fact that the majority of fans were excluded from watching rankled. The unpopularity of Murdoch in many quarters also brought hostility.

Sky has never made Dyke's mistake of saying publicly that it favours the big clubs, yet its preference for showing those with the biggest support makes sense for a broadcaster. So, of course, does showing clubs contending for the title. Over the life of the Premier League, the two have increasingly merged. Sky's consistent preference for showing United, Liverpool, Chelsea and Arsenal has led to the quartet's becoming known as the 'Sky Four'. In 2010–11, of Manchester United's 38 games, 26 were shown live on Sky or ESPN. Nine clubs – West Bromwich Albion, Birmingham, Blackpool, Blackburn, Bolton, Fulham, Stoke, Wigan and Wolves – appeared just 10 times each, the contractual minimum, even though most were embroiled in a tense relegation battle.

Sky was able to remain the only live broadcaster until 2008. Its monopoly drew the frequent scrutiny of British and European authorities. The contracts kept rising in value until 2005, when Sky, the only bidder, paid less. By the next auction, in 2008, the Premier League had done a deal with the European Commission, which broke the rights into packages. Setanta entered the auction. The upward trend resumed.

Setanta paid a backbreaking £393 million for two packages, failed to attract enough subscribers and staggered on long enough to bid again in 2010 when it won just one package but helped push the total value of the deals a little higher.[8] Sky, meanwhile, had more than 10 million subscribers in 2010, of whom around half pay extra for sport.

Tomorrow the World

The arrival of Setanta and then ESPN provided only a small boost to domestic revenues. After all, the Premier League was obliged to sell live rights to more than one company and only two companies were serious bidders. The entry of BT in 2013 dramatically changed the auction. The value of the rights leapt 71 per cent and passed £3 billion.

The growth of domestic rights has been impressive, that of international rights has been stratospheric. Between 2001 and 2010, international rights grew 800 per cent. For 2010–13 they doubled to £1.4 billion, 42 per cent of the Premier League's total television revenue. At the turn of 2013, that growth appeared to be continuing. In October 2012, NBC, a national network, paid $250 million for three years of U.S. rights, more than treble the $80 million Fox and ESPN had paid in the previous deal.[9]

In the international market, the Premier League is in competition with other national leagues. Yet, so far, while Real Madrid and Barcelona clearly have allure, the Premier League has faced negligible competition. The question is whether this is because it has advantages that its rivals simply cannot overcome.

England is still viewed as the home of soccer. It also hosts a league played, broadcast, covered and noisily supported in English, the international language. It has a reputation for competitiveness and unpredictability. Increasingly, this is true only if competitiveness is defined simply as the players running at 100 miles an hour for 90 minutes and kicking each other a lot, but there can be no denying that this translates into plenty of energetic action.

The Premier League and its clubs have cultivated international markets. One simple example is the number of Asia-friendly league games at lunchtime on both Saturdays and Sundays. That gives the Premier League a huge advantage in East Asia over its main global rival, Spain's La Liga, which plays its marquee matches late in the evening.

The revenue came under threat in October 2011, when the European Commission ruled on a case brought by Karen Murphy, a Portsmouth landlady who had baulked at paying Sky's price for a pub subscription and was showing matches from foreign feeds. The Commission found against her but also ruled that the Premier League's practice of selling overseas rights on a country-by-country basis went against the principle that Europe is a single market. Since the vast majority of potential buyers are national broadcasting companies, the ruling could, on the face of it, depress and complicate foreign rights sales, although it might benefit satellite broadcasters with a large European footprint, such as Sky. The ruling also threatens the European resale market for film and other television programming, so the Premier League may be able to sit back and let Mickey Mouse do its lobbying dirty work for it.

Television is a source of paranoia for the top English clubs. They have spent like alcoholics who have won the lottery, developing a taste for expensive foreign imports, and worry that they will wake up one day, hungover, to find that the television bubble has burst. Domestically, the collapse of ITV Digital in 2002, which left many Football League clubs tottering on the edge of bankruptcy, provided an awful warning. The international market, where the Premier League clubs are in direct competition with their leading European rivals in a market that is barely a decade old, is even scarier. The Premier League keeps repeating that it attracts viewers because it offers the most exciting football, but the market is clearly faddish and fickle and no one is really sure if that is true.

Moving Upmarket

Even before Heysel, clubs had erected fences at grounds. After Heysel, pressure from the police and a Conservative government keen on law and order increased. English fans were a national embarrassment. Football seemed powerless to control them. If the fans behaved like animals, then they were to be caged. And in 1989, at the start of an FA Cup semi-final between Liverpool and Nottingham Forest, 96 of them died trapped against the fencing at Hillsborough.

The clubs were forced to refurbish their grounds as all-seater stadia. They knew the potential rewards. Aston Villa had introduced executive boxes, an idea cribbed from North America, in 1977. The disaster put the clubs in a position to squeeze more money out of their fans.

The first Sky windfall coincided with the need to convert the grounds. But, by 1992, clubs had already started to collect money from another source. After Hillsborough, the Conservative government effectively rewarded the clubs for their long and deadly neglect of fan safety. It redirected tax on some competitions run by the pools companies to the Football Trust. Over the next seven years, the trust gave out £150 million in grants to the league clubs. The total expenditure on ground improvement and the construction of new stadia over that period was £500 million.

In their insatiable pursuit of money, the clubs also tried other new sources of financing. Many followed Tottenham's lead. Deloitte estimated in 2009 that Premier League clubs had raised £175 million in stock flotations.[10] It worked for the clubs, and some of their owners, but the stock market should have seen the utility-maximisers coming. The majority of clubs had de-listed by 2010.

Clubs also 'securitised' future revenues: borrowing in exchange for a guaranteed repayment from the anticipated increase in gate and hospitality revenue. Arsenal tried to imitate the American idea of 'seat licences', which it called 'debentures'. The fans were not interested in buying the right to buy tickets. In some cases, the development was paid for by the first of the new wave of super-benefactors. Ewood Park was rebuilt during Jack Walker's reign at Blackburn. Parts of Chelsea's Stamford Bridge were rebuilt with money 'invested' (which, in this case, means 'given') by Matthew Harding. The upgrading of stadia went hand in hand with the publicity being provided by Sky, the rest of the media and the advertisers and sponsors. English football was moving upmarket.

There is nostalgia for the passion of the terraces. But the unimproved grounds could be dangerous, unpleasant places. The terraces were toilets, the toilets were sewers and the food looked, smelled and tasted as if it had come from the toilets. All-seater stadia represent the marketing men's ideal of twenty-first-century British suburban life: jumbo screens, matching coloured seating and souvenir boutiques and fast food outlets every few yards. The stadia also allow an Orwellian level of supervision. There is nowhere for seated fans to hide from the ubiquitous cameras; tickets, now invariably bought in advance, often bear the purchaser's name and can be scanned at the turnstiles. They know where you're sitting and they can see you. Constant anonymous surveillance makes many people understandably uneasy, but a football ground is a shared public space and while no one goes to a match to mix with polite society, few would complain. Violence has been almost entirely eliminated.

In the 1990s, capacity shrank and attendance rose. With a reduced number of clubs, attendance drooped slightly in the first Premier League season. After that it followed a wobbly upward path. By 2008–09 it was 13.5 million compared with 7.8 million 20 years earlier.[11] The cleaned-up product drew not only more but wealthier fans. Between 1991–92 and 1998–99, gate revenues rose from £87 million to £312 million.[12] Investment in stadia paid. According to Deloitte, Premier League clubs spent more, often much more, than £100 million on stadia every year between 2000 and 2009.[13]

Every club has benefited from the stadium boom, but those that have benefited most are the big clubs that have built big stadia and can fill them. In 2009–10, Manchester United and Arsenal generated £4 out of every £10[14] earned by the Premier League teams in matchday revenue.

The nostalgic bemoan the huge drop in the proportion of males aged 16–20 in the crowds. But that was part of the point of the exercise. You need just enough to get the singing going. What adults in their right mind want to spend more time than they have to with large numbers of 16- to 20-year-old males? They can enjoy each other's company, and get as drunk as they like, down the pub watching on Sky.

The glossy, upmarket Premier League, broadcast across the globe, became a magnet for sponsors as well as an international merchandising machine. In 2010, United made €99.4 million in commercial revenue,[15] some 28 per cent of the club's total income. 'Further down the Premier League the market remains challenging with many clubs restricted to low value and/or short term deals,' Deloitte said in its 2011 Money League report.

The Champions League

One growing advantage for the biggest clubs, in all the leading European footballing countries, has been the Champions League. Over the 1990s, the

European Cup gradually evolved from a straight knockout for the champions of Europe's domestic leagues into a competition, which offered broadcasters more matches, in group stages, and more teams from the top nations.

UEFA negotiates the television deals and competition sponsorship centrally. The bulk of that revenue is distributed to clubs under a formula that rewards teams that advance to the later rounds. There is also a 'market pool', which is linked to the television revenues generated by each country. Because British television pays more for rights, English clubs do best from this pool.

In 2010–11, Barcelona, the winners, collected €51.025 million, of which €20.325 million came from the market pool. But that was less than Manchester United, which made €53.197 million. Chelsea went out in the quarter-finals but earned the biggest slice from the pool, €27.023 million.[16] United also reaped the profits of 13 Champions League matches, six of them at home, and the commercial revenue generated by the higher visibility.

Super-Benefactors and Profit-Maximisers

Most of the Premier League clubs continue to be run on the same lines as English clubs always have: by utility-maximisers who spend as much of the club's money as they dare on player transfers and wages. Yet the Premier League era has been distinguished by an influx of foreign owners and two sorts of owner previously largely unknown in English football: the super-benefactors and the profit-maximisers.

The era of the benefactors began in 1991, when Jack Walker, a Blackburn-born steel and aviation millionaire, bought his hometown club. In the next three years he spent £25 million[17] from his own pocket on players, twice breaking the British transfer record. This was something new. Blackburn won the Premier League in 1995. They then dropped out of the top four, and have yet to return. Walker had set the template for others with even deeper pockets.

The rising international profile of the Premier League, the rapid growth in revenue of its clubs and the lack of restrictions on buying them compared with clubs in other European leagues, began to lure foreign purchasers. In March 2003, the Glazer family took a substantial stake in Manchester United. Milan Mandaric's Portsmouth won promotion in May. Then Roman Abramovich appeared. Ken Bates had gambled heavily on Chelsea making the Champions League; when Abramovich bought the club from Bates it was on the verge of financial collapse, but, crucially, had just finished fourth to earn a Champions League berth. Like Walker, Abramovich had money to spend and he was happy to spend it on his football club. He just had a lot more than Walker.

A trend had begun. The crucial foreign acquisitions that followed were by the Glazer family, who increased their stake and gained control of United in 2005, by George Gillett and Tom Hicks, who bought Liverpool, and by members of the Abu Dhabi royal family, who bought Manchester City in 2008.

Chelsea spent more than £100 million on players in the summer that Abramovich bought the club. Within a year, the wage bill, already the fourth highest in the Premier League, more than doubled.[18] Chelsea won the title in 2005, 2006 and 2010. The club's holding company said in 2011 that the club owed just under £739.5 million in loans underwritten by Abramovich.[19]

Manchester City have followed his model. They had finished ninth, 21 points behind fourth-placed Liverpool, the season before the Abu Dhabi takeover; it took three years of wholesale buying at the luxury end of a market already inflated by Abramovich to lift the club to third in 2010–11.

Gillett, Hicks and the Glazers are all Americans. Like their compatriots Randy Lerner, who bought Aston Villa in 2006, John Henry, who snaffled Liverpool from Gillett and Hicks in 2010, and Stan Kroenke, who became the largest shareholder at Arsenal in 2008, they owned, or had owned, franchises in at least one of the four American sports leagues. Apart from Henry, who transformed the Boston Red Sox, none had distinguished themselves as winning owners. Tampa Bay won one Super Bowl under the Glazers, but that was a blip in a generally horrible record. The National Football League has a salary cap designed to guarantee the owners a substantial profit; even so, under the Glazers, Tampa became notorious for staying far below the cap.

Both the Glazers and Gillett and Hicks clearly fit the profit-maximiser model. If they aren't in it for the money, it's not clear what their strategies have been. They leveraged their English acquisitions by loading the cost of the takeovers on their new clubs in the form of debt. In United's case, the leveraged takeover cost £810 million.[20] The club was being run as a money-making operation before the Glazer takeover.

From the start of the Premier League, United generated far more income than any other club. They spent heavily on players, relative to rivals, but uniquely, in the Premier League, consistently generated significant profits. By 2007–08, United's total annual wage bill, at £123 million, was £51 million less than Chelsea's, but was still comfortably the second highest in the Premier League. While Chelsea reported an operating loss of more than £36 million, not counting transfer expenditure of £46 million, United made a profit of £71 million, of which it spent a net £26 million on transfers.[21] The club could support the debt load and still compete.

Liverpool, it turned out, could not. From 2001 to 2008 their wage bill was consistently fourth, sometimes a distant fourth, behind Chelsea, Manchester

United and Arsenal. Under Hicks and Gillett the pattern stayed broadly the same. The result of a fourth-best wage bill was a fourth-place squad. But even that level of spending, combined with the debt load, pushed the club to the edge of bankruptcy, providing Henry with the lever to force Hicks and Gillett out.

The likes of Abramovich and Walker have received the contempt always aimed at the crass and impatient nouveau riche. They are criticised for 'buying' success, as if the traditionally rich clubs do not. UEFA's Financial Fair Play rules, introduced in 2011, are underpinned by a feeling that what the super-benefactors are doing is somehow unfair.

'Rich people like Roman Abramovich have turned everything upside down, both financially and from a sporting point of view,' said Jean-Luc Dehaene, the former prime minister of Belgium, who heads the control panel. 'Their capital should no longer be used to drive up transfer fees and wages beyond the present level, which is abnormal.'[22]

Abramovich is not alone. In 2009–10, Manchester City's wage bill exceeded revenue, and the club then spent the same amount again on transfers. City politely thumbed their nose at the new rules in 2011 when announcing a £400 million, 10-year stadium-naming deal with Etihad, an airline owned by the club's owners, far more than the going rate. Suddenly the break-even number moved up by £40 million a year. Dehaene said he had questions.[23]

Chelsea's spree in 2012, when the club's net transfer spending was almost £80 million, just 12 months before the Fair Play rules were supposed to bite, was eye-catching. Chelsea could spend the windfall of their unexpected, and lucky, Champions League victory. The rules also now allowed Abramovich to kick in more than £36 million of his own money in the first two years of Financial Fair Play. He also signed a sponsorship deal with his old business partner Gazprom, also a UEFA sponsor, the terms of which are 'confidential'. Even so, the long-term financial commitment involved in signing a posse of new players to long-term contracts does suggest Chelsea are gambling on the rules being emasculated either by the courts or by the profound economic problems of Italian and Spanish football.

Yet for all the resentment of Abramovich, between 2004, when Arsenal won the league, and 2010, when City became a threat, only Chelsea's spending stood between United and total domination of the Premier League.

The Future

Between 1994–95 and 2010–11, only three clubs won the Premier League. Even in Spain, where Barcelona and Real Madrid have such a huge financial advantage, five different clubs won La Liga in that span. For seven straight seasons from 2003–04 to 2009–10, the same four clubs qualified for the

Champions League, although Everton joined the party after Liverpool won the competition in 2005 and England gained five places.

With four lucrative Champions League spots at stake, an oligopoly of four clubs appeared self-sustaining. The Big Four used their revenue advantage to buy the players who kept them in the top four. But an oligopoly does not eliminate economic competition or the urge of its members to reduce an oligopoly of four to one of three then two and then one, or of other companies to join, or supplant, them. Leagues may require competition to exist, but that does not mean the members behave that way. Furthermore, the Big Four was not an oligopoly of equals. Liverpool have not won the league since 1990. When Manchester City joined the super-benefactor club in 2008, a fifth club was added to the elite, and five clubs just won't go into four Champions League places.

The Premier League may have helped undercut one of the Big Four's biggest advantages in 2010 when it introduced squad restrictions limiting clubs to 25 players aged over 21. A squad of 25, backed up by a packed youth system, should be big enough for a Premier League campaign but can handicap a team that is also competing in the Champions League.

While the financial disparities, which created the predictability of the Premier League, still exist, the illusion of immutable stability does not. Failure, costly and terrifying, became much more possible. Witness the decline of Leeds United, the last champions before the launch of the Premier League.

The fear is not limited to England. The Champions League and the international television and merchandising markets have created a European elite who see themselves both as truly in competition with each other, not the have-nots in their national leagues, and as having shared interests. Those clubs are under threat. UEFA's Financial Fair Play regulations may have been accompanied by anti-super-benefactor rhetoric, but its core intention is to force clubs to produce transparent accounts and then to punish those who run up debts to fund their playing operations by refusing them entry to UEFA-run club competitions. The three biggest money losers in Europe in 2009–10 were Manchester City, Chelsea and, because of the Glazer loans, Manchester United. They are followed by Barcelona and Inter Milan.

The big Italian and Spanish clubs had the advantage that they could negotiate their own TV deals. But in 2011, Serie A reverted to a collective deal, although with much less equitable revenue sharing than the Premier League, and promptly signed the most lucrative domestic contract in Europe (with Murdoch's Sky Italia). In Spain, where Barcelona and Real Madrid each make an estimated €150 million a year,[24] both clubs have agreed to a collective deal which would allocate the pair 35 per cent of the revenue. The earliest that could start is 2015, but, in a climate increasingly hostile to the big two, some other clubs were baulking at signing, raising the prospect, oh horrors, of an even fairer share-out.

The big two Spanish clubs have increasingly used their revenue to hoover up the biggest stars from across Europe, luring players such as Cristiano Ronaldo and Cesc Fabregas from England. The strategy has paid off, particularly for Real, whose annual revenues have soared to more than €400 million, or £340 million, in 2010 compared to €349.8 million for Manchester United.[25]

When Ian Ayre, the chief executive of Liverpool, suggested in October 2011 that the equal share of international television revenue in the Premier League should be ended because no one in Kuala Lumpur paid to watch Bolton, he recruited Barcelona and Real as bogeymen and suggested that star players, not the tradition or quality of competition in a league, sell international rights. For the good of the Premier League, he contended, Liverpool should be given the means to buy more of them.[26] For that to happen, two-thirds of Premier League clubs would need to approve the change. The turkeys have voted for Christmas in the past when threatened by the rich clubs, but in this context that seems unlikely.

Ayre works for American bosses and his remarks were quickly, and inevitably, followed by a story that the Premier League's American owners wanted to follow the American model and eliminate relegation, which seems bizarre as only one of them, Ellis Short at Sunderland, owns a club that has spent time out of the top division since 1992. But the absence of relegation in North America is one facet of the franchise system, which guarantees markets for clubs. Franchising was, in a sense, part of the agenda of the defunct G-14, a lobbying group of big European clubs.

The prospect of a European Super League, from which most clubs would be permanently excluded, terrifies fans, clubs and domestic leagues alike. John Williams expressed the view that this was inevitable as far back as 1999.[27] The G-14 exploited the fear of a breakaway continental league as leverage in its negotiations with UEFA, and was rewarded with a structure that grants its member clubs almost permanent places in the Champions League. Then the G-14 voluntarily disbanded.

The received wisdom, based on higher attendance for Serie A games on a Sunday than for Champions League games in midweek, is that fans of even the biggest clubs prefer the familiar enemies of their domestic leagues. Yet the Champions League the G-14 moulded has proved it can generate huge revenues for the top clubs and, after a decade, is building a tradition of rivalries.

For those of a paranoid disposition, the European Commission ruling on the international sales of Premier League TV rights was an expression of the innate tendency of the European Union to push soccer towards competition that is an expression of Europeanism rather than nationalism.

Some members of the old G-14 are still publicly pushing a European agenda. In November 2011, Sandro Rosell, the president of Barcelona, suggested that the leading European leagues needed to be cut to 16 teams to allow the Champions League more space to grow into a true European Super League.[28] Barcelona are in an odd position. Support is built on their role as a symbol of Catalonian separatism. That political agenda gives the rivalry with Real Madrid such a lucrative edge. But should fans get their wish, Barcelona would be out of La Liga. Furthermore, Barcelona are likely to be hit particularly hard by the combination of UEFA's financial rules and the changes to Spanish TV rights. For Liverpool, Barcelona and Real Madrid are the sexiest possible playmates. They are certainly more alluring than penurious Everton. A guaranteed place in a franchise-based European Super League is more attractive than having to scuffle for fourth in the Premier League. And Liverpool's history allows the club the illusion that it would not rapidly become the Bolton of the new league. UEFA countered by floating an idea bound to appeal to the great mass of aspirational middle-class clubs. It suggested folding its unsuccessful Europa League into the Champions League and doubling that competition's size.

One potentially pivotal date in this saga is July 2014, the expiration date of the Memorandum of Understanding between UEFA and the European Club Association, the body created after the G-14 disbanded. Signed in 2008, it sets the terms under which clubs release players for national teams. It offers the clubs a powerful potential weapon in dealing with European football's governing bodies.

The natural tendency of successful businesses in the global era is to go multinational. There is a tendency to believe that in the face of big business, the customers, national governments and smaller local companies are powerless. It is that sense of powerlessness and inevitability that first the Big Five and then the Big Four have exploited both on the field and in their dealings off it. The story of the Premier League has been the story of money and the habit of the rich, when unchecked, to get richer. Increasingly, the money in football is international. Yet so far Europe's richest clubs have not dared take the final step. Perhaps money will not write the next chapter.

NOTES

1 M. Lewis, *Moneyball, The Art of Winning an Unfair Game* (New York: W.W. Norton, 2003).
2 S. Dobson and J. Goddard, *The Economics of Football* (Cambridge: Cambridge University Press, 2nd edn., 2011), pp. 151–52.
3 D. Conn, *The Beautiful Game? Searching for the Soul of Football* (London: Yellow Jersey Press, 2005), p. 45.

4 Dobson and Goddard, *The Economics of Football*, p. 172.
5 Ibid.
6 D. Conn, *The Football Business* (Edinburgh: Mainstream, 1997), p. 23.
7 Ibid.
8 Dobson and Goddard, *The Economics of Football*, pp. 173–74.
9 Swiss Ramble, 'When Will the Premier League Bubble Burst?' 28 June 2010, http://swissramble.blogspot.com/2010/06/when-will-premier-league-bubble-burst.html (accessed 15 January 2012).
10 Dobson and Goddard, *The Economics of Football*, p. 189.
11 Ibid., p. 153.
12 Ibid., pp. 164–65.
13 Deloitte, '£3.5bn invested in football stadia over the past 20 years', 3 August 2011, www.deloitte.com/view/en_GB/uk/industries/sportsbusinessgroup/985203 5683a81310VgnVCM1000001a56fooaRCRD.htm (accessed 15 January 2012).
14 Deloitte, 'Football Money League 2011'.
15 Ibid.
16 I am grateful to the UEFA press office which collated Champions League financial statistics going back to 1994–95 in an e-mail on 21 September 2011.
17 R. Savill, 'Local hero who led the Rovers to glory', *Daily Telegraph*, 19 August 2000, www.telegraph.co.uk/news/uknews/1353315/Local-hero-who-led-the-Rovers-to-glory.html (accessed 15 January 2012).
18 I am grateful to Celine Gordine-Wright at Deloitte who provided me with these data, collated from the firm's Annual Reviews of Football Finances, 2001–2011, in a private e-mail on 4 November 2011.
19 P. Kelso, 'Chelsea owner Roman Abramovich counts the cost of European failure: £740 million and rising', *Daily Telegraph*, 8 April 2011, www.telegraph.co.uk/sport/football/teams/chelsea/8436348/Chelsea-owner-Roman-Abramovich-counts-the-cost-of-European-failure-740-million-and-rising.html (accessed 15 January 2012).
20 Dobson and Goddard, *The Economics of Football*, pp. 192–93.
21 Deloitte, 'Annual Reviews of Football Finances', 2001–2011.
22 D. Kent, 'Roman Abramovich and the rest of the big spenders must cut back, says UEFA finance guru', *Daily Mail*, 17 September 2009, www.dailymail.co.uk/sport/football/article-1214026/Roman-Abramovich-rest-big-spenders-cut-says-UEFA-finance-guru.html (accessed 15 January 2012).
23 M. Slater, 'Dehaene "had questions" about Man City's sponsorship deal with Etihad', BBC.co.uk, 12 August 2011, http://news.bbc.co.uk/sport2/hi/football/14505449.stm (accessed 15 January 2012).
24 Deloitte, 'Football Money League 2011'.
25 Ibid.
26 'Liverpool say top clubs should be able to sell their own foreign TV rights', BBC.co.uk, 12 October 2011, http://news.bbc.co.uk/sport2/hi/football/15269831.stm (accessed 15 January 2012).
27 J. Williams, *Is It All Over? Can football survive the Premier League?* (Reading: South Street Press, 1999).
28 'Premier League will not be cut to 16 – Richard Scudamore', BBC.co.uk, 17 November 2011, http://news.bbc.co.uk/sport2/hi/football/15748287.stm (accessed 15 January 2012).

Figure 7.1. Chelsea's Didier Drogba celebrates his winning goal at Wembley, 2009–10 FA Cup Final. Credit: Colorsport/Andrew Cowie.

The Game-Changers: Didier Drogba

On 21 September 2011, a representative of the Ivory Coast's newly established Truth Reconciliation and Dialogue Commission (TRDC) gave an interview to the BBC. The TRDC had been set up to try to bring peace to a country savaged by bloody, destructive violence following the previous year's disputed elections in which about 3,000 people were killed and 500,000 displaced.[1]

Speaking with calm authority, the representative said: 'We need to sit together to speak to know what happened, people from all the different places and say sorry and move forward to the future in the same direction. It's not trying to promote myself. I'm not superman, I can't do it by myself, the only people who can change things are the Ivorians. We have to listen with a lot of humility. You can judge people for what they did or didn't do, we just have to listen to try and send a message and make people understand that this country is better when there is peace.'[2]

A week later, the same man was in Valencia terrorising the home defence. The clothing had changed – the smart suit and crisp white shirt had been exchanged for a tight, blue shirt, shorts and football boots – but the authority remained. Whether in his role as unofficial people's spokesman in the Ivory Coast or up front for Chelsea in the Champions League, opponents have learned not to treat Didier Drogba (Figure 7.1) lightly.

His physicality has a lot to do with it. He's a majestic-looking human being – tall, proud, muscular, leonine. In West Africa you can buy your beer in a glass called 'The Drogba'. It's like a normal mug, but nearly twice the size.

Following Chelsea's 2012 Wembley win over Liverpool – in which Drogba became the first player to score in four different FA Cup finals – Jamie Carragher, the Liverpool defender, described him as unplayable.

'If Chelsea get the ball on to Drogba's chest on the edge of the box and he can bring it down and turn, well, that's it. You can't get round him without fouling him. He's fast enough and so powerful that, even if you catch him, you can't get a foot in to make the tackle. You would have to run around him and you haven't the time to do that. So he's unplayable. In certain positions, there is literally nothing you can do.'[3]

Power. Technique. Speed. Strength. Normally these things are enough, but Drogba's got something else: destiny. On 19 May 2012 Chelsea went to the Allianz Arena to play Bayern Munich in the Champions League final in what was billed as Drogba's last game for the club. They were one down with time fading fast. Who equalised? Drogba. The penalty shoot-out came down to one last penalty. After all the months, all the travel, all the emotion, it all came down to one shot. Who scored? Drogba. 'It was fate,' he said after the final whistle. 'I believe a lot in destiny. I pray a lot. It was written a long time ago. God is wonderful. This team is amazing.'[4]

He is, as Chelsea teammate Frank Lampard said, 'a hero'.[5] There are all sorts of statistics, but this one – nine cup finals for Chelsea, nine goals – says enough.

In 2010, Drogba made *Time* magazine's '100' list: the people they considered the 'most influential' in the world. Necessarily, he was in the 'Heroes' category. He 'has shown the world what's possible when power and grace fuse on the soccer pitch', wrote Eben Harrell. 'Imagine the body of an NBA star with feet as nimble as a prima ballerina's.'[6]

Out on His Own

Born in Abidjan in 1978, he left home when he was five and went to live in Brittany with his uncle Michael, a jobbing footballer who moved wherever the work was. Whenever Michael changed clubs, Didier changed schools, more often than not to a school where he was the only black boy.

Football didn't happen quickly for him. The Le Mans coach he has called his spiritual father was sacked. Marc Westerloppe, now a scout for Lens, said: 'Unlike most footballers, Didier had missed out on the academy system. That could have been a drawback, but in fact it is the reason why he will keep getting better, even now. Didier only started playing every day when he was 18.'[7]

He might have started late, but when he started he didn't stop. In 2002 he left Le Mans for Guincamp for £80,000. The next season he left Guincamp (where, aged 25, he earned £1,400 a week) for Olympique de Marseilles for £3.3 million. A year later Drogba became one of Mourinho's first signings as manager of Chelsea, for £24 million.

Mourinho and Drogba were inextricably linked: both charismatic and unstoppable in equal measure, both intensely talented yet both capable of disappearing in the red mist of their sometimes uncontrollable explosive tempers. In the 2008 Champions League final, Drogba was sent off in extra-time for slapping Manchester United's Nemanja Vidic. The following year, he was banned for six games after the semi-final loss to Barcelona, ranting expletives into a TV camera at the perceived injustices.

The sudden unexpected departure of Mourinho in September 2007 was a blow felt more strongly by Drogba than anyone else. 'I find Jose's "eviction" hard to take. I could not see the blow coming so brutally,' he told the BBC. 'It changes an awful lot of things. At the moment, I am in the sort of nervous state I've never dreamed about before. Many of us used to play first and foremost for the manager. Now we need to forget those feelings and find another source of motivation.'[8]

African Statesman

Drogba doesn't need to find another source of motivation: he's got one. In 2007, he established the Didier Drogba Foundation[9] to raise money to build a clinic for child illness in his hometown, a project made all the more likely to succeed since the announcement that his £3 million fee for becoming the face of Pepsi would go to the Foundation.

The blueprint had been laid down by the Liberian George Weah – another former African Footballer of the Year who also played for Marseilles and Chelsea – who, following his retirement in 2002, went into politics. Drogba is Weah 2.0. A twenty-first-century model. Of late plenty of African stars have graced the world game – Eto'o, Adebayor, Essien, Keita, Yaya Touré – but more than anyone else, Drogba is the face of modern African football. The statesman.

Unlike Weah, he has said that he doesn't intend to go into politics when he retires, that his involvement with the TRDC is simply to deal with the current situation. 'To be honest, I like the place where I am now. I don't have any political opinion. I can say what I want, I'm free. Today my situation is good because when I speak everybody will listen. If I decided to do politics only half of the country will listen. Am I more powerful the way I am? Maybe.'[10]

NOTES

1   J. James, 'Didier Drogba seeks to bring peace to Ivory Coast', BBC.co.uk, 21 September 2011, www.bbc.co.uk/news/world-africa-15001107 (accessed 15 January 2012).

2   A. Croft, 'Didier Drogba works to heal Ivory Coast's wounds', *Reuters,* 21 September 2011, http://uk.reuters.com/article/2011/09/21/uk-ivorycoast-drogba-idUKTRE78J6NB20110921 (accessed 15 January 2012).

3   M. Samuel, 'Didier Drogba – Why the Chelsea striker is simply unplayable', *Mail Online*, 19 May 2012, www.dailymail.co.uk/sport/football/article-2146013/Didier-Drogba-The-Chelsea-striker-unplayable.html#ixzz1vKoprvKG (accessed 19 May 2012).

4 M. Sanghera, 'Drogba's belief key to Chelsea's Champions League glory', BBC. co.uk, 20 May 2012, www.bbc.co.uk/sport/o/football/18134607.

5 Ibid.

6 E. Harrell, 'The 2010 Time 100', *Time Specials,* 29 April 2010, http://www.time. com/time/specials/packages/article/0,28804,1984685_1984949_1985240,00. html (accessed 15 January 2012).

7 K. McCarra, 'Rough Diamond Drogba adds the polish', *Guardian,* 25 November 2006, www.guardian.co.uk/football/2006/nov/25/newsstory.sport4 (accessed 15 January 2012).

8 'Drogba dismayed by Mourinho exit', BBC.co.uk, 29 September 2007, http:// news.bbc.co.uk/sport1/hi/football/teams/c/chelsea/7017657.stm (accessed 15 January 2012).

9 The Didier Drogba Foundation, www.thedidierdrogbafoundation.com (accessed 15 January 2012).

10 J. White, 'Didier Drogba is the Chelsea striker who possesses more power than Ivory Coast's president', *Daily Telegraph,* 16 February 2012, www.telegraph. co.uk/sport/football/teams/chelsea/9085118/Didier-Drogba-is-the-Chelsea-stri ker-who-possesses-more-power-than-Ivory-Coasts-president.html (accessed 16 May 2012).

Figure 8.1. Alex Ferguson (Manchester United manager), Charlton Athletic v Manchester United, 07/02/1987. Credit: Colorsport.

8

COLIN SHINDLER

The Boss: A Very British Convention

Who needs a manager? No spectator pays to watch a man gesticulating in a dugout or even kicking water bottles in the technical area. The players are the focus of the crowd's attention, not the manager. The game began as a team game for 11 players whose captain effectively managed the side's tactics. The chairman ran the club and the captain managed the team, formulating the most basic of tactics and organising the training walks which players would take in their Sunday-best clothes with bowler hats placed carefully on their heads and watch-chains rakishly displayed in waistcoat pockets, the nineteenth-century equivalent of the snood, the shaved head and the disfiguring tattoo.[1] What need did they have of a manager?

Ironically, as the twenty-first century moves into its second decade there is a renewed move to sideline the manager. Owners of the richer football clubs have affirmed their power by adopting the principles of the system traditionally used in American football and baseball of a general manager buying the players and a field manager or head coach training them. George Steinbrenner, who owned the New York Yankees from 1973 until his death in 2010, ran the club as his personal fiefdom, hiring and firing with abandon. Indeed he employed and sacked Billy Martin as manager no fewer than five times. Jesus Gil, president of Atlético Madrid for 16 years, though of more pronounced extreme right-wing views than Steinbrenner, enjoyed a similarly volatile relationship with his staff (to say nothing of the players and the supporters). This dictatorship by the front office is, of course, anathema to the traditional manager who struggled for most of the twentieth century to achieve his position of power throughout the club. How did this tortuous process begin?

Major William Sudell made the transition from a Preston North End player to chairman of the club in the early 1880s. It was he who recruited good players from Scotland to play for Preston, finding them employment in his local cotton mill until the Football Association eventually bowed to Sudell's advocacy and authorised the start of professionalism. Sudell was the man whose foresight resulted in Preston's becoming the first club to win the League Championship and the FA Cup in the same season and to go unbeaten (playing 22 matches) throughout an entire season. However, as an indication that recent scandals in football's business dealings are not an aberration, Sudell's connection with football ended unhappily when in 1895 he was found guilty of fraudulently redirecting funds from the mill to the football club and was sent to prison for three years.[2]

Birth of a Cult

The cult of the manager effectively began in England in the 1920s with Herbert Chapman, who managed to reverse Sudell's career trajectory by starting with a financial scandal and ending it as a lauded high achiever. An ordinary inside forward, plying his trade mostly in the Southern League, Chapman was about to retire to become a mining engineer when a chance remark in the dressing room after his last game led to his appointment as the player/manager of one of his former clubs, Northampton Town. Within two seasons Northampton were champions of the Southern League and Chapman was soon on his way to Leeds City, struggling at the foot of the Second Division and doomed to apply for re-election.

Again he revolutionized the club's playing style with instant success but after only eight matches of the first postwar season City were convicted of making illegal payments and closed down. Chapman was alleged to have burnt the books and was banned for life, although when Huddersfield Town took him on in 1921 they pleaded with the authorities that Chapman had been manager of a munitions factory when the offences had been committed and the ban was overturned.[3] Huddersfield were soon rewarded for their enterprise. Over four seasons, Chapman led them to the FA Cup and two League Championships, profoundly influencing the boyhood of Harold Wilson, the future prime minister, who could recite the names of Chapman's team as easily as any economic statistics.

In 1925 Chapman moved to Arsenal at the same time the offside law was changed so that only two opposition defenders, rather than three, needed to be between the attacking forward and the goal. It was Chapman, along with his influential first signing, the 34-year-old Charlie Buchan, who moved the centre-half from his traditional place in the middle of a 2–3–5 formation to become a 'stopper' in the middle of the back line, changing the formation to the 'WM' which survived in England for 40 years. Jack Butler, whom Chapman inherited at centre-half, was unable to adapt and was replaced by the more dependable Herbie Roberts, signed from Oswestry Town to perform this new role. He was soon joined by Jack Lambert, Joe Hulme, Cliff

Bastin, Alex James and David Jack, who became the basis of Chapman's team that went on to win the FA Cup in 1930 and the League Championship in 1930–31 and 1932–33.

Chapman was certainly responsible for tactics in his coaching capacity but he also conducted transfer negotiations, selected his teams and generally ruled the club in such an autocratic way that nobody had any doubt who was in charge. Unlike the traditional xenophobes who populated British football Chapman was openly interested in the European game and cultivated the friendship of Hugo Meisl, the coach of the Austrian national team whose unbeaten run of 14 games between April 1931 and December 1932 gained them the sobriquet of the 'Wunderteam'. Meisl, a Jewish intellectual, born in Bohemia and raised in Vienna, was not unlike Arsène Wenger in his beliefs and attitudes.[4] He reciprocated the English manager's admiration although his position was essentially that of a coach rather than a manager.[1]

Chapman's other significant managerial contemporary was Vittorio Pozzo, the equally Anglophile manager of the Italy sides that won the World Cup in 1934 and 1938, but although Pozzo, like Meisl, did not experience the day-to-day running of a club, his time as national coach coincided with the high point of Italian Fascism. The prevailing political ideology encouraged Pozzo in his desire to exert control over selection and management of the national side. No England manager received similar licence until Alf Ramsey in 1962. Pozzo was a shrewd man-manager, emphasizing the primacy of the team ethic and the importance of defence with his insistence on man-marking and the efficiency of the swift counter-attack. His fervent nationalism was the motivating factor behind his team's visit to the battlefields of the First World War on their way to a 5–0 victory over Hungary in Budapest.[5] It was a tactic repeated by Steve Waugh when he led his Australian cricket side to Gallipoli before the Ashes tour of 2001 without attracting the sort of adverse criticism that pursued Pozzo after the fall of Mussolini.

Chapman had bought and constructed his Arsenal championship side but he died suddenly of pneumonia in 1934 before he could begin to establish a successful youth policy. The managers who developed their profession in the Football League thereafter, Buckley, Busby and Cullis, all set out to build their own youthful teams. Major Frank Buckley ran Wolverhampton Wanderers as completely as Chapman had dominated Arsenal but he added to the autocracy a variety of innovations 30 years in advance of general practice. In an attempt to intimidate the opposition, he told the press that he had had his players inoculated with extract of monkey gland to aid

---

[1] For more on Hugo Meisl, see Chapter 3 in this volume, 'Austria and Hungary: The Danubian School', by Huw Richards.

performance, though it transpired subsequently that they were ordinary vitamin injections.[6]

Buckley ordered the watering of the Molineux pitch before home games because he felt heavy pitches suited the stamina of his team, whom he also sent off to a psychologist in the search for elusive sporting self-confidence. He turned an inherited overdraft of £115,000 in 1927 into a profit by selling players who had attained their peak level of performance, 70 years before Billy Beane was lauded for doing the same thing at the Oakland A's. Bryn Jones fetched a record transfer fee of £14,000 from Arsenal in June 1938 and Jimmy Mullen made his First Division debut at the age of 16 the following season. His real legacy to the club which he left in 1944 after a 17-year stay was this elevation of a successful scouting system and youth policy. Chief among his successes were Billy Wright, whom he left behind at Wolves, and John Charles, whom he signed almost immediately after arriving at Leeds United in 1948.

The Tartan Invasion

Sir Matt Busby is generally credited with the innovation of a team constructed entirely with home-developed players, and Buckley suffers by comparison; but there is no doubt that what Busby did in the early 1950s – dismantling the team of mature players who had won him the FA Cup in 1948 and the League Championship in 1951–52 and replacing them with what became universally known as the Busby Babes – deserves all the accolades it has consistently attracted. Like so many other successful managers of the 1950s and 1960s (Cullis, Shankly, Mercer, Nicholson, Stein) Busby had learned his trade as a player in the underpaid, insecure days of the 1930s and 1940s. The martinet side of all of these men originated in their instinctive recreation of the relationship of mutual suspicion they had endured with the manager in their own playing days.

Busby initiated no new tactical advance. His players would later talk about his exhortation of 'Give the ball to another red shirt' as the extent of his advice but they questioned Busby's authority at their peril.[7] Charlie Mitten, outside-left in his 1948 Cup-winning team then seduced by the promise of riches in Bogota, was not allowed back into the fold when he realized his mistake and wished to return with his tail between his legs after the Colombian adventure misfired. In 1966, when Denis Law questioned his meagre wages (allegedly £35 a week) at a time when the quicksilver Scottish striker was at the height of his powers, Busby responded instantly by transfer-listing him. The shaken Law soon came back into line.[8] He later revealed he had been quietly granted his pay rise but from Busby's point of view his star player had been seen to submit to the manager's omniscience. Busby was also shrewd enough to ensure that any player whom he transferred, even if improbably he actually made a success of the move, went to a club in a town where the *Manchester Evening News* was not the local paper. Only Johnny Giles, who went to the nascent Leeds United in 1963, returned to haunt him.

It was Busby's belief in his fecund youth policy, and his determination to seize the chance of European football in 1956 when the Football League was advising against Manchester United's entry into the second season of the new European Cup tournament, that established his reputation. It was his survival amidst the wreckage of the plane crash at Munich in February 1958 and his triumph at Wembley ten years later in the competition that had taken the lives of eight of his players, as well as 15 other victims, that cemented that reputation.

He wasn't, of course the first Scottish manager to win the European Cup. That honour had gone the previous year to Jock Stein when his Celtic team, who became known as the Lisbon Lions and who had all been born within 30 miles of Glasgow, had defeated Inter Milan 2–1. It was a victory that was widely regarded as a triumph of attacking free enterprise over the spirit of dour defensiveness promoted by Helenio Herrera, the Inter Milan manager who had developed the sweeper system known in Italian as *catenaccio* (translated as a chain that locks the front door of a house). Herrera was undoubtedly defensively minded but he did make his team both triumphant and feared before Celtic's famous victory.

Stein was a Protestant and was told in so many words that his success in charge of Celtic's reserve team was not going to advance his career at a club whose employees and supporters were almost exclusively Roman Catholic. Stein had to approach the manager's chair at Celtic via successful spells in charge of Dunfermline and Hibernian. When first offered the job he was asked to share it with the Catholic Sean Fallon but Stein stood firm and eventually not only assumed his new role in sole charge but demanded that he be free to sign Protestant players if in his opinion they would help the club. (It was, however, Graeme Souness, as late as July 1989, who made the most significant cross-religion signing when he persuaded the former Celtic player and Catholic Mo Johnston to play for Rangers.)[9] Stein's domineering manner and unshakeable belief in his own ability, confirmed by an unparalleled run of success for 10 years from the mid-1960s, was influential in the subsequent managerial style of Alex Ferguson (Figure 8.1).

No Guru, No Method, No Teacher

There has never been any one way of managing a football club that could be guaranteed to produce success. Stan Cullis took Wolverhampton Wanderers to two FA Cup wins and three League Championships between 1949 and 1960 as well as famous victories in 'friendly' matches under the new Molineux floodlights against Honved and Moscow Spartak in a hail of impassioned vituperation.[10] Although he famously did not swear and spoke in an incongruously thin voice, Cullis drove his players on with explosive belligerence demanding a high work rate and constant pressure. In contrast Arthur Rowe won the championship with Tottenham Hotspur in 1951 by arguing calmly and logically the merits of the 'push-and-run' quick passing system. Rowe might well have benefited from the current coaching arrangement because it was the relentless administrative pressure on a manager who wanted to control everything at the club that caused his health to break down.[11]

Internationally, the most successful and least recognized English manager of the immediate postwar years was a Yorkshireman called George Raynor. Again, an undistinguished playing career in lower league clubs in the north of England was followed by an entirely unexpectedly triumphant managerial career. Recommended to the Swedish FA by Stanley Rous, Raynor took his newly adopted country to a gold medal in the 1948 Olympics and in the 1950 World Cup, while England lost to the United States, Sweden finished third. In the 1958 World Cup played in Sweden, Raynor steered the host nation to the final where they were beaten 5–2 by Brazil. Raynor followed his best players into Italian football, briefly managing both Lazio and Juventus before returning to England where he managed Doncaster Rovers and Skegness Town, surely the first manager from Serie A to do so.[12] In November 1953 in Budapest, days before Hungary were due to play England at Wembley, Sweden nullified the great Hungarian side in a 2–2 draw. Raynor's attempts to pass on the benefits of his tactical awareness were rejected by England, who continued to underestimate his skills.

Ignoring Raynor's advice, England lost 6–3 at home and 7–1 in Budapest six months later. Geoffrey Green, writing in the *Times* the day after the Wembley encounter, called it 'Agincourt in reverse'.[13] The players were famous, the manager was unknown. Gyula Mandi was nominally in charge but the de facto manager was the deputy minister of sport, Gusztav Sebes, his former MTK team-mate. It was Sebes's decision to withdraw Hidegkuti, who played with the centre-forward's number nine on the back of his shirt, into a position which would today be known as an attacking midfielder. The English formation, unchanged since Chapman withdrew his centre-half, was unable to cope with a system that did not correspond to the traditional numerical symmetry.

Yet was even Sebes in any real sense the manager, a title that implies a degree of power? Certainly he was the master tactician but he was a faithful Communist and it could be argued that the Communist Party was the real manager of that Hungarian side. Sebes's ideological purity could not, however, save him from the obloquy that followed his side's unexpected defeat by West Germany in the 1954 World Cup final and he was replaced by a five-man committee. Having defeated England because, according to the bewildered England centre-half Syd Owen, they played like 'men from outer space', Hungary decided to return to earth by emulating the English FA.[14]

Bela Guttmann, the other Hungarian manager to make his mark on world football, was a very different character. He was a Jew, destined by religion and attitude to wander the world, inspiring players and crowds but alienating officials and employers. He left the pre-Nazi anti-Semitism of 1920s Budapest to join the Jewish club Hakoah and the intellectual football café society of Vienna which had embraced Hugo Meisl and his philosophy. Most of Guttmann's family died in the concentration camps but Guttmann survived in Switzerland then resumed his travels as an eccentric, innovative, wandering football manager passing through Hungary, Rumania, Italy, Argentina and Cyprus before finding himself in Brazil after the Uprising, staying to manage São Paulo. It was, at a very simple level, Guttmann's Hungarian 4–2-4 which provided the tactical basis of the 1958 Brazil team, although by then Guttmann was in Portugal with Porto, followed by Benfica, where he was the first to spot the flowering talents of the Mozambique-born Eusébio. Guttmann's fiery relationship with directors, his readiness to depart if he could not run the club his own way, his determination to be paid what he felt he was worth and his success in so many different countries make him a significant contributor to the developing cult of the manager.[15]

Sheepskins, Cigars and the Rise of the Assistant Manager

In England the manager grew in influence after the war principally through the triumphs of Busby and Cullis. When the great Real Madrid team won the first five European Cups the club employed no fewer than five managers, none of whom left a significant legacy. By contrast Busby managed Manchester United from 1946 until 1969, Cullis was at Wolves from 1948 until 1964, Bill Nicholson at Spurs from 1958 until 1974, and Bill Shankly was the manager of Liverpool from 1959 until 1974, two years longer than Don Revie remained manager of Leeds United. All found considerable success, benefiting considerably from their longevity, but all found success within the first two or three years of their appointment thus avoiding summary dismissal before their ideas could be demonstrably seen to have failed.

During the 1960s a new pattern began to emerge in which the manager devolved a certain amount of power to his assistant. Bertie Mee, formerly Arsenal's physiotherapist, led the club to its famous double in 1971 but all the coaching was delegated first to Dave Sexton and then to Don Howe. Joe Mercer, a highly popular player for Everton and Arsenal until he retired in 1954 after breaking a leg just before his fortieth birthday, was only intermittently successful as manager of Sheffield United and Aston Villa, where he suffered a serious breakdown in health. Lured back to the manager's office in 1965 by the fallen giant Manchester City, Mercer was still suffering from hypertension and knew that he would not survive a second similar breakdown so he hired the boisterous, charismatic Malcolm Allison as his assistant. Allison was a brilliant coach, greatly influenced by his time doing National Service in Austria in 1949–50 and by European football in the wider sense. Although Mercer reserved the right to buy and sell players and pick the team himself, in reality he knew when to listen to Allison.

For five years the partnership brought Manchester City the most sustained period of success in its history but after winning the European Cup Winners' Cup and the League Cup in 1969–70, Allison started to resent his junior position. Mercer proved unwilling to move over and let Allison enjoy his time in the sun; Allison's resentment turned to vindictive scheming. Finally he succeeded in changing the board of directors, ousting Mercer and installing himself in the long-coveted manager's chair where he lasted just 18 months. For all his many coaching talents he was, though he was the only man to refuse to recognize the fact, a poor manager. The jobs are very different and the tragedy of Allison's career was that he was the one who proved it. Together Mercer and Allison were the perfect managerial partnership. Apart they were much less than the sum of their individual parts.[16]

As Mercer and Allison began their decline, another managerial partnership of equally combustible chemical elements was forming in Derby. Brian Clough was the manager and Peter Taylor his assistant but this partnership was not split along the familiar manager/coach lines. 'I'm the shop window. Pete's the goods in the back,' Clough would say self-deprecatingly and, in later times, mendaciously.[17] Instead, Taylor's great gift was to spot youngsters and those whose talents were not being recognized elsewhere; there was no great competition to secure the services of Kenny Burns, Larry Lloyd or Peter Withe. Clough was no tactical genius either but a man whose ability to motivate players has rarely been matched.[18] In 1968 he bought the fading Dave Mackay and built a new team around him. He turned ordinary players like John McGovern and John O'Hare into good ones, good ones like Roy

McFarland and Colin Todd into great ones. Crucially, unlike Allison, Taylor held no deep-seated yearning to manage on his own.

After falling out with the Derby chairman and a spectacularly unsuccessful 44 days alone in charge of Leeds United after Revie's departure to manage England, Clough reunited with Taylor at Nottingham Forest. There they fell easily into the same roles that had propelled Derby to success. They turned Burns, a striker with Birmingham City, into an outstanding defender and signed the unheralded Ian Bowyer, an unspectacular left-winger at Manchester City who became a midfield fulcrum at Forest, and most spectacularly took an overweight transfer-listed winger, John Robertson, and turned him into a player whose significant contributions won Nottingham Forest two successive League titles and two successive European Cups. This success did not, however, ameliorate Clough's critical description of Robertson as 'a very unattractive young man. If one day I was feeling a bit off-colour I would sit next to him. I was bloody Errol Flynn compared to him. But give him a yard of grass and he was an artist, the Picasso of our game.'[19]

Clough bewildered players with his unpredictable behaviour. He might encourage them to have a drink or visit a sex club on a pre-season tour and lighten up to ease the tension of a cup final the following day or he might, without a word of explanation, seek out the young Roy Keane in the dressing room at the end of a game and punch him in the mouth as a response to a poorly judged back pass from which a goal had resulted.[20] Directors as well as players were reluctant to question his authority. Unlike his elder contemporaries Busby, Revie, Nicholson and Alf Ramsey, Clough liked the media (it lay behind his bitter disagreements with Sam Longson, the Derby chairman) and in return the media adored him. He was the first British manager to understand how the media worked and how its power could be turned to a manager's advantage. Shankly embraced the media, unlike his rival, the Everton manager Harry Catterick, whose significant successes were never lauded to the same degree because of his deeply entrenched suspicion of the fourth estate.

Ramsey, who managed England to a World Cup victory in 1966, was another manager who loathed the media, newspaper reporters in particular, which is probably why when England failed to qualify for the 1974 World Cup he had no friends in the press to make his case before he was sacked by the FA. He had, however, changed the national side and the national game. He refused to leave Ipswich Town to take the job in 1962 until he had been assured that he would have complete control over selection, hitherto the preserve of a selection committee whose individual selections perforce dictated the formation that Walter Winterbottom, the nominal manager, could employ.[21] Secondly, he developed, with great success, the 4–4–2 formation which essentially dispensed with wingers and expanded the number of bodies in the midfield. It was reputed that he favoured work rate over flair but the team that won the World Cup contained three players who were undisputedly of world class – Gordon Banks, Bobby Moore and Bobby Charlton.

When Charlton retired in 1973 he, like his brother Jack, began a career in management. Despite his undoubted skill as a player, his popularity and his desire to succeed, Charlton left Preston North End after two seasons with the rueful realization that his talents did not extend far in that direction. His brother Jack, with fewer playing talents, understood the earthy side of the job and prospered accordingly at Middlesbrough, Sheffield Wednesday and pre-eminently as manager of the Republic of Ireland, where he was honoured not just with the freedom of Dublin and an audience with the pope during the 1990 World Cup finals but also with a life-size statue outside Cork Airport.[22]

A manager does not need a captain to be successful but an analysis of the relationship between Nicholson and Danny Blanchflower, Ramsey and Moore, Revie and Billy Bremner suggests that a strong relationship benefits both. Such a relationship certainly existed between Rinus Michels and Johann Cruyff. Forged initially at Ajax in the late 1960s, it blossomed in Barcelona when Cruyff followed his manager to Catalonia and most visibly during the 1974 World Cup in Germany. The seductive style of football propounded by Michels and perfectly executed by Cruyff, Neeskens and the rest of that dazzling Holland side was called 'Total Football'. In essence, in its fluidity and with every player capable of playing in any position, it wasn't too far removed from the football played by the Magical Magyars twenty years earlier or even that of the Austrian Wunderteam twenty years before that. Again, Michels is perhaps best classified as an influential coach although in his autocratic behaviour in Holland and Spain he certainly displayed many of the accepted traits of the traditional manager.

A New Order

Football management, rather like film directing, looks easy but remains deceptively complex because it involves the seamless interweaving of so many disparate elements, the failure of any one of which can destroy the entire operation. The successful demand for total control, which appears to be a prerequisite, does not guarantee good results and neither does an appointment with a thriving club. In the 1980s, building on the legacy bequeathed by Shankly, Liverpool became one of the most successful and respected clubs in the world. When Kenny Dalglish resigned as manager in February 1991 they had won 10 of the past 15 League Championships, 4 of the nine European Cups for which English clubs were eligible, 4 League Cups and the UEFA Cup. Management had passed smoothly from Shankly to Bob Paisley to Joe Fagan to Dalglish, all of them schooled in the famous Liverpool 'boot room'.

Graeme Souness seemed a logical continuation of this heroic tradition. He was captain of that all-conquering Liverpool side of the 1980s and had already cut his managerial teeth at Glasgow Rangers. He had been an uncompromising player and seemed likely to maintain the discipline that had been at the heart of the Liverpool ethic. In fact, the three years Souness lasted at Anfield, despite the 1992 FA Cup victory, were by the standards of what he had inherited quite disastrous, with bad results resulting in rumours of dressing-room arguments, which had never leaked out of Anfield previously. Many signings were overpriced failures and the bond between manager and crowd, such a feature at Anfield since Shankly's appointment over 30 years before, started to fray. The managers who followed – Roy Evans, the last of the boot-room appointees, Gerard Houllier and Rafael Benitez – were unable to return Liverpool permanently to its days of glory, and the prizes were transported 30 miles down the East Lancs Road to Old Trafford where Manchester United inherited Liverpool's robe and crown and the manager reigned unchallenged.

Sir Alex Ferguson survived his early years of disappointment and unrest to establish himself as the true heir to Busby, a manager who managed every aspect of the club. In many respects the role had changed a great deal by the end of the century. In mid-century the manager's principal anxieties were his relationships with his board of directors and the local reporter. Television had made no inroads and radio reporting was not intrusive. Bad results leading to crowd disaffection and low attendances were, as ever, usually the reasons for dismissal but the financial element did not control the game as it was later to do.

The chairman of the board of directors tended to be a man of local influence. Bob Lord at Burnley was a butcher, and although he exerted significant power at the club for many years, his trade rather symbolized the parochial nature of it. In 2003 Roman Abramovich acquired Chelsea and changed that nature permanently, adopting the autocracy of Steinbrenner but rejecting the public profile of Jesus Gil. He was to be followed by other excessively wealthy owners: the Abu Dhabi Royal Family bought Manchester City and the Glazer family had access to enough money to acquire Manchester United. Other American sports franchise holders followed – John W. Henry at Liverpool, Ellis Short at Sunderland, Stan Kroenke at Arsenal and Randy

Lerner at Aston Villa. These were men who were used to hiring and dismissing coaches, not men who would be greatly restrained by their managers should their ideas clash. It was as if the battles fought and won by Shankly, Revie, Busby and Clough had been rendered entirely irrelevant.

The manager now served at the whim of the owner, beneath whom also served various executives. The temptation to meddle with matters in what had previously been regarded as the manager's sphere was now overwhelming. The owner was frequently foreign and not necessarily affected if he provoked an adverse reaction from supporters because he did not live locally. The manager was now well remunerated but his position, with few exceptions, especially in the Premier League, was even more insecure. Even the Special One, José Mourinho, arguably, and certainly by his own lights, the best manager in world football, could not survive his owner's displeasure at Chelsea.

It was reported by the BBC in 2011 that in the 2010–11 season managers who were sacked in the English League Two had survived in their jobs for an average of just over 18 months; in League One it was 16 months and in the Championship less than a year. The Premier League kept its managers for just over two years but it was the Premier League that was largely responsible for the £99 million paid out in compensation to managers whose contracts were terminated.

The increasing demands for instant success and constant availability to the media has made the cult of the successful manager more intense whilst restricting entry to this charmed circle to the very few. When players earned two or three times the average wage of the working man, the fear of unemployment was so great that a manager who was a shrewd disciplinarian could handle them with some ease. When players started to earn salaries beyond the ordinary dreams of avarice, the manager found his authority difficult to sustain. Successful managers may still demand and receive the money, facilities and coaching staffs that would make managers of previous generations weak with envy, but the price they pay in pressure, anxiety and insecurity of employment would undoubtedly give them pause for thought. What hasn't changed is that ultimately their fate is decided by 11 fallible human beings on the pitch. The cult of the manager is of limited duration. On the day he leaves his post his successor is anointed. The car keys are returned and the name on the door is re-painted. *Sic transit gloria mundi* – even for football managers.

NOTES

1   T. Pawson, *The Football Managers* (London: Eyre Methuen, 1973), p. 27.
2   P. Vasili, *The First Black Footballer, Arthur Wharton, 1865–1930* (London: Routledge, 1998), p. 56.

3 S. Page, *Herbert Chapman: The First Great Manager* (Birmingham: Heroes Publishing, 2006), pp. 97–98.

4 J. Wilson, *Inverting the Pyramid: The History of Football Tactics* (London: Orion, 2008), p. 60.

5 Ibid., pp. 68–69.

6 Ibid., p. 137.

7 John Aston interview 2003 with author for *George Best & 21 Others* (London: Headline, 2004).

8 R. Adamson, *Bogota Bandit: The Outlaw Life of Charlie Mitten* (Edinburgh: Mainstream, 1996), pp. 118–20; D. Law with B. Harris, *The King* (London: Bantam Press, 2003), pp. 170–71.

9 A. McPherson, *Jock Stein: The Definitive Biography* (Compton, Berkshire: Highdown, 2004), pp. 96–97.

10 Wilson, *Inverting the Pyramid*, pp. 135–37.

11 Pawson, *The Football Managers*, pp. 38–39.

12 Ibid., pp. 40–43.

13 *Times*, 26 November 1953.

14 Wilson, *Inverting the Pyramid*, pp. 88–89.

15 Ibid., pp. 95–100.

16 C. Shindler, *The Worst of Friends: The Betrayal of Joe Mercer* (Edinburgh: Mainstream, 2009), pp. 287–88.

17 D. Hamilton, *Provided You Don't Kiss Me: Twenty Years with Brian Clough* (London: Fourth Estate, 2007), p. 48; pp. 69–70.

18 Hamilton, *Provided You Don't Kiss Me*, pp. 162–63, pp. 148–49.

19 'The things they say: Brian Clough', Fifa.com, 1 May 2009, www.fifa.com/worldfootball/news/newsid=1053374.html#the+things+they+say+brian+clough (accessed 15 January 2012).

20 Hamilton, *Provided You Don't Kiss Me*, pp. 153–54; R. Keane with E. Dunphy, *The Autobiography* (London: Michael Joseph 2002), p. 38.

21 L. McKinstry, *Sir Alf* (London: HarperSport, 2006), pp. 199–200.

22 L. McKinstry, *Jack & Bobby* (London: Collins Willow, 2002), pp. 451–52; pp. 397–98; p. 439.

WILL TIDEY

The Game-Changers: Sir Alex Ferguson

On 6 November 1986, Alex Ferguson inherited a bloated, underachieving Manchester United team slumped in the relegation zone. It was 19 years since the planet's best-known football club had won a league title, and the excesses of the Ron Atkinson era had left them no closer to emulating Liverpool's dynasty of success at home let alone in Europe. In Ferguson, United sought the long-awaited heir to Sir Matt Busby, and tasked him with returning the club to the halcyon days of George Best, Denis Law and Bobby Charlton.

It would take a man of strong convictions to do it, and Ferguson's reputation as a driven leader with a fierce will to succeed made him the obvious candidate. Here was a man raised on the raw, working-class streets of Govan – a shipyard worker's son who had scrapped his way up to play for Rangers, then punctured the Old Firm duopoly as a manager with Aberdeen.

Charlton was a staunch advocate of Ferguson's approach and had already sounded him out for a move south of the border during Ferguson's brief stint managing the Scottish national team at the 1986 World Cup in Mexico. United's chairman Martin Edwards didn't need convincing. He was won over when he watched Ferguson criticise his players following victory in the Scottish Cup final: 'His fury showed the sort of standards he set. Just to win was not good enough. He wanted to win in style.'[1]

Ferguson's first contribution was to rein in United's legendary drinking culture: 'I told them they would have to change their ways, because I certainly wasn't going to change mine.'[2] Cultures gradually shifted, but the success Ferguson needed to justify his revolution would not arrive overnight. 'Three years of excuses and it's still crap ... ta-ra Fergie'[3] read a banner that captured the prevailing mood at Old Trafford in December 1988. 'Under you we've had shit football, shit atmosphere, shit boardroom shenanigans, our support is drifting away,'[4] wrote Teresa McDonald the following autumn in a special, crisis edition of the *Red News* fanzine.[1]

---

[1] For more on Ferguson's relationship with the media, see Chapter 12 in this volume, 'Sheepskin Coats and Nannygoats: The View from the Pressbox', by Rob Steen.

Ferguson needed a stay of execution, and he got one by leading his team to FA Cup glory the following May. Mark Robins and Lee Martin proved the unlikely heroes, while Ferguson betrayed his ruthless ambition by dropping his first-choice goalkeeper, and good friend, Jim Leighton for the FA Cup final replay against Crystal Palace. Leighton has never forgiven him, but Ferguson was vindicated with his first major trophy at United.

A second followed 12 months later, with victory against Barcelona in the Cup Winners' Cup final. Ferguson's squad by now included a teenage Lee Sharpe, and with the emergence of a 17-year-old Ryan Giggs, among others, was beginning to take on a youthful air that channelled the legendary Busby Babes. The press dubbed them the 'Fergie Fledglings', and as Jim White pointed out, Ferguson was instilling a belief system in United's youth team that would reap its reward in years to come. 'This,' wrote White, 'was a manager prepared to play young players.'[5]

In 1993, Ferguson finally ended United's 26-year wait for a league title. The success coincided with the dawn of the Premier League era and owed everything to the chance acquisition of Eric Cantona from Leeds. Ferguson enquired on a whim about the Frenchman, and United were gifted a £1.2 million signing who would alter the club's destiny. With Cantona for inspiration, and a snarling Roy Keane installed in midfield, Ferguson topped his first title with a Double in 1994. It was Ferguson who coaxed Cantona back after the man dubbed 'Le Nutter' by the press leapt into the crowd, and infamy, at Selhurst Park in January 1995, and on his return from an eight-month suspension cast him alongside the teenagers the BBC pundit – and former Liverpool defender – Alan Hansen said you couldn't win anything with. They won the Double. 'Ferguson is one of the best managers of all time,' Cantona would reflect. 'I was very lucky … He is like Gandhi on the game side, a genius. He had so many different generations of players now. He's 70 and works with players 18 years old, but adapts himself to all generations.'[6]

It was ever thus in the 1998–99 season, which would define Ferguson's career and deliver United an unprecedented, and improbable, Treble. It began with Ferguson rebuilding the fragile confidence of David Beckham, who returned from the 1998 World Cup the most vilified man in the country. Nine months later Ferguson looked on as Beckham orchestrated one of the most remarkable comebacks seen in a major final as United scored two late goals to take the European Cup. Ferguson had his holy grail, not to mention a knighthood, and with Busby emulated, set about collecting titles and meeting his greatest challenge –'knocking Liverpool off their f**king perch'.[7]

A second European Cup followed in 2008, achieved with the talents of Wayne Rooney and Cristiano Ronaldo in irresistible union, before Ferguson finally saw United eclipse Liverpool's haul of 18 league titles in 2011: it was the 37th major trophy of a quite epic reign. At the time of writing, Ferguson was the longest-serving active manager in English football, and the most successful Britain had ever produced.

'The Best Psychologist in the World'

The defining characteristic of Ferguson's success has been his ability to relate to players with contrasting personalities. From the eccentric showman Cantona to the understated and insular Paul Scholes, Ferguson fostered close relationships with too many players to mention. In return he earned their trust, and in most cases the very best of their talents were on display in the team he ruled. 'He wanted to kill me at times, I'm sure,' Beckham said. 'But he was a father figure to me and he was also the man who gave me the chance of playing for my dream club.'[8]

And so, as Ferguson's 25th anniversary celebrations got underway in earnest, the media he so often warred with dropped to their knees in tribute. 'People who don't know him probably hear all the hair-dryer stories and think he is some sort of ogre, but in fact his ability to connect with people is extraordinary,' wrote the former England cricket captain, Michael Vaughan, in the *Daily Telegraph*, having attended a gala 25th dinner in Manchester. 'What came across is the way he has turned Manchester United into one big family. Everyone who has ever played for the team still feels part of the club ... I think he's the best psychologist in the world.'[9]

NOTES

1 P. Barclay, *Football – Bloody Hell: The Biography of Alex Ferguson* (London: Yellow Jersey Press, 2010), p. 186.
2 A. Ferguson, *Alex Ferguson: Managing My Life – My Autobiography* (London: Coronet Books, 2010), p. 241.
3 J. White, *Manchester United: The Biography* (London: Sphere, 2008), p. 279.
4 M. Crick, *The Boss: The Many Sides of Alex Ferguson* (London: Simon & Schuster, 2002), p. 314.
5 White, *Manchester United*, p. 286.
6 'Cantona: Ferguson Is Like Ghandi', FourFourTwo.com, 24 February 2011, http://fourfourtwo.com/news/england/74188/default.aspx (accessed 15 January 2012).
7 D. Taylor, 'The greatest challenge of Ferguson's career is almost over', *Guardian*, 9 January 2011, www.guardian.co.uk/football/2011/jan/09/sir-alex-ferguson-manchester-united-liverpool (accessed 15 January 2012).
8 J. Breeze, 'Beckham pays tribute to "father figure" Ferguson', Goal.com, 4 November 2011, www.goal.com/en-gb/news/2896/premier-league/2011/11/04/2742300/former-manchester-united-star-david-beckham-hails-father (accessed 15 January 2012).

9 M. Vaughan, 'Sir Alex Ferguson has turned Manchester United into one big loyal family says Michael Vaughan', *Daily Telegraph*, 5 November 2011, www.telegraph. co.uk/sport/football/teams/manchester-united/8870467/Sir-Alex-Ferguson-has-t urned-Manchester-United-into-one-big-loyal-family-says-Michael-Vaughan.html (accessed 15 January 2012).

Figure 9.1. David Beckham celebrates his goal. Manchester United v Newcastle United, FA Charity Shield, Wembley, 11/8/1996. Credit: Colorsport.

9

JED NOVICK

David Beckham and the Celebrity Phenomenon

They say that stars give you something to dream about ... [the] screen idols are immanent in the unfolding of life as a series of images. They are a system of luxury prefabrication, brilliant syntheses of the stereotypes of life and love. They embody one single passion only: the passion for images, and the immanence of desire in the image. They are not something to dream about; they are the dream. And they have all the characteristics of dreams.[1]

David Beckham (Figure 9.1) is as Baudrillard described: he is not something to dream about; he *is* the dream. He is as his own new fragrance 'Homme' describes:

> David Beckham Homme encapsulates the spirit of David Beckham, the man, the footballing sensation, the sporting ambassador, the style leader, the father and husband. Successful and confident, David is the epitome of masculinity. From his innate sporting soccer talent to his ambitious determination, his sensual new fragrance captures all that makes David unique.[2]

He's the ultimate billboard – from Manchester to Madrid to Milan to LA; he's even turned his tattooed body into a canvas. When Naomi Klein wrote in 1999 how celebrities 'now mirror the corporate structure of corporations like Nike and Gap'[3] and how the 'processes of commodification have become so ubiquitous and commonplace that the idea of unbranded space has become almost unthinkable', she could have been writing Beckham's career plan.

Behind a thousand 'Brand it like Beckham' headlines talking about 'Beckonomics' is a multifaceted icon, not just a brand, not just a portfolio of brands. He's not just a shelf in the supermarket, not even an aisle, and he has spread far beyond his original sportsman constituency to somewhere between fashionista and political mover. His global appeal is such that he has appeared in 150 countries in Gillette shaver advertisements. The Japanese Meiji Seika company made a three-metre-high chocolate statue figure of Beckham as part of his endorsement of their confectionery before the 2002 World Cup finals. If that were not enough, monks at a Buddhist shrine in Thailand made a gold-plated Beckham where people can worship. In 2005, the sum total of Beckham's brand portfolio value was estimated to be approaching $400 million.[4]

Yet alongside all this, he can't let go of his first love. When, in March 2010, aged 35, he tore an Achilles tendon he not only turned a career-threatening injury into a new career opportunity – he became England manager Fabio Capello's right-hand man during that summer's World Cup in South Africa, acting as liaison between players and management. Other 35-year-olds might have said 'OK, enough's enough', but Beckham doesn't do what others might do. He trained, he recovered, he got back into the team, he played. And then, in November 2011, he inspired LA Galaxy to win the MLS (Major League Soccer) Cup.

As a footballer, he had reached the top. He had played for three of the biggest, most famous, most prestigious clubs in the world – Manchester United, Real Madrid and AC Milan. He had 115 international caps. He had won six Premier League titles, one Champions League, two FA Cups, the InterContinental Cup, the FA Youth Cup, La Liga, the Supercopa de España. He was England captain for six years and 58 matches. He became a UNICEF Goodwill Ambassador in 2005 and was awarded the Order of the British Empire in 2003.

While doing all this he's cut through – seemingly effortlessly – the often brutish macho world of professional football. In March 2009, Beckham overtook Bobby Moore's haul of 108 caps, making him the record holder of England international appearances for an outfield player. Three months later, a mural six storeys high was unveiled outside Macy's in San Francisco picturing him naked except for a pair of tight, very tight, white Armani underpants. He popularized the notion of metrosexuality.[5] In a world where there had been but one 'out' gay player in the British game – the late, unhappy Justin Fashanu, who later hanged himself – Beckham openly courted the gay world. And we're not just talking about a designer sarong. He's appeared on the cover of the gay magazine *Attitude* (June 2002). He's posed outrageously in underpants. He advertised Police sunglasses looking like one of The Village People. And in 2002, he posed for *GQ* magazine – promoted as 'his most outrageous shoot' – with facial makeup, baby oil on his uncovered chest, wearing a white silk scarf – and nail varnish. The shoot was headlined 'Camp David'.

He's half of a pop star couple who captained England while sporting a Mohican haircut. He has somehow managed to transcend every prejudice, every barrier, every hostility. It's easy to talk about a pop star or an actor being 'metrosexual'. But this is a professional footballer and we're talking about a world where not so long ago a player – Graeme Le Saux – was nearly destroyed for reading the *Guardian*.

When he arrived in Los Angeles in 2007, Tom Cruise and Will Smith threw a party for him at the Museum of Contemporary Art. 'At the outset,' Tom Dart wrote in the *Times*, 'his move seemed less like a transfer than product placement on an epic scale, a grand marketing gambit for player and league.'[6] Galaxy failed to make the play-offs in his first two years and the suspicion, not helped by his loan to AC Milan, was that he was there not necessarily for sporting reasons.

The naysayers weren't shy in making the point. Publicist Michael Levine said that Beckham's move to Los Angeles was a 'tremendous opportunity. LA is the world's best celebrity platform location. This is a great brand extension opportunity for him, and soccer is largely irrelevant.'[7]

But Beckham, as he always has, turned it round. The 'Go home, fraud' posters are long forgotten, In late 2011 MLS commanded about $40 million from prospective owners for a new franchise, four times higher than on his arrival five years earlier. From 2012, there would be 19 teams, five more than when he arrived. And Galaxy won the cup.

'It's dangerous to say David Beckham has changed soccer in America,' says Alexi Lalas, former general manager of LA Galaxy and the man who was key to Beckham's move there. 'People were kicking a ball before he came and they will be after he has gone. But he has changed MLS and Galaxy forever.'[8] Becks is the pop star who doesn't make bad albums, the film star who can open a film anywhere in the world, the ad man's dream.

Beckham, Becks, 'Golden Balls' … It's entirely appropriate that he went to Los Angeles – La La Land, the City of Angels – for he bestrode a mythic land where your surname is entirely unnecessary, entirely redundant. Kylie, Britney, Mick, Keith, Becks. One of Klein's new breed of branded humans.

Posh and Becks

I'll tell you what I want, what I really really want
So tell me what you want, what you really really want
I'll tell you what I want, what I really really want
So tell me what you want, what you really really want
I wanna, I wanna, I wanna, I wanna, I wanna really
Really reallywannazigazig-ha[9]

On 26 June 1996 EMI released the first single by a new all-girl pop band called The Spice Girls. The *New Musical Express*, that most reliable arbiter of pop taste, said: 'It's not good, it's not clever, but it is fun.'[10] As a pop conceit,

The Spice Girls were perfect. Five ordinary girls, not particularly special or talented. Each had her own name, her own look, her own persona, but what they wanted was universal. They wanted 'it'; they wanted life. They wanted '*zigazig-ha*'. An immediate success, within a week 'Wannabe' was Number 1 in the British pop charts. Seven weeks later it was still Number 1.

Meanwhile, in a different universe entirely ... It was 17 August 1996, the first day of a new season. Manchester United were playing Wimbledon at Selhurst Park. It was bright and sunny, lovely but unremarkable. A routine day and a routine match. Beckham picked up the ball just inside the United half. He looked up and saw that the Wimbledon 'keeper Neil Sullivan had wandered off his line. He pulled his right foot back and ... that was when it happened. That was the moment the God of Celebrity decided to sprinkle his fairy dust on David Beckham. As his perfectly placed long-range lob dipped over the hapless Sullivan and into the net, Beckham turned round and raised his arms. His floppy fringe framed his boyish face and, as one, the world was drowned in the sound of clicking cameras. He might not have known it then, but that was the moment David Beckham found out what 'zigazig-ha' meant, what it really, really meant.

'My wife picked me out of a soccer sticker book. And I chose her off the telly ... It felt straight away like we'd always been meant to be together.'[11] Crucially, when David met Victoria Adams in November 1996, he didn't only meet her, he met her manager, Simon Fuller, chief executive of 19 Entertainment. David and Victoria became Posh 'n' Becks.

If individually David and Victoria were icons, together they were something much, much more. 'By becoming part of (and party to) the cultural capital which Victoria Adams possessed, David Beckham transcended the boundaries of his own occupational locale and was thrust into a much broader consumptive space: one not typically reserved for athletes.'[12] Filling the vacuum left by the death of Princess Diana (31 August 1997) they became The Story. As Piers Morgan, a former editor of the *Mirror*, said, 'On a slow news day we used to lead the paper on the royals, now we go for Queen Posh and King David.'[13]

Beckham entered the arena at just the right time. Looking back, it might seem as if there was a collision in the sky, a coming together of celestial forces. The Manchester United youth team he played in – the near-mythical 'Fergie's Fledglings' including Nicky Butt, the Nevilles, Paul Scholes, Keith Gillespie and (spiritually) Ryan Giggs – won the FA Youth Cup in May 1992. At the end of that month the Premier League was formed. In September that year, Sky Sports was encrypted and sold as a subscription TV channel. Less than a year later, *OK!* magazine was launched. Tony Blair and Gordon Brown hadn't yet made their pact at Islington's Granita restaurant, but already the pieces were in place for Blair's vision of Cool Britannia. The early to mid-1990s changed football forever. In these few short years, a monochrome world found itself swathed in technicolour. Football became gentrified; it moved out of the ghetto and into the mainstream. In 1994, the *Daily Telegraph* became the first British newspaper to launch a daily sports supplement and it didn't take long for the rest of Fleet Street to cotton on.

Everything was in place. What was needed was a face: a trailblazer, a new kind of footballer to spearhead this new kind of world. According to Ellis Cashmore, professor of culture, media and sport at Staffordshire University: 'The rise of Sky was coterminous with the rise in celebrity culture and the whole degradation of hard news and its substitution with soft news, with lifestyle, was the result not so much of a conspiracy but Sky's attempt to sabotage the news market.'[14]

Sky not only changed TV; it changed our appetites, creating what Cashmore calls 'the feedback loop' – a media which feeds itself, which generates its own stories and creates its own stars. 'The stories come from the newspapers and they feed into football and Sky benefits from that and that feeds back into the newspapers. And it's not only the red tops, but all the papers because they're all in the same market.'[15] Football, Sky, the newspapers. The perfect circle.

Thanks to Sky, leading footballers in England were suddenly super-rich and super-exposed and Beckham wasn't the only one caught in the headlights; he was just better at it than anyone else. Steve McManaman, one of Liverpool's 'Spice Boys', was managed by Simon Fuller, the Spice Girls' manager and svengali. Jamie Redknapp, his team-mate, married a pop star, Louise Nurding of the Spice Girls' rivals, Eternal. Neither came close. Where others looked clumsy and ill-at-ease, Beckham simply looked effortless. As Patrick Barclay says: 'He's pretty flawless – pretty and flawless.'[16]

A New Man for a New World

A new kind of footballer to spearhead this new kind of world. Not even Rupert Murdoch could have imagined Beckham. The footballer as celebrity wasn't a new concept. 'England captain marries pop star' wasn't a new headline. Billy Wright was the first footballer to play for England 100 times. He ended his career in 1959 with 105 international caps, including 90 appearances as captain – and in stark contrast to today's stars, this was in an era when the calendar wasn't littered with meaningless friendlies and substitutes were not allowed.

On 28 July 1958, Wright married Joy Beverley of the Beverley Sisters pop group. 'When we arrived at the register office, there were six or seven thousand people outside,' recalled Wright in his autobiography. 'We lost the aerial of our car and on the way through the crowds one of the brides-maids lost her shoe! We attended a small luncheon afterwards before driving to Stratford-on-Avon for the shortest honeymoon ever. Twenty-four hours later, Joy was working in Bournemouth and I resumed training with Wolves!'[17]

The prototype football celebrity was another iconic Manchester United Number 7: George Best. Blessed and cursed with looks and skill, Best had to cope with life in the goldfish bowl before the celebrity age: 'I spent a lot of money on booze, birds and fast cars. The rest I just squandered.'[18] It wasn't just his money he squandered. While Best had no Team Best – there was no Simon Fuller, no Victoria, no Simon Oliveira (Beckham's PR) – mostly what he didn't have was Beckham's discipline.

Many of Beckham's virtues are those precisely not associated with celebrity or media stardom. He has been very durable, he works hard and he's very disciplined. His lifestyle has been far more of a distraction to journalists than it has been to him. We don't hear of Beckham being a disruptive influence, missing training or acting like a prima donna. He's clearly good at compartmentalising his life and in the football element of it – which is the base for it all – he appears to be the epitome of the good pro. It would seem that far from being the next evolutionary development of George Best as is often supposed, there's a much bigger case for seeing him as a modern version of Billy Wright – someone who maximised his talent through the qualities of the archetypal pro, and a famous showbiz wife.

Beckham is, to use marketing-speak, a hyphenate – who he is on any given day depends on which media platform you choose to hook him into. It's an art which has made him not only the ultimate hyphenate, but also the ultimate survivor. 'I'm a good Darwinian and I believe in the adaptive capacity of creatures,' says Cashmore. 'Survival is the right term and you need intelligence to survive and intelligence means an ability to adapt to changing environments and she's done that and she's survived and prospered.'[19] Beckham may well be, to use Mark Simpson's term, a metrosexual, he may well have grabbed the headlines for wearing a sarong and there may well have been rumours about wearing his wife's underwear, but ... 'she'?

She. Victoria. As Posh Spice, she had a fairly low-key start to life. Of the five Spice Girls, she was the only one who didn't sing a solo on that first single. She missed most of the session and communicated with the group via mobile phone. 'I just couldn't bear not being there. Because whatever they said about how it didn't matter, it did matter. Saying "Yes, I like that" or "Not sure about that" down the phone is not the same.'[20] Posh Spice, Pushy Spice, Mute Spice ... Svengali Spice?

'I really think that she is the mastermind behind it,' says Cashmore. 'Because you've got to think that she came from a show business background and had been very skilfully managed by Simon Fuller and she knew all the ins and outs of how to create and maintain a celebrity in the absence of particular talent.'[21] Could he have been David Beckham without her? 'No, no,' argues Cashmore. 'He'd have been a footballer and he'd have been internationally recognised, but if he hadn't married her he would be known as we know Michael Owen or Steven Gerrard – as someone who's in the news for football but not a global phenomenon.'[22]

'The people around him are all very efficient,' says Barclay. 'And Beckham himself is very, very good at it, he's pretty sure-footed. He likes sleeping with the big beasts. If you could have an audience with God, that's what he'd do. Because he's a star. But being associated with those very big people is another trait of his and has helped project him onto the world stage to the point where he wouldn't look out of place between, I don't know, Bill Clinton and Henry Kissinger.'[23]

Or between David Cameron and Prince William, as he was during England's fruitless bid to host the 2018 World Cup. 'Absolutely,' says Barclay. 'In fact I'm sure they'd both worry about being slightly diminished. Who was the most fêted? Not the best looking because that's a given, but who was the most famous?'[24] As Turner, Bonner and Marshall argue in *Fame Games*, 'the distinction between celebrity and other kinds of social or political elite status is becoming less clear as the signs of celebrity drive out less powerful alternatives'.[25] So let's ask the question again. Who was the most famous?

But for all the trappings and all the show, for all the endorsements and all the tattoos, for all the outrageous outfits and sarongs and Beckingham Palace parties (but only seen in *OK!*– thanks to an exclusivity rights deal) and all the purple wedding thrones and all the Spice Girls records, there was only one time the public turned against him.

St Etienne 1998

Argentina. It had to be Argentina. The history between England and Argentina, both on and off the pitch, had been chequered. There was the 1966 World Cup where Argentinian captain Antonio Rattin refused to leave the field after being sent off and Sir Alf Ramsey refused to let his players swap shirts, reportedly calling the opposition 'animals'. There was the 1986 World Cup, Maradona and the 'Hand of God'. In between there had been the Falklands War and the sinking of the *Belgrano*. When the countries met in the second round in St Etienne at the 1998 World Cup, the scene was set. Maybe the England manager, Glenn Hoddle, should have seen it coming.

Just after the break, in the 46th minute, Diego Simeone crashed into Beckham. Lying on the ground, he flicked a leg up and … Simeone went down as if shot by a squadron (before facing Beckham in a European Cup quarter-final the next year, the Inter Milan midfielder would admit to having faked injury). Danish referee Kim Milton Nielsen reached into his pocket and sent Beckham off. Hoddle didn't look at Beckham as he left the pitch, Argentina went on to win 4–3 in a penalty shoot-out and England were out. No one cared about the two players who missed the penalties. There was only one story.

The *Daily Mirror* headline read '10 Heroic Lions, One Stupid Boy'.[26] Inside the paper was a dartboard with a picture of Beckham's face on it. Outside the Pleasant Pheasant pub in South Norwood, London, a sarong-clad effigy was hung by a noose. Such was the frenzy that the *Observer*'s Paul Wilson feared that the 'hate mob' might compel the player to 'escape this poisonous atmosphere by playing abroad'. *When Saturday Comes* even felt compelled to lecture its readers that 'neither football, nor England should matter that much'.

It takes a certain kind of genius to turn such a setback into a PR triumph – but that's exactly what Team Beckham did. Beckham responded by saying nothing. 'Here again, I think you'll find the hidden hand of his wife,' says Cashmore. 'Another athlete, unguided, might have had an agent like Max Clifford or someone like that who might have said something like, "What you've got to do is go out there and set the record straight", but Victoria said "Silence" – and, of course, it worked like a charm.'[27] It's probably no coincidence that Fuller never says anything. Unlike his one-time partner, sometime nemesis Simon Cowell, Fuller never says anything.

To quote Denis Thatcher, another successful man who married a driven woman: 'Better keep your mouth shut and be thought a fool than open it and remove all doubt.' Crucially, Beckham didn't only not say anything. He also played like a dream, inspiring Manchester United to an unprecedented Treble – Premier League, FA Cup and Champions League. It was a remarkable rehabilitation.

This rehabilitation peaked in April 1999 when *Time Out* magazine went as far as to portray Beckham as a pseudo-Christ-like figure and featured him on the front cover in white trousers and see-through shirt in a pose evocative of Christ and the crucifixion. The caption read: 'Easter Exclusive: The Resurrection of David Beckham'.[28]

Barclay also points to that time as a turning point. 'The sending-off against Argentina showed the mettle of the man. He had to put up with a lot of things which could have made him retreat into his shell. He could very well have backed off, but he set about winning the nation round by apologising, by enduring the hideous chants that all footballers get when they display a hint of vulnerability, and came through it. You can call it courage, you can call it doggedness, but it certainly made the most unbelievable commercial success – because it marked him out as a man of greater strength.'[29]

In March 2007, Beckham reclaimed the event in the way he knows best. He recreated the effigy scene for an ad for a new Adidas boot.[30]

The Most Famous Footballer in the World

He can't kick with his left foot, he can't head a ball, he can't tackle and he doesn't score many goals. Apart from that he's all right.

– George Best[31]

There's a suspicion about Beckham, that he's an empty vessel, used by Simon Fuller, by his wife, by the marketing departments ... by the moneymen. Beckham wore the No. 7 shirt, traditionally the shirt of the outside-right – the winger – but he wasn't fast enough to be a real winger. More, he didn't have 'a trick', a shorthand phrase used by football writers to describe wingers who have speed and skill – the ability to beat their man, to get past players. In football, Beckham didn't have a trick. He had a peach of a right foot, but didn't have pace, couldn't really beat his man.

Off the field, though, every time he's been faced by an opponent, he's dropped a metaphorical shoulder, thrown a sidestep and skipped past. In life, Beckham has had more than enough tricks and has made a habit of not only skipping past potential problems, but stopping by to turn those problems into friends. But then again, his detractors might say he's made a living out of turning tricks. They'll talk about shirt sales and economic forces without stopping to say what exactly is wrong with selling shirts, with attracting new fans. They'll wheel out Best's well-worn quote without even pausing to acknowledge how good that right foot is.

Having said that, he does fulfil his end of the economic bargain. Tim Leiweke, the president and CEO of Anschultz Entertainment Group, which owns LA Galaxy, claimed that within three months of signing, Beckham had already 'paid for himself'. Since Beckham's arrival, the club had sold out their luxury suites, attracted 11,000 season ticket-holders, inked a groundbreaking shirt sponsorship deal worth an estimated $20 million with Herbalife, and had increased merchandise sales by 700 per cent for the Galaxy and by 300 per cent for the league.[32]

'The level of his fame far outweighs his football ability,' says Barclay. 'But his popularity is genuine. It was noticeable at an England match that he came on for three minutes and got a bigger cheer than the player who's just scored a hat-trick. His popularity is genuine, particularly with children.'[33]

He has been – and even in the age of Cristiano Ronaldo and Lionel Messi may still be – the most famous footballer in the world. Every previous holder of that title also had a very strong claim to be the best player as well – we've celebrated most of them in this book. But not even Beckham's most devoted admirer would claim that for him. For all the dexterity of that right foot, he dictated play for neither United nor England. He was no Beckenbauer, Cruyff or Zidane. Nor did he stamp his class on a major international tournament at either club or national level.

While Beckham might not be 'great', he is, in the classical sense, a hero. Think Brad Pitt as Achilles. His one moment of greatness was against Greece in 2001, where he single-handedly secured England a place in the 2002 World Cup finals. The set-up was perfect. If England didn't beat Greece, there was the prospect of a difficult play-off against Ukraine. Beckham had tried with five of his characteristic free-kicks. They all missed. Was Golden Balls' golden boot going to let us down? Then, deep into injury-time in the 93rd minute ... there was time for one last free-kick. 'Brilliant Beckham averts Greek tragedy' read the inevitable headline.[34]

Prince Charming

Don't you ever, don't you ever
Stop being dandy, showing me you're handsome
Prince Charming, Prince Charming
Ridicule is nothing to be scared of.[35]

I asked Patrick Barclay if there really was anything that made Beckham extraordinary. 'I remember going on an away trip with Man United and we were waiting at the back of the plane for a pee. I saw him and said, "David, I actually know your father. I watched you play in the youth team". The way he spoke to me, I thought "this is not a footballer". He's one of the five or ten footballers I've met in my life who were remarkable, who would have been remarkable if they'd been bank clerks, for their manners. In fact, no, make that five in my whole career who are exceptional. Most people are reasonably well-mannered, but very few stand out – and Beckham was one.'[36]

'Everyone who knows him from those early days at United, everyone's got a little story about him being personable and polite,' says Laura Williamson of the *Daily Mail*. 'Our chief photographer remembers that Beckham always remembered his name. It made him feel good, of course. It might be a technique of course, but it works.'[37]

He's polite. It's a wonderful quality. As an extension of this, he never criticises anyone. If he's written off – as throughout his career he often has been – he simply gets on with it, practises some more, and wins them round.

In August 2006 the England manager Steve McClaren axed him from the team. 'I told David I was looking to change things, looking to go in a different direction, and he wasn't included within that. He took the news very well, although he was disappointed.'[38] Less than a year later, McClaren was singing a different tune. 'Everybody's professional and we've a squad that will blend together that will get us a result and I'm sure everyone will welcome David back. Everyone knows David's attributes and he's a big-game player who can help us win.'[39] In his comeback game, a friendly against Brazil at Wembley, Beckham made an instant impact, supplying a deep free-kick for John Terry to head England in front.

At Real Madrid in 2007 Fabio Capello said Beckham would never play for him again. But his continued efforts in training and professional attitude forced Capello to change tack and, within a month, recall him. Beckham responded by transforming Real, inspiring them to a late-season surge to dramatically win La Liga on the final day of the season. Capello, recalls Barclay, 'became a big, big mate, and got him to go to Milan'[40] and later, as England manager, engineered Beckham's international resurgence. In June 2008, Capello reinstated him as England captain.

And if anyone picks a fight with him, it never lasts. He turns it round. In February 2003 Arsenal beat Manchester United 2–1 at Old Trafford in the fifth round of the FA Cup. Sir Alex Ferguson, not a man to treat defeat lightly, took his frustrations out in the dressing room by kicking Ole Gunnar Solskjaer's boot at Beckham's head. Beckham said nothing but – in the closest he has ever come to making a statement – allowed himself to be photographed leaving the ground with a face like thunder, his long blond streaked hair held back by an alice band exposing two surgical strips over his left eye.[41]

Now Beckham only talks about Ferguson as a father figure. 'No matter what has been said in the past, whether good or bad, I only remember the good times,' he said the day before his new club AC Milan faced Manchester United in the Champions League. 'Sir Alex was the man who gave me my chance to play for the club I'd always dreamed of playing for. There's definitely no score to settle. He's an incredible man. He always was and always will be a father figure to me.'[42]

It's November 2011, eight years since David Beckham left United for Real Madrid. Yet Beckham is everywhere. The day I went to London to interview Patrick Barclay, then chief football commentator of the *Times*, the back-page lead story of his paper (22 July) was Beckham (a list of the clubs who might be interested in signing him). When I went to London to interview Laura Williamson (25 August), Victoria train station was plastered with a series of life-sized posters of Beckham for 'Homme'. A head shot, black jacket, white shirt, black tie. Immaculately coiffured, his perfectly contoured face dressed in the perfect designer stubble last seen on George Michael in the early 1990s.

When I interviewed Cashmore (15 September), the lead story on 'Today', the BBC Radio 4 flagship news programme, was Beckham (about how he topped the newly published 'Football Rich List'). When I sat down to write this chapter, in the week beginning November 1, the BBC Sport website had a Beckham story four days of the week: how he wanted to be part of the proposed Olympic football team ('It's my dream to play for Team GB'), a tribute to Sir Alex Ferguson to mark his 25 years as Manchester United manager ('To have played under a manager like Sir Alex Ferguson, every player dreams of that') and about where he might play next year (he's 'flattered' by the interest and, at the time of writing, the clever money was on Paris St Germain). By Friday 4 November, we got to the inevitable 'Beckham: "I'm not finished yet"'.[43]

Why Beckham?

David Beckham exemplifies indulgence in the consumer market. His image has become the dominant icon of sport representation, yet it is a strangely elusive and anchorless image – a floating signifier which can become attached to a range of discursive elements with equal plausibility.

– Garry Whannel[44]

So – why Beckham? How did Beckham become Beckham? Was it Simon Fuller, the silent svengali pulling the strings? Or was it Victoria Adams, who went from Spice Girl to Spouse Woman using Becks as her sword? Or was it Sir Alex Ferguson, the best British manager of his generation? Or was it Sky and the Murdoch press, or was it Fabio Capello or was it his father? The answer is 'All of the above'. He was the perfect person at the perfect place at the perfect time. He was at Manchester United, the biggest club in the biggest football market at a time when both were getting far bigger and reaching far wider audiences than ever before. If all of those things are true – and they are – maybe he's just ... lucky. Right person, right place, right time. Best bear in mind a quote usually attributed to the legendary American film producer Samuel Goldwyn: 'The harder I work, the luckier I get.'

The only person not on that list is Beckham himself. He's good, but not too good. He's very polite. He appeals to everyone. He's embraced black culture, gay culture, fashionistas. He's the working-class boy made good, the devoted dad and loving husband. He's smart, sharp and ambitious enough to surround himself with incredibly smart, sharp, ambitious people. He also clearly enjoys the flash of the camera in a way that, generally, pop stars do and sports stars don't. He ticks every box.

As Cashmore says: 'Beckham reverberates with inclusiveness. White, but with Black tastes; straight, but adored by gay men; male, but with a penchant for nail varnish, body-waxing, and androgynous attire.'[45]

Much has been made of Beckham's alleged lack of intelligence, but like most other charges against him, it doesn't stand up. What's the evidence? He doesn't say much and he's got a high-pitched voice. 'We don't expect our intellectuals to be great footballers, but for some reason we expect our great footballers to be intellectuals,' wrote Julie Burchill. 'But when it comes to having one's life "sorted", as the young folk say, he is in a class of his own, considering his youth and his degree of fame. And this in itself bespeaks intelligence.'[46]

He's brave. Sport is full of people who, for one reason or another, are afraid to stick their head above the parapet. Sadly, examples – and victims – abound. The gay sports star who stays in the closet. The depressive. The anxious. In the rough, tough world of football it pays not to display something that might be seen as weakness. Beckham has – seemingly – never considered that. Maybe he's very brave. Even if we say the judgement was that of his advisers, he'd still have to be very brave. Maybe the experience of the aftermath of St Etienne in 1998 taught him that nothing could touch him. What could anyone say that would be as bad as that? You want to laugh at me because I'm wearing a sarong? Go ahead.

And he had Posh. Warren Beatty said of Madonna in the 1991 film *Truth or Dare*: 'She doesn't want to live off-camera, much less talk. There's nothing to say off-camera. Why would you say something if it's off-camera?'[47] But Posh and Becks, for all the headlines and endorsements and publicity, aren't the showbiz couple who live, as the Robbie Williams album title has it, life through a lens. As omnipresent as they have sometimes seemed, as controlling as she sometimes might appear, there has never been a question about their togetherness, about their commitment to family. And if she sometimes appears crass – too in thrall to fame – he is never less than dignified. Even when Rebecca Loos, his personal assistant during his time in Madrid, gave an interview to the *News of the World* in April 2004 claiming that she'd had an affair with Beckham, it only made their marriage stronger.

Have we missed anything? Patrick Barclay: 'Looks. It sounds simplistic, but looks will get you a long, long way. If he looked like Nicky Butt or Phil Neville he wouldn't be Beckham. He has that swagger that doesn't look like a swagger, that confidence that comes from always being good-looking.'[48]

Maybe Beckham has got a trick after all. His trick is knowing what he's got and how to use it. It's knowing who to surround himself with and how to utilise their skills. Maybe it's not great, maybe it's genius.

NOTES

1 J. Baudrillard, *Selected Writings* (Oxford: Polity Press, 1988), p. 56.

2 Advert for David Beckham 'Homme', www.cheapsmells.com/beckham-homme-at-great-prices.

3 N. Klein, *No Logo* (Canada: Knopf, 2000), http://ems30i.weebly.com/uploads/2/8/9/5/2895302/thebrandexpands.pdf (accessed 15 January 2012).

4 C-C. Yu, 'Athlete Endorsement in the International Sports Industry: A Case Study of David Beckham', *International Journal of Sports Marketing & Sponsorship*, 6, 3 (2005), 189–99.

5 M. Simpson, 'Here Come the Mirror Men', *Independent*, 15 November 1994, www.marksimpson.com/pages/journalism/mirror_men.html (accessed 15 January 2012).

6 T. Dart, 'Star quality Continues to burn bright in a Galaxy far, far away', *Times*, 19 November 2011, www.thetimes.co.uk/tto/sport/football/article3231378.ece (accessed 15 January 2012).

7 'Beckham to Leave Real Madrid for LA Galaxy', Foxsport.com (2007), quoted in J. Vincent, J. Hill and J. Lee, *The Multiple Brand Personalities of David Beckham: A Case Study of the Beckham Brand* (Belmont, CA: Cengage Learning, 2009), www.thefreelibrary.com/The+multiple+brand+personalities+of+David+Beckham%3A+a+case+study+of...-a0216352321.

8 Dart, 'Star quality continues to burn bright in a Galaxy far, far away'.

9 Lyrics to 'Wannabe' by The Spice Girls (Rowe, Stannard, The Spice Girls).

10 D. Fadele, *New Musical Express*, 23 November 1996.

11 T. Watt, *Beckham – Both Feet on the Ground: An Autobiography* (London: Harper, 2003), p. 83.

12 E. Cashmore and A. Parker, 'One David Beckham? Celebrity, Masculinity and the Soccerati', *Sociology of Sport*, 20, 3 (2003), 214–31.

13 A. Morton, *Posh and Becks* (London: Michael O'Mara Books, 2000).

14 Author's interview with Ellis Cashmore, 15 September 2011.

15 Ibid.

16 Author's interview with Patrick Barclay, 22 July 2011.

17 L. Topham, 'Matches of the Day: How footballing marriages of yesterday compare to Colleen and Wayne's lavish nuptials', *Daily Mail*, 12 June 2008, www.dailymail.co.uk/femail/article-1025838/Matches-Day-How-footballing-marriages-yesterday-compare-Coleen-Waynes-lavish-nuptials.html (accessed 15 January 2012).

18 'Best: Decline of the Golden Boy', BBC.co.uk, 14 June 2005, http://news.bbc.co.uk/1/hi/uk/4090840.stm (accessed 15 January 2012).

19 Author's interview with Cashmore.

20 V. Beckham, *Learning to Fly* (London: Penguin, 2001), p. 128.

21 Author's interview with Cashmore.

22 Ibid.

23 Author's interview with Barclay.

24 Ibid.

25 D. Turner, F. Bonner, and D. Marshall (eds.), *Fame Games: The Production of Celebrity in Australia* (Cambridge: Cambridge University Press, 2000), p. 11.

26 'UK Press Attacks Beckham Petulance', BBC.co.uk, 1 July 1998, http://news.bbc.co.uk/1/hi/uk/123759.stm (accessed 15 January 2012).

27 Author's interview with Cashmore.

28 G. Seenan, 'David Beckham, from football savior to the new Messiah', *Guardian*, 14 September 2005, http://football.guardian.co.uk/News_Story/0%2C1563%2C1569434%2C00.html (accessed 15 December 2011).

29 Author's interview with Barclay.

30 M. Sweeney, 'Beckham spearheads Adidas push', *Guardian*, 6 March 2007, www.guardian.co.uk/media/2007/mar/06/advertising (accessed 15 January 2012).

31 George Best quote from redmanchester.com, www.redmanchester.com/wiki/George_Best_Quotes (accessed 15 January 2012).

32 C-C. Yu, 'Athlete Endorsement in the International Sports Industry: A Case Study of David Beckham'.

33 Author's interview with Barclay.

34 C. Malam, 'Brilliant Beckham averts Greek tragedy', *Daily Telegraph*, 6 October 2001, www.telegraph.co.uk/sport/football/teams/england/3014197/Brilliant-Beckham-averts-Greek-tragedy.html (accessed 15 January 2012).

35 'Prince Charming' by Adam and the Ants (Ant/Pirroni), September 1981.

36 Author's interview with Barclay.

37 Author's interview with Laura Williamson, 25 August 2011.

38 'McClaren ends Beckham England era', BBC.co.uk, 11 August 2006, http://news.bbc.co.uk/sport1/hi/football/internationals/4782613.stm (accessed 15 January 2012).

39 'Beckham recalled to England squad', BBC.co.uk, 26 May 2007, http://news.bbc.co.uk/sport1/hi/football/internationals/6694743.stm (accessed 15 January 2012).

40 Author's interview with Barclay.

41 S. Roach, 'Will Becks give Man Utd the boot?', BBC.co.uk, 18 February 2003, http://news.bbc.co.uk/sport1/hi/football/teams/m/man_utd/2775269.stm (accessed 15 January 2012).

42 R. Williams, 'David Beckham refuses to put the boot into Sir Alex Ferguson', *Guardian*, 15 February 2010, www.guardian.co.uk/football/2010/feb/15/david-beckham-alex-ferguson-manchester-united (accessed 15 January 2012).

43 D. Bond, 'Beckham flattered by interest from Premier League and Paris', BBC.co.uk, 2 November 2011, http://news.bbc.co.uk/sport1/hi/football/15554291.stm (accessed 15 January 2012).

44 G. Whannel, *Media Sports Stars: Masculinities and Moralities* (London: Routledge, 2002), p. 202.

45 E. Cashmore, *Celebrity/Culture* (New York: Routledge, 2006), p. 233.

46 J. Burchill, 'The boy done good', *Guardian,* 20 October 2001, www.guardian.co.uk/books/2001/oct/20/features.football (accessed 15 January 2012).

47 *In Bed with Madonna: Truth or Dare* (Keshishian and Miceli, 1991).

48 Author's interview with Barclay.

Figure 9.2. George Best of Manchester United, 1963–64 season. Credit: Colorsport.

ROB STEEN

The Game-Changers: George Best

Manchester United. Two words that reek, not just of football, but football as style and self-expression. If the Old Trafford institution can be considered the game's best-known brand name, it is because its players have long been seen, from Southampton to Sydney, as the personification of glamour, exponents of the game at its most expressive and creative, an image whose roots can be traced back, primarily, to the swaggering sides managed by Matt Busby in the mid-to-late 1960s.

Bobby Charlton and Denis Law were two of the crown jewels but both were outdazzled by George Best (Figure 9.2), the winger-cum-inside-forward widely regarded as the finest player produced by Britain over the past 50 years and, along with Alfredo di Stéfano, the finest never to grace the World Cup finals. Pelé, always gracious if a tad wayward in his views, once told Best that he, not the Brazilian, was the planet's foremost player. As the saying in his native Northern Ireland goes, 'Maradona good; Pelé better; George Best.' Few, certainly, have so effortlessly fulfilled the promise of their name.

'With feet as sensitive as a pick-pocket's hands, his control of the ball under the most violent pressure was hypnotic,' attested Hugh McIlvanney. 'The bewildering repertoire of feints and swerves, sudden stops and demoralising spurts, exploited a freakish elasticity of limb and torso, tremendous physical strength and resilience for so slight a figure and balance that would have made Isaac Newton decide he might as well have eaten the apple.'[1] 'Best played like an angel,' marveled Brian Glanville. 'A football was almost too ludicrously large to test his skills.' And yes, he admitted it: beating a full-back gave him a sexual charge.[2]

Yet Best is also remembered as a tragic figure, both for the way he is perceived to have frittered away his career – after walking out on United for the first time at 27 he was largely a spent force – and because, like his mother, he descended into alcoholism and thence an early grave.

Di Stéfano once told him he had to decide whether football was a business or a game: to Best it was 'always a game'.[3] The first footballer to achieve tabloid notoriety, a fixture on front page and back, he was the free spirit and so-called fifth Beatle who embodied the purported freedom of the so-called Swinging Sixties, especially disdain for authority and caution, but didn't really know what to do with it bar make enough money to enjoy himself.

The shoulder-length mane and penchant for fashion, discos and dolly birds, even the hint of androgyny, made him as appealing to men as to women. He appeared on *Top of the Pops*, opened his own boutique and nightclub. The proto-Beckham,[1] he transcended the sport but floundered under the twin weight of adulation and envy, not to mention a self-professed disenchantment with the game itself. 'Frankly, I don't know how he stood up to it all,' sympathised Paddy Crerand, midfield prompter in United's first European Cup-winning run. 'OK, he buggered it up, but it wasn't altogether his fault. We've got to take some of the blame. Society if you like, the people who expected too much of him, the hustlers who wanted to make a few quid out of him, the people who brought their sick kids to him and asked him to cure them. The girls who threw themselves at him, the players who fed off him and then rubbished him on the way down.'[4]

By Permission of Busby

In their manager's heart, Best was twinned with Duncan Edwards: whether he benefited is moot. 'Every manager goes through life looking for one great player,' said Busby. 'I found two – Big Duncan [Edwards] and George.'[5] Edwards was just 21 when he died from injuries sustained in the 1958 Munich air crash, whereupon, some have theorised, Busby, himself badly injured, lost his severity: more willing to indulge Best's individualistic, artistic bent, he was less inclined to curb his excesses. 'Perhaps a man who has seen so much exuberance crushed in a single, frightful moment,' suggested Arthur Hopcraft, 'could not be expected to be harsh when it appeared, even more showily, in a later generation.'[6]

The son of a shipyard iron turner, brought up on Belfast's Cregagh housing estate, Best 'made himself into a two-footed player', noted Michael Parkinson, 'to the point where he had forgotten which was his natural foot'.[7] He first imposed himself on a wider audience in 1966 when, in what Glanville hailed as 'one of the finest exhibitions'[8] by a British team in Europe, he inspired United to a 5–1 victory in a European Cup tie against Benfica, finalists in four of the five previous seasons and hitherto unbeatable in Lisbon. Nicknamed 'El Beatle' by the appreciative Portuguese, he was the

---

[1] For more on football and celebrity, see Chapter 9, this volume, 'David Beckham and the Celebrity Phenomenon', by Jed Novick.

heartbeat of two League title wins and the first victorious European Cup campaign by an English club. Renewing hostilities with Benfica at Wembley, he put United ahead for good in extra-time with a flamboyant solo goal, sealing his anointment as European Footballer of the Year – a trophy he would sell at auction. While rounding the goalkeeper, he would reflect, it felt as if he was the only man on the pitch for whom time had not stopped. Indeed, as he admitted to me when we met at his Mayfair club shortly before the 25th anniversary of that historic defeat of Benfica, it was all he could do to resist the temptation to apply the finish lying on the ground.[9] Cruelly victimised by the unscrupulous defenders of the era, who resented his fearlessness as much as his legerdemain, arguably his greatest goal came, nonetheless, in a League Cup tie against Chelsea, when he somehow resisted a tackle by Ron 'Chopper' Harris that threatened to sever both legs.

His disillusionment gained impetus when he stepped down in 1969: never less than wide, the philosophical divide separating Charlton and Best, old world and new, became a chasm. The point was reinforced with typically acidic whimsy: 'When Bobby looks at himself in the mirror in the morning and combs what's left of his hair, he knows that's as good as he's going to feel all day.' Not for nothing did Best express approval for Raich Carter's dictum: 'Old footballers should be shot.'[10]

'When I was playing,' he explained, 'I wasn't going out to deliberately drink myself into oblivion. After I stopped playing I did.'[11] Publicly at least, he seldom sounded regretful until the end: his last public appearance was on the front of the *News of the World* the weekend before he died in 2005. He wanted people to see how ravaged he was, to warn them of alcohol's demons.

Acute intelligence all too often forgotten amid memories of the intoxicated, slurring guest on a thousand talk shows, his instinctive response, whenever accused of being a wastrel, was to paint a sardonic, probably apocryphal scene. 'There I am, lying on a hotel bed with a leggy blonde and a caseful of banknotes, when in comes room service. "So, George," he goes, "where did it all go wrong?"' After his death, Alex Higgins, snooker star and soul brother in self-destruction, launched a campaign to remove the three middle letters from Belfast and rename it 'Best City'. It failed, but the name now conjoined with Belfast City Airport isn't C. S. Lewis, Van Morrison, Mary Peters or Edward Carson, but Best. Nobody made that benighted city smile quite like Georgie.

NOTES

1 H. McIlvanney, 'The Best years of our lives', *Observer*, 18 October 1992, www.kilmarnockacademy.co.uk/famoushmcilvanneybestyears.htm (accessed 15 January 2012).

2 B. Glanville, *Champions of Europe – The history, romance and intrigue of the European Cup* (London: Guinness, 1991), p. 54.

3 G. Best with R. Benson, *The Good, the Bad and the Bubbly* (London: Pan Books, 1990), p. 166.

4 M. Parkinson, *Best – An Intimate Biography* (London: Arrow, 1975), pp. 138–39.

5 G. Burn, *Best and Edwards: Football, Fame and Oblivion* (London: Faber, 2006), p. 20.

6 A. Hopcraft, *The Football Man – People and Passions in Soccer* (London: Penguin, 1971), p. 114.

7 Burn, *Best and Edwards*, p. 110.

8 Glanville, *Champions of Europe*, p. 55.

9 Interview with author, Mayfair, London, April 1993.

10 G. Best with R. Benson, *The Good, the Bad and the Bubbly*, p. 173.

11 Ibid., p. 125.

10

JEAN WILLIAMS

Football and Feminism

Emma Byrne: The Arsenal Ladies' goalie who bakes her own bread.[1]

England's World Cup victory of 1966 has been constantly re-interpreted, reappraised and revised as a historic moment in the history of association football, particularly in Britain. One of the myths frequently peddled about 1966 as a media moment in English cultural history is that it inspired a new generation of women to play football. There seems some evidence to support the argument: for example, the Women's Football Association (WFA) was formed in 1969. For some important international players and coaches in England, such as Sue Lopez, 1966 did seem to be some sort of catalyst; but the general situation was considerably more complex and the perception of women remains problematic.[2]

When Fanny Blankers-Koen won four gold medals to become the most famous athlete at the 1948 London Olympic Games, it was reported that the 'World's Fastest Woman is an Excellent Cook'. In 2011, Emma Byrne, the Arsenal Ladies' Irish goalkeeper, was also congratulated on having good culinary skills. That a magazine such as *Sky Sports* should feature a woman footballer at all is indicative of the changes in the sport in the last 60 years: that her domestic abilities are a main focus of the article illustrates how little has changed.

Sport, we are often reminded, is a peculiar business and we make exceptions for it that we do not accept in other areas of our lives. For female football players today, biology is indeed destiny. Like much sport, the language we use to describe female participation is in itself problematic. 'Football' usually means the game as played by men and boys: 'women's football' is, observers insist, a different variant. 'The women's game' and other descriptors therefore express gender difference in ways that are both symbolic and embodied.[3] The FIFA president, Sepp Blatter, has been on record more than once insisting that women players have a duty to look more 'feminine' to break football into new markets: perhaps more mindful of beach volleyball than Kevin Keegan in the 1970s, Sepp would like to see women in shorter shorts.[4]

The fact that many people on the street would be able to identify Karren Brady, Delia Smith, Julie Foudy, Birgit Prinz or individual women employed in football should not obscure the more widespread and fundamental exclusion of women from football's elite. UEFA has grown from an administrative body where three people worked full-time in 1960 to an organization of over 340 employees functioning across multiple languages and cultures. It first had a European women's competition in 1984. When Karen Espelund, a respected Norwegian player and administrator who headed the women's committee, was 'co-opted' on to the executive board in 2011 it was another important first.[5] FIFA has yet to have a woman permanently appointed to its own, more controversial and powerful, executive board. Lydia Nsereka, the president of the Burundi Football Association, became the first woman ever to sit on the executive as a co-opted appointee in May 2012.

The supposed 'newness' factor is an invented tradition relating to women players. The first official Women's World Championship (later to be called a World Cup) took place in the People's Republic of China in 1991, backed by FIFA and sponsored by confectionery company M&Ms. China also hosted the 2007 Women's World Cup (WWC); the United States has held two such competitions in 1999 and 2003 and Sweden one in 1995. There are now also two youth versions: the Under-20 and Under-17 WWC tournaments were held in Germany and Trinidad and Tobago respectively in 2010. The 2011 WWC, hosted by Germany in 2011, was intended as a record-breaking female-only sports tournament on the continent. It certainly created a new high for Twitter social networking traffic with over 7,100 messages a second for the final: more than for the Royal Wedding, the death of Osama Bin Laden or the Japanese tsunami the same year.[6]

The crowded playing calendar also includes Olympic tournaments since 1996 and confederation, regional and national competitions. This is, in itself, divisive, since English women would represent the female Great Britain team in 2012, much to the consternation of the Scottish, Welsh and Northern Irish individuals who might be eligible. Katie Taylor, a former member of the Irish women's national team and the 2005 Irish Youth Footballer of the Year, won the Republic's first gold medal of the 2012 Games, beating Russia's Sofya Ochigava in the lightweight boxing final. Her commercial endorsements in 2011 included a Lucozade promotion with Travis Barker (formerly drummer of Blink 182) and British pop-rapper Tinie Tempah.[7] Evidently, it is sometimes easier to earn a media profile as an individual athlete than as part of a team, which relies on being selected and navigating the politics of national associations.

While the rise in the number and variety of international fixtures for women players is football's most conspicuous move toward equality in the last 20 years, there is much continuity in the change. The Football Association in England had full control of women's football as late as 1993; Scotland did not fully affiliate the Scottish Women's Football Association until 1998. Dramatic change seemed to follow incorporation. In 2002 football overtook netball as the most popular participation sport among women in England, by some indicators, and there are now over 150,000 FA-affiliated female players.[8] In both Scotland and England, we are constantly told that it is the 'Fastest Growing Team Sport' for females.[9] Kelly Simmons reported a combined total spent on girls' and women's football of £11.5 million in 2003.[10] In addition, £60 million had been put into grassroots football, from which girls and boys were to benefit.

Empowerment but Little Diversity

Advocates have developed a progressive rhetoric in the last 20 years. This narrative is determinedly ahistorical and it is not in the least militant in its political intent. I do not want to be curmudgeonly and suggest that the very real changes that have happened since the inception of a Women's World Cup are of little import. Thankfully, there is much to applaud in what might be termed practical feminism and this includes men and women who facilitate female involvement. I have met few women football players who would call themselves feminists, but there are quite a few men I would call feminist fathers (or partners, or coaches and so on). Soccer moms, aunties and sisters should not be underestimated. However, women's involvement in male sport and men's participation in women's sport is one of the most under-written topics in the academic literature on the topic.

Shouty chauvinism, likely to be heard on BBC Radio 5 *Live* phone-in shows, seems to drown out this quietly supportive volunteer culture. This is a depressing aspect of football's present reality in Britain but not as dangerous as the outright homophobia of the 'corrective rapes' which have hurt and killed, among others, Eudy Simelane, former star of South Africa's acclaimed Banyana Banyana national female football squad.[11] The lack of transparency and opportunity at elite levels of administration and play are therefore polite forms of exclusion compared with such ignorance and violence. As Jayne Caudwell's important work on gender, sexuality and race reminds us, the tendency to suggest that women fall into a category of their own can divert attention from the differences between them.[12] While Simelane was killed for her equal rights activity, some lesbian teams and players have found empowerment and self-determined expressions of team identity in football and so diversity is one of the aspects of football remaining to be more celebrated.

The death of Justin Fashanu in 1998 reminds us that this is not just an issue for women players. While rugby had its Gareth Thomas moment in 2009, when the Welsh rugby international with over 100 caps came out to widespread admiration, and cricket was equally as supportive of Stephen Davies in February 2011, football's understanding of sexuality and gender is less progressive. Any sense of irony was completely absent, however, when a newly appointed equality and diversity officer at the FA recently assured me that football had one of the best track records on this issue in sport. Another new equality and diversity appointment at the Professional Footballers Association, which for many years excluded women from its annual gentlemen's dinners, told me much the same thing.

Why do we know so little about the history of women's participation in sport, football in particular? The primary aim of a recently published survey aimed at Britain's growing number of family historians was to convey the range and diversity of women's work spanning the last two centuries and to suggest ways of finding out more about what often seems to be a 'hidden history'.[13] *Women in European Culture and Society*, an academic survey by Deborah Simonton, does makes reference to the rise of the female global sports star, beginning with Suzanne Lenglen's rather shocking appearance in short skirt, bandeau and sleeveless dress at Wimbledon from 1919 onwards. There is, however, no mention of football until page 386.[14] The book's argument concludes on page 393. Given that the subtitle of that book is *Gender, Skill and Identity from 1700*, we are reminded that football as a sport has often stood for modernity since its codification from 1863 onwards.

Courtly Love and Curt Rejoinders

Evidence of women's football can be traced back to folk and courtly forms. A recent pamphlet for the world women's invitational in Beijing detailed a Song Dynasty (960–1279) three-day contest, where a women's squad composed of 153 members, all in elaborate costume, played with embroidered balls to the accompaniment of a musical band.[15] After codification, more fixtures were arranged, for example, between teams calling themselves Scotland and England, who played in Edinburgh in 1881.[16] Opposition was widespread but the Hopewell sisters, Mabel, Maude and Minnie, deserve their place in football's hall of fame as pioneers nevertheless. The British Ladies Football Club in 1895 combined the talents of middle-class Nettie Honeyball as player-secretary with the non-playing president, Lady Florence Dixie. However, most of the women seem to have been enthusiasts who had been introduced to football, enjoyed playing and did what they had to do to participate.[17]

The Lancashire United Transport Company based in Atherton had a team as early as 1915 and the women of the Preston Army Pay Corps had already played at Deepdale by 1916. Most of the early twentieth-century teams were founded either by workers, such as the most famous British example, the Dick, Kerr Ladies of Lancashire, formed in 1917, or, as in the French case of Fémina in July 1912, by sports enthusiasts. This Parisian club formed by Pierre Payssé, the Olympic gymnast, diversified its sporting range and in 1917 added association football.[18] Fémina toured England in March 1920, first playing Dick, Kerr's in Preston. The image of the kiss of welcome between the two captains at the first match, though very chaste, was widely circulated across Europe: from this moment on mediated international matches and regional competition were an important part of the story of women's football.

Female football migration was very evident in this early period. In its coverage of what was effectively a women's international tournament, where Dick, Kerr's were the unofficial 'England' team, playing 'France' as represented by the Fémina club, the *Daily Mirror* of 18 May 1921 had two photographs of Lily Parr on page eight, the first an action shot of her 'beating the French goalkeeper for the fifth time' and the second showing team-mates 'chairing Miss L Parr after the match. She scored all five goals'.[19] By the end of 1921 Lily Parr was famous, in part, for being famous. To a degree this was because she was playing for a club that had wanted to be known as the best from its first public game, on Christmas Day 1917, when Dick, Kerr's had beaten the Arundel Coulthard Foundry 4–0 at Deepdale at a 'Great Holiday Attraction' in front of 10,000 people.[20] The coming of war had seen the Strand Road tram building and light railway works, originally founded by W. B. Dick and John Kerr of Kilmarnock, become a munitions factory in late 1914.

Grace Sibbert is said to have taken the initiative to found the team during work breaks, and although it played first against male colleagues, it soon became part of a spectacle in which women played against women for charitable purposes – a pattern which lasted until the team disbanded in 1965. Quite quickly the team drew upon the reputation of Preston North End and their ground at Deepdale in order to stage these events (there and in other major stadia) in front of large crowds. This encouraged the image of Dick, Kerr's Ladies' as *the* team in the country and with it grew the fame of the company they represented. Competitive rivalry extended by 1921 to 150 British teams, including Birmingham, Bath, Cardiff, Edinburgh, Liverpool, Manchester, Newcastle, Plymouth and Stoke. If Preston was proud, it was also pioneering.

These home games combined with 'internationals' against France and Belgium, at least one played in Spain. A Dick, Kerr's tour to the United States and Canada took place in late 1922 against male professionals, with Lily Parr as captain and star draw. Parr is thought to have earned 10 shillings a game for her entire playing career, until she retired in 1951. Alice Mills, who had never previously been out of Britain before this tour, followed many other Lancashire cotton migrants and moved to the Pawtucket area the year after, retiring from football to raise a large family and remaining in the United States for the rest of her life.

The combined interests of civic charities, the local press, the factory owners and the professional club were contributory factors in this early popularity. However, as the case of Lily Parr shows, the team pursued a fairly aggressive policy of transferring in the best players: relatively few regulars were Prestonians by birth. On Boxing Day 1920, 53,000 watched the Dick, Kerr Ladies beat St Helen's Ladies 4–0 at Goodison Park. A moot point, of course, is the extent to which these migrants were semi-professional: Dick, Kerr's certainly drew playing personnel from outside the immediate area, with French (Louise Ourry) and later Scottish players (Nancy 'The Cannonball' Thomson) moving to Preston and working while they played.

By 1921, the FA had banned women from the fields of Football League and Association clubs, in part because players' 'expenses' absorbed too much from charity money raised and because it was 'unsuitable'.[21] If male professional players were to be controlled by maximum wage caps and the 'retain and transfer' system, however difficult these were to police, female professionalism was not to be tolerated. As has been seen, this antipathy towards women's football permeated most of Europe but did not always lead to an outright embargo. Women in France began playing at a similar time to those in Britain and promoted the popularity of the sport internationally in part via the Women's World Games of 1921–36, pioneered by Alice Milliat in protest at female exclusion from many disciplines at the Olympic Games. Jules Rimet, for example, had assisted in two matches played by women's teams in front of 10,000 spectators in 1920.[22]

Expansion and the Struggle for Identity

Women's football also developed in Germany and Austria after the First World War and there seems to be evidence of a game in Russia. The United States and Canada have had college-based soccer programmes for women since the early 1920s, at least, and there seems to have been evidence of female college players in Hong Kong. Certainly it became sufficiently established in the United States and Canada to produce books such as Frost and

Cubberley's *Field Hockey and Soccer for Women* and the *Smith Book of Soccer*.[23] In 1919 the Austrian weekly *Allgemeine Sport-Zeitung*, based in Vienna, reported matches. By 1925 there were debates in *Sport und Sonne* about the essentially masculine nature of football, as one article headline indicated, 'Das Fussbalspielist Männerspiel',[24] but notions of the body and permissiveness were changing: the elegant 'sport girl' exemplified by the willowy tennis player in whites and the 'new woman' of boxing and athletics in the Weimar Republic graced the covers of *Sport und Sonne* in the 1930s.[25] In contrast, pioneers of women's football, such as 19-year-old Lotte Specht, were making the Frankfurt weekly press looking very much like they had just played a hard match.[26]

Cultural, social, economic and political changes spread and increasing numbers of women participated in sport, including football, giving rise to what can appear to be the late modernity of female interest. A West German Women's Football Association in Essen was formed in August 1955 with 22 clubs. This was followed by the 2–1 victory in an international with the Netherlands in 1956 in front of a crowd of 18,000 in Essen and then, in 1957, to a European Women's Championship with the final in the 40,000-seat Poststadium, a 4–1 victory for 'England' over 'West Germany'. FIFA, by its own admission, only began researching early women's football matches during the last few years and its claims that the 'first' official international was played between France and the Netherlands in April 1971 are open to debate.[27]

Interest by business and commercial sponsors pre-dated the creation of an official World Cup by 20 years. In November 1969, for example, the Fédération Internationale Européenne de Football Féminine (FIEFF) ran a 'world cup' tournament with the support of drinks company Martini and Rossi. In the four-team tournament in Turin, Italy, Denmark, England and France were provided with kit, equipment, all-expenses-paid travel and accommodation. This was another milestone in a European-wide awareness. The resulting women's world championship in Rome in 1970 and another (unofficial) tournament in Mexico in 1971 showed that businessmen independent of the governing bodies had begun to explore the commercial potential of female football at the elite level. This prompted FIFA to accept responsibility for all football activities or see the women's game go its own way. The ban on women's football was lifted piecemeal by national associations in the 1970s: in England in 1971 and in Brazil in 1975.

This new attitude to female players coincided with the 1972 Equal Rights Amendment of the American constitution. In the same year Title IX of the Education Amendments to the Civil Rights Act of 1964 committed to gender equity for federally funded education programmes in the United States.

The broad application of this later led to the 1979 Title IX Athletics Policy Interpretation. The correlation between the introduction of Title IX and an increase in both female sport and participation in education is compelling. By the late 1990s, women who had come through college soccer programmes and been selected for the women's national team were becoming aspirational role models.

Mia Hamm shared the limelight with Michael Jordan in the so-called consciousness industries of commercial sporting products and their media spin-offs as the second-most important Nike-sponsored athlete.[1] The 1999 World Cup final was a record-breaking event with 93,000 spectators and worldwide TV coverage; shortly afterwards, the 20 members of the victorious U.S. squad were sufficiently well known to found the WUSA professional league in what has been called the most competitive sports market in the world. Perhaps uniquely, Mia, Julie, Joy, Kristine, Brandi, Michelle (along with Briana, Tiffeny and Carla) rose to levels of fame with the U.S. public which make surnames unnecessary.

Americanisation and the Women's Super League

This brief historical survey is intended to contextualise the attempt by the FA to launch the first professional league for women in England in 2011. Licensing by the national association is the model for the newly launched Women's Super League (WSL) of eight teams. At around £3 million spent on the project so far, the national association is also the major stakeholder. Women's football has helped the association's Corporate Social Responsibility programme, in addition to its equity and diversity agenda, by targeting areas of government concern to draw in external income streams. English women national team players were offered central contracts for the first time in 2008–09. Twenty England women's contracts of £16,000 per annum were available, centrally issued by the FA and annually negotiated from 1 December to 30 November each year. A player can only work up to 24 hours a week in another job and hence, rather than being a full-time professional agreement, it is seen as providing the 'freedom to train'. This is because the fitness of so many England players was in need of improvement, holding down employment as they did and training in what free time was left. Freedom to train is not, however, an entitlement to play or a right to selection.

The drift across the Atlantic by female European players is one of the clearest migration patterns in the women's game. None of the American-based

---

[1] See the interchapter 'The Game-Changers: Mia Hamm' following this chapter.

England national team players for 2009–10 had central contracts (these included Kelly Smith and Alex Scott at the Boston Breakers; Eniola Aluko at Saint Louis Athletica; Anita Asante and Karen Bardsley at Sky Blue FC and Karen Carney, Ifeoma Dieke and Katie Chapman at the Chicago Red Stars). There is a clear message from the English Football Association that returning women players to domestic football is a priority. In order to have a central contract there is a stipulation that a player must be home-based in order for her training to be monitored and so she 'must be registered to play for a football club affiliated to an English County FA'. I was told that while the application process is open to all, none of the U.S.-based players applied. Paradoxically, earning a living as a player in the United States would not exempt that person from the 24-hour rule. Controlling both the league and the national team is, however, meant to increase synergy for the English female elite of the game.

The situation in the United States is not entirely stable either: the Chicago Red Stars had to suspend operations for the 2011 Women's Professional Soccer (WPS) season. While some players negotiated contracts elsewhere in the United States as 'free agents', others, such as Carney, returned to England. Carney felt that the 2009 move to Chicago was 'fantastic, one of the best experiences of my life. I went over there young, just out of university, and got to play professional football. It opened my eyes to so many things.'[28]

The motivations for creating the WSL stem in part from wanting England players to play full-time in England, but also to provide a more stable platform for greater competitiveness in the Women's Premier League (which the FA took over in 2004). The WSL launched with eight teams because Hope Powell, the national team coach, has prioritized the quality of football that is played in a 'less is more' strategy. The North and North East in particular are therefore not included and there have been accusations of a southern bias. Doncaster Belles' first game against Lincoln on 13 April 2011 attracted 750 spectators, while the more publicized Arsenal-Chelsea match saw 2,200 supporters pay between nothing and £6 a ticket. Slow and conservative growth are the key messages of the WSL. Each club may pay four players each year in excess of £20,000 (central England contracts are excluded).

How, then, has the Women's Super League been conceptualized as a product and brand to sell the idea of young female football players to the paying public? Marketing rationale began with the premise that the Women's Premier League is not a tangible product to sell, and so there was a need to create a fan base, mostly comprised of girls aged 9–15. ESPN identified a slot on Tuesdays for a highlights package and also bought rights to production and cross-league footage. Each of the eight clubs has a website of similar standard, design, product and branding perspective.[29]

Gender has been downplayed as part of the media story and the 'new' product emphasis has been on a summer league as a differentiating factor. This has been perceived within the FA as news for the media, at a quiet time for football, although the first game was played during a busy time in the fixture list in domestic leagues and international competitions. A break was scheduled after the seventh match on 12 May 2011, so games resumed in late July and the schedule completed in August: the Women's World Cup finals began in Berlin on 26 June and ended on 17 July in Frankfurt, where Japan were crowned World Champions for the first time.

This is not so very different from the way that the two United States professional leagues, the Women's United Soccer Association and Women's Professional Soccer, launched in 2001 and 2007 respectively. Mark Noonan, speaking at the same 2003 Symposium as Kelly Simmons referenced earlier, called his presentation 'Before They Were Champions: Developing the 1999 U.S. Women's Champions National Team Brand'.[30] Noonan's message was a simple one: 'A big event, a special team, a moment in time. We see them as a group of sport and gender pioneers: we present them to the audience in lots of games, in lots of cities with the players very connected to their audience.' The WSL live experience is also intended to borrow from the grassroots marketing that proved such a successful ticket sales strategy for the 1999 World Cup final, drawing the largest live audience ever for a women's game. Yet negative stereotypes, while diminishing, continue to surround female participants. Clichés such as 'On the ball with the beautiful game – here come the girls' still abound in marketing, as the World Cup in Germany made clear.[31] Similarly, FIFA promotional campaigns used models such as Adriana Sklenarikova, wife of Christian Karembeu, who helped France win the 1998 men's World Cup, even though she has never played the game.[32]

There is evidently some way to go before 'a right to train' becomes full professionalism in a commercially vibrant league in England. Whatever the civil processes at work here, the emerging model of English professional women's soccer offers interesting examples of leagues that combine aspects of North American franchises with the traditional models of football. As such, they have wider implications for how the sport is presented to a European and worldwide audience. The Women's Super League can be seen as perhaps the most Americanised example of a professional football league in Europe, although the summer scheduling also draws on the Sky-supported models of rugby league and netball's Super League. This suggests that the holy grail for women's football would not be landing a deal with ESPN for highlights viewers but Sky for live coverage. There are possibilities as the suspension of the WPS season in the United States in late 2011 saw many of the British players forced to seek jobs in Europe. England was the biggest beneficiary.

For example, Kelly Smith returned to Arsenal, who took the WSL title for the second season in a row in September 2012: a predictable outcome, given their previous dominance.

Cautious Optimism

The Olympic Closing Ceremony in Athens in September 2004 could be interpreted as marking the end of a chapter for women's association football in the United States. The U.S. team flag-bearer was the triple Olympic medallist Mia Hamm. The women's national team had won gold, a victory that made up in small part for the semi-final exit in the 2003 World Cup in Los Angeles (defeated by the winners Germany 3–0). The following 10-game 'Fan Celebration Tour' served as a last opportunity to see Hamm, Julie Foudy and Joy Fawcett in a women's national team that had transcended sport and had made front-page news. Kristine Lilly and Brandi Chastain also toured, though Michelle Akers did not.[33] Members of the '91ers' team that won the inaugural Women's World Cup had begun to step down. Though Akers had retired from international football after the 1999 World Cup, she preceded Hamm as the figurehead in a team which at that point had never placed below third in any of the seven senior women's events and had won two World Cups and two Olympic gold medals. The success in 2011 of the Nadeshiko Japan national squad (the nickname comes from a delicate pink flower, symbolic of national female beauty) may see them reach heights in their own country to match this. It is as well to remember, though, that national associations routinely under-fund their women's national teams. In 2011, for example, the Iron Roses of China were noticeably absent from the World Cup finals for the first time.

A recent project on female migration, 'Women, Football and Professionalisation 1971–2011', identified some trends relating to player migration in football's global gendered labour market.[34] There is a gradual but widening public recognition of women who pioneered professional and semi-professional roles in football, in part due to the increasingly European-wide practice of electing key individuals to respective Halls of Fame. With an estimated 26 million female players globally, of whom 6 million are based in Europe, the evolution of football as a sport and as an industry over the past 60 years has been dramatic.[35] However, there are reasons to be cautious amid the optimism. The same survey claims only a total of 21 million *registered* European players, male and female, compared with an educated guess of 62 million unregistered participants. It is not uncommon, for example, to include those who intend to participate in the next year, as well as those who actually do play. Globally, even by FIFA's own enthusiastic figures, women make up 10 per cent of the total number of football players *at best*.

When we look at elites able to earn a living from the game, the gender disparity is amplified: if there are 60,000 professional players registered in Europe, for example, very few are women. This is striking because the idea of amateurism has, to a large degree, defined what it is to be a professional: under FIFA rules, if players earn more for their football-playing activity than the expenses that are incurred in performing those duties, they must have a written contract and are thereby considered professionals. While those who do not meet these criteria are considered amateurs, the word 'professional' encompasses a considerable range of activity, from the essentially casual participants supplementing their main income through football to the multi-millionaire players of Europe's big five leagues.

So, the following 'big' question remains: how many women are involved in what kinds of professionalism in world football? We recognize that most of the growth of female participation has developed in the last 40 years, yet we know very little about any attendant professionalization. I await the first female president of FIFA with anticipation. I am more impatient to hear the multiple stories of the world's female players.

NOTES

1 'Emma Byrne: Away from the Game', *Sky Sports*, April/May 2011, p. 17.
2 S. Lopez, *Women on the Ball* (London: Scarlet Press, 1997), pp. 42–43; S. Lopez, *UEFA Europe, Professionalisation and Women's Football 1971–2011 Questionnaire Response*, 30 December 2010; J. Williams, *A Game for Rough Girls: A History of Women's Football in England* (Oxford: Routledge, 2003); 'An Equality Too Far? A Thematic Review of European Issues Relating to Women's Football', *New Approaches in Football History Themenheft von Historical Social Research* 1 (2006), 34–43; *A Beautiful Game: International Perspectives on Women's Football* (Oxford: Berg, 2007).
3 M. Kunz, 'The Female Figure: Vital Statistics from the Women's Game', *FIFA World* (Zurich: FIFA, March 2010), pp. 44–45.
4 J. Blatter, 'President's Corner', *FIFA World: For the Game, for the World* (Zurich: FIFA, 28 May 2010), p. 27.
5 'UEFA Executive Committee Concludes June Meeting', UEFA.com, the official website for European football, 17 June 2011, www.uefa.com/uefa/aboutuefa/organisation/executivecommittee (accessed 27 September 2011).
6 E. Fanning, 'Women's World Cup final between USA and Japan sets Twitter record', *Guardian*, 18 July 2011, www.guardian.co.uk/football/2011/jul/18/womens-world-cup-twitter-record (accessed 15 January 2012).
7 The video is widely available on YouTube and the range of comment it provokes is interesting, www.youtube.com/watch?v=kOiZr93zz7c (accessed 15 January 2011).

8   J. Oatley, 'English Women's League Prepares for Re-Boot', *FIFA World*, March 2011, pp. 39–43.

9   J. Macbeth, 'Attitudes towards Women's Football in Scottish Society', *Scottish Affairs* 63 (2008), 89–119.

10 K. Simmons, 'Women's Football in England', *FIFA Second Symposium for Women's Football*, Long Beach, USA, 4 October 2003 (Zurich: FIFA Archive).

11 A. Kelly, 'Raped and Killed for Being a Lesbian: South Africa Ignores "Corrective" Attacks', *Guardian*, 12 March 2009, www.guardian.co.uk/world/2009/mar/12/eudy-simelane (accessed 28 September 2011).

12 J. Caudwell, 'Queering the Field? The Complexities of Sexuality within a Lesbian-Identified Football Team in England', *Gender, Place and Culture: A Journal of Feminist Geography* 14, 2 (2007), 183–96; '"Bend It like Patel": Centring "Race", Ethnicity and Gender in Feminist Analysis of Women's Football in England' (with S. Scraton and S. Holland), *International Review for the Sociology of Sport*, 40, 1 (2005), 71–88.

13 M. Ward, *Female Occupations: Women's Employment 1850–1950* (Berkshire: Countryside Books, 2008), p. 3.

14 D. Simonton, *Women in European Culture and Society: Gender, Skill and Identity from 1700* (Oxon and New York: 2011), p. 386.

15 'Women's Football in Ancient China' *National Women's Soccer Invitational Brochure*, Beijing 1982, p. 17.

16 P. Brennan, 'England v Scotland 1881', www.donmouth.co.uk/womens_football/1881.html (accessed 15 January 2012).

17 Williams, *A Game for Rough Girls*, p. 43.

18 L. Prudhomme-Poncet, *Histoire du Football Féminin au XXe Siècle* (Paris: L'Harmattan, 2003), pp. 5–10.

19 'Women's "International": Dick, Kerr's, the Women's "Soccer" Side, Defeated the French Women's Team 5–1 (Exclusive)', *Daily Mirror*, 18 May 1921, p. 8. I am grateful to Neil Carter for all references to the *Daily Mirror*.

20 P. Brennan, *The Munitionettes – A History of Women's Football in North East England during the Great War* (Northumberland: Donmouth, 2007), p. 25, www.donmouth.co.uk/womens_football/1881.html (accessed 15 January 2012).

21 Williams, *A Game for Rough Girls*, p. 20.

22 Williams, *A Game for Rough Girls* and *A Beautiful Game*; P. Dietschy, *Histoire du Football* (Paris: Librairie Académique Perrin, 2010), p. 503.

23 H. Frost and H. Cubberley, *Field Hockey and Soccer for Women* (New York: Charles Scribners and Sons, 1923); M. Knighton, 'Development of Soccer for Girls', *American Physical Education Review*, 34 (1929), 372.

24 E. Nendza and J. Hoffmann, *Verlacht, Verboten und Gefeiert* (Auflage: Landpresse, 2006), p. 14.

25 E. Jensen, *Body by Weimar: Athletes' Gender and German Modernity* (Oxford: Oxford University Press, 2011).

26 Nendza and Hoffmann, *Verlacht, Verboten und Gefeiert*, p. 24.

27 S. Duret, 'First Ladies', *FIFA World* (Zurich: FIFA, April 2011), pp. 34–39.

28 J. Oatley, 'Q and A', *FIFA World* (Zurich, FIFA, March 2011), p. 41.

29 Football Association, www.thefa.com/Leagues/SuperLeague (accessed 15 January 2012).

30 M. Noonan, 'Before They Were Champions: Developing the 1999 US Women's Champions National Team Brand', FIFA Second Symposium on Women's Football, Long Beach, USA, 4 October 2003 (Zurich: FIFA Archive).

31 D. Smith, 'On the ball with the beautiful game – here come the girls', Professional Footballers' Association, www.givemefootball.com (accessed 25 February 2011).

32 FIFA, 'Adriana Karembeu: A Passion for Women's Football: FIFA.com Caught Up with the Beautiful Game's Most Glamorous Standard-bearer', 3 January 2011, www.fifa.com/womensworldcup/news (accessed 2 November 2011).

33 B. Chastain, *It's Not about the Bra: Play Hard, Play Fair, and Put the Fun Back into Competitive Sports*, Harper Collins 2004, and the related website itsnotaboutthebra.com. See also L. Gregg, *The Champion Within: Training for Excellence* (Burlington: JTC Sports, 1999).

34 J. Williams, 'Women's Football, Europe and Professionalisation 1971–2011', unpublished UEFA-funded research project, De Montfort University (2011).

35 FIFA, 'FIFA Big Count 2006: 270 Million People Active in Football', fifa.com, 31 May 2007, www.fifa.com/aboutfifa/organisation/media/news/newsid=529882/index.html (accessed 15 January 2012).

HUW RICHARDS

The Game-Changers: Mia Hamm

Quite where cartoons fit into the equation that reckons a picture is worth 1,000 words is a matter for debate, but at their best they catch the zeitgeist with the crisp economy of both. The U.S. victory in the 1999 Women's World Cup final had few better memorials than Christopher Weyant of *The New Yorker* captioning his drawing of a girl talking to a boy beside a football pitch with the words 'Jason, I'd like to let you play, but you see it's a girls game'.[1]

The image of the moment was certainly Brandi Chastain triumphantly whirling her shirt above her head – revealing, not so coincidentally for some observers, a black Nike sports bra – after converting the decisive spot-kick in the penalty shoot-out that followed the drawn final against China. It was, though, Mia Hamm who gave her name to the largest building on the Nike campus and was, in the words of Grant Wahl, 'Not merely the face of a sport ... but the sound of it as well.' The soundtrack to American matches for much of her 18-year, 275-match, 158-goal international career was that of vast numbers of young fans, many wearing replicas of her no. 9 shirt and imitating her pony-tailed hairstyle, chanting 'Miiiiii-aaaaaa'.[2]

Her popularity has endured. Hamm can now literally be described as iconic, since her image was the logo for the latest, albeit failed, attempt to create a professional women's league in the United States. A Harris poll in 2010, six years after she retired, found that she was still the fourth most popular female athlete in the United States, surpassed only by the tennis-playing Williams sisters and the auto-racing driver Danica Patrick.[3]

While great sporting performers bestride their age, they also exemplify it. Much in Hamm's story is strictly personal: the birth in March 1972 with misshapen feet and bowed legs, the good fortune of spending much of her childhood with her U.S. Air Force family in soccer-conscious Italy and being spotted at 15 by national coach Anson Dorrance, who even then was struck by her 'incredible ability to shred people and get to the goals' and put her straight into the U.S. squad.[4]

None of this would have had much impact beyond the personal but for the unprecedented opportunities provided for women under Title IX, a 1972 Nixon administration measure demanding that federally funded education institutions devote equal funding to both sexes. Between 1972 and 2004 the number of female athletes taking part in high school sports multiplied seven times, from 290,000 to 2 million.[5] Soccer, as it is invariably called in the United States – where 'football' is reserved for the indigenous mutation of rugby – was the main sporting beneficiary. In 1981 there were 80 college teams; by 1999 there were 926.[6]

This created reservoirs of talent and fans. The talent came first as the United States won the initial World Cup in 1991 with Hamm – still at the University of North Carolina – playing in midfield. She and four team-mates – Chastain, Kristine Lilly, Julie Foudy and Joy Fawcett – played together in every major tournament until 2004. Team understanding, and giant totals of caps and goals, were enhanced by, in the absence for most of that time of a professional women's league, playing large numbers of international matches.

Support and recognition took a little longer. Those pioneering World Cup winners returned to 'a reception committee of three', while in 1996 NBC covered their Olympic final victory for only a few minutes before cutting away to rhythmic gymnastics.[7] But by 1999 the World Cup final packed out the Rose Bowl with 85,000 fans, while $40 tickets were scalped for $1,000. NBC's 40 million audience was twice as large as for the men's final played at the same venue in 1994.[8]

Hamm was both the symbol and chief beneficiary of this wave, by 1999 of sufficient celebrity to appear in adverts alongside basketball hero Michael Jordan, America's supreme male sports icon of the time. When in 2003 she married baseball player Nomar Garciaparra, then apparently destined for the Hall of Fame, it was unclear which partner brought greater stardust.

Why Hamm? It could be argued that dynamic midfielder Michelle Akers was a more accomplished player. Goalscorers are of course likely to be exalted in any footballing culture, with the additional possibility that her career totals were the number most obviously accessible and meaningful to a public accustomed to the statistical fixations of other U.S. sports.

Hamm did not pursue fame. Foudy recalled her as 'always team-first' and 'content to let other people take centre-stage'.[9] Wahl diagnosed 'exceptional talent laced with epic self-doubt' while *Sports Illustrated*, in a rare cover story featuring a woman in sports kit rather than a bikini, called her 'The Reluctant Superstar'.[10] But as Wangerin points out: 'The commercial appeal of a white, middle-class, graciously humble Olympic heroine was not lost on corporate America.'[11]

So she both bestrode and exemplified her times. She could not, though, transcend them. She contributed hugely to the WUSA professional league set up in 2001. Matches involving her Washington team attracted crowds conspicuously higher than the league's highly respectable average of 6,500.[12]

She remained a world-class player – FIFA's player of the year in 2001 and 2002, and second in 2004 when she retired along with Foudy and Fawcett after adding a second Olympic gold and carrying the U.S. flag at the closing ceremony. But her career outlived WUSA, suspended in 2003. It had, reckoned Wangerin, 'seemed to stem as much from emotion as much as solid business principles'.[13] Both television and, in consequence, potential commercial backers continued to be less impressed by live attendances than by research showing that the bulk of keen sports fans were men, who much preferred to watch male performers.[14]

It remains to be seen whether 1999 was a peak, or a mere step on an upward ascent for U.S. women's football. Either way Hamm, 'perhaps the most important female athlete of the last 15 years' for Michael Wilbon, and 'the first female team-sport superstar' for *Sports Illustrated*'s Gary Smith,[15] was an entirely logical choice of icon for Women's Professional Soccer, whose problems lay elsewhere.

NOTES

1   *The New Yorker*, 19 July 1999.
2   G. Wahl, 'A Woman in Full', *Sports Illustrated*, 20 September 2004.
3   G. Wahl, 'Mia Hamm Keeps Busy in Retirement', *Sports Illustrated*, 11 August 2010.
4   S. Guard, 'How to Hammstring the Opposition', *Sports Illustrated*, 14 December 1992.
5   'Last Hurrah for US Women', BBC Sport website, 3 September 2004, http: bbc. co.uk/sport/hi/football/world_football/3622770.stm (15 January 2012).
6   D. Wangerin, *Soccer in a Football World* (London: When Saturday Comes Books, 2006), p. 293.
7   Ibid., p. 291; G. Smith, 'The Secret Life of Mia Hamm', *Sports Illustrated*, 22 September 2003.
8   Wangerin, *Soccer in a Football World*, p. 300.
9   Wahl, 'A Woman in Full'.
10 G. Wahl, 'O Sole Mia', *Sports Illustrated*, 6 October 2003; *Sports Illustrated* cover, 22 September 2003.
11 Wangerin, *Soccer in a Football World*, p. 296.
12 Ibid., p. 311.
13 Ibid.
14 Ibid., p. 313.
15 Smith, 'The Secret Life of Mia Hamm'; Wilbon cited in D. Zirin, *What's My Name Fool? Sports and Resistance in the United States* (Chicago: Haymarket, 2005).

II

JOHN WILLIAMS

Fans: Consumers, Hooligans and Activists

The Destitution of Fandom

'Let's face it we all know it's sad.' The opening line from Liverpool FC fan Alan Edge's ruminations on the essential nature of late-modern football fandom. His is a neo-theological text, reflecting on an act of cultural devotion. And this is unquestionably a bad start. It immediately raises the unpleasant but undeniable possibility (routinely repeated) that a central outcome of much obsessive football watching is the righteous self-loathing it both promotes and rewards.[1] Edge goes on, 'The thing is, though, none of us have any say in it. It controls us and we can't do the slightest thing about it.' This is an overstatement, surely, a denial of free will itself. But here comes the killer line: 'The worst of it is none of us really want to anyway.'[2]

In short, being a committed football fan is – for Edge at least – to inherit the equivalent of a socio-cultural gene or be engulfed by a neo-religious tribal fervour: to be inducted into an addictive, blissful form of ecstatic torture, based on the exclusion of the 'other'. We all recognise this state, of course, one in which the object of obsessive fandom in the late-modern world has come to function, perhaps unhealthily, as a narcissistic extension of the self.[3] It also provides meaning for the apparently irrational insistence of a Boca Juniors fan in Buenos Aires that he be laid on his deathbed in the shirt of the rival River Plate club he had hated all his life. That way, he explained, he could celebrate with his final breath the death of 'one of them'.[4]

This may be a rather clichéd take on football support today – that it is only fully realised in relation to one's enemy and it feels so bad it must be good – but is certainly no unique view. A more recent fan's biography about football support in England, for example, argues that the inadequacy of one's chosen football club, allied to the collective emotional fan investment involved in its relative failure, can actually be more therapeutic and more rewarding than following any winning outfit. According to this view, adopting a *losing* club works best to stave off depression and other forms of mental illness.[5] 'The football fan is not just a watcher,' the perceptive Arthur Hopcraft observed. 'His [sic] sweat and his nerves work on football, and his spirit can be made rich or destitute by it.'[6] But mostly destitute.

Indeed, the Uruguayan football writer Eduardo Galeano has recently observed of the football fanatic that he is invariably hopelessly at sea: 'a fan in a madhouse. His mania for denying all evidence finally upended whatever once passed for his mind, and the remains of the shipwreck spin about aimlessly in waters whipped up by a fury that gives no quarter.'[7] This is a poetic way of outlining our collective inadequacy as sports fans. Edge goes on to relate the story of a foreign summer holiday which is entirely – irrationally – ruined when a single piece of news leaks out that a preferred transfer target has inexplicably refused to join *his* club, Liverpool, in the close season. Misery follows. How else are football supporters to know that they are truly alive, if not through contrasting the depthless misery of failure with the occasional unexpected flicker of real achievement? How else, indeed …

Another Liverpool fan, 'Nico', a continental Elvis Costello lookalike and a guy very well known to the club's most committed supporters, routinely travels from his home in the Low Countries to watch Reds matches. He follows Liverpool around the globe to improbable locations and 'meaningless' (but not for him) pre-season matches in the Far East and Asia. There are thousands of football supporters around the world like Nico. Who can make sense of their long-distance love? For such fans, the sheer scale of their spending of time and money on football signals an effective withdrawal from the formal logic of capitalist exchange in which use value has spiralled out of relation to exchange value.[8] Supporters like these will spend 10 times – or more – the face value of tickets to attend key matches. Who could blame them?

Locally based football fans often consider themselves to be 'superior' or more 'loyal' than distant travellers, asking why these intruders do not support their *own* domestic clubs?[9] But, perhaps counterintuitively, it is actually these committed foreign interlopers who also most often prize the importance of place, tradition and the 'local' in their adopted football clubs.[10] They snarl at the mention of intrusive sponsorships and 'inappropriate' fan styles; they typically reject the alleged 'prostitution' of the club brand, and the sale of stadium naming rights. They are also usually among the first onto the barricades to fight hostile buy-outs, or proposals from dubious owners to relocate a stadium from a cherished historic site. In short, they 'get' the significance of place and tradition in football, even if occasionally they are the schematic versions marketed at them by clubs.

All these global fan developments are part of the alleged recent 'Disneyisation' and 'McDonaldisation' of the elite levels of the sport in

England and elsewhere.[11] The fervour with which non-locals defend the local in this context implies that they may be darkly aware of suggestions that they might actually be ersatz 'day trippers' after all. That it is their own presence which most threatens what it is they claim to love so deeply. It is also a reminder – as if one were needed – that even the elite, the so-called super football clubs from the European game, continue to derive much of their meaning and especially their 'authenticity' – a key concept in recent debates about football fandom – from the fact that, in the end and even in an increasingly de-centred world, football clubs do, and must, always come from *somewhere*.[12]

When Is a Fan not a Fan?

In the earlier history of the professional game, when television coverage of football was either non-existent or severely curtailed almost everywhere, when club owners were usually local businessmen, major employers or minor public figures and were overwhelmingly frugal in their football affairs, and when club merchandising and corporate markets remained imaginary or little developed, expressing one's football fandom *outside* of match attendance and local connections was deeply problematic: there was simply no substitute for 'being there'. Active local supporters, additionally, often raised cash to help clubs build new stands and improve basic facilities.[13] Today, they are rather more likely to raise money for celebration and nostalgia; for the erection of commemorative football monuments and statues. But this arrangement, in which being a fan meant being local and physically present at matches, also worked culturally, in terms of providing opportunities for working people to generate a sense of meaningful collective place identity, and to engage directly with the sport and its stars – most of whom were still within touching range of their followers. Things have changed.

It is easy of course to make the mistake that everything in the game is different for football fans today; to focus only on the elite, the global and the 'new', and to miss the crucial continuities of the local role of football in 'everyday life'.[14] But the term 'fan' or 'supporter' is a label which is palpably no longer easily confined these days to those who live locally and/or who turn up to watch football directly inside the stadium. Since the late-1980s what academics have called the 'hyper-commodification' of elite-level football has been fuelled by huge and different volumes of new capital from oligarchs, TV companies and an array of sponsors. It has also produced a distinctive new set of social and cultural relations around the sport and new forms of cultural encoding of football, mainly orchestrated via the impact of new media technologies.[15]

As a result, message boards, fan blogs and fanzine forums, game updates and, most importantly of all, consumption-powered club websites, real time and match highlight Internet coverage (both official and illicit), and also the extensive selling of football TV rights abroad have all extended the global reach of the larger European clubs. They have 'fans' around the world today. All this has occurred in an era characterised by the growing importance and volume of de-territorialised communication flows and the decline of the regulatory impact of more traditional national cultural and economic institutions. According to some theorists, the major football clubs in Europe are becoming the nodes of a new European 'network society', one based much more on a constant flux of interactions between these powerful global actors than the much more static 'state-centred' worldview implies.[16]

As a result of these changes, signs of familiar football affinities can now crop up in strange and disarming locations: witness the recent armed anti-Gaddafi rebels in Libya advancing on Tripoli wearing – you guessed it – English Premier League and Italian La Liga replica football shirts. To give another, more benign, example, in January 2007 around 75,000 people watched 'live' a Manchester United v Arsenal Premier League match at Old Trafford. Up to 6 million more watched the match on BSkyB TV in the United Kingdom, with an estimated 2 million more tuned in via the 40,000 pubs and clubs taking the live coverage. But the match was also televised 'live' in another 201 countries, a reported global reach into 613 million homes worldwide.[17] In this sense, the cultural meaning of football – and of fandom – has been rapidly transforming.

New Dimensions of Football Fandom

These sorts of statistics and relationships, of course, are often dismissed by traditionalists and domestic live football attenders as being essentially consumer-based and therefore peripheral to their own much deeper engagement with their respective local football clubs. Family ties and connections of place are still most strongly prized here. But such developments are actually implicated in producing a much more complex range of different, new fan types which now demand our urgent attention.

Amir Ben Porat, for example, argues that local fandom as a source of identity formation in the Israeli *Primer League* is indeed assailed by the impact of globalisation and the seductive appeal of the stronger European football clubs – but even in this new competitive context it manages somehow to survive. It is formed out of three interconnected domains of experience which produce a 'bounded' or indestructible 'cradle to the grave' form of local football fandom, one which is in near-constant tension with other identity struts involving relations with work, family members and friends. Expressing true support of this kind means a fandom with no real exit: a *real* fan cannot shop for another, superior model.[18]

These domains collectively constitute a practice of identity around football that is also familiar elsewhere. They are the *emotional-affective* domain, in which football acts as a mechanism that moulds individual fans into a satisfying and secure collective; the *cognitive* domain, which divides fans in terms of their levels of commitment to clubs between passive and involved, between the 'we' and the 'they'; and the *symbolic* experience in which fandom might embody locally specific social categories or relations – for example, the way in which support for Glasgow Rangers in Scotland might embody Protestantism, or that following Bnei Sachnin (an Israeli Arab club) is likely to embody locally important ethnicity/nationalist sentiments and attachments.[19]

The American cultural studies theorist John Fiske (1992) takes a rather different route in delineating the meaning of late-modern fandom. He contends we must analyse different types of fan *productivity* to understand what it means to be a fan and to make sense of how fans act upon – and thus also help to 'create' – the object of their fandom. Firstly, he identifies *semiotic* fandom: the creation of meaning involved in the fan's individual relationship with and consumption of the text (in this case, the club, match or home stadium). No matter how standardized the match experience or the home stadium might seem to non-fans, it is its supporters who occupy and transform stadia into places and events of particular emotional significance.[20]

Secondly, *enunciative* fandom has its roots in the creative appropriation and use by fans of club merchandise and also in the social interaction and fan talk which occurs around the game, in bars, pubs and the homes of fans and on the slew of supporter phone-in shows on radio and television.[21] Finally, *textual* fandom involves the materials or texts (songs, fanzines, websites, blogs and other materials) which are now routinely produced by football fans. Even in the digital age, the capacity to craft a chorus of original songs is still regarded in supporter circles as an important signifier of cultural distinction.[22] In some instances, football songs can renegotiate collective identities and also be wielded as tools of domination, both culturally and physically, for example in hooligan conflicts or to intimidate rival spectators.[23]

These three dimensions of fandom combine to make a sort of crucible in which the mass culture of football consumption is turned into the popular culture of socially meaningful football club support.[24]

The sociologist Richard Giulianotti has also usefully begun to explore these new possibilities for fandom in the global era, firstly by examining the ways in which globally displaced communities of fans work creatively in unfamiliar cultures to maintain their original club ties,[25] and then by producing a useful fan typology drawn across 'traditional/consumer' horizontal and 'hot/cool' vertical axes. He highlights, for example, contrasts between the 'hot'/traditional match attender, and the 'cool' consumer football *flaneur* of today: someone who has a casual and rather distant relationship to the game, and an identity established 'through a depersonalized set of market relations, particularly interactions with the cool media of television and the Internet'.[26]

Despite their obvious sophistication, these new fandom accounts still seem somewhat fixed. They lack the required flexibility and specificities to be able to accommodate the wide range of fandoms and variations in existing attachment to clubs. As Tom Clarke puts it, in relation to an English football minnow: 'What it means to be "Scunthorpe 'til I die" will vary from person to person: the re-located student, industrial worker, the out-of-towner, will all have different experiences of being Scunthorpe, despite the town's shared identity.'[27] Such accounts also often seem to be talking only or largely about *male* fans, when we know that today's growing band of female football supporters express their own subjectivity as fans in ways that make it clear that they do not fit comfortably into either the traditional/authentic supporter couplet, or its opposite, the new consumer/inauthentic arriviste.[28]

Cornell Sandvoss identifies the peculiarly self-reflective quality of football fandom which accounts for some of the 'cognitive' distinctions identified earlier by Ben Porat and the fact that following a particular football club may mean very different things to different fans.[29] Supporter loyalties in the era of global television sport and increased social and geographical mobility are rather more complex than is suggested by the conventional wisdom that all fans will 'support you ever-more'.[30] Much football support today is selective, contingent and insecure; the game is a product to be marketed and sold and although most supporters reject the type of marketing rhetoric that seeks to reduce their status to 'customer', they also exhibit a pragmatic accommodation to football's hyper-commercialization.[31]

But Sandvoss has also argued, convincingly, that in a period of increasingly 'mobile privatization' characterized by the impact of globalisation and by the profound restructuring of everyday (post-) industrial life in developed societies, football fandom has, necessarily, also had to perform much more important identity work than in the past, evoking emotionally significant notions of 'home'.[32] As Chris Stone and others have similarly argued, the recent loss in developed societies of the social anchors that once made identity seem 'natural' and 'non-negotiable' has meant a desperate search for a 'we' experience through football club support.[33]

Recent empirical research on football fans in England would seem to confirm the importance for fans of seeing and experiencing the local football stadium as an emotionally 'special place' and one which is indeed evocative of these deep and intensive feelings of 'home'.[34] Hooligan fans also often enhance their reputation for 'hardness' and local loyalty of course by stoutly defending the 'home' patch from outsiders. A recent, different, example of the intensity of such 'home' affiliations is the case of supporters of SV Hamburg in Germany who successfully established a supporters' cemetery a mere 50 metres from the club stadium. 'If you think about people supporting a club for 30, 40, 50 years, it's part of their life,' commented stonemason Uli Beppler, 'so why shouldn't it be part of their death?'[35]

The Age of the Virtual Fan

Suggestions by Richard Giulianotti and others that 'global media' football fans are somehow less committed or less engaged by their clubs than other supporters – are 'cooler' in their support – have recently been challenged by researchers who have begun to explore the intensive new virtual networks of football fan cultures.[36] In fact, the English Premier League (EPL) recently floated the idea of hosting a '39th' fixture in a range of market-appropriate locations abroad, thus rendering local fans – temporarily at least – as 'virtual' spectators. The response was less than positive. No matter: the idea was soon ridiculed by the man who had proposed it, the EPL chief executive Richard Scudamore, as 'old fashioned and passé'.

Instead, he told the world's press that new 'immersion technology' would soon offer global football fans of the EPL the simulated '*Avatar*' experience of actually 'being in the stadium'. All this was allied to the ultimate proposition in terms of consumer choice – the satellite TV match choice red button: 'You could be on a Saturday evening in Hong Kong, 3pm in England, deciding whether you want to be on the Kop or in the Holte End at Aston Villa. You'll be able to decide where you want to be and watch the game,' explained Scudamore in August 2011. 'The possibilities are endless. There could be cafes and bars creating a virtual reality stadium, with tickets being sold to use the technology for those who do not subscribe.'[37]

Even 'endless possibilities' can never satisfy unregulated desire, and we are already in the era in which high ticket prices and increasingly passive stadia mean that football spectators' demand for immediate proximity to the event – the 'being there' element – is being challenged, and possibly even replaced for some, by the attractions of a rather different fan experience. Watching on giant screens in chaotic football fan parks or collectively gathering in pubs and bars may no longer routinely be regarded as second best to the experience of hyper-regulated and sterile football arenas.[38]

The EPL's vision of virtual fandom – reportedly only a few years away – will also offer credence to the 'boosterism' claims made on behalf of elite European clubs about the sheer *scale* of their international cultural influence and the scope of their new economic power. Manchester United are argued to have some 331 million fans worldwide, including 9.5 million Facebook fans.[39] These sorts of extravagant claims are limited to a small number of European super-clubs, of course, but available technology and the devouring ambitions of sponsors mean that such potential global exposure is actually no longer confined to the giants of the game. In August 2011, for example, a preliminary English FA Cup tie between two minor non-league clubs was streamed live on Facebook by competition sponsors Budweiser, thus making it available, free of charge, to a potential global audience of some 700 million.[40] In the internet age even very local football can become global.

More significantly perhaps, in 2007 the MyFootballClub (MYFC) website offered football fans around the world direct involvement in the management of a *real* football club – the non-League outfit Ebbsfleet United in Gravesend in the United Kingdom. Some 32,000 members drawn from 70 countries initially subscribed, thus allowing MYFC to use digital media to 'camp in the front garden of its subscribers'.[41] MYFC bought control of Ebbsfleet and promised a synthesis of 'grass roots' and 'high tech' in intimate connections with an 'organic' local football club, thus subverting, it was argued, the era of football oligarchs, culturally distant millionaire players and multi-billion-pound TV contracts. In fact, of course, MYFC was doing something much more complex and contradictory: it placed digital media technology 'at the centre of its claims that it revives lost football supporter traditions, the very demise of which have been attributed to the growth and influence of media.'[42] MYFC struggled to maintain its legitimacy as Ebbsfleet flat-lined: by June 2011 subscribers had fallen to a reported new low of 1,350.

The Price Is(not) Right

Actually, in societies characterised by this sort of vortex of media effects, even physically *being* at the match today – something beyond the wildest dreams, of course, of the vast majority of these global fans, hangers-on and new internet investors – can itself seem like an increasingly surreal and profoundly mediated sporting experience. Post-modern stadia (including weather-free, roofed venues) which attempt to replicate the safety and individualised consumer comforts of home and where spectators are also watched, micro-managed under the silent gaze of closed circuit TV cameras, can feel like very rarified spaces. One recent convert likened attending a European club match in England to 'going to the theatre or opera, and with similar prices'.[43] Academic and fan organizer Rogan Taylor has suggested instead that the new regimes of control by culture, price and surveillance have meant the increasingly precarious presence of 'ordinary people who must be stretching to afford it' and the relative exclusion of both older and younger fans.[44] But such developments have also marginalised another figure: the football hooligan.

English hooligans were a role model in the 1970s and 1980s for young fans in Holland and Germany and for 'radical' members of organised *ultra* fan groups in Italy and supporter *penas* in Spain.[45] The hooligan nadir for the English came at the Heysel stadium in 1985, when 39 mainly Italian fans were killed at the European Cup final following a charge by Liverpool supporters and a stadium wall collapse. English clubs were banned from European competition.[46] The later television-funded reconstitution of the English game in the 1990s as a fashionable cultural product meant that hooligans were also squeezed: by price, by video technology, and by the new safety cultures of all-seated stadia, as well as by police intelligence gathering and even new 'dialogue and facilitation' approaches to managing hooligan gangs.[47] Fan conflict in England was increasingly displaced to lower leagues, to locations away from the stadium and out of the cameras' glare – but also into the symbolic realm of the internet and popular media.[48] Meanwhile, the epicentre of the hooligan phenomenon in Europe had moved south and east.

In Italy, for example, organised and expressive fan violence, extremism and racism among *ultras* continue to dog the game, threatening both its popularity and safety.[49] In the Balkans and in parts of the old Eastern Europe, meanwhile, the strains of new nationhood, high unemployment and the re-emergence of old ethnic divisions in extremist political clothes both dramatise and feed hooligan outbreaks. In Poland, youth alienation is argued to be a key cause of rising hooliganism,[50] while in October 2010 political orchestration from Belgrade was said to be behind the abandonment of a Euro 2012 qualifier between Italy and Serbia after widespread nationalist-inspired violence and Albanian flag-burning by known Serbian hooligans and agitators.[51]

In September 2011 the Turkish football authorities inventively highlighted the problematic masculinities that continue to lie at the heart of football hooligan cultures all over the world. After crowd trouble at Fenerbahce, the Turkish FA banned all adult male fans from the club's next home match – which attracted instead an enthusiastic, well-behaved crowd of 41,000 women and children. Perhaps there was an alternative, after all, to stadium Disneyisation, ticket price rises and intensive video surveillance for countries still riddled by hooliganism.[52]

At club level, twenty-first-century ticket prices in Europe were being impressively restrained in some places – the German Bundesliga, for example, has large, flexible and peaceful standing terraces and a modernist regulatory and licensing model as a stabilising feature, producing Europe's largest average and most varied football crowds in the process.[53] In Italy, Spain and especially in England, however, elite football had embraced more the core values of neo-liberal globalisation and marketization – with global player rosters, stratospheric salaries and ticket prices to match. England leads the way here, with match ticket prices in the EPL climbing over a 20-year period for some clubs by a staggering 1,025 per cent. By 2011 the average age of all live EPL attenders had climbed to a decidedly middle-aged 41.[54]

Living the Football Life

But this 'post-modern' tale of television, commercialization, globalisation and exclusion is not the whole story, of course. Football remains deeply embedded in the daily lives of millions of 'ordinary' local people, young and old. The game continues to carry prized memories of embodied shared experience and place, and its influence extends into homes, workplaces and public spaces, connecting supporters within and across spatial boundaries.[55] Millions of supporters of clubs outside the elite levels – and many within them – continue to experience and enjoy football as a lifetime version of 'serious leisure', one still defined largely by ties of family and place, and where the material costs to individuals of group membership continue to exceed their visible rewards.[56] At lower levels, too, football fans remain deeply committed to more local, less marketized, forms of the game, often derogating the affluent clubs and the global 'network leagues' that are more obviously driven and directed, not by fans and local interests, but by global sponsors and television.[57]

Indeed, we have already examined the enduring *emotional* importance of football for its committed followers in an increasingly uncertain world and how football fans display a realist acceptance of the game's commercial tropes, but they also hold on to their own affective, non-market understanding of their identities as fans.[58] And when this tension becomes simply too great, there has been both accommodation but also brave resistance among fans around the globe to football's recent excessive commodification. Creative accommodation has occurred, for example, in the ways in which mediated versions of football – in pubs and bars – have become a favoured site for excluded fans symbolically to re-enact and re-invent a 'lost' and mythologized standing terrace culture.[59]

However, the existing 'membership' models of spectator engagement and the democratic fan involvement at some of the larger clubs in Spain and elsewhere in Europe – in Germany, foreign ownership is still largely resisted and clubs are run as members associations in which supporters hold 51 per cent of the shares – have not yet been replicated in England. They may never be. But at many smaller English clubs, new patterns of involvement of supporters in running, or even owning, clubs, in the shape of government-backed Supporter Trusts, have produced a potentially progressive new dynamic and a local community focus. But even these are not free from contradictions and the charge that they often end up being incorporated into the commercial activities of the club hierarchies they seek to replace.[60]

At a few larger European clubs, protesting supporters have also had some recent successes. The *Spirit of Shankly* fan group played a part, in 2010, in ridding the Liverpool club of the ownership shackles of the Americans, Tom Hicks and George Gillett, though the global economic downturn did much of the crucial work.[61] At neighbours and rivals Manchester United, a 'resistance identity', as Castells might describe it, has emerged among some fans in response to the ownership of the club by new American (dis)investors, the Glazer family.[62] This opposition has been manifested in the formation of an entirely new club, FC United of Manchester, initially as a protest against the alleged corporate destruction of more organic football affinities. Following the apparent fracturing of fan communities around United – though the club has quickly replenished its lost support – new formations have emerged. The club marketing rhetoric of 'customer base' seems wholly inadequate to describe the cultural democracy at FC United, which is now rising fast up the English league structure.[63]

These local patriotisms and fierce struggles, co-ordinated by fans, over the 'ownership' and meaning of some of the world's most valuable and important football clubs confirms the enduring significance of the *affective* ties that bind, even at the very largest outfits. But it also illustrates that football fandom, especially today in the newly globalized world of sport, comes in an increasing number of sizes and forms: from the friendship and family groups active at the smallest local football clubs to the foot soldiers and leaders of the *ultras*, *penas* and kops at the European super-clubs; from the committed local attender to the distant internet observer; and from the obsessive fanatic to the more casual football *flaneur*.

But it is also true that in the bafflingly complex and rarefied domain of late-modern football fandom, supporters of all football clubs, big and small, old and new, distant and local, will probably continue to characterize the elusive and still highly prized notion of fan 'authenticity' in pretty traditional and reassuringly comforting ways. In other words, 'by looking into a metaphorical mirror and defining their own traits and habits'.[64] And, ultimately, all supporters know – and Liverpool's Alan Edge is as good a judge as any on this – that even in the digital age of mediation and simulacrum, for the 11 heroes on the field to consider playing *without* their fans in the stands in the future is really like dancing without music.[65]

NOTES

1 M. Hyde, 'Forget the freebies, keep us in misery', *Guardian*, 1 September 2011.

2 A. Edge, *Faith of Our Fathers: Football as a Religion* (Edinburgh: Mainstream, 1997), p. 5.

3 C. Sandvoss, *Fans: The Mirror of Consumption* (Cambridge: Polity Press, 2005), p. 16.

4 E. Galeano, *Football in Sun and Shadow* (London: Fourth Estate, 2003), p. 109.

5 J. Crace, *Vertigo: One Football Fan's Fear of Success* (London: Constable, 2011).

6 A. Hopcraft, *The Football Man* (Harmondsworth: Penguin, 1971), p. 197.

7 Galeano, *Football in Sun and Shadow*, p. 7.

8 Sandvoss, *Fans: The Mirror of Consumption*, pp. 115–16.

9 S. Bridgewater, *Football Brands* (Basingstoke: Palgrave Macmillan, 2010), p. 143.

10 R. Nash, 'Globalised Football Fandom: Scandinavian Liverpool FC Supporters', *Football Studies*, 3, 2 (2000), 5–23.

11 V. Duke, 'Local Tradition versus Globalisation: Resistance to the McDonaldisation and Disneyisation of Professional Football in England', *Football Studies*, 5, 3 (2002), 5–23.

12 R. Giulianotti and R. Robertson, 'The Globalisation of Football: A Study in the Globalisation of Serious Life', *British Journal of Sociology*, 55, 4 (2004), 545–68.

13 R. Taylor, *Football and Its Fans: Supporters and Their Relations with the Game* (London: Leicester University Press, 1992).

14 C. Stone, 'The Role of Football in Everyday Life', *Soccer and Society*, 8, 2/3 (2007), 176.

15 R. Giulianotti, 'Supporters, Followers, Fans and Flaneurs: A Taxonomy of Spectator Identities in Football', *Journal of Sport and Social Issues*, 26, 1 (2002), 29.

16 R. Levermore and P. Millward, 'Official Policies and Informal Transversal Networks: Creating "Pan-European Identifications" through Sport?', *Sociological Review*, 55, 1 (2007), 150.

17 'Premiership's worldwide pot of gold', *Independent*, 23 January 2007.

18 A. Margalit, '"You'll Never Walk Alone": On Property, Community and Football Fans', *Theoretical Inquiries in Law* 10 (2008), 226–27.

19 A. Ben Porat, 'Football Fandom: A Bounded Identification', *Soccer and Society*, 11, 3 (2010), 277–90.

20 Sandvoss, *Fans: The Mirror of Consumption*, p. 59.

21 J. Williams, 'Protect Me From What I Want: Football Fandom, Celebrity Cultures and "New" Football In England', *Soccer and Society* 7, 1 (2006), 96–114.

22 P. Schoonderwoerd, '"Shall We Sing a Song for You?": Mediation, Migration and Identity in Football Chants and Fandom', *Soccer and Society* 12, 1 (2011), 132.

23 B. Power, 'Justice for the Ninety-six: Liverpool FC Fans and Uncommon Use of a Football Song', *Soccer and Society*, 12, 1 (2011), 42–43; T. Clarke, 'I'm Scunthorpe 'til I Die: Constructing and (Re)Negotiating Identity through a Terrace Chant', *Soccer and Society*, 7, 4 (2006), 504.

24 Sandvoss, *Fans: The Mirror of Consumption*, p. 43.

25 R. Giulianotti, 'Sport Spectators and the Social Consequences of Commodification: Critical Perspectives from Scottish Football', *Journal of Sport and Social Issues*, 29, 4 (2005), 386–410.

26 Giulianotti, 'Supporters, Followers, Fans and Flaneurs', p. 38.

27 Clarke, 'I'm Scunthorpe 'til I Die', 500.

28 S. Pope, '"Like Pulling Down Durham Cathedral and Building a Brothel": Women as "New Consumer" Fans', *International Review for the Sociology of Sport*, 8 (2010), 13, http://irs.sagepub.com/content/early/2010/10/07/10126902 10384652.

29 C. Sandvoss, *A Game of Two Halves: Football Fandom, Television and Globalisation* (London: Routledge, 2003).

30 A. Tapp, 'The Loyalty of Football Fans – We'll Support You Evermore?' *Database Marketing and Customer Strategy Management*, 11, 3 (2004), 212.

31 Giulianotti, 'Sport Spectators and the Social Consequences of Commodification', p. 406.

32 Sandvoss, *Fans: The Mirror of Consumption*.

33 Stone, 'The Role of Football in Everyday Life', p. 179; K. Dixon, 'A "Third Way" for Football Fandom Research: Anthony Giddens and Structuration Theory', *Soccer and Society* 12, 2 (2011), 279–98.

34 S. Charleston, 'The English Football Ground as a Representation of Home', *Journal of Environmental Psychology*, 29 (2009), 144–50.

35 Margalit, 'You'll Never Walk Alone', p. 222.

36 T. Gibbons and K. Dixon, '"Surf's Up!": A Call to Take English Soccer Interactions on the Internet More Seriously', *Soccer and Society* 11, 5 (2010), 599–613.

37 J. Burt, 'Premier League to Enter the Avatar Age', *Daily Telegraph,* 3 August 2011.

38 J. Bale, 'Virtual Fandoms: Futurescapes of Football' in A. Brown (ed.), *Fanatics! Power, Identity and Fandom in Football* (London: Routledge, 1998), pp. 265–78.

39 Forbes, 'The World's Most Valuable Sports Team'(2011), www.forbes.com/ pictures/mli45fdhk/no-1-manchester-united.

40 R. Bagchi, 'FA tie to be broadcast on Facebook by sponsor', *Guardian Sport*, 18 August 2011, p. 5.

41 A. Ruddock, B. Hutchins and D. Rowe, 'Contradictions in Media Sport Culture: The Re-Inscription of Football Supporter Traditions through On-Line Media', *European Journal of Cultural Studies*, 13, 3 (2010), 328.

42 Ibid., p. 325.

43 D. Orr, 'My trip to the Arsenal game was more like a night at the theatre than a football match', *Guardian*, 18 August 2011.

44 D. Conn, 'Young fans and old pay biggest price for football inflation', *Guardian Sport*, 17 August 2011.

45 R. Spaaij and C. Vinas, 'Passion, Politics and Violence: A Socio-Historical Analysis of Spanish Ultras', *Soccer and Society* 6, 1 (2005), 79–96.

46 J. Williams, *Red Men: Liverpool Football Club the Biography* (Edinburgh: Mainstream, 2010), pp. 368–71.

47 J. Williams, 'The Cost of Safety in Risk Societies', *Journal of Forensic Psychology*, 12, 1 (2001), 1–7; C. Stott, J. Hoggett and G. Pearson (2011), 'Keeping the Peace: Social Identity, Procedural Justice and the Policing of Football Crowds', *British Journal of Criminology* (2011), 14.

48 E. Poulton, '"Fantasy Football Hooliganism" in Popular Media', *Media, Culture and Society*, 29, 1 (2006), 151–64.

49 D. Gould and J. Williams, 'After Heysel: How Italy Lost the Football "Peace"', *Soccer and Society*, 12, 5 (2001), 586–601; M. Guschwan, 'Riot in the Curve: Soccer Fans in Twenty-first century Italy', *Soccer and Society*, 8, 2/3 (2007), 250–66.

50 P. Piotrowski, 'Coping with Football-Related Hooliganism: Healing Symptoms versus Cause Prevention', *Journal of Applied Psychology*, 36, 3 (2006), 629–43.

51 P. Bandini, 'Italy v Serbia called off after seven minutes due to crowd trouble', *Guardian*, 13 October 2010.

52 L. Taylor, 'Women and children first, with the men nowhere, works at Fenerbahce', *Guardian Sport*, 21 September 2011.

53 J. Jackson, 'How the Bundesliga puts the Premier League to shame', *Observer Sport*, 11 April 2010, Section 8.

54 Conn, 'Young fans and old pay biggest price for football inflation'.

55 Stone, p. 181; Clarke, 'Scunthorpe 'til I Die'; Dixon, 'A Third Way for Football Fandom Research'.

56 I. Jones, 'A Model of Serious Leisure Identification: The Case of Football Fandom', *Leisure Studies*, 19 (2000), 293–98.

57 Clarke, 'Scunthorpe 'til I Die'; Jones, 'A Model of Serious Leisure Identification'.

58 Giulianotti, 'Sports Spectators and the Social Consequences of Commodification', p. 405; D. Kennedy and P. Kennedy, 'Towards a Marxist Political Economy of Football Supporters', *Capital and Class*, 34, 2 (2010), 181–98.

59 Ibid.; M. Weed, 'Exploring the Sports Spectator Experience: Virtual Football Spectatorship in the Pub', *Soccer and Society*, 9, 2 (2008), 189–97.

60 D. Kennedy and P. Kennedy, 'Preserving and Extending the Commodification of Football Supporter Relations: A Cultural Economy of Supporters Direct', *Sociological Research Online*, 12, 1 (2007), 4.4. Available online at www.socresonline.org.uk/12/1/kennedy.html.

61 J. Williams and S. Hopkins, '"Over Here": "Americanisation" and the New Politics of Football Club Ownership – the Case of Liverpool FC', *Sport in Society*, 14, 2 (2011), 160–74.

62 M. Castells, *The Power of Identity* (Oxford: Wiley-Blackwell, 2009), pp. 8–10; P. Millward, *The Global Football League: Transnational Networks, Social Movements and Sport in the New Media Age* (Basingstoke: Palgrave McMillan, 2011).

63 A. Brown, '"Not for Sale?" The Destruction and Reformation of Football Communities in the Glazer Takeover of Manchester United', *Soccer and Society*, 8, 4 (2007), 624.

64 J. Rockwood and P. Millward, '"We All Dream of a Team of Carraghers": Comparing "Local" and Texan Liverpool Fan Talk', *Sport in Society*, 14, 1 (2011), 48.

65 Galeano, *Football in Sun and Shadow*, p. 6.

ROB STEEN

The Game-Changers: Franz Beckenbauer

The best teams never to win the World Cup were by general consent Hungary in 1954 and Holland in 1974. That the unexpected victors, in both instances, wore white and black may well be the most resplendent of the many feathers in the cap that sits so jauntily on the head of German football. Hungarians have cause to grouse about the teeming rain and sodden pitch in Berne – and there have been allegations that some members of Sepp Herberger's side were injected with a stimulant, pervetin[1] – but they and the Dutch were both out-thought as much as outplayed. That the German captain on the second occasion was Franz Beckenbauer, the Caliph of Cool, was in no sense a coincidence.

No nation, not even Brazil, has appeared in more World Cup finals than Germany's seven. No nation has appeared in more semi-finals than their remarkably clean dozen. Yet the German contribution to football is often downplayed, a curious state of affairs attributable, perhaps, to the fact that no sensible German would ever characterise the game as beautiful. To Bavarians and Hamburgers and Westphalians, it is a test of skill, strategy and strength, of head and heart, body and soul. As an emblem of the country's post-1945 re-invention, nothing, not even Adi Dassler's stripes or Levi Strauss's jeans, stands prouder.

For all the counterevidence supplied by Einstein, Beethoven, Göethe, Albrecht Dürer, Werner Herzog, Rainer Werner Fassbinder and the Hutter brothers, few populations have been subjected to quite as many thoughtlessly stilted characterisations as Germany's. Tacitus's infamous *Germania* may have inspired the Third Reich but its Roman author never felt obliged to actually visit those strange northern territories. In the last third of the twentieth century, planet sport was invaded and graced by three very different German sportsmen – Beckenbauer, Boris Becker and Michael Schumacher, sons, respectively, of a post office worker, an architect and a bricklayer. Schumacher was the most dominant, the most willing to flout the rules,

Becker the most athletic and apt to shock, Beckenbauer the one hailed as an 'unrivalled moral authority'.[2]

Beckenbauer's countrymen came to see him as 'Der Kaiser' after he was photographed at a post-match banquet in Vienna standing next to a bust of Emperor Franz-Joseph (a magazine, indeed, had previously likened him to the eccentric Bavarian King Ludwig).[3] During the 1974 World Cup he averted strike action by persuading his fellow players to accept bonuses of DM70,000 per man, some way below the six-figure sums promised by the Italian and Dutch FAs. One *Financial Times* reporter characterized him as 'the imperial smoothie'.[4]

Affection, nonetheless, was not unconfined. He alienated the German Left, supporting the conservative Christian Democratic Union, and had a symbiotic relationship with the widely reviled Bayern Munich, a provincial club-turned-superpower and the chief symbol of how German football was beginning to shed its 'regional-cultural embodiment' amid the political upheavals of the 1970s, an era that witnessed an economic surge by a once-agrarian state, Bavaria, and, especially, Munich, Germany's 'secret cultural capital'.[5] Bayern, the most dominant single club in any major football nation over the past 50 years, and by extension Beckenbauer, 'a culturally provocative figure',[6] divided national opinion in a manner perhaps rivalled only by their counterparts in Spain and Scotland.

With the ball at his feet, invisible baton in hand, the default view elsewhere was awe. Among de facto post-1945 defenders, only Bobby Moore exuded such command. My first sighting came during the BBC's monochrome coverage of the 1966 World Cup group match between West Germany and Switzerland. The trim, dark mane, lean frame and certainty of movement hinted at inner balance and precocious poise. Surging forward as if on castors, he executed a nimble one-two then tucked his shot beyond the goalkeeper with a self-assurance that bordered on disdain: a first impression that proved utterly reliable. If some regarded him as naïve, as Ulrich Hesse-Lichtenberger testified in his engrossing history of German football, *tor!*, nothing Beckenbauer has ever done in a footballing capacity has betrayed the remotest hint of self-doubt, not even when he damaged a shoulder and played on with his right arm in a sling during the epic 1970 World Cup semi-final against Italy.

As such, he symbolized German football, Europe's dominant force for most of the twentieth-century's final quarter. In 1974, Bayern won the Bundesliga and the first of three consecutive European Cups while supplying more than half the national side. Bassett's would have been proud of such allsorts: magisterial Beckenbauer; the lithe if mildly potty Sepp Maier, goalkeeper and glove pioneer; Paul Breitner, the Maoist with the Black

Panther afro; clever Uli Hoeness and his mad professorial blond hair; Georg Schwarzenbeck, a bird-dog of a full-back, and that impossibly stealthy thiever of goals, Gerd Muller. Throw in Günter Netzer from Bayern's chief rivals, Borussia Mönchengladbach, et voila, raved *L'Equipe* after England had been dissected and discarded at Wembley, here was football 'from the year 2000'[7]. A triumph, some might say, for the anti-Teutonic Way.

Trailblazer

Widely cited as the first attacking sweeper, or libero, Beckenbauer was 20 when he helped West Germany reach the 1966 World Cup final, exhibiting close control, a searching pass, crisp shooting and a brand of acute positional awareness that yielded interceptions rather than necessitating tackles. Schön, however, assigned him to mark Bobby Charlton – a negative statement and a craven waste. The coach did not make the same mistake twice. Six years later, Beckenbauer held aloft the European Nations Cup after the hosts had thrashed Russia 3–0 with an irresistible display that typified Rinus Michels' 'Total Football', a concept that flowered during the Dutchman's time coaching Ajax and Holland but which made the Germans (creative director F. Beckenbauer) the brand leaders. Michels credited Beckenbauer with trailblazing two new formations – 5–3–2, the 'defensive variation', and 3–5–2, the 'building-up variation'.[8] The notion of two man-markers in the middle backed up by a mobile sweeper was his, as was the full-back entrusted, whether in attack or defence, with patrolling an entire flank.

Beckenbauer, moreover, remains proudly alone in captaining and managing a World Cup–winning team (Mario Zagallo, the Brazilian, is the only other man to play in and manage both). This, though, said less about his coaching qualifications (none) than the unquestioning way he was regarded. In fact, in the wake of the national side's dismal performance at the 1984 European Championships – which had moved the French newspaper *Liberation* to suggest that 'the brute animal' of German football 'deserved to be drowned in its own urine' – it took a story fabricated by his agent (in *Bild*, Germany's biggest-selling tabloid, headlined 'Franz: I am ready') to coax him to take over as manager. Latterly, he led his country's bid to host the 2006 World Cup, devised new playing formations and continued, as an ambassador, television pundit and newspaper columnist, to exert a considerable grip on footballing perceptions.

At FIFA's centennial annual congress in 2004, Beckenbauer and Pelé were both awarded the organisation's highest honour, its Centennial Order of Merit. As a twin nod to science and art, it seemed one of that body's less debatable decisions.

NOTES

1   Reuters, 'West Germany's 1954 World Cup win may have been drug-fuelled, says study', *Guardian*, 27 October 2010, www.guardian.co.uk/football/2010/oct/27/west-germany-1954-drugs-study (accessed 15 January 2012).
2   U. Merkel, 'The 1974 and 2006 World Cups in Germany: Commonalities, Continuities and Changes', *Soccer and Society*, 7, 1 (2006), 14–28, www.informaworld.com/10.1080/14660970500355553.
3   U. Hesse-Lichtenberger, *tor! The Story of German Football* (London: WSC Books, 2003).
4   P. Chapman, *The Goalkeeper's History of Britain* (London: Fourth Estate, 1999), p. 279.
5   W. Pytra, 'German Football: A Cultural History' in A. Tomlinson and C. Young (eds.), *German Football: History, Soccer, Society and the World Cup 2006* (Oxon: Routledge, 2006), p. 16, http://books.google.co.uk/books.
6   Ibid.
7   Hesse-Lichtenberger, *tor! The Story of German Football*.
8   R. Michels, *Team Building – the Road to Success* (Spring City, PA: Reedswain, 2001), p. 44.

12

ROB STEEN

Sheepskin Coats and Nannygoats: The View from the Pressbox

Much football writing is done when the reporter is in a state of some excitement, when the din of a huge crowd is making his temples twang. This was not the sweet, contemplative atmosphere in which cricket reporters may place their adverbs with the infinite care of a late cut. The football reporter is frequently frozen to the bone, so that words become petrified in his head like that famous toothpaste tube advertised in a block of ice. Press boxes are not the ivory towers that some critics perceive when they sit down to write their thousand-word letters of sneering comment to our editors. The boxes may often be quite high up in the air, but they induce more lifted pulses than lofty thoughts.[1]

While it is conceivable that politicians despise their chroniclers every jot as much as football folk detest theirs, it is hard to imagine a more adversarial journalistic relationship than that between football reporters and their subjects, offering as it does a stark and curious contrast to those enjoyed by other cultural journalists. In his 2012 book *Family – Life, Death and Football: A Year on the Frontline with a Proper Football Club*, Michael Calvin, formerly chief sportswriter at the *Sunday Mirror*, recounted his experiences of a year at Millwall FC, a rare insider's look behind the scenes facilitated by his longtime friendship with Kenny Jackett, the club manager. It was here that he confirmed what he had always suspected: 'As a journalist I was deemed to occupy a place on the evolutionary scale somewhere between a sloth and a sewer rat.'

In 1968, long before those who make their living from the game convinced themselves that they were far too wealthy and important to be questioned, Arthur Hopcraft outlined the sheer absurdity of it all. A general reporter and feature writer who had worked in Brazil, India and West Africa for the *Daily Mirror* and the *Guardian* before turning his gaze to football, Hopcraft's perspective was also that of someone who grew up in a Midlands mining village, someone to whom the clubs' self-aggrandisement was notably nauseating.

'Football clubs get the sort of publicity from newspapers which is granted to no other sport,' he reasoned.

> No newspaper can afford not to write about football but there are several with the resources and ruthlessness to dig up and overstress all kinds of little sins scattered about the game should they feel sufficiently provoked ... Newspapers do not delve into matters like these any more deeply than is sufficient to handle the stories when they occasionally emerge because sports staffs are in the main much more interested in the game. What is more they accept that a degree of this kind of blemish is inevitable in any commercial enterprise as glamorous and fiercely contested as professional football. The League's display of pious horror when a vulgar newspaper occasionally tells all about very little is a grotesque mistake. I suspect the public wonders what the League is frightened of rather than agrees that the newspaper should be censured.[2]

Had he still been alive four decades later, Hopcraft would have appreciated the irony: in an age when attention from traditional, electronic and social media means that the game is reported to an extent inconceivable even 25 years ago, the paranoia and misplaced priorities that prompted an eruption of public relations departments (the Fifth Estate?) means that access to players has never been more strictly restricted.

Yet just as the emphasis once shifted from print to television and thence to the internet, the latest transformation has come courtesy of the Twittering classes. Freed from the tyrannical leash of mundane cliché and PR-speak, media-trained footballers have used the new medium to cut out the middleman, bypassing print and television and communicating directly with anyone who has the vaguest interest in their utterances. Journalists, as a consequence, are on perpetual Twitter-watch. This cuts both ways. While what ensues is largely a bonfire of the inanities, exceptions, refreshingly, are on the rise. Take Javi Poves, a well-rewarded defender with Sporting Gijon in Spain's La Liga, who in tweeting his retirement assailed his profession as 'putrid' and 'corrupt'. To continue in this 'circus' would offend his principles: 'Footballers are valued too much by our society compared to others who should be the true heroes. The system is based on being sheep and the best way to control them is to have a population without culture.'[3] Amid the riots that panicked England in the summer of 2011, to the delight of many and the ire of more, prominent players such as Rio Ferdinand even dared to defy the first law of the modern sporting jungle and take a stance that could easily be construed as political. The backlash was inevitable: clubs imposed fines. It was an indication of differing priorities, and the arrogance of those who run football, that in September 2011, Steve Elworthy, head of marketing at the England and Wales Cricket Board, claimed that 'the general awareness' of the national team had never been higher, attributing this, in part, to 'the digital media such as Facebook and Twitter allowing followers to get closer to their heroes'.[4]

While the media's love affair with sport in general, and association football overwhelmingly in particular, can be seen in daily sports papers such as *L'Equipe* (France), *Corriere dello Sport* (Italy) and *AS* and *Marca* (both Spain), all obsessed with the Great God Soccer, this chapter focuses on British football journalism primarily because of that satanic beast known as Fleet Street, a collection of London-based and London-centric 'national' newspapers otherwise dubbed 'The Street of Shame'. It says much for the power of that perception that these warring papers continued to labour under those collective names long after their relocation to the concrete-and-steel towers of Canary Wharf and the vast portakabins of Wapping. It is the plurality and depth of coverage offered by these papers that has defied all efforts to successfully launch an English *L'Equipe* or even *Sports Illustrated*. They also operate in a uniquely competitive market that has wrung the best and worst from journalists and journalism.

The very worst, because it disdained any sense of the responsibility that comes with power, was the front page of the *Sun* on 19 April 1989, four days after the Hillsborough disaster that saw 96 Liverpool supporters crushed to death (though it should be stressed that the sins, as in the vast majority of the more sensationalist stories, were those of general news reporters and editors rather than football writers). 'THE TRUTH' vowed the headline. Beneath ran three subheads: 'Some fans picked pockets of victims ... Some fans urinated on the brave cops ... Some fans beat up PC giving kiss of life'. The basis for all this were unsubstantiated allegations made by South Yorkshire police 'sources' in a palpable attempt to divert blame from their own culpability for the chaos and ensuing tragedy. The chief cause of fury was the headline, not the allegations themselves; they had already been published elsewhere, even in Liverpool's own *Daily Post*, which ran an article headlined 'I blame the yobs'.[5] For all the groveling apologies and cap-in-hand pilgrimages to Liverpool made by the paper's executives, the boycott of the country's best-selling daily by the city's inhabitants was still going strong more than two decades later. After the findings of the Hillsborough Independent Panel, published in September 2012, revealed that 164 police statements had been substantially altered, Kelvin MacKenzie, the editor of the *Sun* who composed the notorious headline against the advice of colleagues, finally apologized yet persisted in blaming the 'trusted' agency whose allegations he had printed, unforgivably, as fact.

The late 1980s, affirmed Roy Greenslade, the *Daily Mirror* editor turned professor of journalism and media commentator, were a 'wild west' period for the tabloids, leading directly to the creation of both the Press Complaints Commission and a code of ethics (not that either would prevent the phone-hacking of the following decade). Another key factor was Wapping, home to Rupert Murdoch's papers since the 1986 move from Fleet Street and the defeat of the print unions. 'MacKenzie's power to do as he liked increased to worrying proportions,' wrote Greenslade. 'He took greater and greater risks, leading to the paper's libel of Elton John and the publishing of the Queen's Christmas speech before she had had the chance to deliver it.'[6]

It can be fairly argued, therefore, that the history and antics of Fleet Street encapsulate the development of what some might call a profession, others a trade, and one of its finest practitioners, Hugh McIlvanney, 'a scruffy vineyard'.

The Trailblazers

Famed in his own time as Ubique and later Tityrus, the sort of classically hewn pen names that gave early journalists both protection and gravitas, James Catton is widely, if wrongly, cited as the first football journalist of consequence. If previous accounts are to be believed, he began writing about the game for the *Preston Herald* in 1875 – no mean feat given that he was just 15, at most. By 1868, however, Charles Alcock had already launched and edited *The Football Annual*.

Celebrated as 'the inventor of modern sport' by Dr Eric Midwinter and 'the father of association football' by Catton himself,[7] Alcock was secretary, simultaneously, of both the Football Association and Surrey County Cricket Club, a man whose foresight and enterprise sired the FA Cup and the County Cricket Championship in addition to official international cricket tours and The Ashes.[1] In 1882, he also found time to launch *Football*; Alcock believed he and his co-editor, Nicholas 'Pa' Jackson, then assistant secretary of the FA, were meeting a growing need. 'The want of a Journal specially representing the interests of our National Winter Game has long been an admitted fact, as Football is becoming more popular every year, the necessity for such a periodical becomes more apparent.'[8] According to Heiner Gillmeister of the University of Bonn, meanwhile, this influence soon extended to Germany: in the late nineteenth and early twentieth centuries, three Britons edited sporting journals there – John Bloch on *Deutsche Ballspiel-Zeitung* from 1891, Andrew Pitcairn-Knowles and Fred Manning on *Sport im Bild*.[9]

---

[1] For more on Alcock's role in the game's development, see Chapter 1 in this volume, 'Kicking Off: The Origins of Association Football' by Dave Russell.

Catton was in the right place at a fortuitous time, covering Preston North End during what was immeasurably the Lancastrian club's most fruitful era. 'The reports were brief and there were none of the personal paragraphs, garrulous items, and more or less sensational news which are now part not only of weekly periodicals, but of morning and evening newspapers.' As yet, even the very notion of a pressbox had yet to gestate, the legacy of a generation of correspondents beset by severe colds and rheumatism. The lack of shelter also exposed the reporter's work to the elements; reports due to be telegraphed might be sodden or simply blown away. 'When I first attended football matches as a reporter,' remembered Catton, 'it was necessary to walk about the ground, to keep outside the touchlines, of course, or to stand behind the goal-posts, if the custodian was a genial man and free from nerves and small irritabilities ... Up and down the touch-line and round about the goals the reporter had to wander like a restless spirit.'[10]

At length, wooden benches or desks were provided, bordering the touchline around halfway. Catton could not remember when or where the first pressbox was erected, 'but when one secretary was asked for such accommodation his reply was: "Dear me! I suppose you would like nicely glazed windows, an armchair, a foot-warmer, a cigar, and a glass of whisky at intervals."'[11]

Charles Buchan, a powerful centre-forward for Arsenal, Sunderland and occasionally England either side of the First World War, recalled being interviewed by Catton in 1925: 'Jimmy was a little tubby fellow, not five feet in height. He was, however, the greatest writer of his day, knowledgeable, benevolent and respected by all the soccer authorities.'[12] Buchan would carve his own mark in this arena: becoming a journalist on retirement, he founded the Football Writers' Association as well as *Charles Buchan's Football Monthly*, a staple for schoolboys in the third quarter of the twentieth century.

For the first half of the century, match reports formed the bulk of newspaper coverage. As the chief football correspondent of the *Times* from 1948 to 1976 – he was reputedly the first to be so anointed by any newspaper, though he was not bylined under his own name until he had been doing the job for nearly two decades – Geoffrey Green experienced the extremes of the spectrum. In 1964, he and the rest of the press corps, seated along a touchline as Argentina drubbed their Brazilian hosts in Sao Paolo, were attacked by the crowd. Eleven years earlier came a happier memory:

> The only time I ever saw a press box show its feelings almost to a man was during the last dramatic stages of the Matthews cup final of 1953. When Blackpool's winning goal went home in the dying seconds ... and Matthews had at last gained his Cup winners medal, the Wembley press box simply exploded. Pens, pencils, notebooks, writing paper and even typewriters went

flying. Journalists were standing on their chairs cheering, some even with tears in their eyes. My Sports Editor, sitting beside me, threw his hat to the wind. Calm was a stranger as Matthews was carried shoulder high.[13]

Insularity prevailed beyond the Second World War, dictated in part by lack of column inches and in part by the prohibitive costs and logistics of sending reporters overseas. The *Times* did not see fit to publish news about any of the first three World Cups until the third final, in 1938. Even then, as Fabio Chisari has noted, the only reference came courtesy of a minimalist five-line report from the news agency, Reuters: '*The Times* ... with its conservative clientele, continued covering equitably both amateur and professional sports, and avoiding the World Cup.'[14] Nevertheless, the public thirst for football news and reports was mounting to such an extent that the paper expanded its coverage in the 1960s, following the lead of the *Daily Express* and the *Daily Mirror*. This was a direct response to a report by the accountants Cooper Brothers and Company, commissioned in a quest to broaden the publication's appeal as the circulation war began to bite; the 50 per cent rise in the average daily sale, from 254,000 to 388,000, has been credited in part to this expansion, though it was the deep pockets of Herbert Thomson, the Canadian tycoon who bought the paper in 1966, that made the changes practicable. Then again, as Chisari also observed, 'the focus on football, although necessary ... was, in many ways, alien to the ethos of *The Times*'.[15] Over the ensuing decades, sports pages, seen as a way to readers' hearts, were multiplying everywhere. In 1990, to the astonishment of many, Fleet Street's first dedicated daily sports section would be published not in the *Sun* or *Mirror* but in the archly conservative *Daily Telegraph*.

Fear and Loathing in Milan and Manchester

By the time he retired, Green was lamenting the decline of the match report, a direct consequence of the tabloid-led emphasis on personalities and quotes; this decline would accelerate as live television broadcasts began to beat the press to the punch. 'The pressures now seem greater and the competition keener in a contracting industry. The growing pains of new technology have led to various strikes and have certainly added to the burden of meeting earlier edition times. But the scoop, the backstage story, and the quotes are now paramount at the expense of a straight match report.'[16]

This accent on individuals, heightened by the tabloid circulation war, exacerbated the growing mistrust between the media in one corner, and officials, managers and players in the other. In the 1960s, Burnley banned reporters and newspapers from the pressbox because Bob Lord, the chairman, was angry at what he saw as intrusion into club affairs; Arsenal banned Danny

Blanchflower, now reporting for the *Daily Express*, though whether this had anything to do with his having captained Tottenham while they were ruling the North London roost is unclear; the Football League called upon all 92 clubs to deny accreditation to the *People*, who'd published a story about 'the drinking capacity and bedroom manners' of a Stockport County player.[17]

In 1973, just seven years after England had won the World Cup, Brian James was among the journalists accompanying Sir Alf Ramsey's squad on an ill-fated summer tour that brought three matches in nine days in Chorzow, Moscow and Turin; of the two losses, against Poland and Italy, the first would lead directly to the end of an era: Poland ultimately took England's place at the following year's World Cup, hastening both Ramsey and his captain, Bobby Moore, to the exits.

> At Moscow Airport Jeff Powell of the *Daily Mail* is ill-advised enough to drift into the company of several players. He leaves, red-eared, a minute later after a player threatens to 'stick one on you – and the rest of your bunch of blanks'. Another pressman, Frank Clough of *The Sun*, is without a visa and is ordered to get back on the plane and fly home. 'Effing good job,' calls a player. 'And take the rest of these effers with you.'
>
> [*On the flight home after losing to Italy, Ramsey sits facing the players and with his back to the press*]
>
> It is hard to say who has been right, for the problem is a total lack of understanding. The writers do not know what he is trying to achieve with his teams, for he seldom theorises and never explains. Equally, he is so absorbed in his own function that he simply doesn't pretend to comprehend the pressmen's preoccupation with deadlines, communications or their nagging necessity to have something fresh to write about every day.
>
> At Heathrow the party splits. Ramsey makes a point of going around thanking every player in turn. Only very few of the journalists shake his hand.[18]

Even those who knew how to play this particular game came a-cropper. Terry Venables, a shrewd, personable, publicity-conscious coach and manager of Tottenham, Barcelona and England among others, forged a more mutually productive relationship with the press than most, but this availed him naught once the climate changed, especially when some shady business dealings came to light. Where once 'El Tel' would think nothing of spending an evening in the company of reporters, tabloid and broadsheet alike, wariness set in:

> To an extent I still do socialise with journalists, but there is much more nervousness now than there used to be, a feeling that whatever you say, whatever the circumstances, will go in the paper the next day. When I was out with Ken [Jones], Brian [James] and Peter [Lorenzo], I could relax with them, without

worrying that any off-the-cuff remark I might make would be taken down and used in evidence against me in the papers the following day. Unlike some of their counterparts now, those guys got by on the quality of their writing, and did not have to sell newspapers on crap and side-issues; not that I blame the guys today, because the pressure they are under nowadays is enormous ... almost as much as football managers.

That is still the case in Spain, to some extent. The Spanish press run acres of stories and there is never any shortage of copy, because one or two Barcelona directors, for example, would give stories to their favourite journalists. They would soften them up by feeding them bits of information, in the hope of stopping the press from writing about them and slaughtering them, at some stage. Over there, it is a simple system. If the team is winning, you are the best, and if it is losing, you are the worst. That is how you are judged. While that is also true in Britain, the journalists who cover football in Barcelona are not interested in your private life or outside activities.[19]

Seldom can this schism have found a more disquieting voice than in a television documentary, 'Do I Not Like That – The Final Chapter', which followed Graham Taylor's doomed efforts to manage England's passage to the 1994 World Cup finals, culminating in a near-hysterical exchange with my former colleague at Hayters sports agency, Rob Shepherd. Glanville had seen it coming. 'You're a liar, you write lies!' he reported Taylor ranting after the then-Watford manager had refused to shake hands with him following a game at Queens Park Rangers ('I can't, I can't'). 'What was he talking about?' Glanville wondered as the tirade continued and the pair continued to argue outside the press room. 'Gradually, as the smoke cleared, I realised he was talking about a criticism I'd made of him fully three years before in *World Soccer* magazine, when, during a youth international in Tel Aviv, he substituted a young full back who'd disagreed with his tactics.'[20] To Glanville, it 'seemed a classical Freudian instance of displacement ... In my case, my sustained criticism of Taylor's long-ball tactics, which seemed to me to be tainting the essence of English football, because Watford initially made such positive use of them.'

In 1990, the England World Cup squad in Italy refused to talk to the press following tabloid stories about alleged sexual indiscretions by both the manager, Bobby Robson, and his captain and namesake Bryan; to Glanville, this was 'both irrational and unfair'[21] since the offending articles had been written by general news reporters – the players did not distinguish between different branches of what they saw as the same rotting tree. Such mutual antipathy was by no means confined to British shores. In 1982, the Italian squad refused en masse to speak to reporters during the World Cup after

one paper published a 'scurrilous' story about two players having a homo-
sexual affair. The general manager, Gigi Peronace, who also, perversely, happened to be an agent, depicted the press as 'giornalista d'assalto'.[22]

Peronace was not alone in regarding the journalist as a pariah rather than
a conduit. It says little for one of the most successful and respected managers
in the game's history, and much for his limitless contempt for the media – or
rather the non-compliant members of that fraternity – that no football figure in recent times has challenged the journalist's capacity for dispassionate
observation quite like Sir Alex Ferguson.

Half a century ago, even less, journalists would be encouraged to travel
and socialise with the Manchester United players; Sir Matt Busby instructed
them to 'treat the press the same way you would treat a policeman'.[23] This,
of course, impacted severely on disinterested reporting, but at least supporters felt informed. Ferguson lives in a more prying, less trusting age. He
counts a number of journalists among his close friends – including Hugh
McIlvanney, who ghosted his autobiography – but woe betide those who
incur his wrath. Here is a man, noted one reporter, who 'hoards grudges like
other people collect stamps'.[24]

Witness Daniel Taylor, a Manchester-based *Guardian* reporter whose
even-handed 2007 book, *This is the One – Sir Alex Ferguson: The Uncut
Story of a Football Genius*, was described by Patrick Barclay, author of a
full-fledged biography of Ferguson, as 'intelligent, fair and, in places, verging
on the affectionate'; the 'genius' still banned the author from Old Trafford,
though what the book reveals makes it easy to understand why. 'We journalists regale our friends with anecdotes and enjoy the certain social cachet that
comes from dealing with [Ferguson],' confessed Taylor. 'But we know, deep
down, that he doesn't like what we do.'[25]

In some ways it is hard to blame him. Taylor readily admits that corners are cut and chances taken, trivialities exaggerated, quotes spun, transfer gossip reported as fact. The culprits even have their own name for
it –'twirling'. Ferguson summed up his rationale thus: 'I don't get the press
coverage I think I'm entitled to and I no longer see it as part of my job
to fulfil their interests.'[26] Even when he does relent, he mislays his manners. When, at the end of a rare trophy-free season, the man from the
Daily Telegraph asked what had gone awry, Ferguson grinned: 'That's a
good question. But it would take a whole interview to get it and that's an
interview you're never going to fucking get.' Prior to one World Cup, the
Manchester press corps asked Ferguson whether he intended attending.
'None of your business,' he snapped. 'Do I ask if you're still going to those
fucking gay clubs?'[27]

Gabriel, Hughie and Brian

While credible claims could be made on behalf of Barclay, whose emailed proposal to Ernie Walker, then president of the Scottish FA, prompted the latest change to the offside laws,[28] the most influential football journalist to date has probably been Gabriel Hanot, the administrator and erstwhile French international who wrote for *L'Equipe* and *France Football* and was the mainspring behind the launch of the European Cup. 'His mind, well into old age, was always awash with new ideas,' marvelled Glanville. Indeed, Sir Stanley Rous, when president of FIFA, was once heard to express the fervent desire, given a New Year's wish, that Hanot would stop publishing half-baked ideas. 'Some of them might have been,' conceded Glanville. 'The European Cup emphatically wasn't.'[29] Yet while Hanot was 'always the idealist, a figure from another, more altruistic, less financially frenetic time', he came to regard himself 'as something of a Frankenstein'. His brainchild metamorphosed into something wholly unintended: victory became more about money than glory, which in due course led to what Glanville has characterised as 'the notorious years of the Golden Fix' in the 1970s, when referees were bribed and results pre-ordained.[30]

Perhaps the most fêted football journalist, and certainly the most decorated, is McIlvanney, a proud, genial Scot who for the past half-century has served the *Kilmarnock Standard*, the *Scotsman*, the *Daily Express*, the *Observer* and latterly the *Sunday Times* with eloquent and serious-minded distinction (though stories of his hell-raising are legion). Better known across the Atlantic for his boxing writing (he was inducted into the International Boxing Hall of Fame in 1999), and in Ireland for his musings on horse racing, the fact that football has been just one of the strings to his mellifluous bow has probably been a boon.

Elected to the *Press Gazette* Hall of Fame as one of the trade magazine's 40 greatest journalists of modern times, he was, until 2012, the only sportswriter to have been voted Journalist of the Year and, in the estimation of David Randall, author of *Great Reporters*, is 'simply the best writer ever to apply words to newsprint'.[31] No journalist I have worked with, or read, has taken quite so much care over his choice of words or punctuation. In 2005 McIlvanney confessed to enduring agonies while composing a tribute to the newly deceased George Best: 'I don't go into the writing of any piece with dreams of triumph. I go in with a neurotic fear of a screw-up, and that obviously applies to that piece.' He was inhibited by the 'anxiety of doing it justice' and by the conviction, given the time he had spent with and watching Best, that he 'had a responsibility of a kind'.[32] Typically, that sense of responsibility cut both ways. The Ulsterman, he reasoned, was inferior to Pelé, Maradona and others: they were superior team-players.

As someone who spent a number of years as his 'personal sub-editor' at the *Sunday Times*, I can readily testify to McIlvanney's meticulous and gentlemanly ways. Fear of error was indeed a driving force: 'I'm a real brow-clutcher when a mistake gets through. It's a neurosis ... I should have a much more mature and sensible attitude but the neurosis is too deeply implanted.' Hence the obsessive fact-checking. Once, heading home from a game in northern England after filing his copy, he learned from a fellow reporter that a shot against the bar had been deflected, albeit barely, and resolved to phone in a correction: the desire to do right by the goalkeeper and the principles of his trade persuaded him to leave the last train to London, obliging him to spend the night in distant, dismal Crewe.

'To watch McIlvanney at work is not a pretty sight,' attested the journalist and author Norman Giller, who shared pressboxes with him while working for the *Daily Express* and *The Sun*:

> He carves slowly like Leonardo, chiselling out every word with care and consideration. He is often the last to leave the press box, having worried every word to the newspaper destination like an anxious parent seeing his kids off to their first day at school. Havana cigar in hand like a conductor's baton, he becomes lost in a cocoon of concentration as he weighs each sentence with Shylock-style money-lending deliberation. His words are his currency and he will not relax until every dot and comma is accounted for. Hughie cannot write anything without total commitment; even a note to the milkman produces the agony of creation.[33]

The result, happily, was almost invariably worth the angst. Witness his running report of the fabled 1960 European Cup final at Hampden Park, delivered in sections as the game progressed, thwarting considered reflection:

> Fittingly, the great Glasgow stadium responded with the loudest and most sustained ovation it has given to non-Scottish athletes. The strange emotionalism that overcame the huge crowd as the triumphant Madrid team circled the field at the end, carrying the trophy they have held since its inception, showed they had not simply been entertained. They had been moved by the experience of seeing sport played to its ultimate standards.[34]

Barclay and David Lacey, acclaimed pounders of the daily beat, both regard Glanville as the benchmark of excellence. 'Most football writers fall into two categories,' Barclay once contended: 'those who have been influenced by Glanville, and those who should have been.' When I asked him why, the reasons bubbled over: 'Brian's got absolutely no snobbery. I couldn't believe how helpful he could be to a young reporter. I adore the elegance of his writing, and his judgement of footballers is fantastic.' Lacey counted him as an inspiration: 'I was always impressed by his use of language. He was very good at quotes, at capturing someone in what they say.'[35]

Glanville, like Green a public–schoolboy, was still firmly in the saddle when he turned 80 in 2011, still effortlessly reeling off match reports for the *Sunday Times*, obituaries for the *Guardian* and columns for *World Soccer*. Always welcoming, like McIlvanney, of starstruck young reporters, he needed no invitation to regale them with accounts of uproarious times with Lenny Bruce, the delights of Yiddish folklore and scriptwriting for the groundbreaking satirical TV show *That Was the Week That Was*, not to mention the curse of *catenaccio*, one of many Italian words to which he introduced teenagers struggling to tell 'its' from 'it's'. He agonised less than McIlvanney and wrote more flamboyantly, as befits both an extrovert character and a much-quoted essay he wrote for *Encounter* magazine in the 1950s,[2] wherein he chided his countrymen for failing to emulate the example set by the best American sportswriters:

> British sports journalism is still looking for an idiom ... still waiting for the columnist who can be read by intellectuals without shame and by working men without labour. Meanwhile it is afflicted by dichotomy: a split between mandarin indulgence and stylised stridency, this in itself a valid reflection of the class structure.[36]

It would be fascinating to know whether McIlvanney, three years Glanville's junior, read those words at the time. Among contemporary sportswriters, Jason Cowley has observed, 'Perhaps only McIlvanney, with his long, baroque sentences, metaphorical reach and belief in the heroic potential of sport ... would not be out of place in the pages of, say, the *New Yorker*', the weekly magazine and longtime home to his spiritual and literary counterpart, Roger Angell.

Glanville, who has never attempted to match McIlvanney's sporting breadth, is more driven in his pursuit of those he believes to be the scourge of the game, most relentlessly the so-called Hungarian fixer Dezso Solti. Peter Stead praises his fiction elsewhere in this volume, but suffice to say that his journalistic outlook has always been firmly that of the passionate internationalist. In writing and constantly updating *The Story of the World Cup*, a definitive volume reprinted for the eighth time shortly before the 2010 tournament, the fourteenth he had covered, he brought far-away matches and far-flung figures to the attention of aspiring journalists.

[2] See Chapter 13 in this volume, 'Brought to Book: Football and Literature' by Peter Stead.

Best known for his trenchant work as chief football correspondent of the *Sunday Times* for 30 years, his love of Italy saw him base himself in Florence and Rome, reporting and writing columns for *Corriere Dello Sport*, *La Stampa* and *Corriere della Sera*.

To watch him compose a runner in those pre-laptop, pre-lapserian days was an education: producing a piece of A4 paper which he had divided into a grid, the number of boxes precisely allotted according to the number of words he had been asked to submit, he proceeded to write a word in each box, the better to save the sub-editor any cutting and hence ensure every word found its way into print. Once he had phoned his copy over, he would make a collect call to his second home and dictate, in apparently perfect Italian, an off-the-cuff report to *Corriere Dello Sport*. 'There was no one quite like him,' reckoned Cowley. '*Football Memories*[his 1999 memoir], with its rapid, staccato sentences, non-sequiturs and jumpy, anecdote-rich style, captures something of the essence of this restless football intellectual, who has perhaps spent more time watching the game than is wise for any sane man.'[37] The same, of course, could be said of so many fellow toilers in that grubby vineyard.

NOTES

1 A. Hopcraft, *The Football Man* (London: Collins, 1968, Penguin reprint 1971), p. 181.

2 Hopcraft, *The Football Man*, pp. 179–80.

3 G. Marcotti, 'Footballers and ideology combine for curious mix', *Times*, 15 August 2011, *The Game* supplement, p.15

4 J. Gillespie and S. Wilde, 'Cricket's big hitters cross £1 m boundary', *Sunday Times*, 18 September 2011.

5 R. Greenslade, 'The Sun's Hillsborough source has never been a secret – it was the police', *Guardian*, 17 October 2011, www.guardian.co.uk/media/greenslade/2011/oct/17/sun-hillsborough-disaster

6 Ibid.

7 K. Booth, *The Father of Modern Sport: The Life and Times of Charles W. Alcock* (Manchester: Parrs Wood Press, 2002), p. ix.

8 From *Football*, 4 October 1882, quoted in Booth, *The Father of Modern Sport*, p. 85.

9 H. Gilmeister, 'English Editors of German Sporting Journals at the Turn of the Century', *Sports Historian*, May 1993, pp. 1–15, www.la84foundation.org/SportsLibrary/SportsHistorian/1993/sh13c.pdf.

10 J. A. H. Catton, *The Story of Association Football* (Cleethorpes: Soccer Books, 2005, reprint).

11 Ibid.

12 C. Buchan, *A Lifetime in Football* (London: Phoenix House, 1955), quoted in 'The Encyclopedia of British Football', Spartacus Educational, www.spartacus.schoolnet.co.uk/Fcatton.htm.

13 G. Green, *Pardon me for Living* (London: George, Allen & Unwin, 1985), pp. 179–80.
14 F. Chisari, 'Definitely Not Cricket – *The Times* and the Football World Cup 1930–1970', *Sports Historian*, Vol. 20, No. 1, May 2000, p. 48, www.la84foundation.org/SportsLibrary/SportsHistorian2000/sh201f.pdf.
15 Chisari, 'Definitely Not Cricket', p. 47.
16 Green, *Pardon me for Living*, p. 181.
17 Hopcraft, *The Football Man*, p. 179.
18 B. James, 'A sad breakdown of communication: diary of a grim tour', *Sunday Times*, 17 June 1973, reprinted in *The Sunday Times Sports Book* (London: World's Work, 1979), pp. 38–39.
19 T. Venables, *Venables: The Autobiography* (London: Penguin, 1995), pp. 89–90.
20 B. Glanville, *England Managers – The Toughest Job in Football* (London: Headline, 2007), p. 169.
21 Glanville, *England Managers*, p. 44.
22 Glanville, *England Managers*, p. 42.
23 D. Taylor, *This is the One – Sir Alex Ferguson: The Uncut Story of a Football Genius* (London: Aurum 2007), p. xxi.
24 Taylor, *This is the One*, p. xxii.
25 Ibid., p. x.
26 Ibid., p. xix.
27 Ibid., p. xi.
28 Interview with author, 17 July 2011.
29 B. Glanville, *Champions of Europe – The history, romance and intrigue of the European Cup* (London: Guinness, 1991), p. 5.
30 Glanville, *Champions of Europe*, p. 9.
31 D. Randall, *Great Reporters* (London: Pluto 2000), www.greatreporters.co.uk/reportershmcilvanney.html.
32 I. Burrell, 'Hugh McIlvanney: A giant among sporting greats', *Independent*, 5 December 2005, www.independent.co.uk/news/media/hugh-mcilvanney-a-giant-among-sporting-greats-518223.html.
33 N. Giller, 'Hugh McIlvanney remains the matchless Master', Sports Journalists Association, www.sportsjournalists.co.uk/the-giller-memorandum/hugh-mcilvanney-remains-the-matchless-master/.
34 *Scotsman*, 19 May 1960, quoted in Giller, 'Hugh McIlvanney remains the matchless Master'.
35 Interview with author, 17 July 2011.
36 Quoted in J. Cowley, 'Kicked into touch', *New Statesman*, 5 March 1999, www.newstatesman.com/199903050048. See also Peter Stead's essay in this volume, 'Brought to Book: Football and Literature', Chapter 13.
37 Ibid.

ROB STEEN AND JON VALE

The Game-Changers: Havelange, Blatter and Platini – The Ruling Class

Joao Havelange

Picking on a nonagenarian is seldom considered a virtue in polite or even philistine circles, not least when said elder has been nominated for the Nobel Peace Prize. Then again, since those who run football almost invariably have to be dragged from their thrones kicking, screaming and ranting, many would argue that there are justifiable exceptions, and that Joao Havelange, in particular, deserves every sling and arrow. Such is the pluralism of football realpolitik in the twenty-first century, however, that there are also many, primarily but not exclusively from the Third World, who regard the Brazilian with respect and gratitude. To Hugh McIlvanney, he is 'to moral leadership what General George Custer was to military prudence'.[1] The only unanimity is that he will be remembered, whether fondly or bitterly, as the modern game's most influential mover and shaper.

It was Havelange who expanded FIFA from a shoestring operation to one which he claimed, at the end of his reign, was worth around $250 billion; Havelange who wrested football's reins from Northern Europe, established lucrative partnerships with Coca-Cola and McDonald's, and (as Paul Darby relates in Chapter 6 of this volume) globalised the game, giving Asia and Africa their say. It was Havelange, moreover, who eased the future IOC president Juan Antonio Samaranch's passage into the Olympic fraternity and facilitated his rise. Havelange also saw himself as promoting world peace through football, waxing lyrical about the positive impact on East Asia of staging the 2002 World Cup in Japan and South Korea, and claiming to have helped bring China 'into the world's economic and political embrace'.[2]

On 21 June 2011, nearly a decade and a half after he (theoretically) ceased calling the shots at FIFA, I googled the words 'Havelange' and 'corruption' and generated 79,400 responses. This vast number could be traced to the fact that five days earlier, in the wake of allegations by the BBC's *Panorama* programme that he had accepted $1 million in bribes, ostensibly on behalf of FIFA, the IOC, somewhat belatedly, began investigating Havelange, an IOC member since 1963 and president of football's governing body from 1974 to 1998. The allegations centred on the 95-year-old's relationship with FIFA's erstwhile marketing partner, International Sport and Leisure (ISL), the company founded by his late friend Horst Dassler.

Following the collapse of ISL in 2001, the Swiss liquidator Thomas Bauer advised Andrew Jennings, the English investigative reporter, that he had found evidence of 'football-related' payments to FIFA officials to secure lucrative television and sponsorship rights contracts stretching back over two decades. Jennings claimed that the slush fund, channelled through a bank account held in Liechtenstein, was only discovered after a payment worth 1 million Swiss francs was accidentally sent to a FIFA executive in Zurich.[3] In June 2006, Jennings, interviewed on BBC's *Panorama* programme, alleged that the intended recipient was Havelange himself. In December 2011, with an International Olympics Committee (IOC) inquiry imminent, Havelange resigned from the committee; wary of the legal constraints, Keir Radnedge, chairman of the football arm of AIPS, the International Sports Press Association, contented himself with declaring it a 'glaring coincidence'. The following July, court documents revealed that FIFA officials had knowledge of the bribes paid to Havelange and suggested that his right-hand man, Sepp Blatter, had also been aware. The ruling body agreed to pay 2.5 million Swiss francs (£1.64 m) in compensation but only if criminal proceedings against Havelange and the Brazilian executive committee member Ricardo Teixeira were dropped. Jennings, meanwhile, reasserted his claims, first published in the *Daily Mail* in 2002,[4] that Havelange had actually pocketed $60 million from ISL and that Blatter had knowledge of this.

Moral Flexibility

Born Jean-Marie Faustin Godefroid Havelange in Rio de Janeiro, to Belgian parents, there was early evidence of moral flexibility – he joined his father's arms trading company – but there was one thing about which he soon became rigid: he could never work for anyone else. As Brazil embraced modernity, he built a business empire in transport and finance. For a man of unimposing build, he possessed a remarkable capacity for intimidation. There was 'such an aura about him', testified David Will, a Scottish lawyer and veteran FIFA committeeman, 'people were actually physically scared of him'.[5] To Guido Tognoni, a former FIFA media director, he was 'a master of power' apt to 'make you believe that the sky was red when it was actually blue'.[6]

If the honours have flown fast and thick – the Order of Special Merit in Sports (Brazil), Commander of the Cavaliers of the Order of Infante D. Henrique (Portugal), Cavalier of the Vasa Orden (Sweden) and the Grand Cross of Elizabeth the Catholic (Spain) – perhaps the most ludicrous, and revealing, was the Swiss Football Association's 1988 decision to nominate him for the Nobel Peace Prize, for turning FIFA into 'a world power binding all nations'.[7] It may have been mere coincidence, but the Swiss were contemplating a bid to stage the 1998 World Cup. During his successful presidential campaign, however, Jacques Chirac claimed that Havelange, who voted for Barcelona ahead of Paris to stage the 1992 Olympics, had promised him *France* would be hosts, something FIFA's executive had yet to even consider. Countering the Swiss, President Mitterand awarded Havelange the Légion d'Honneur, his country's highest decoration. Checkmate: the Coup du Monde went to France.

Until his death in 1987, Havelange's trump card was Horst Dassler, son of Adidas founder Adi, whose factories supplied footwear to Jesse Owens and a venomous anti-tank rocket-launcher to the Nazis. The man from FIFA, claimed Jennings, 'promised an expansion in coaching and tournaments. It would all benefit football. The problem was that he did not have the money to keep his election pledges. Dassler solved his problem. He was given the marketing contract, sweet-talked the Coca-Cola company to back the alien sport of soccer – and everybody got rich.'[8]

It was Havelange who, with his pals at Adidas and ISL, attested David Goldblatt, 'transformed Fifa from a penurious cottage industry into the owner of the world's greatest commercial and sporting spectacular';[9] Havelange who hand-picked the profoundly unloved Blatter to succeed him, an election reportedly facilitated by kickbacks, vote-rigging, finance from the Gulf and undue use of FIFA resources. And Havelange who, upon succeeding Sir Stanley Rous as FIFA president, expanded the World Cup. The 1974 tournament in Munich featured 16 teams; come 1998, the field had doubled. Africa, Asia and North and Central America and the Caribbean were the main beneficiaries, and he was adored for promoting their interests. The developed countries were less enamoured, livid, as they saw it, that the competition, and their dominance, had been diluted.

Lennart Johansson, Blatter's lone rival to succeed Havelange, hailed him as 'the right man at the right time and in the right place'[10] yet likened to him a dictator increasingly interested only in trumpeting his own achievements and enjoying the fruits of his dubious labours. As spokesman for the United States' ailed bid to host the 1986 World Cup, Henry Kissinger's experience of Havelange made him feel 'nostalgic for the Middle East'.[11]

Sepp Blatter

For all the mercurial brilliance practised by football's most astounding on-field artists, the legacy of Joseph 'Sepp' Blatter, FIFA's long-reigning and sublimely cunning president, will probably reverberate through the ages with far greater potency. The enormity of the modern game, its global grasp, financial force and commercial capabilities have all been honed by this wiliest of Swiss administrators who – despite countless allegations of political and financial corruption – remains firmly embedded as the most powerful figure in world sport.

A business and economics graduate from the University of Lausanne, Blatter's true talents lay in the slicker domain of public relations, with his winning charm and easy smile earning him roles across a variety of organisations, including the dubious title of 'President of the World Society of Friends of Suspenders', an organisation formed to protest at 'women replacing suspender belts with pantyhose'.[12]

It was in 1972 that he struck lucky. While working for Longines, a Swiss watch and race-timing company, he was spotted by Horst Dassler, who was slowly creating a monopoly of control over the world's sporting administrators desperate for his lucrative corporate connections. Dassler, who held particular sway over Havelange, embraced the young Swiss as a protégé. 'Blatter was trained at the Adidas headquarters at Landesheim,' said another of Dassler's old allies, Patrick Nally, the British entrepreneur and specialist consultant widely acknowledged as the 'founding father' of modern sports marketing. 'He spent his time there getting to know the Adidas operation. Horst and Blatter became very close during the months he lived in Landesheim. He was very much cemented into the relationship.'[13]

Havelange followed Dassler's lead and set about grooming Blatter in the dark arts of diplomacy. Without consulting his executive committee, in 1981 Havelange appointed Blatter as his general secretary, making him virtual second in command only six years after joining FIFA. This axis of power became impregnable, with a variety of stakeholders deploring their 'autocratic and unaccountable style'.[14] Despite their dominance, Blatter wanted more. 'After years in the shadows, Sepp had had enough,' wrote Andrew Jennings. 'Churning in his guts, Sepp lusted to be President.'[15]

In 1998, Blatter's patience was rewarded by election as president following Havelange's retirement. In keeping with the controversy of his subsequent tenure, his election was dogged by rumours of foul play and bribery of African officials, who before the election seemed certain to vote for Blatter's opponent, Lennart Johansson. While nothing has ever been proved, such allegations have been ever-present throughout Blatter's presidency.

The collapse in 2001 of ISL, FIFA's long-term partner, cost FIFA $116 million according to then-general secretary Michel Zen-Ruffinen. Jennings claims that Blatter was involved in illicit dealings between FIFA and the ISL, sanctioning the transfer of 1 million Swiss francs to the private account of a FIFA official.[16] Then there was a dossier from Zen-Ruffinen, once seen as a likely future president, lambasting Blatter's absolute dominance of the supposedly democratic organisation. 'FIFA today is run more like a dictatorship. FIFA is not a decent and structured organisation anymore. It has been reduced to a Blatter organisation.'[17]

Then, in 2010, came the bidding for the 2018 World Cup. The 'Cash for Votes' saga led to the suspension of two FIFA members following a *Sunday Times* investigation, although similar charges brought by the English FA against four other delegates, including former FIFA vice-president Jack Warner, were dismissed. The subsequent removal of both Warner and Mohamed bin Hammam, who was running against Blatter for the presidency, allowed Blatter to be re-elected unopposed. While the allegations against bin Hammam were serious – he was accused of attempting to bribe Caribbean voters with $40,000 to support his presidential campaign – the way Blatter sauntered back into the hot seat did little for his already damaged reputation, welcome as his denouncing of the trafficking of young African players was.

Blatter's gaffes have also landed him in hot water. Apparently, none of football's minority groups are safe from his bigoted critical eye. After airing his views on the women's game – 'Let the women play in more feminine clothes like they do in volleyball' – and gay footballers – 'They don't declare it because it will not be accepted in these macho organisations. But look at women's football – homosexuality is more popular there'[18] – Blatter's archaic rhetoric plunged to even greater depths with comments in 2011 suggesting that racist abuse of players could be settled 'with a handshake'. Such views sit oddly with the vast, multicultural span of FIFA's governance.

Yet Blatter clung on to power. His survival instincts are acute. A subconscious reflex is to scan a room in seconds to beam friendly glances to faces he knows, even if he and the smile's recipient are not on good terms.[19] Plus, his stage management skills are superb. If he faces scrutiny from a particular section of a forum, whether major European nations or probing reporters, he will orchestrate support from the floor, excluding difficult questions and weathering any potential storm. When Blatter managed to avoid a vote of no-confidence proposed by disgruntled European members, Franz Beckenbauer conceded the move was 'pure Blatter. Brilliant'.[20]

This command of political techniques has steered Blatter through a presidency mired in allegation. He has maintained the commercial drive instigated by Havelange and brought successful World Cups to the virgin territories of Asia and Africa, reinforcing football's identity as the one true global game. Yet for all his savvy politics, his reign will be remembered for corruption, unaccountability and farcical statements that have turned FIFA into an administrative laughing-stock. Then again, with a man once in charge of the 'World Society of Friends of Suspenders' at the helm, is anyone really that surprised?

Michel Platini

While Michel Platini may be far from unique among footballers in combining an illustrious playing career with prominence in other arenas – Pelé, Zico and George Weah, for instance, all became politicians – no iconic figure has come so close to running the game, something he is threatening to do as president of UEFA and Blatter's heir apparent. If the closest parallel in global sporting terms lies with Lord Sebastian Coe, how the Frenchman must sometimes wish the only thing on his plate was a mere Olympic Games.

In 1987, his final year in boots, Platini gave an extensive interview to the radical newspaper *Libération*. His inquisitor was Marguerite Duras, feminist doyenne of the French literary establishment and a disciple of Georges Bataille, the controversial and infamously convoluted existentialist. The following is not satire:

> DURAS: *What kind of a game is this? Both demonic and divine?*
> PLATINI: *Football is loved by everyone, everywhere, because it has no definitive truth …*
> DURAS: *And if men were perfect, there would be no football?*
> PLATINI: *Yes, the result would always be 0–0; there would be no goals because no one would be making a mistake.*[21]

Two decades later, Platini remained mystified: 'Quite frankly I have no idea what she was on about. But it was extremely good fun. And it got me known with intellectuals … But I am a football man.'[22] In this, to a degree, he was being disingenuous. Few 'football men' have thought so deeply about the game's direction or assailed its ills with such passionate eloquence.

Take the booming international market for players under 18, in his eyes a form of 'child trafficking' that should be prohibited by law. What is killing the game, he argued in 2008, are youth academies, 'football factories where young players are force-fed a diet of over-training and financial cynicism'.[23] Football, he insisted, has 'a social role, which is not just about taking young lads from third-world countries and making them into superstars'.[24] He has advocated wage caps and curbs on transfer spending and foreign ownership of clubs, as well as on non-nationals in club sides (the '6+5' plan, subsequently reborn as '9+9'). His laudable, socialistic goal is a level playing field, or a reasonable approximation thereof. Whatever the outcome, this is one revolution that is certain to be televised.

Talisman for all Seasons

Much as *realpolitik* should dictate caution, it is sorely tempting to invest hope that the resurrection of FIFA's reputation and practices can lie in someone who has already given the game so much. Born in 1955 to an Italian father amid the coalmines of Lorraine, Platini, like so many other luminous French footballers – Marcel Desailly (Ghanaian), Luis Fernandez (Spanish), Just Fontaine (Moroccan), Raymond Kopa (Polish), Jean Tigana (Malian), Zinedine Zidane (Algerian) – was of foreign descent. Making his professional debut for Nancy in 1973, the budding playmaker scored on his international bow two years later and enhanced a burgeoning reputation for talismanic qualities with the decisive goal of the 1978 French Cup final. That summer, having helped France reach their first World Cup finals since 1966, he gave further notice of the versatility that would leave an indelible impression. As Gabriel Hanot so memorably put it, 'Platini's centre is everywhere, his circumference is nowhere.'[25]

Where Argentina 1978 had hinted at renewal, the 1982 World Cup testified to the rising tempo of a French revival that would enchant and refresh, culminating in resplendent victories for a proudly multiracial side at the 1998 FIFA showpiece and the 2000 European Championships. In reaching the last four in Spain, 'Les Bleus' were indebted to a lavishly tooled midfield quartet, one that, according to Jonathan Wilson, 'shifted shape according to the opposition': sometimes Platini played as a centre-forward, sometimes 'in the hole' and sometimes as a *regista* [instigator]. Significantly, coach Michel Hidalgo asked him 'to adjust to the demands of the system, rather than building the side around him'.[26] Team first, ego second.

Instead of the anticipated crescendo, however, came defeat and near-tragedy when Harald Schumacher, ostensibly keeping goal for West Germany but seemingly bent on defending every tributary of the Rhine, all but caved in Patrick Battiston's skull with a reckless airborne charge that the referee, unaccountably, failed to punish, even with a free-kick. Reflecting on that titanic semi-final, won on penalties by the Germans after a 3–3 draw, Platini declared that football, in essence, was 'about good and evil'.[27] Mme Duras doubtless approved.

Leaving St Etienne for Juventus, where he led all Serie A scorers in his first three seasons, good prevailed in stirring style at the 1984 European Championships. Diego Maradona at the 1986 World Cup aside, it is difficult to conceive of one man dominating a team event quite so completely as Platini did that June. Not only was he France's captain and fulcrum but also principal scorer: seven in the opening phase, including two 'perfect' hat-tricks (one with the left foot, one with the right, one with that cool head); the winner in a 3–2 semi-final defeat of Portugal, and the first in the final, supplying a lead that was only extended in injury-time. Feared for his free-kicks, he practised them against a wall composed of six-foot clothes-maker's dummies.

Coaching success at club and national level ensued, but that was never going to be a second act gripping or challenging enough. It remains to be seen what impact Platini can have: can he revive ethical values and banish match-fixing, betting scandals, administrative corruption and the overwhelming stench of greed? In 2011 he seemed at pains to remind us of his priorities, exalting Lionel Messi and Cristiano Ronaldo, adamant that he remained 'a player at heart, not a politician'.[28] Should he succeed Blatter, it may not be excessively optimistic to anticipate a game in more trustworthy hands. However, as Matt Dickinson suggested, the fact that Qatar's 2022 World Cup bid even found favour with Platini – 'supposedly the one "suit" the fans can relate to', the man whom one trusts feels honoured at being branded a 'dangerous little faggot' by one of Blatter's less noble aides, Peter Hargitay[29] – leaves the heir apparent 'for ever compromised'.[30]

NOTES

1 H. McIlvanney, *Observer*, 6 July 1986, reprinted in 'Jewels in a Dung Heap', *McIlvanney on Football* (Edinburgh: Mainstream, 1997), p. 267.
2 J. Sugden and A. Tomlinson, *Badfellas* (Edinburgh: Mainstream, 2003), p. 71.
3 A. Jennings, *Foul! The Secret World of FIFA: Bribes, Vote-Rigging and Ticket Scandals* (London: HarperCollins 2006).
4 A. Jennings, 'Blatter knew about Havelange bribes 15 years ago!', Transparency In Sport, 13 July 2012, http://transparencyinsportblog.wordpress.com/2012/07/13/blatter-knew-about-havelange-bribes-15-years-ago-2/.
5 Sugden and Tomlinson, *Badfellas*, p. 63.
6 Ibid., p. 68.
7 Ibid., p. 69.
8 A. Jennings, 'Havelange to Blatter– the Dynasty Based on Corruption', ESPN.com, 28 February 2002, http://soccernet.espn.go.com/archive/global/news/2002/0228/20020228featjenningsmain.html (accessed 15 November 2011).
9 D. Goldblatt, 'Kickbacks but no penalties', *Independent*, 9 June 2006.
10 G.L Jones, 'Time Finally Up for FIFA's Havelange', *Los Angeles Times*, 7 June 1998.
11 Sugden and Tomlinson, *Badfellas*, p. 68.
12 S. Ingle, 'Wrong Again', *Guardian*, 29 June 2006, http://blogs.guardian.co.uk/worldcup06/2006/06/29/wrong_again.html (accessed 15 January 2012).

13   A. Jennings, *Foul! The Secret World of FIFA: Bribes, Vote Rigging and Ticket Scandals* (London: HarperCollins, 2006), p. 28.
14   J. Sugden and A. Tomlinson, *FIFA and the Contest for World Football* (Cambridge: Polity Press, 1998), p. 65.
15   Jennings, *Foul! The Secret World of FIFA*, p. 35.
16   Ibid., p. 6.
17   J. Sugden and A. Tomlinson, 'Not for the Good of the Game: Crisis and Credibility in the Governance of Football' in Lincoln Allison (ed.), *The Global Politics of Sport: The Role of Global Institutions in Sport* (Oxford: Routledge, 2005), p. 34.
18   S. Rice, 'Sepp Blatter Gaffes and Outbursts', *Independent*, 17 November 2011, www.independent.co.uk/sport/football/news-and-comment/sepp-blatter-gaffes-and-outbursts-1896594.html (accessed 15 January 2012).
19   Jennings, *Foul! The Secret World of FIFA*, p. 78.
20   J. Sugden and A. Tomlinson, 'Not for the Good of the Game', p. 30.
21   Quoted in P. Delbourg and B. Heimermann, *Football and Literature* (Paris: Editions Stock, 1998) and P. Shaw, *The Book of Football Quotations* (Edinburgh: Mainstream 1999).
22   A. Hussey, 'This Man Can Save English Football: UEFA President Michel Platini', *Observer*, 26 October 2008, www.guardian.co.uk/football/2008/oct/26/england-football-platini (accessed 15 January 2012).
23   Ibid.
24   Ibid.
25   Quoted in H. Gordon (ed.), *International Football Book No. 26* (London: Souvenir Press 1984), p. 32.
26   J. Wilson, *Inverting the Pyramid – A History of Football Tactics* (London: Orion 2008), p. 268.
27   Hussey, 'This Man Can Save English Football'.
28   O. Gibson, 'Uefa President, Michel Platini, Worries Game Is Going Pear-shaped', *Guardian*, 26 August 2011, www.guardian.co.uk/football/2011/aug/26/michel-platini-uefa (accessed 15 January 2012).
29   Merciades, Bonita, *Secrets of the Battle to Host the World Cup*, 2012, extract published at transparencyinsport.org, November 2012, http://www.transparencyinsport.org/Michele_Platini_is_a_dangerous_little_faggot/PDF-documents/THE_BID_Secrets_of_the_Battle_to_Host_the_World_Cup_Extracts.pdf
30   M. Dickinson, 'Savour Europe's Best in Battle before Mediocrity Kicks In', *Times*, 3 December 2011.

13

PETER STEAD

Brought to Book: Football and Literature

The development of competitive professional football on a national scale in late Victorian Britain had coincided with the coming of mass education, mass literacy and the widespread distribution of newspapers, magazines and stories by publishers fully attuned to popular taste. Fans talked about the game and were given every opportunity to read and fantasise about it. Over the decades a football literature of match reports, pen portraits, biographies and fictional stories accrued. The nature of football was to be shaped and coloured as much by this literature as by personal memory.[1] The game had created something bigger than itself, but was this a sub-cultural phenomenon, something for the working classes only, or rather a concern of those who conceived of a national culture? Was football to be written about exclusively for its fans? Were football themes worthy of consideration by those who valued good writing and who wondered whether both literature and sport were capable of reflecting and shaping a national cultural identity?

The twentieth century saw the establishment of a political democracy in Britain and the democratisation of its culture. Within that context an undercurrent of dissatisfaction developed regarding how football was perceived and written about. Some writers wondered whether it would ever be possible to write popular culture, including sport, into that widening national culture. The whole issue was best articulated in two essays published by Brian Glanville in 1965 which neatly summed up the difficulties facing sports writing in Britain and did much to shape subsequent attitudes.[2] Glanville argued that the British had not found a successful idiom for writing about sport and this is why both its sports reporting and fiction had been so lacking in quality. This failure he attributed to the factor of class – the class divisions and attitudes that had prevented the British from writing freshly, precisely and memorably about sport in general and football in particular. Two themes ran through his essays. First there was the judgement that in literary terms football, for all its popularity, could not compete with cricket (the 'Establishment game', just the ticket for the 'belletrist and literary romantic') or boxing (a sport 'nearer the bone', less contrived and one admired by some great American writers). It was baseball that took Glanville to his second theme. Why was it that football, which is 'indubitably our national sport as baseball is America's', had not similarly generated fine writing or become associated with national identity?

Glanville made his points succinctly and did not explain the process whereby middle-class and literary taste, with Bloomsbury very much in the van, had relegated popular culture and its writers to a subsidiary role. There had been some significant British football writing but it had occurred in literary cul-de-sacs. Arnold Bennett should certainly be a 'hero', as John Carey suggests, for his writings offered a 'systematic dismemberment of the intellectual's case against the masses'.[3] In his 1911 novel *The Card,* a mayor 'who knew nothing about football' is replaced by an opportunist who uses a local football club in a campaign aimed specifically at 'the great football public'.[4] Bloomsbury had no time for Bennett but his novels were eagerly read by D. H. Lawrence. Whereas Bennett had been fascinated by new urban energies, Lawrence explored the psychological pressures of industrial society. His story *Strike Pay* (1914) is a brilliant account of a striking miner, Ephraim Wharmby, and his friends who spend a day walking the nine miles to Nottingham.[5] They spend their strike pay, drink beer, witness a fatal accident and 'see a good match'. Not only does their team Notts beat Aston Villa but 'Flint, the forward for Notts, who was an Underwood man well known to the four comrades, did some handsome work, putting the two goals through'. Later Wharmby is berated by his mother-in-law but his wife quietly supports him. Football had been beautifully incorporated into a worker's day. By 1919 the only great modern British novelist from a working-class background had abandoned Britain; by 1930 he was dead.

P. G. Wodehouse, a former public schoolboy, was possibly a more influential football writer than either Bennett or Lawrence. The game of football that enraptured the masses had been shaped and codified by the upper classes in their public schools, and a literature generated within that context of muscular Christianity was to determine the role of football in countless imaginations. The *Boy's Own Paper* was launched in 1879 and it was in such publications and their public school stories that the winning of cups and the scoring of dramatic goals were established as the basic elements in football fiction and private dreams. Eventually it was rugby that won out in the public schools but it was the round ball that had wider cultural potency.[6] The plot of Wodehouse's 1906 story *Petticoat Influence* rests on a young lady confusing rugby and soccer, but happily her brother wins his soccer Blue for Oxford. The narrator provides vivid reportage: when her brother runs out he has the look 'of a dog that's just going to be washed'. Initially 'there was a lot of running about and kicking' and he fails to impress. However, our hero has his moment of glory: he 'began to play really splendidly' and from his shot 'the ball whizzed into the net'. Now the masterful Wodehouse allows his narrator to overhear the comment, 'all the same, he ought to have passed'.[7] In time the public school settings went but the basic tropes remained, fundamental yet limiting. The challenge to all football writers was that of transcending a formula.

The Role of Popular Culture

The power of middle-class taste and values was evident in the great battle over popular culture that occurred during the interwar years. The battle focused mainly on the role of cinema in national life. This tremendously popular form of entertainment was overwhelmingly associated with the working classes and those preponderantly American showmen who catered to their needs. In the 1930s it was J. B. Priestley, sharing Bennett's Dickensian holistic notion of a national culture, who pointed to the ways in which American film and literature had refreshingly transcended class barriers, a fact readily appreciated by the British working class. Unlike politicians and intellectuals on the right or left, he could see that the fulfilment afforded by popular culture was essential to Britain's democratic future.[8] His 1929 novel *The Good Companions* provides as rich a description of what a local football club means to factory workers as any in the language. Describing the crowd leaving a Bruddersford United match he reflects that 'to say that these men paid their shillings to watch twenty-two hirelings kick a ball is merely to say that a violin is wood and catgut, that *Hamlet* is so much paper and ink'.[9] In his 1934 travelogue *English Journey,* Priestley is rather more pompous as he reports on a visit to a derby match in Nottingham (a city destined for football literary stardom) and welcomes what he calls 'this uproarious Saturday plaything'. He writes with prescience on 'how everything has been done to spoil the game' but admits that it was 'still good ... to see that quick comradeship engendered by the game's sudden disasters and triumphs'.[10] By 1939 Priestley, having won the argument over film, was poised to become the recognised spokesman for the working class during what became 'the People's War'. The culture was filling out but sport, and in particular football, had yet to be fully analysed within that culture.

Glanville's 1965 frustrations were to appear in the wake of two decades in which the status of popular culture had been transformed. A. J. P. Taylor's judgement that in the War 'the British people came of age' explains how, after 1945, with full employment, a Welfare State and a new system of secondary education, the country could begin to come to terms with matters of class and regional identity.[11] Popular culture played a vital role in both creating and reflecting this process. Broadcasting, the press, the arts and leisure generally assumed fuller roles within a substantially more democratic culture. Football crowds were huge and with the arrival of the BBC's *Sports Report* (1949), the launch of *Charles Buchan's Football Monthly* (1951) and enlivened press coverage the game was contributing significantly to a national vibrancy. There was a new crop of stars whose images were widely reproduced and whose ghosted autobiographies were published by firms such as Stanley Paul and Pelham. Football fans felt well catered to and undoubtedly it was a subsequent nostalgia for what Peter Jeffs has termed *The Golden Age of Football* that was to take football writing out of the shadows.[12]

Meanwhile, the traditional literary subcultures had played their part in the Golden Age. The comics were still important although football had been eclipsed by the Sgt Matt Braddock and the *Tough of the Track* stories. The strip cartoon brought new life, and with the coming of *Roy of the Rovers* in 1954 a sacramental status was given to the ideal of charismatic centre-forwards scoring cup-winning goals.[13] Readers of all ages could now find countless novels that cherished the same formula. Football writers had noted the appeal of cricket stories that had achieved an English authenticity by exploiting the village game.[14] The pastoral format allowed for a range of bucolic characters whilst neatly avoiding the professional game's urban actualities. In his 1951 novel *The Whistle Blew*, Eric N. Simons presciently named his village's charismatic and frequently scantily clad centre-forward 'George Best'; Best imagines himself as 'a wild, tempestuous batterer at the gates of the citadel' but in clinching victory he is 'transformed into an exalted warrior'. At inside-left Zachary Brown has '*Boy's Own Paper* dreams of sinuous dribbles ending in brilliant goals' and is only truly happy with 'legs, legs, and yet more legs, as defenders rushed upon him'.[15] The village format came to fruition in 1954 with Robin Jenkins's *The Thistle and the Grail*, a story beautifully written in the Scottish kailyard (cabbage patch) tradition. The novel examines the playing out of class, family and religious issues in a depressed 1930s village, and the case for football being 'the only substitute for a faith and a purpose' is well made. Inevitably, *Boy's Own* conventions are deployed in the telling of how Drumsagart Thistle win the Cup, the Holy Grail. Star forward Alec is fancied by the pub landlord but in fact everyone saw him as 'enhaloed, aureoled, empanoplied'. An early 7–0 defeat for Thistle is an 'amaranthine humiliation'. There had been 'former glory' but all readers would recognise the truth that 'faith could gnaw on that dry bone no more'.[16] In 1975 J. L. Carr elegantly satirised football reporting in *How Steeple Sinderby Wanderers Won the Cup*, a succinct and amusing tribute to the village format.[17]

Towards a New Realism

In the 1960s football writers were determined to reach a more demanding readership. Glanville himself had forced the issue and it is with his 1963 novel *The Rise of Gerry Logan* that football fiction entered the modern age.[18] He was delighted when a professional footballer who had read *Gerry Logan* commented 'that's how it is'. There is indeed a remarkable documentary quality to the story of the Glasgow-born Logan who plays successfully in London and Italy, develops a glamorous lifestyle, befriends journalists and is taken up by television. We have moved well away from Drumsagart. Many readers were struck by the similarities between Gerry and the author's real-life friend Danny Blanchflower. When in 1968 Glanville wrote of the great Spurs player that 'there is a core of something secret, held back, concealed ... he is intelligent, humorous, ambitious, competitive, even egocentric, but the inwardness of the man is elusive', one knew that football writing had entered a new era and that fiction and analysis were advancing hand-in-hand.[19]

Football writers responded to cultural changes but also to events on the field. Glanville's 1965 essays had been written the year before England won the World Cup. Very soon there were signs that football writing was evolving, not least by becoming fashionable. Glanville had already noted that 'football for some years has been "in" in London: intellectuals go to see it'. He was not labouring alone. John Moynihan's *The Soccer Syndrome* (1966) recalled the immediate postwar austerity. As a boarder at a rugby-playing school he had been captivated by Chelsea, whom he saw as 'a side of such reckless disposition that at times they seemed more like a household of characters from a nineteenth century Russian novel', and by Tommy Lawton, a centre-forward who 'provided one of the few pin-ups of a jaded metropolis'.[20] Arthur Hopcraft's *The Football Man* (1968) was subtitled *People and Passions in Soccer* and to a possibly unrivalled extent examined individual responses to the joys and difficulties of the game. He wrote of 'that unique altering of the senses' experienced when going into a match and memorably brought to life another great centre-forward: Bolton's Nat Lofthouse, a former miner, 'had a navvy's forearms and shoulders and a special darkness of expression when he was playing which reflected his intention of single-minded antagonism for the other team's defenders'.[21]

Hopcraft had written a classic, but perhaps more influential in the short term were Michael Parkinson's *Sunday Times* articles, published in 1968 as *Football Daft*. Parkinson's Barnsley-inspired recollections were an acquired taste but there is no doubt that his talk of goalkeepers being 'like things that go bump in the night' and his image of Skinner Normanton's 'billiard-table legs' encouraged a new generation of quality-press readers to start thinking of how football had shaped their own identity.²²

Football fiction was becoming more ambitious. This was an age in which the children of working-class fathers were achieving professional qualifications, although it was the Royal Air Force (RAF) that had taken Alan Sillitoe away from working-class Nottingham. His superb 1959 story *The Match* deservedly stands comparison with Lawrence's *Strike Pay*, although it is darker and the domestic conclusion less comfortable. The grim mood is set at the start of a Notts County match which Lennox knows his side would lose 'not through any prophetic knowledge ... but because he himself hadn't been feeling in top form'. 'Why,' he wonders, 'did he make Saturday afternoons such a hell on earth?'²³

In 1960 a massive challenge had been thrown out to football followers by David Storey's *This Sporting Life*, in which the author, the son of a miner and himself both an art school graduate and former professional rugby league player, used his sport for the setting of a powerful working-class story.²⁴ Football's response came from Barry Hines, a Barnsley miner's son, once an accomplished player and afterwards a teacher. In *The Blinder* (1966) the story of a schoolboy star becomes increasingly melodramatic as sexual and financial opportunities arise. More impressive was *A Kestrel for a Knave* (1968), a brilliant depiction of a troubled Yorkshire teenager. A year later the story was filmed by Ken Loach as *Kes*. Here, actor Brian Glover created the most treasured moment in the whole imagined history of the game by capturing all the pomposity and petty vindictive cruelty of sad physical education masters. The scene is less crisp in the book, but Hines had given Glover gold to work on. The master forces young Billy to play in a match and announces that his own red-shirted side are Manchester United and, as he wears the number nine shirt, he would be Bobby Charlton. When the boys ask why he was not Denis Law as usual, he confusingly replies that he would now be adopting a more scheming role and 'anyway, Law's in the wash this week'.²⁵

In 1969 B.S. Johnson published a box containing 27 unbound sections that constituted his fascinating novel, *The Unfortunates*. Jonathan Coe later explained that the book was a study of 'randomness' and 'disintegration' and in real life had been triggered by Johnson's mind wandering during a match that he was reporting in Nottingham. The fictional Johnson's melancholy is fuelled both by the tedium of the match and thoughts on the inanity of reporting. As he struggles to find anything to say he thinks of the 'well-paid pseuds who write their reports from prepared telling phrases, and make the football fit whatever it is they imagine their readers want them to say'.²⁶

More immediately influential in the short term were two novels in which Glanville returned to his almost documentary approach to the realities of the game. His *Goalkeepers Are Different* (1971) traces the rise of a 'keeper from parks football to the England team and *The Dying of the Light* (1976) follows the fall from grace of a retired English 'keeper.[27] The writing is far more ambitious in the later book and there is a striking intensity in the initial mood of betrayal and death. In his 1965 essays, Glanville had urged writers to take more heed of the often vivid language of players they interviewed. The public were made more aware of that language by Hunter Davies's 1972 account of a year spent with the Spurs team. *The Glory Game* taught us more about players than we had ever known and we learned that British footballers found most refereeing decisions, tackles, foreign players and countries 'diabolical'.[28] Both Glanville and Davies were inviting players to speak for themselves. In 1976 the former Millwall player Eamon Dunphy duly obliged with *Only a Game?,* a book (suggested Glanville) that took us beyond 'ghosted pap'. Acknowledging a debt to a book by baseball pitcher Jim Bouton,[29] Dunphy's diary demonstrated that 'relationships in football are tenuous' and that in the Second Division 'battle is what the game is all about'.[30] The game had been stripped of romance and fans taken considerably closer to the action. The players had found their voice: the question now was whether it was time for the fans to be heard.

The View from the Terraces

In the years since 1945 the nature and quality of football writing had evolved in the context of a considerable intensification of football culture generally. That culture had been consistently stoked by events both on and off the field with performances in World Cups and European club competitions providing the main debating points. This process, which came to a crescendo in the last decades of the century, was best summed up by Harry Pearson in 1994 when he pointed out that the actual playing of the game was 'only the kernel of something greater ... the core, you might say, of the Game'.[31] Mark Perryman boldly argued that 'no other sport matches the culture that football fans have created around their game'.[32] Many aspects of that culture had become unattractive as in the 1970s and 1980s gates plummeted, hooliganism became the headline story and many clubs experienced financial difficulties. Football was undeniably in crisis. Yet with hindsight it can be suggested that it was precisely during these difficult days that the seeds were planted for a revival and substantial redefinition of the place of football in the national culture. The historian Dave Russell has referred to the game's 'reinvention' whilst David Conn saw football being 'rebranded from filthy habit in the 1980s to legitimised state religion in the 1990s'.[33] A new football literature was to be at the heart of this new sense of 'the Game'.

The difficult years had produced their own literature and in particular they saw the publication of James Kelman's *A Disaffection* (1989), a magnificent account of a crisis in the life of Patrick Doyle, a Glasgow teacher. Kelman's novel is a reminder of the sheer intensity of Scotland's working-class football culture, where violence, partisanship, personal tragedies and sheer magic had existed cheek by jowl. After a few pints Patrick ends up at a junior match where he hears some choice language ('Gone ya fucking dumpling ye va cunt ye couldni score in a barrel of fannies'), looks down and so misses the only goal, considers whether a mournful neighbour is a journalist or an MI5 agent and reflects on how football crowds create the ideal circumstances for assassinations. But Patrick spots that the visiting side 'had a small boy out on the wing who was really good with the ball at his feet': his own side then attacked – 'Exciting stuff … it was good'.[34] For all the vagaries of Scottish football it has always had a cultural complexity envied throughout the United Kingdom.

It was the novelist Kevin Sampson in his 1998 non-fiction account of a Liverpool season who best summed up what was happening to football's following. He explained that 'we never used to sit for hours debating all that was wrong with the club … We do now'. Now the local press and radio stations had provided 'a thriving Merseyside forum for disaffected fans' where 'all the would-be managers and amateur psychologists indulge themselves'. To use Peter Terson's phrase, crowds had grown out of their rattle.[35] Everyone had become an expert on every aspect of the game whether it was the form of individual teams, players, managers or commentators. Phone-ins, fanzines, magazines, phones and the internet had allowed the ultimate extension and democratisation of Sampson's forum. There was an open opportunity to make public one's expertise and also, of course, one's loyalties. And it was that element of loyalty that guaranteed credentials for any degree of authority. It was in the years of crisis that the distinctive individuality of British clubs became appreciated as never before. In 1986 the American author Charles Korr concluded his pioneering history of West Ham by explaining that 'the Hammers have been part of something much larger than the club'. These qualities of authority and loyalty appealed to intellectuals and fans alike. The novelist Irvine Welsh was to regret it deeply, but perhaps at last things were moving towards one big Football Culture?[36]

Two books published in the aftermath of Italia '90 were to trigger off a new national interest in the game and a new era for football writing. There was a degree of irony about this. As Jonathan Wilson commented, England had not played well and yet 'this somehow led to football's middle-class revolution'.[37] But the television images of Paul Gascoigne's tears and the fatal penalty shoot-out, added to the superb packaging of the tournament, had given England's efforts a heroic dimension that Pete Davies was to immediately harness in *All Played Out*. Davies uses his talents as a novelist and reporter to create a huge canvas in which he can incorporate details on the perplexing matters of English tactics, the mood changes of individual players, the shenanigans of the press and the ultimately honourable contribution of the maligned England manager Bobby Robson. At the heart of Davies's epic story is the contrast between the World Cup's 'Planet Football', where people's spirits 'go speeding down the tunnel of the game and, smashing, release subatomic primal frenzies of hope, joy and despair', and the pre-tournament behaviour of the British press and the FA that was 'dismally modern-English – mismanaged and sloppy, noisy and oafish'. The words that came to his mind that, he felt, could be equally applied to 'our schools, our hospitals, our railways, our government' were 'tired and stupid ... a whole way of thinking that's all played out'.[38]

Fever Pitch and the Deluge

No football book has been more widely acclaimed outside or more influential inside the community of fans than Nick Hornby's *Fever Pitch* (1992). Hornby vividly communicates a young fan's obsession with his club and scrupulously connects his own moods and development to that club's fixtures. This was a serious memoir and one that presented general readers with fresh insights into how young people had negotiated what were difficult decades in England. For dyed-in-the-wool fans, however, the fashionable success of the book created a sense of unease. The young Hornby had lived in leafy Maidenhead, far from the working-class milieu of Highbury, and his father's alighting on Arsenal seemed fortuitous: there is little sense of history. The author tries too hard to strike an attitude: he was 'an Arsenal fan first and a football fan second' and one who felt that 'complaining about boring football is a little like complaining about the sad ending of King Lear: it misses the point somehow'. Was football being used by a writer looking for a subject, and could that subject have been *any* aspect of popular culture?[39] One certainty was that there were many fans asking themselves why they hadn't written in this vein. The opportunity was already at hand. Since 1986 the magazine *When Saturday Comes* had been providing 'a voice for intelligent football fans'. In *My Favourite Year* (1993), a collection of essays inspired by the magazine (and edited by Hornby himself),[40] D.J. Taylor examined the un-Hornby-like syndrome of an obsessive father, and

Giles Smith reassuringly explained that being 'preposterously anal' about collecting programmes and the like was the norm.

And so the deluge came. Now it was books that had to be collected and for the first time it was possible to think in terms of a proper football library. There was quality writing and in-depth analysis on all aspects of the game by both academics and journalists, with perhaps the most exciting development being the international dimension offered by authors such as Simon Kuper, David Winner and Jimmy Burns.[41] On the domestic front, books by Colin Shindler and Gary Imlach fleshed out the intimate details that had been omitted from all those ghosted biographies.[42] The most pleasurable development was the proliferation of what was identified as the 'confessional genre'. The poet Blake Morrison recalled having 'to play alone' and in his garden he kicked the ball around his own 'stadium of dreams' whilst providing a 'Ken Wolstenholme commentary'.[43] Shindler with *Manchester United Ruined My Life* confessed what was to be increasingly thought 'but ne'er so well expressed'.[44] Every prospective writer in the country had now been licensed to sum up personal dilemmas, family histories and a world-view from the perspective of the terraces.

Perhaps nobody has rooted his fandom so firmly in a social context as Harry Pearson. His 1994 *The Far Corner* is a bleak, sardonic and amusing tour of the football grounds of north-east England. The tone is set by his confession that he supports Middlesbrough, 'because I'm a glory seeker'. The country described is clearly 'played out' but he remains mindful of how his grandfather had communicated a love of the game. On a map of the area his hand would circle various towns 'stirring up soccer wherever it went'. This was a place where for manual workers 'football was a means to show they were capable of more than their jobs allowed: of brilliance and creativity' and 'where sport was not an education in reality but an escape from it ... a glimpse of something better.'[45]

Three decades had passed since Glanville had outlined the difficulties of writing football fiction and, at the century's end, it seemed as if the bookshelves would be largely stocked with serious journalism and 'belletrist' memoirs, the labours of the so-called soccerati. Was football writing merely confirming the wider claim that British novelists seemed incapable of tackling ambitious issues? Had the nation generally taken to alternative literary forms (such as biographies, memoirs and travel books) as a substitute? Perhaps it really was the case that football did not lend itself to imaginative writing? Thinking of football writing generally, Ed Horton had commented that 'one melodrama is much like another' and the editors of an anthology of sports writing excluded fiction on the basis that stories 'with teams with made-up names are always unsatisfactory'.[46]

One way around this last point was to have fictional characters react-ing to real-life matches. In Roddy Doyle's *The Van* (1991), the Irish team's adventures in the recent World Cup occasion comic events back home. But better by far to convey the joy of playing the game. In his brilliant depiction of a childhood, *Paddy Clarke Ha Ha Ha* (1993), Doyle describes an epic street game in which Northern Ireland beat Scotland 42–38. Paddy admits that his younger brother was 'a brilliant dribbler' and that he 'hated him'. Sometimes there is the pleasure of suddenly encountering a match in the middle of a non-football novel. In David Mitchell's intriguing study of ado-lescence,[47] *Black Swan Green* (2006), young Jason has realised that 'games and sports are about humiliating your enemies' and he participates in the humiliation of another officious track-suited (Wolves) PE master. A boy vio-lently tackles an opponent and explains, 'Now I've remembered it's football. But when I made the tackle, I thought it was rugby.'[48] Other writers have more fully deployed matches, imaginary or otherwise, to establish their role in shaping either individual personalities or communities. In *For Whom the Ball Rolls* (2001), Ian Plenderleith ingeniously uses short stories to reveal how aspects of the game affect a wide range of social types.[49] In Anthony Cartwright's novel *Heartland* (2009), football is a key component of the social life of the multiracial Black Country town. One of his characters was at Molineux in 1954 to see the Hungarians serve up 'football like water, like dancing, like light'.[50]

The New Cultural Dispensation

The Britain of the early twenty-first century is a country blessed with a rich football literature, and the signs are things can only get better. David Peace's *The Damned United* (2006) took the football novel into new territory: a novelist who specialised in creating bleak urban landscapes brilliantly rec-reated that infamous flashpoint of manager Brian Clough arriving at Leeds United in 1974. Peace uses prose, verse, dialogue and flashbacks to inject an unprecedented degree of emotion into the day-to-day-routine of foot-ball which takes on an Old Testament intensity.[51] The beauty of football's new cultural dispensation is that this challenging novel can be read along-side several excellent non-fictional accounts of those bitter events, including Anthony Clavane's superb cultural and political history of football in Leeds, *Promised Land* (2011).[52]

A number of writers have highlighted Eric Cantona's arrival on the English football scene in 1991 as a distinct turning-point.[53] In his autobi-ography Cantona wrote of how he had always had a 'feeling of being free' and of how music, poetry and the lives of 'fragile people ... who managed to remain strong' had inspired him.[54] Perhaps it is something resembling Cantona's sense of artistic freedom that readers are now looking for. Now, almost half a century after Glanville's reflections on sports writing, the British can enviously consider the centrality of novelists in the football culture of other lands. The Argentine journalist Jorge Omar Perez listed 20 writers, including Albert Camus, Mario Vargas Llosa, Gabriel Garcia Marquez, Gunter Grass, Naguib Mahfouz and Eduardo Galeano, who had written about the game and would be worthy contenders for a notional 'Nobel Prize in football writing'.[55] Meanwhile, Irishman Seamus Heaney, a genuine Nobel laureate writing in English about the actual playing of the game, captured those Cantona dimensions that many of us want explored in our football literature:

> *Youngsters shouting their heads off in a field*
> *As the light died and they kept on playing*
> *Because by then they were playing in their heads*
> *And the actual kicked ball came to them*
> *Like a dream heaviness, and their own hard*
> *Breathing in the dark and skids on grass*
> *Sounded like effort in another world ...*
> *It was quick and constant, a game that never need*
> *Be played out. Some limit had been passed,*
> *There was fleetness, furtherance, untiredness*
> *In time that was extra, unforeseen and free.*[56]

NOTES

1   T. Mason, *Association Football and English Society 1863–1915* (London: Harvester Press, 1980), pp. 187–95; D. Russell, *Football and the English* (Preston: Carnegie, 1970), pp. 103–13.

2   B. Glanville, 'Looking for an Idiom', *Encounter,* July 1965 and 'Sport in Fiction', *New York Times Book Review,* 18 July 1965. See also Rob Steen's chapter in this volume, 'Sheepskin Coats and Nannygoats: The View from the Pressbox', Chapter 12.

3   J. Carey, *The Intellectuals and the Masses 1880–1939* (London: Faber and Faber, 1992), pp. 152–81.

4   A. Bennett, *The Card* (London: Penguin Books, 1975), pp. 206–9.

5   D.H. Lawrence, 'Strike Pay' in *The Prussian Officer and Other Stories* (London: Duckworth, 1914).

6   J. Richards, *Happiest Days: The Public Schools in English Fiction* (Manchester: Manchester University Press, 1988).

7   P.G. Wodehouse, 'Petticoat Influence (A Football Story)', *Strand Magazine,* No. 182, March 1906, http://arthursclassicnovels.com/wodehouse/petcot10.html.

8   P. Stead, *Film and the Working Class* (London: Routledge, 1989), pp. 101–5.

9   J.B. Priestley, *The Good Companions* (London: Penguin Books, 1962), p. 13.

10 J.B. Priestley, *English Journey* (London: Heinemann, 1934), pp. 143–45.

11 A.J.P. Taylor, *English History* (Oxford University Press, 1965), p. 60.

12 P. Jeffs, *The Golden Age of Football* (Derby: Breedon Books, 1991).

13 'Tough of the Track' and 'I Flew with Braddock' appeared in *The Rover*. For 'the alternative universe' of football comic stories see A. Mitten, *The Rough Guide to Cult Football* (London: Rough Guides, 2010), pp. 208–11.

14 See H. De Selincourt, *The Cricket Match* (London: Jonathan Cape, 1924) and A. G. Macdonell, *England, Their England* (London: Macmillan, 1933).

15 E.N. Simons, *The Whistle Blew* (London: Werner Laurie, 1951), pp. 36, 132, 216.

16 R. Jenkins, *The Thistle and the Grail* (Edinburgh: Polygon, 1997). Discussed in J. Hill, *Sport and the Literary Imagination* (Bern: Peter Lang, 2006), pp. 35–51 and by A. Bairner in *Sport in History*, 29, 2 (2009), 171–89.

17 J.L. Carr, *How Steeple Sinderby Wanderers Won the FA Cup* (London: Prion, 1999).

18 B. Glanville, *The Rise of Gerry Logan* (London: Secker and Warburg, 1963).

19 B. Glanville, 'Danny Blanchflower' in John Arlott (ed.), *The Great Ones* (London: Pelham, 1968), pp. 143–60.

20 J. Moynihan, *The Soccer Syndrome* (London: Sportspages, 1987) p. 17, p. 61.

21 A. Hopcraft, *The Football Man* (London: Penguin Books, 1971), p. 32.

22 M. Parkinson, *Football Daft* (London: Stanley Paul, 1968), p. 17, p. 90.

23 A. Sillitoe, 'The Match' in *The Loneliness of the Long Distance Runner* (London: Allen, 1959).

24 D. Storey, *This Sporting Life* (London: Penguin Books, 1962).

25 B. Hines, *The Blinder* (London: Michael Joseph, 1961); B. Hines, *A Kestrel for a Knave* (London: Penguin Books, 1969), p. 114.

26 B.S. Johnson, *The Unfortunates* (London: Picador, 1999).

27 B. Glanville, *Goalkeepers Are Different* (London: Hamish Hamilton, 1971) and *The Dying of the Light* (London: Secker and Warburg, 1976).

28 H. Davies, *The Glory Game* (London: Sphere Books, 1973).

29 Jim Bouton's revealing and pioneering baseball diary *Ball Four* was first published in 1970.

30 E. Dunphy, *Only a Game?* (London: Penguin Books, 1977), p. 98, p. 127.

31 H. Pearson, *The Far Corner* (London: Abacus, 1997), p. 152.

32 M. Perryman, *The Ingerland Factor* (Edinburgh: Mainstream, 1999), p. 17.

33 Russell, *Football and the English*, pp. 209–34; D. Conn, *The Beautiful Game* (London: Yellow Jersey Press, 2005), p. 59.

34 J. Kelman, *A Disaffection* (London: Picador, 1990), pp. 91–104.

35 K. Sampson, *Extra Time* (London: Yellow Jersey Press, 1998), p. 1. See also Sampson's novel *Awaydays* (London: Jonathan Cape, 1998).

36 C. Korr, *West Ham United* (London: Duckworth, 1986), p. 207; I. Welsh, Introduction to M. King and M. Knight, *The Naughty Nineties: Football's Coming Home?* (Edinburgh: Mainstream, 1999).

37 J. Wilson, *Inverting the Pyramid: The History of Football Tactics* (London: Orion, 2008), p. 5.

38 P. Davies, *All Played Out* (London: Mandarin, 1991), p. 4, pp. 132–33.

39   N. Hornby, *Fever Pitch* (London: Victor Gollancz, 1992), p. 135. Hornby's approach owed much to F. Exley, *A Fan's Notes: A Fictional Memoir* (New York: Harper & Row, 1968).

40   N. Hornby (ed.), *My Favourite Year* (London: H.F. & G. Witherby, 1993).

41   The British Society of Sports History, their journal *Sport in History* and their conferences facilitated an unprecedented coming together of academics and professional writers.

42   C. Shindler, *Fathers, Sons and Football* (London: Headline, 2001); G. Imlach, *My Father And Other Working-Class Football Heroes* (London: Yellow Jersey Press, 2005).

43   B. Morrison, *Too True* (London: Granta, 1998), pp. 68–69. See also J. Coe, Introduction to Johnson (1999).

44   C. Shindler, *Manchester United Ruined My Life* (London: Headline, 1998).

45   Pearson, *The Far Corner*.

46   E. Horton in Hornby (ed.), *My Favourite Year*, p. 55; N. Coleman and N. Hornby (eds), *The Picador Book of Sports Writing* (London: Picador, 1996), p. 4. See I. Preece, 'Fact Versus Fiction', *When Saturday Comes*, No. 288 (2011), pp. 30–31.

47   R. Doyle, *The Van* (London: Secker and Warburg, 1991) and *Paddy Clarke Ha Ha Ha* (London: Vintage, 1998), pp. 165–73.

48   D. Mitchell, *Black Swan Green* (London: Sceptre, 2006), p. 7, pp. 252–55.

49   I. Plenderleith, *For Whom The Ball Rolls* (London: Orion, 2001).

50   A. Cartwright, *Heartland* (Birmingham: Tindal Street Press, 2009), p. 92.

51   D. Peace, *The Damned United* (London: Faber and Faber, 2006).

52   A. Clavane, *Promised Land* (London: Yellow Jersey Press, 2010).

53   D. Winner, *Those Feet: An Intimate History of English Football* (London: Bloomsbury, 2006), p. 36; S. Maconie, *Hope & Glory* (London: Ebury, 2011), p. 244.

54   E. Cantona, *Cantona: My Story* (London: Headline, 1994), pp. 3–4.

55   J. O. Perez, *Los Nobel del futbol* (Barcelona: Meteora, 2006), discussed in J. Turnbull, T. Satterlee and A. Raab (eds.), *The Global Game* (Omaha: University of Nebraska Press, 2008), p. 295.

56   S. Heaney, 'Markings' from *Seeing Things* (London: Faber and Faber, 1991).

Figure 13.1. Johan Cruyff and Franz Beckenbauer of the Cosmos during a game in Giants Stadium, New York, 30/8/1978. Credit: Colorsport.

JON VALE

The Game-Changers: Johan Cruyff

Holland, a country enriched with a proud history of creative eccentricity, was always destined to provide European football with its most marvellous maverick. Johan Cruyff (Figure 13.1), universally recognised as the finest footballer the continent has ever produced, played the role superbly.

Here was a player who retired, aged just 31, as the sport's outstanding talent, only to return a year later in the unheralded surroundings of American soccer. He was sent off in only his second international appearance, chose clubs based on political preference and revelled in defying conventional or popular thinking.

While Cruyff was a bona fide radical, he possessed an eloquence and a mentality that inspired an increasingly sceptical generation of 1960s Dutch youth. Hermut Smeets, a columnist with Dutch newspaper *NRC Handelsbad*, said of the time: 'We experienced a cultural, social and political revolution, with Johan Cruyff as the main representative.'[1] Karen Gabler, who grew up in this Cruyff-inspired generation, was similarly aware of his importance. 'Cruyff was a kind of model for us, maybe like John Lennon was in England. He got into all kinds of conflicts because he started asking the question which the whole generation was asking: "Why are things organised like this?"'[2]

How he transferred this attitude to the game made him an icon. For Cruyff, winning was not all. How you won, that was what counted. 'There is no medal better,' as he put it, 'than being acclaimed for your style.'[3] He was absolutely devoted to his mentor Rinus Michels's concept of 'total football', an innovative system where players were not restricted to specific tactical duties; by Cruyff's reckoning, a proper footballer should be competent in all of the game's arts.

Like all great mavericks, Cruyff got away with it because no matter how loud his voice, no matter how outrageous his attitudes, his talent was louder and more outrageous. He was football's equivalent of a stealth bomber. Playing as a centre-forward with licence to roam, his movements appeared almost serene. He didn't just run. He glided. He didn't just jump. He soared, seemingly beyond gravity's all-conquering reach. To Brian Glanville he was 'tormentingly elusive'.[4] David Miller, former chief sportswriter at the *Times*, labelled him 'Pythagoras in boots'.[5] Michels, the man who honed Cruyff's extraordinary talents, was only a little less gushing: 'When you saw Cruyff off the pitch he was like a thin boy. But on the pitch, he was from another planet.'[6]

Having been named European Footballer of the Year in both 1971 and 1973, the years spanning Ajax's hat-trick of European Cup titles, he moved to Barcelona at the start of the 1973–74 season for a world-record £922,300. Their investment was instantly and handsomely rewarded: the Dutchman inspired them to their first league title since 1960.

But in an era before the riches of club competition, the World Cup was king. Elected heir apparent to Pelé as the world's greatest player, Cruyff arrived in West Germany in 1974 expected to justify such prestigious status. He didn't disappoint. The Dutch team of 1974 remains one of international football's most fabled, pressing, preventing and probing in blissful synchro-nisation, shifting from expansive to compact with ease and befuddling teams overwhelmed by a smooth cascade of orange. When they reached the final against the hosts, pre-match talk was of how many Holland would score.

Such predictions were premature. Cruyff, named the player of the tour-nament, won his team a first-minute penalty but was thereafter shackled by Berti Vogts in what is commonly remembered as football's greatest display of tenacity. Starved of their talisman and faced with the imperious efficiency of Franz Beckenbauer's Germany, Holland wilted. They lost 2–1, matching the Mighty Magyars of 1954 as the best team to never win the World Cup.

It was to be Cruyff's final act on international football's grandest stage. Four years later, still at the peak of his powers, he elected to miss the World Cup in Argentina following an attempted kidnap in 1977. 'I had a rifle at my head, I was tied up, my wife tied up, the children were in the apartment in Barcelona,' he told Radio Cataluyna in 2008. 'To play a World Cup you have to be 200%. There are moments when there are other values in life.'[7] Never again would he wear his country's distinctive livery.

He eventually called time on his playing career in 1984, taking his first steps into management with Ajax a year later. Despite critics deeming him too volatile to command such responsibility, his unrelenting commitment to footballing aesthetics made him a formidable manager. During his three sea-sons at Ajax he helped nurture the considerable talents of Frank Rijkaard, Danny Blind and Dennis Bergkamp, but it was at his next job – as manager of Barcelona – that these principles would provide the foundations for foot-ball's most successful breeding ground.

In the short term, he turned Barcelona into European football's aristocrats, harnessing the sublime attacking talents of Romario, Hristo Stoichkov and Michael Laudrup to create the perfect example of his free-flowing vision, but it was Cruyff's insistence on youth development that ranks as his greatest triumph. He drove the club's focus towards La Masia, the academy centre – located only a stone's throw away from the Camp Nou – where modern masters such as Xavi, Andres Iniesta and Lionel Messi learned their trade, totally engrossed in a lifestyle more spiritually intense than any other football academy in the world.

The man later charged with overseeing La Masia, the Barcelona coach Pep Guardiola, credits Cruyff as his chief inspiration: 'All the coaches I had in my career were important but Cruyff was the most important of all. He was without equal on training and tactics and he helped me to understand the million details that decide why some matches are lost and some matches are won.'[8] Anyone who witnessed the beauty of Guardiola's team will testify that Cruyff, who gave Guardiola his Barcelona debut in 1990, has left his legacy in safe hands. 'Winning is one thing,' he once contended. 'But to have your own style, to have people copy you, to admire you. That's the greatest gift.'[9]

NOTES

1 H. Smeets, 'Cruyff Gave Form to the Netherlands', *Hard Gras*, April 1997.
2 D. Winner, *Brilliant Orange: The Neurotic Genius of Dutch Football* (London: Bloomsbury, 2000), p. 19.
3 Ibid., p. 144.
4 B. Glanville, *The Story of the World Cup* (London: Faber & Faber, 2001), p. 199.
5 S. Kuper, 'Holland, a Country of Clubs' in A. Raab, T. Satterlee and J. Turnbull (eds.), *The Global Game: Writers on Soccer* (Lincoln: University of Nebraska Press, 2008), p. 41.
6 Quoted in FIFA, 'Johan Cruyff – I Was There', *FIFA Classic Football*, www.fifa.com/classicfootball/players/player=1043/quotes.html (accessed 6 December 2011).
7 P. Doyle, 'Kidnappers made Cruyff miss World Cup', *Guardian*, 16 April 2008, www.guardian.co.uk/football/2008/apr/16/newsstory.sport15 (accessed 15 January 2012).
8 R. Draper, 'Ronald Koeman: How Pep Guardiola created the greatest football team in the world', *Daily Mail*, 22 May 2011, www.dailymail.co.uk/sport/football/article-1389541/Ronald-Koeman-How-Pep-Guardiola-created-greatest-football-team-world.html (accessed 15 January 2012).
9 Quoted in M. Dickinson, 'Barcelona owe Cruyff big debt', *Times*, 3 January 2012.

PART THREE

Where We Are

14

HUW RICHARDS

What Took You So Long? Spain Conquers the World

Nothing summed up the mood in Spain before the 2006 World Cup in Germany better than a feature in the daily sports paper *Marca*. The pictures and profiles of the 26 tournament referees, labelled 'men with no mercy', were accompanied by a headline which in effect translated as 'Which one of them will put us out this time?' While the refereeing paranoia echoed Spain's elimination by co-host South Korea in the 2002 tournament, the dominant note was fatalism. Something, the article argued as it detailed *Mundial* exits back to the loss against hosts (and eventual winners) Italy in 1934, was certain to derail Spain's hopes.[1]

In the same week blogger Juan Jose Anaut reported that only 32 per cent of *marca.com* users thought Spain could win the trophy – while this struck him as excessive optimism, it compared to 80 per cent who had believed they would win four years earlier.[2] *Marca* commented: 'We don't have a Zidane or a Henry, a Ronaldo or a Ronaldinho.'[3]

While it only took the opening 4–0 victory over Ukraine to transform journalistic discourse into excitedly plotting Spain's route to a final against Argentina, personal observation in Seville suggested no trace of the bacchanalia that would have accompanied a comparable performance by England, and *La Roja* did indeed fall short, losing to the rejuvenated French in the quarter-final.

Only a few years ago, but in football terms another age. Now other countries contemplate the talent at Spain's disposal – not only Andres Iniesta, Xavi Hernandez, David Villa and Iker Casillas but players such as David Silva and Juan Mata who look giants in foreign leagues but are unable to command a regular national team place back home. They envy their victories at Euros 2008 and 2012, and the 2010 World Cup, and wonder how they can possibly compete. *Marca* bullishly headlined its report of victory in the European under-19 championships 'Spain Always Win'.[4]

It is tempting when comparing the national team's record and Spain's long history of success at club level – winning more European titles (32), including more European Cups/Champions Leagues (13) than any other country, while Real Madrid and Barcelona rank first and second in matches and trophies won – to channel a Spice Girl who did not marry David Beckham and ask 'What Took You So Long?'[5]

Spain won a medal at the 1920 Olympics when that was the most significant international football tournament and in 1929 were the first non-British team to defeat England. But initial promise was not maintained. Fourth place at the 1950 World Cup, in which none of the final four had been World War II combatants (Spain had suffered as badly as most in its civil war, but had had six years longer to recover), and a European Nations Cup win in 1964, at home and when the competition was still so little-regarded that Marcelino's winning header against the Soviet Union scarcely registered elsewhere, was the full list of achievement.

Spain failed even to qualify for the World Cup four times between 1954 and 1974 or to progress beyond the pool stage between 1950 and an insipid display as host in 1982. Joining England among the World Cup's recurring quarter-finalists after that represented progress, but their departures from global and continental championships struck recurrent notes. They were wont to run into France at their best (Euro 84 and 2000, World Cup 2006), couldn't beat Italy when it mattered (Euro 88 and World Cup 1994 joining the earlier loss in 1934) and had an unfortunate habit of losing penalty shoot-outs to host nations (Euro 96, World Cup 2002).[6]

Contested Identity

But why *should* Spain have done better? Size does matter. Spain is a middle-sized European country, significantly smaller than France, Italy or even pre-unification Germany. It was also traditionally poorer.

On top of all this is contested and fractured national identity. Much of Spain's footballing strength has always been concentrated in Catalonia and the Basque country, whose relationship with the Spanish state has been equivocal at the best of times and (with good reasons) one of outright detestation for four decades from 1936. Pep Guardiola, Barcelona coach from 2008 to 2012, supports the existence of a Catalonia representative team and had an uneasy relationship with the other outstanding midfielder of his time, Real Madrid's Fernando Hierro, a conservative Andalucian. But that he still played 47 times for Spain underlined Phil Ball's contention that Catalans, Basques, Madrilenos and Andalucians have generally played together without serious difficulties.[7]

More suggestive is the mismatch between where Spain finds players and where it plays. Barcelona and Athletic Bilbao rank first and third for players capped by Spain, but that representation is not remotely reflected in the Spanish Federation's choice of match venues. That Madrid dominates even in the absence of a Stade de France-type national stadium is no great surprise or outrage, but it is striking that Seville and Valencia are the most-used alternatives. Neither Barcelona's Camp Nou, one of Europe's largest and best-appointed stadiums, situated in Spain's second city and home to the best team in Europe, nor Bilbao's 'Cathedral of Football', the San Mames, has seen *La Roja* in action as frequently as La Rosaleda, Malaga (which has a capacity below 30,000 and is located in a city with an impressive history of footballing insolvencies), either of the two main grounds in Seville, or even Dalymount Park, Dublin.[8]

If the success of Spain's clubs is in sharp contrast to the fortunes before 2008 of the national team, it is also equally logical. While Spain is a medium-sized country, Madrid and Barcelona are very large cities – seriously outweighed in Western Europe only by London and Paris – and focus the bulk of their economic and emotional resources on a single dominant club, leaving Español and Atletico as undoubted second strings.

This mismatch of club and country fortunes echoes England, and with good reason. The strongest English club teams have usually been, in football terms at least, multinational. Liverpool's best teams fully reflected their city's strongly Celtic flavour. So too have Real and Barça, who, as Manuel Vázquez Montalbán wrote, 'fielded an authentic foreign legion, without losing their identity as national symbols'.[9] The Ballon d'Or award for Europe's (since 2010 the world's) footballer of the year has been won 15 times by somebody playing in Spain, but once only by a Spaniard, Luis Suarez in 1960.[10] While Real's victories in the first five European Cups owed much to foreigners of the quality of Ferenc Puskas, Alfredo Di Stéfano, Raymond Kopa and Hector Rial, Barça were reinforced by a Hungarian diaspora begun by Ladislao Kubala, and joined after 1956 by Zoltan Czibor and Sandor Kocsis. Spain banned imports for a decade from 1962, and it seems no coincidence that its most fallow period in European competition was the trophy-less years between 1966 and 1979.[11]

Real v Barcelona

Contemporary Real and Barcelona offer the extreme example of the way television habitually strengthens the strongest, commanding a huge share of Spanish domestic TV money. While demonstrably less fair than the English system, this has the paradoxical effect of making La Liga competitive from third place down – enabling the European exploits of upstart Villarreal – compared to sixth or seventh in England. Combined with huge home grounds, this income flow enables Real and Barça to pay the highest salaries in world sport. A 2011 ESPN survey showed that the basic annual pay of the average Barça first-teamer was close to $8 million, and for their counterparts from Real it was more than $7.3 million, higher than their counterparts at the New York Yankees and Los Angeles Lakers and with a comfortable edge on the highest other payers in football, Chelsea and Inter Milan, both around $6 million.[12]

Like all the most vehement sporting rivalries, Real v Barça expresses forces that extend far outside, and long predate, football. For Vázquez Montalbán, a proud but clear-eyed Catalan, it was a 'necessary enmity' and 'an escape valve for the mutual antipathy of Barcelona and Madrid, an authentic storehouse of historic ill-will', with Barça representing 'the unhappy history of Catalonia, in perpetual armed or metaphorical conflict with the Spanish state since the 17th century'.[13] Spain's civil war and military dictatorship supplied a fresh layer through the murder of Barça president Josep Sunyol by Franco's forces and the dictator's subsequent clear preference for Real.[14]

Supporting Barça was, Vázquez Montalbán points out, a comparatively safe way for Catalans to express anti-Francoism, and it is no fluke that the spectacular growth of the club's membership towards the current roll of 170,000-plus began in the 1940s.[15] There are echoes of the Celtic-Rangers relationship in Barcelona's collective self-image as underdogs battling against an oppressive established power, victims of constant discrimination by referees. Yet to supporters of other teams they look like partners in an overbearing duopoly, resembling their supposedly mortal enemy much more than they do any other club. As Ball points out, if anybody has had a consistently bad deal from referees it is smaller Spanish clubs.[16] If football under Franco had been simply a *Madridista* conspiracy, Barça would hardly have been allowed to dominate the period between 1949 and 1953, still less win later titles that jeopardised Real's run of European Cup appearances.

The Guardiola Era

The beauty and brilliance of the football played by Guardiola's team and the self-regarding '*Mes Que Un Club*' motto picked out in the Nou Camp seating obscures some less beguiling realities. That glorious football, and the huge wages of its practitioners, are purchased by running into massive debt. Club administration has offered the *Animal Farm*–like spectacle of former revolutionaries becoming simulacra of their previous oppressors. The promise of the *Elefant Blau* pressure group, an inspiration to the nascent British supporter trust movement when representatives came to London in 1998, fizzled out once in power. Leader Joan Laporta so alienated former allies that all but three of the other *Elefant Blau* representatives who joined the club administration when he was elected club president in 2003 resigned within five years. After losing a vote of confidence among members he retained the presidency by resorting to procedural devices for which he had rightly criticised Josep Núñez, the autocratic president from 1978 to 2000.[17] That Laporta not only survived but could later use the presidency as a springboard into Catalan nationalist politics was attributable entirely to the successes of Guardiola.

Barcelona's current style and ascendancy are an echo of wider forces: post-Franco Spain's modernisation and comfort with the modern world, the extent to which (at least until the current economic downturn regenerated tensions) the 'uneven devolution' of the modern political settlement eased Catalonia's relationship with the Spanish state and the self-confidence of Barcelona itself, often seen as an ideal for other cities to emulate. It has been accompanied by a wider pattern of success for Spanish sport epitomised by the tennis stars led by Rafa Nadal (whose uncle Miguel Angel played alongside Guardiola for Barça and Spain through the 1990s), Formula One champion Fernando Alonso and dominance of cycling's greatest Tours. *Marca* proclaimed a sporting golden age before Guardiola's team had played a competitive match.[18]

In December 2011, the same paper, contemplating Barça's evisceration of South American champions Santos, was asking seriously if they were the best club side ever. That this question was informed by more thought and substance than the British media's habitual designation of the Premier League's flavour of the month as immortals was shown by a long list of alternatives going back to the River Plate teams of the 1930s, and that *Marca* retained its knee-jerk loyalty to Real with a story in the same issue arguing that because they had taken a point more than Barça from league games during the calendar year, they were the true champions of 2011.[19]

Nor was the question ridiculous. The first three and a half years of Guardiola's tenure saw Barça claim 13 trophies, mixing voracity for achievement with football of incomparable artistry. Their only notable setbacks were against teams coached by José Mourinho, who organised his Inter Milan team into a defensive effort that, even without home-bred players, evoked the most rigorous traditions of the Italian game. That Champions League semi-final triumph in 2010 had much more substance than Real's Copa del Rey victory in 2011, a mere punctuation point in a series of hammerings inflicted by Barça. Guardiola's players consistently rose to great occasions, twice humiliating very good Manchester United teams in Champions League finals. Even if Real's victory in the 2011–12 Liga and Chelsea's almost comically heroic Champions League semi-final display at Camp Nou halted that inexorable run of success, they did not detract from the overwhelming quality, both aesthetic and practical, of what went before.

Each club has been peculiarly well incarnated by its current leading figures. Real's are expensive imports – the rowdily attention-seeking Mourinho and his fellow-Portuguese, the sublimely gifted but charmlessly preening Cristiano Ronaldo, extracted from Manchester United for a world record fee. Barça offered the joyously exuberant Lionel Messi and, until his resignation, the coolly cultured Guardiola. Both are homegrown, even if Messi had to cross the Atlantic from his native Argentina to join the Barça nursery at La Masia.

If Spain's current global ascendancy has its roots anywhere, it is at Barça's training centre, founded by Nunez at the prompting of Johan Cruyff, the bridging figure in the transfer of coaching sophistication from the Netherlands that is an essential element in both Barça and Spanish hegemony. Cruyff argued that 'the greatest teams have six or seven players they grew themselves' and sought to graft those Dutch traditions on to his second home in Catalonia. Guardiola, then coach of Barça B, oversaw some reformation of the La Masia 'laboratory' in 2007, aimed at ensuring a continued flow of top-class talent inculcated with the distinctive club culture and style.[20]

But if quality of player education was the sole source of playing success, Crewe Alexandra would have been perennial Premier League champions. If ability to apply the Barcelona style were enough in itself, Swansea City would have won the 2011–12 title. Barcelona, like Manchester United, also have the income and charisma of a great club. They can attract the best raw talent and have the resources with which to develop it. But even given that, the sheer innate talent represented by a group including Messi, midfielder Sergio Busquets and World Cup final winner Iniesta has a once-in-a-generation quality. If Messi, in 2011 the first footballer to be named *L'Equipe*'s 'Champion of Champions' in a non–World Cup year, is the brightest star, Guardiola's coaching mentor Juanma Lillo points to the complementary attributes of one key lieutenant: 'For me, there's no one like Iniesta. He receives, he passes, he interprets, he evaluates the necessities of the team, he is constantly adapting. He could be a goalkeeper, he is so aware. Messi produces the best *jugadas* (runs, moves) in the world but Iniesta is the best *jugador* (player).'[21]

Barcelona players were the core of Spain's triumphs of 2008, 2010 and 2012, but they did not do it by themselves. Real supplied a magnificent goalkeeper in Iker Casillas and the top-quality defending, if less than sure-handed care of trophies, of Sergio Ramos. Basque traditions were superbly represented by Xabi Alonso, a midfielder whose quality has been evident as much in its absence from Liverpool – who undervalued him and have failed to replace him in kind or quality – as in its calmly accomplished presence with Real since he changed clubs in 2009. Valencia contributed the two Davids – both since departed. Midfielder David Silva was the best player in the English Premier League in the first half of 2011–12 while David Villa, a striker combining the technique of a top-class midfielder with the predatory instincts and precision of a sniper, has fitted seamlessly into Barça's flow. Nor should we forget the contribution in 2008 of a player representing a notable Spanish footballing tradition, the import. Brazilian-born midfielder Marcos Senna vitally brought the composure of a veteran and a precision valuable at any age to the Euro-winning team. His Villareal team-mate Juan Capdevila offered a similar veteran steadiness in 2010.

Vicente del Bosque, coach after spiky veteran Luis Aragones had achieved the initial breakthrough in 2008, also represented converging forces. He was the son of a Republican railwayman imprisoned by Franco, but had played for and coached Real Madrid. A lifelong *Madridista*, he fielded teams dominated by Barça players. His benevolent walrus-like appearance reflected genuine warmth, but cohabited with an acute football brain and a gift for getting the best out of world-class players. He had previously given Real four brilliant years, before getting sacked for offering only genuine substance to a club management demanding ostentatiously meretricious style.

One might argue that Spain were fortunate in their opposition, with several of the usual suspects below their best. Traditional *bestias negras* Italy and France were both in decline, Germany in transition, Brazil non-vintage and a hugely gifted Argentinian generation entrusted to the erratic hands of Diego Maradona.

But there was no doubt which was comfortably the best team in all three tournaments. Spain grew into each competition, developing irresistible momentum by the end. They coped with the pressures created by a formidable pre-tournament record and that national inheritance of disappointment and pessimism – no small thing as successive England teams and New Zealand Rugby World Cup squads could confirm. In 2010 the opening defeat by Switzerland meant that every subsequent match was potentially tournament-ending for Spain, but they had the mental strength to maintain confidence in their methods and underlying quality. There is, as Jonathan Wilson rightly points out, always an element of the contingent about results. Had Paraguay converted a second-half penalty during the quarter-final or any of Arjen Robben's lethally quick breaks in the final forced a breakthrough, the outcome might have been further disappointment. But it was not. Winning one tournament might be contingent. Winning three in a row, none of them on home ground and after resounding qualification campaigns and consistent victories elsewhere – Spain won 49 out of 54 matches, losing only 2, between the start of 2007 and the World Cup final – most certainly is not.[22]

The Italian bogey was laid in 2008 under the nerve-wracking circumstances of a penalty shoot-out at the end of a match in which Spain were clearly superior but failed to score. Germany, the ultimate tournament players, were beaten in both 2008 and 2010. The most striking tribute of all to their supreme technique, domination of possession and mesmeric movement was that the Netherlands, of all nations, were intimidated into an ugly World Cup final display summoning up David Lacey's immortal reminder that 'the Dutch invented the clog'.[23]

'All things must pass' not only sums up the philosophy of teams who move the ball better and more frequently than any recorded predecessor, but also reminds us that competitive advantage is of its nature transitory. Knowledge transfer has at times been slow in football – nothing sums up the insularity of British football for much of the twentieth century better than Willi Meisl's anecdote of the Swede Karl Gustafson, who thought English training sessions outdated on a visit in 1912 and returned 40 years later to find them unchanged.[24] But the best are always under scrutiny, with the sharpest minds among their opponents seeking to learn and apply the lessons of their success. Knowledge travels faster nowadays, and while Spain's run of successes in age-group competitions shows that displacing it will not be easy, somebody will catch up. It will probably be one of the larger, longer-established giants – perhaps Italy or Brazil. Or it might be some wholly new contender as unexpected as Uruguay in the 1920s or the Netherlands half a century later. Simon Kuper and Stefan Symanski have made an intriguing and logical case for the eventual rise of Turkey.[25]

For the moment, though, the best football in the world speaks Spanish with a pronounced Catalan accent and a hint of Dutch ancestry and is played in a manner that compels admiration and affection like no hegemon since the Brazilians of the 1958–70 era. Whoever follows will not only have to be very good, but will do well to be half as compelling.

NOTES

1 Quoted in H. Richards, 'Spain braced for everything except success', *Financial Times*, 14 June 2006. '*Hombres sin Piedad*' is also the Spanish title for the film *Twelve Angry Men*.
2 J.J. Anaut, A La Contra blog, Marca.com, 9 June 2006.
3 Richards, 'Spain braced for everything except success'.
4 D. Shaw, Deutsche Presse Agentur, 2 August 2011, www.monstersandcritics.com on 30 December 2011.

5 *Guia Marca de la Liga 2011* (Madrid: Grupo Unidad Editorial, 2010), p. 385.

6 Ibid., p. 414, pp. 420–27.

7 P. Ball, *Morbo* (London: When Saturday Comes, 2011 edn.), pp. 230–34.

8 *Guia Marca de la Liga 2011*, p. 428.

9 M. Vázquez Montalbán, *Fútbol, una Religion en busca de un Dios* (Barcelona: De Bolsillo, 2006), p. 24.

10 *Guia Marca de la Liga 2011*, p. 394; 'Argentina's Lionel Messi wins Fifa Ballon d'Or award', BBC.co.uk, 10 January 2011.

11 *Guia Marca de la Liga 2011*, p. 392. D. Goldblatt, *The Ball Is Round: A Global History of Football* (London: Penguin, 2007) pp. 415–17.

12 N. Harris, 'The 200 Best-paying Teams in the World', *ESPN The Magazine*, 2 May 2011.

13 Montalbán, *Fútbol, una Religion en busca de un Dios*, p. 64, p. 150, p. 159.

14 J. Burns, *Barça: A People's Passion* (London: Bloomsbury, 2000), pp. 107–14.

15 Montalbán, *Fútbol, una Religion en busca de un Dios*, p. 65, p. 73.

16 Ball, *Morbo*, p. 141.

17 'Why La Liga has taken a kicking', *Financial Times*, 30 August 2008.

18 D. Melero, 'La "Edad de Oro" del deporte espanol es una realidad', *Marca.com*, 7 July 2008.

19 'El Real Madrid gana la Liga 2011' and G. Herrero and J.M. Rodriguez, 'El mejor equipo de la historia?' *Marca.com*, 19 December 2011.

20 M. Perarnau, 'La Masia, como un laboratorio', *Sport.es*, 18 June 2010.

21 'Messi, premio "Campóon de Campeones" 2011', *Marca.com*, 24 December 2011; S. Lowe, 'The Brain in Spain', *The Blizzard*, 1 (2011), p. 63.

22 *Guia Marca de la Liga 2011*, p. 427.

23 P. Shaw, *The Book of Football Quotations* (London: Ebury, 2003), p. 133.

24 W. Meisl, *Soccer Revolution* (London: Phoenix House, 1955), p. 159.

25 S. Kuper and S. Szymanski, *Why England Lose: And Other Curious Phenomena Explained* (London: HarperCollins, 2009), pp. 1–2.

The Game-Changers: José Mourinho

'Please don't call me arrogant, but I'm European champion and I think I'm a special one.' So said José Mourinho in June 2004 at his first press conference as Chelsea manager, and as he sat there bathed in the flash of popping cameras it was difficult to disagree. He's won the Champions League with two different teams and the league title in four different countries. Without having to say anything else, that's special enough.

He's articulate, bright and smart enough to be charming/insulting/charismatic/abusive in five languages (English, Portuguese, Spanish, Italian and French). He's rakishly good-looking, immaculately dressed and wears just the right amount of designer stubble. Not for nothing is he known as the Iberian George Clooney. The Portuguese man of phwoar. Throw in the self-confidence, the haughty arrogance and the ability. It's a heady combination. We really are a long way from sheepskin coats. And when he sat down at that press conference and anointed himself the Special One, yes, he was being mischievous, yes, he was wilfully creating the myth, and yes, he was playing with the press like a cat might play with a mouse, but he got away with it because he was right. He knew it and so did everyone else.

We had already seen the manager-as-character: Shankly, Clough, Allison – managers who knew one end of a soundbite from the other, characters who knew who the real star of the show was; and as the 1990s turned into the 2000s and media coverage went into overdrive, more characters were needed for the global soap opera that was modern football. Players were either muzzled, media-trained to death or simply dull – someone whose greatest academic achievement was an educated left foot was never going to be that interesting to the wider population. Increasingly, the press turned to managers and coaches for the stories and quotes. There was Sir Alex with his hairdryer; Arsène the *professeur* who never saw anything; Harry the wheeler-dealer. All good characters, all provided good copy. But José Mário dos Santos Félix Mourinho was something else. The football manager as 'character' turned up to 11. Not for nothing did the Spanish edition of *Rolling Stone* magazine pronounce him 'Rock Star of the Year' in December 2011.[1]

The Two Mourinhos

'If I wanted to have an easy job ... I would have stayed at Porto – beautiful blue chair, the UEFA Champions League trophy, God, and after God, me,' he said at another early Chelsea press conference. The looks, the attitude, the quotes ... it's all as designed as the stubble, weapons in the arsenal, something else to give an edge.

What makes a special one special? Didier Drogba talks of his 'charming smile', attention to detail and ability to create a father-son bond between player and manager, but more intriguingly describes him in almost spiritual terms. 'On the bench I've heard him describe what would happen in an almost surgical way. Sometimes this was almost disquieting. As if he could see the future.'[2]

Like many managers, Mourinho revels in creating an 'us and them' siege mentality, picking fights and protecting his team at any cost. While often tiresome to the outsider, this cartoon-like prickly aggression clearly works. And if it has the added effect of putting all the attention on him, well, that's just a bonus.

Just as clearly, sometimes he goes wildly over the top: gouging the eye of Barcelona's assistant coach Tito Vilanova during a brawl at the end of the final of the 2011 Supercopa de España wasn't big or clever. But, as Grant Wahl wrote, 'There is a reason his $12 million annual salary is the highest of any coach on the planet. He's the best in the world.'[3]

Away from the arena, when no one's looking, he's religious, cultured, happily married, a devoted father, doesn't drink or smoke – and probably still charming. Before he became a football coach, he was a teacher of special needs children. Where does the real Mourinho begin and end?

'Even he himself says that there are two José Mourinhos,' says Patrick Barclay, who wrote the biography *Anatomy of a Winner*. 'There is the charming private man and there is the coach we see, a coach who has an inability to apologise for anything that he or one of his players says and does. Desmond Morris [anthropologist and author of *The Football Tribe*] told me he was convinced that having film-star looks helped Mourinho take [control of] the Chelsea dressing room. Because look at it this way. What do footballers like? They like money and women and the fact that most of their girlfriends would rather sleep with José than them, it gives him that cachet among the lads.'[4]

Mourinho got his break in July 1992 when Sir Bobby Robson was appointed manager of Sporting Lisbon and decided that he needed a good local coach, someone who spoke the language and knew the ground. That was where he acquired the pejorative 'The Translator', a name neither he nor his detractors have ever forgotten. But he was much more than a skilled linguist. 'He'd come back and hand me a dossier that was absolutely first class. I mean first class,' Robson said. 'As good as anything I've ever received. Here he was, in his early thirties, never been a player, never been a coach to speak of either, giving me reports as good as anything I ever got.'[5]

In management his attention to detail is legendary, but he knows that preparation can only get you so far. 'I think the genius will always make the difference. And the genius in my sport is about some unbelievable players that can break every organisation and every work you can do. Genius in managing also exists. For me the most important thing is man management. Football for me is a human science, it is about man.'[6]

Mourinho followed Robson to Barcelona before bowing to the inevitable and becoming a boss in his own right with Porto. Just as Sir Alex Ferguson is immune to the criticism that he can only do it at a big rich club, having broken the Scottish domination of Celtic and Rangers with Aberdeen, so too Mourinho. Porto were, in European terms, a small team with small resources. Fresh out of the equivalent of managerial high school and within two years of taking over, Mourinho had made them European champions. A special one.

When he joined Inter Milan from Chelsea in 2008 it was described as 'arguably the most difficult club in the world to manage'.[7] Massimo Moratti had hired and fired 14 managers since buying the club in 1995. Yet two years later, Inter won a remarkable treble – the Italian league and cup and the Champions League, taking Mourinho's haul to 17 major trophies in eight seasons. That year he was named FIFA World Coach of the Year. Special? Less than a year later, and under a new manager (his old nemesis Rafa Benitez), Inter failed to progress past the group stage of the Champions League.

Inter won the Champions League in the Bernabeu, Real Madrid's cathedral. Within weeks that would be his new home for, as he said, 'It's a unique club and I believe that not to coach Real leaves a void in a coach's career.'[8] As ever, it wasn't going to be easy, because for all their resources and for all their history, one thing stood in his way: Pep Guardiola's Barcelona, the best club side there's ever been. 'Real Madrid wants to be again the best – of the present and of the future. That's my challenge.'[9] If anyone could rise to that challenge, it's Mourinho. He is, after all, special.

And so it came to pass. In 2011–12, Real Madrid broke the record for the most goals in a season (121) as well as the most points in a season (100). More importantly, on 21 April, Real beat Barcelona 2–1 in the El Clásico at the Camp Nou, effectively sealing their first La Liga title since 2008. It was Barcelona's first defeat in 55 games. Guardiola resigned as Barca coach and announced he was taking a year off. Mourinho signed a new contract. Maybe he's not special. Maybe he's whatever the next word along is.

NOTES

1 *Rolling Stone*, December 2011, http://rollingstone.es/noticias/view/mourinho-rockstar-de-2011-en-la-portada-de-rolling-stone.

2 D. Drogba, *Didier Drogba: The Autobiography* (London: Aurum Press, 2008).

3 G. Wahl, 'What's So Special about Jose Mourinho?', *Sports Illustrated*, 7 March 2011, http://sportsillustrated.cnn.com/vault/article/magazine/MAG1182630/index.htm (accessed 15 January 2012).

4 Interview with author, 22 July 2011.

5 J. Crowley, 'NS Man of the Year', *New Statesman,* 19 December 2005, www.newstatesman.com/200512190026 (accessed 15 January 2012).

6 *Daily Telegraph*, 27 December 2011.

7 P. Nathanson, 'Jose Mourinho faces the toughest job in Europe at Inter Milan', *Daily Telegraph,* 3 June 2008, www.telegraph.co.uk/sport/football/teams/chelsea/2302278/Jose-Mourinho-faces-toughest-job-in-Europe-at-Inter-Milan.html (accessed 15 January 2012).

8 'Real Madrid unveil Jose Mourinho as their new coach', BBC.co.uk, 31 May 2010, http://news.bbc.co.uk/sport1/hi/football/europe/8708315.stm (accessed 15 January 2012).

9 Wahl, 'What's So Special about Jose Mourinho?'

15

TOBY MILLER

Where Next? Football's New Frontiers

Football is more popular than Jesus and John Lennon combined. One in every two living people, we are told, watched the 2010 men's World Cup on television.[1] More than ever, football is a universal currency, a lingua franca – the common ground of culture. In the words of the prominent U.S. journalist Dave Zirin, 'Soccer is the great global game: the closest thing we have to a connective cultural tissue that binds our species across national and cultural borders.'[2] Go anywhere in the world with a ball under your arm or a ripping sporting yarn next to your glass and you'll never walk, sit or stumble alone.

We are accustomed to such shibboleths about the universal popularity of the game. But are they true of the three countries that account for much of the world's population, knowledge, armaments, wealth – and sport: the United States, China and India? These are crucial sites for a sport that claims ecumenicism/hegemony. Why have they resisted football's appealing blandishments and seemingly inexorable march? And what about virtual frontiers – the likely impact of new media technologies on the game's future? Will football's geography and means of reception both change markedly as gigantic countries and innovative genres enter the field of play?

Conversely, one might ask why the growth of football's popularity, whether spatially or textually, is even an issue. Can't a sport simply emerge and exist organically? The answer is sonic and onomatopoeic. The sound of football is no longer the whoosh of a ball rippling a net. It's the ker-ching of an international cash register.[3]

Bosman and Beyond

Consider the wealthiest and most powerful part of the world game: European professional football clubs. Once small city businesses, for much of their lives, they were run rather like not-for-profits, drawing upon and representing local cultures. By the 1990s, many had been commodified and made into creatures of exchange. In the course of this radical transformation, they fell prey to fictive capital, becoming sources of asset inflation used by rentiers to service other debts through the cash flow of television money and gate receipts, at the same time as their *embourgeoisement* solved a policing problem for states about what to do with the public and its passions.

Many factors produced these phenomena, notably the game's globalization, governmentalization, commodification, televisualization and position within the New International Division of Cultural Labor (NICL).[4] Multiple stakeholders are committed to football's expansion, from managers and players to network executives and institutional investors. An example of this change is the shift in the NICL that derived from the midfield player Jean-Marc Bosman's appeal to the European Court of Justice (ECJ) against his suspension in 1990 by the Union Royale Belge des Sociétés de Football for seeking a transfer overseas. Bosman's case was based on the right to freedom of movement for European Union (EU) workers. The Court decided in his favour five years later. Facing the threat of fines from the European Commission, in 1996 FIFA discontinued rules restricting the number of foreigners who could play. Within a few months, cross-European player mobility increased sharply, and a gap in talent between wealthy teams and also-rans widened.

At the same time as the Bosman decision, huge amounts of money became available to football as television was deregulated across Europe, new communications technologies and consumer electronics proliferated and elite competitions maximized their media exposure. In the decade from 1990, European football rights costs grew by 800 per cent, during a period of minimal macroeconomic inflation. The amounts paid to televise the sport may seem large, but they are risible when compared to producing drama or even original news and current affairs because most development costs and star salaries are borne by the sports themselves rather than TV stations. In addition, securing rights to popular leagues is a popular means of securing subscribers to new services such as cable and satellite.[5]

As in the Bosman case, these economic developments are not solely the result of market forces. They also reference the world of states. For example, during the first five years of the English Premier League, which commenced in 1992, 60 matches were televised each season; by 2006, the number was 138. As Sky television cordoned off more and more games, the European Commission expressed concern about lack of competition for coverage. This opened the way to Setanta, a satellite channel that sought to expand beyond its limited diasporic home in Irish pubs around the world to private homes around the British Isles and the United States. Setanta and Sky paid £2.7 billion for UK and international rights between 2007 and 2010, a deal that was ultimately shared with Disney's ESPN when Setanta overreached and collapsed.[6]

Football is also a crucial component in the new kind of corporate citizenship avowed by capitalists who want to smell nice. Corporations invoke citizenship ideals to describe themselves while principally pursuing their economic interests. This is part of a restless quest for profit unfettered by regulation, twinned with a desire for moral legitimacy that is based on doing right while growing rich through a respect for law and a desire to meddle. Two hundred and fifty-five public, private and mixed projects of international development utilized sport in 2008 – a 93 per cent increase over five years. A high proportion involved corporations, frequently via astroturf – faux grassroots – organizations such as the Vodafone Foundation. Using football permits corporations to act as if they were governing agencies operating with the public good in mind, even as they heighten North-South imbalances, promote their own wares, commodify sports, distract attention from their environmental and labour records, and stress international/imperial sports over local ones.[7]

The wider point is this: for football clubs, national associations and international organizations, growth has become a watchword. So when considering where football goes next, the powers-that-be will not only ponder introducing goal-line technology, tweaking the rulebook or presenting the game to a smart-phone world. Their political-economic priority will be selling the game in sizeable and affluent territories.

India and China

Why has India, with a population of over a billion people, never appeared in the World Cup finals? Why is its national team ranked in the hundreds internationally? How can a sport that was hugely popular and successful in the early days of Olympic football, and attracted over 130,000 spectators to the 1997 Kolkata Derby between East Bengal and Mohan Bagan, not produce players of international note?[8]

If it is a mystery why a sporting nation so influenced by British imperialism, and whose national league can be traced back to the 1880s, hasn't embraced football, it is unlikely to remain so for long. The International Monetary Fund (IMF) estimated that India's GDP in 2013, while declining, would still be 4.9 per cent.[9] That figure is as interesting to FIFA as scorelines at the Bernabeu or the San Siro. It is stimulating numerous studies and anecdotes seeking to explain and improve football's profile.

Indian TV audiences for the 2010 World Cup were disappointing. The average viewership for live games was 1.5 million, with a peak of 5.6

million. Audience reach plummeted 53 per cent from 2006, and the national broadcaster Doordarshan did not feature supporting programmes such as magazine shows. The country does now have a television network dedicated to football, Ten Action+, which covers the principal European leagues and may have been a marketing factor, along with other Asian broadcasters, in Spain's decision to play La Liga games at earlier hours. Ten Action+ sees the national football audience as very particular in regional and linguistic terms – it is urban, English-speaking and hence middle class, with potential expansion to include the mofussil. The domestic league suffers from inadequate stadia, the absence of major teams in key areas such as Delhi and the predominance of cricket.[10]

The triumph of cricket as India's defining sport derived from a complex field of media deregulation, televisual investment, middle-class expansion and satellite innovation, which it managed more effectively than other sports.[11] For football to compete, it needs to control this constellation rather than accept being crowded out.

Another statistic that's likely to catch the eye of FIFAcrats is the IMF figure of 8.2 per cent annual growth in GDP for China in 2013.[12] Hence the governing body's fantasy of an East Asia dominated by football.[13] Arguably the last great footballing frontier, China has hinted that it may bid for the World Cup in 2026. In 2010, Wei Di, head of the local Football Association, boasted that China had the venues and the rail network needed to host a big event and that the FIFocracy was positive.[14] China's TV ratings for the 2010 World Cup saw an average live match audience of 17.5 million and a peak of 66 million. Audience reach was up 17 per cent on 2006, which represented an additional 48.5 million viewers. Regional broadcasters became involved for the first time and there was more non-live primetime coverage.[15]

Thus far, however, crime is limiting the development of football in China. Match-fixing and gambling – the latter is illegal – are rampant at the highest levels of administration and, allegedly, among referees. Of course, these tendencies and problems are everywhere, but the Chinese public and state have exhibited intense irritation with them and claim the issue is systemic rather than occasional. There have been repeated attempts to reform management of the game, including high-profile arrests and the formation of a China Anti-Football Gambling Alliance.[16] Critics also point to the absence of promotion to young children, 'a soccer tradition less pronounced than that of Europe', and struggles between commercial leagues and state sporting bodies, such that the state socialism of Olympic training is incompatible with the managed capitalism of cartel clubs.[17]

The Chinese FA says the number of players fell from 500,000 in 2000 to 50,000 in 2011. In 2009, it launched a schools promotion across dozens of cities, the 44 Cities Project, but the schools were slow to cooperate. In addition, there is a lack of city venues. In 2011, a large real-estate concern committed to sponsor an elite youth academy, but this came just weeks after major corporations had fled the sport due to its corrupt image, and China Central Television was reconsidering coverage of the national league.[18] So the patchwork of civil, state and commercial bodies involved paints a complex picture of this most desired of commercial fetishes.

The United States Problem

Let's consider in detail now the object of FIFA's desire since the year dot, the world's lumbering, tumbling empire – the United States. We'll find that the future has already arrived – in fact it's been here quite a while. Football is massively important in that country, across the spectrum from cultural signage to economic investment. But this fact is largely denied by the bourgeois media, macho nativism and reactionary academia.

During the 2010 World Cup in South Africa, the glossy lounge-lizard magazine *Vanity Fair* ran a blog called 'Fair Play'. In best Derridoidal style, the editors printed the word 'soccer' with a deconstructive line across it – suddenly subject to erasure by 'football'. Nike, McDonald's and Coca-Cola saw the World Cup as a much bigger deal than the Olympics. Coke's biggest promotion yet was at the 2010 tournament. It included a deal with YouTube whereby viewers across 17 languages and 120 nations posted their goal celebrations. Anheuser-Busch and Visa were heavily involved, too: the Visa Match Planner smart-phone application provided scores and retail information, articulated to the tournament. MTV ran spots around the world with the tagline 'We understand why you aren't watching MTV'. ESPN Deportes, Disney's U.S. Spanish-language TV sport channel, didn't have the rights either, but it dispatched 25 reporters to South Africa to realize the promotional campaign '*90 minutos no son suficientes*' (90 minutes aren't enough), troping the duration of matches to indicate the importance of background and synoptic material.[19] This all looks like a mature market where football is a leading light.

But the sport receives fewer column inches, phone-in rants and breathless commentary than the nation's staples of professional men's sport: ice hockey, 'American' football, baseball and basketball. Explanations for football's ambivalent stature in the United States vary, but many local accounts, whether scholarly, journalistic or political, rely on a potent brand of amateur intellectualism and reactionary theorization that celebrates a putative 'American exceptionalism' that supposedly makes U.S. sport an export rather than an import culture.

The concept of exceptionalism began as an attempt to explain why social-ism had not taken greater hold in the United States. It has since turned into an excessive rhapsody to Yanqui world leadership, difference and sancti-mony. So we encounter claims made – in all seriousness – that 'foreignness' can make a sport unpopular in the United States, and the media will not accept practices coded as 'other'.[20] We even have academics telling us that because basketball and football are both played in the air and involve goals, they are too similar for people to follow syntagmatically and must instead be paradigmatic alternatives, and that U.S. sports do not connote national-ism in the same way as football (Mandelbaum, 2004 and 2010). Perhaps the most appalling instance of 'American exceptionalism' was provided by the Reaganite Republican Jack Kemp, who derided football before Congress as a 'European socialist' sport by contrast with its 'democratic' U.S. rival.[21]

The *Village Voice* denounced football thus: 'Every four years the World Cup comes around, and with it a swarm of soccer nerds and bullies remind-ing us how backward and provincial we are for not appreciating soccer enough.'[22] During the 2010 World Cup, this anti-leftist xenophobia saw Glenn Beck, one of the right's pitchfork men in the bourgeois media, refer to Barack Obama's policies as 'the World Cup of political thought'. He advised listeners that 'the rest of the world likes Barack Obama's policies, we do not' and 'we don't want the World Cup, we don't like the World Cup, we don't like soccer'. Convicted Watergate conspirator G. Gordon Liddy derided the game on his talk show because it 'originated with the South American Indians' and asked 'Whatever happened to American exceptionalism?' His guests from the coin-operated Media Research Center said it was 'a poor man or poor woman's sport' that 'the left is pushing … in schools across the country'.[23]

The Latin@ Factor

Football has always been popular in the United States – but the key is that its popularity lies with people whose interests have not been important for mainstream sports marketers, newspapers and so on, for example, the Bolivians and Salvadorans who crowd into DC United games in the Barra Brava section. So impoverished are many football fans that, for example, Los Angeles has perhaps 200 unaffiliated amateur adult leagues with half a million players who cannot afford to join the national system. Almost 6 million women and more than 8 million men play regularly, two thirds of whom are adults. Because football is loved by an unusual cross-class alli-ance of very poor, working-class Latin@[24] immigrants and relatively affluent, college-educated white parents, it is complex to research and promote.[25]

Of course, anti-immigrant and specifically anti-Latin@ feelings can run very deep. When the United States and Mexico contested the 2011 Confederation of North, Central American and Caribbean Association Football (CONCACAF) Gold Cup final in Pasadena before 93,000 people, the presentation of the trophy was made in Spanish. Tim Howard, the United States goalkeeper who plays in the English Premier League, erupted: 'CONCACAF should be ashamed of themselves. I think it was a [expletive deleted] disgrace that the entire post-match ceremony was in Spanish. You can bet your ass if we were in Mexico City it wouldn't be all in English.'[26]

These prejudices run against the economic interests of both the country and the sport. Internationals between the United States and Mexico in the United States are run by Soccer United Marketing (SUM), a subsidiary of Major League Soccer. SUM connects touring Mexican teams with U.S. sponsors such as Coca-Cola, Home Depot and AT&T, which rely on this marketing to target Latin@s. Conversely, the United States Soccer Federation, which runs the national team, is conflicted. To make money, it hosts matches in California or Texas in order to attract Latin@ crowds. To encourage nativist support when matches are qualifiers for major tournaments, it is tempted more by New England and the Midwest.[27]

Regardless, the numbers all point in one direction. During his time with the Los Angeles Galaxy, David Beckham won three Teen Choice awards over native athletes.[28] Visit YouTube[29] and recall the winning penalty of the Women's World Cup final in Pasadena in 1999, attended by 90,000. Or wind forward to Los Angeles 2009, when 93,000 turned up to watch Barcelona and saw Beckham score,[30] then on to the 60,000-plus who attended 2007 expansion team Seattle's last home game of 2011.[31] The play-off rounds of the 2006 and 2010 World Cup finals both drew larger U.S. TV audiences than baseball's World Series. And there were more citizens of the United States at the South African tournament than of any other country apart from the host.[32]

The clouds have grown heavy and thick around elderly, inadequate ways of understanding the U.S. sporting market that obey the simp(eria)listic dictates of 'American exceptionalism'. Average attendance at the 1994 World Cup, held in the United States, was just under 70,000 – the highest ever in any country. Television viewership for the 2006 World Cup was up 90 per cent on 2002. And when television and radio rights to the 2018 and 2022 World Cup tournaments went up for sale, Fox bought the Anglo version and NBC's Telemundo the Spanish for a combined U.S.$1.2 billion, more than twice the previous amount. Telemundo's principal rival among Spanish-language broadcast networks, Univisión, frequently the top-rated

TV station across all languages, out-rated Anglo competitors in 2010 with its coverage of a U.S.-Mexico international match, which 60,000 attended. Since 2005, the United States has had English- and Spanish-language TV networks dedicated to football, covering leagues in Britain, Germany, Asia, Africa, France, Spain, the Netherlands, Australia, Latin America – and the United States (men's and women's from 2009). There are numerous podcasts, radio shows, fans and players.[33]

The niche cable and satellite station Fox Soccer Channel attracts men aged 18–34 with annual household incomes over $75,000 ('Fox Soccer', 2008). The hint as to how it identifies viewers to advertisers comes from its TV commercials, which are about regaining and sustaining hair-growth and hard-ons, losing and hiding pimples and pounds, and becoming and adoring soldiers and sailors. In 2007, the matches it covered drew between 50,000 and 70,000 viewers; four years on, the average was 100,000. In 2011, the station's biggest-ever ratings for an English Premier League game amounted to 418,000 viewers and 285,000 households, while 954,000 watched a U.S.-Mexico fixture.[34] The ratings for English matches are mostly achieved very early in the morning (in much of the country) and nowhere near prime time anywhere. The Champions League final of 2011 set a ratings record with 2.6 million watching, Fox Soccer and Fox Deportes were attracting ever-larger audiences and it was an obvious move to shift these programmes to stations available to everyone. Fox decided to show English Premier League games on its broadcast station, including a live match on the day of the 2012 Super Bowl.[35] The future for football in the United States was headed in one direction – consolidation of long-standing tendencies denied by gormless nativists.

Old, Middle-Aged and New Media

This chapter has focused on television as both a source of numbers to indicate football's popularity and as an evolutionary force in the game's changes. That emphasis has largely excluded old media, such as newspapers, and new media, such as the internet. The emphasis on middle-aged media (TV) does not derive from the author's age, however. Television remains crucial to the way football is run and the way it is watched. But this is because TV itself is changing in productive ways. Technological and legal transformations are siphoning sports away from broadcast and onto cable, satellite and pay-per-view. And powerful teams and leagues are establishing their own televisual networks: Manchester United, Benfica, Barcelona, Middlesbrough, Olympique de Marseille, AC and Inter Milan, Real Madrid and Chelsea boast channels, inter alia.

Among members of the Organisation for Economic Cooperation and Development (OECD), 52 per cent of TV households received only broadcast signals in 1995. By 2002, that number had dropped to 37 per cent, as cable in particular proliferated. Synchronized moving images and sounds can now be sent to and received from public spaces, offices, homes, shops, schools and transportation. The devices include TVs, computers, smartphones, tablets and personal digital assistants. The networks vary between broadcast, satellite, cable, telephone and internet. The stations may be public, private, community or amateur. The time of watching is varied, from live to on-demand. These technologies increasingly transgress the boundaries and policing established by nations. The spread of some transmission systems is very limited – perhaps 2.5 million homes worldwide had internet television in 2005 – but others are on the move: cable and satellite channels in the OECD almost doubled between 2004 and 2006. In 2008 there were 1.1 billion TV sets in the world, with 43 per cent receiving signals from broadcast and 38 per cent from cable.[36] Television is more diverse, more diffuse, more popular, more powerful and more innovative than ever. Our spanking new flat-screen TVs will soon be tossed cavalierly away if the next generation takes off – sets from Sony, Samsung, LG, Toshiba, Sharp and Panasonic, with streaming movies and Yahoo!/Intel widgets for internet connections with information about weather and stock prices, or Blue-ray players that access the internet. The lesson of new technology remains the same as ever: as per print, radio, and television, each medium is quickly dominated by centralized and centralizing corporations, despite its multi-distributional potential. This centralism is obviously less powerful in the case of the internet than technologies that are more amenable to being sealed off.

The idea is laughable that audiences using several different communications technologies while watching TV are more independent of, for example, commercials. No fewer than a third of sports audiences who send instant or text messages while viewing refer to the commercials they have been watching, and almost two-thirds have greater recognition of those commercials than people who simply watch television without reaching out in these other ways to friends/fellow-spectators.[37]

Dedicated sports cable stations such as ESPN use interactive TV for such as 'My Vote' and 'My Bottom Line'. These adjuncts to conventional television-watching uncover more and more data about audience drives in the name of enabling participation and pleasure in watching via new media add-ons. Internationally, ESPN has sought to purchase broadband portals that ensure global dominance and now owns Cricinfo, Scrum.com and Racing-Live.[38] People who watch TV on different devices and via different services are watching more, not less, television. Television still dominates as the mode of production, distribution and reception. A shift to internet dominance will only come with massive, dependable, fast, high-resolution screens capable of comfortable use by households together. Which will essentially be televisions.

Is Growth Good?

Let's finish by turning an eye to the notion that growth in football is good anyway, by examining the impact of the sport's globalization on the environment. The World Cup is of particular concern. FIFA boasts that it

> is dedicated to taking its environmental responsibility seriously. Issues such as global warming, environmental conservation and sustainable management are a concern for FIFA, not only in regards to FIFA World Cups™, but also in relation to FIFA as an organisation. That is why FIFA has been engaging with its stakeholders and other institutions to find sensible ways of addressing environmental issues and mitigate the negative environmental impacts linked to its activities.[39]

From solar-powered stadiums to free public transportation, the 2006 World Cup featured a 'Green Goal', which claimed to make the event 'climate-neutral' by saving 100,000 tonnes of carbon dioxide via climate-protection projects in India and South Africa.[40] But the data excluded international travel, part of the difference between environmental audits that focus on one country rather than a wider ecological impact.[41] Environmental audits of global events are meaningless if they don't look at travel and the media.

Because the claims made about the 2006 tournament rang hollow, FIFA set up an Environmental Forum. Its task has been to 'green' stadia, training grounds, accommodation, amenities and so on, in accordance with the UN Environmental Program. For the 2010 tournament, South Africa used biogas from landfills, wind farms and efficient lighting, and proudly proclaimed that nine teams had their jerseys made from recycled polyethylene terephthalate bottles. Coincidentally, these teams were themselves sponsored by a major sporting goods company, which remorselessly promoted its good deed.[42] The 2014 tournament in Brazil will supposedly be played out in green stadia.[43] But beware greenwashing, since post-event calculations disclose that the South African World Cup carbon footprint was twice that of the 2008 Beijing Olympics.[44]

Such initiatives do not confront the real issue. Mostly fuelled by European tourism, the 2010 World Cup had the largest carbon footprint of any commercial event in world history: 850,000 tonnes of carbon expended, 65 per cent of it due to flights.[45] The Cup's environmental initiatives did not

Table 15.1. *Predicted environmental impact of 2010 World Cup*

	Component emissions (tCO2e)	share (%)
International transport	1,856,589	67.4
Inter-city transport	484,961	17.6
Intra-city transport	39,577	1.4
Stadia constructions and materials	15,359	0.6
Stadia and precinct energy use	16,637	0.5
Energy use in accommodation	340,128	12.4
Total tCO2e Excluding international transport	896,661	
Total tCO2e Including international transport	2,753,250	100

Source: Republic of South Africa et al. (2009).

address the unsustainability of air travel, where the very prospect of corporate media publicity and public-image beneficence depend on environmental despoliation. This is a step too far – or too close – to take. It would signal serious intent for media organizations, sports and states to diminish the worst carbon footprint in the world outside the Pentagon's.[46]

Before the 2010 finals, the South African and Norwegian governments conducted a study of the likely environmental impact, coming up with the data in Table 15.1.

Those responsible knew the implications. The South African government generated tender documents inviting competition to offset the flight footprint, but issued no contracts.[47] The externalities of tourism and foreign currency were always going to outweigh such concerns.

One can argue that both these aspects – air travel and media electricity – are beyond the jurisdiction of FIFA or governments or fans. To which I can only recommend the wisdom of Kissy Suzuki as offered to James Bond in *You Only Live Twice* (Lewis Gilbert, 1967): 'Think again, please.' FIFA and local organizers strike deals with airlines, airports and media organizations. That endows them with power and responsibility alike in ways that are much more important than tourism or football. And fans must be aware of their own complicity in this travesty.

Plutocracy Rovers v Footocrats United

FIFA's growth evangelism is problematic. Given the fervour accompanying the organization's self-anointed omniscience and omnipotence, it comes as no surprise that the doctrines of economic growth that it follows have religious origins. When the Trinity was being ideologized within Christianity, something had to be done to legitimize the concept at the same time as dismissing and decrying polytheistic and pagan rivals to the new religion's moralistic monotheism. Hence *oikonomia*, a sphere of worldly arrangements that was to be directed by a physical presence on Earth representing theology's principal superstition, the deity. God gave Christ 'the economy' to manage, so 'the economy' indexically manifested Christianity.[48] When FIFA arrogates to itself the right to make and break laws, to buy and sell territories, and to pollute the world, it is invoking just such magical origins and justifications. We should not be in thrall to this self-anointed elect's control of football's future, especially when it is deeply connected to commercial dictates and surveillance. In Zirin's wise words:

> only in a world so upside down could 'the Beautiful Game' be run by an organization as corrupt as FIFA and by a man as rotten to the core as FIFA President Sepp Blatter. Only Sepp Blatter, whose reputation for degeneracy approaches legend, would hire ... Henry Kissinger to head 'a committee of wise persons' aimed at 'rooting out corruption' in his organization.[49]

FIFA and its fiefdoms are painful hangovers from the amateur good-old-boy networks that ran the sport before its wholesale commercialization, at the same time as they represent the ultimate in contemporary commodification and governmentalization, with transparency a word rather than a rule. The world of football relies on obsessive desires to know and control players, competitions and audiences, in keeping with this bizarre blend.

A few clubs are increasingly powerful and the majority increasingly fragile as financial pressure to win slots in the Champions League intensifies because of TV money. This sets management of the game on several possible collision courses with ruling associations. For example, FIFA's committee on club football features representatives from Saudi Arabia, New Zealand, South Africa, Egypt, Ivory Coast and Honduras and almost no one from teams that provide major World Cup players or characterize the sport globally. And of the $3.7 billion that FIFA received from the 2010 World Cup finals, just $40 million went to clubs.[50] Meanwhile, Michel Platini, head of UEFA, claims to stand against greedy clubs, corrupt FIFAcrats and crass commodification, saying, 'We are the guardian of European football. Our role is to protect the game from business.' In 2007, Platini wrote to each EU head of state asking them to help deliver football 'from the rampant commercialism which assails it'. This was a direct criticism of the EU's attitude to football – the EU regards it as basically a business (see the Bosman case) – and of the English Premier League's norms. Platini spoke of the need to 'defend the European sporting model based on financial and social solidarity between rich and poor'. The Premier League's chief executive/creature of the wealthy, Richard Scudamore, retorted that Platini's arguments 'don't rise much above the view of people in the corner of the pub'. Platini replied: 'I prefer to speak as a guy in the pub than the assistant referee Scudamore was.'[51] Platini is introducing financial fair play rules, 'which will force clubs in its competitions to break even' from 2011, albeit with caveats.[52] And he speaks as one of the world's greatest players, as opposed to an English shopkeeper.

For now, the power to shape football rests very much with European leagues, FIFA, UEFA and television stations. With European teams overstretched financially by increasing salaries and competition to qualify for UEFA's lucrative trophies, clubs being bought up by new money from the United States, Russia, Asia and the Arab world, and China and India confronting their code's corruption and inefficiency, the landscape is likely to change. Global plutocracy may unsettle corrupt footocrats as much as pre-capitalist fans.

Rationalization and centralization will surely chart football's future, albeit leavened by the very pulsating, passionate energies that are its raison d'être to control and channel, and that so engaged Weber in his wish to answer and confound Marx's interest in

> foul and adventures-seeking dregs of the bourgeoisie … vagabonds, dismissed soldiers, discharged convicts, runaway galley slaves, sharpers, jugglers, lazzaroni, pickpockets, sleight-of-hand performers, gamblers, procurers, keepers of disorderly houses, porters, literati, organ grinders, rag pickers, scissors grinders, tinkers, beggars.[53]

Those leftover people, in our corners, *favelas*, underpasses and streets, are also and equally the future of football. They are not niche-channel cable subscribers or frequent-flyer business-class passengers. But it is their world, too.

NOTES

1 'Almost Half the World Tuned in at Home to Watch 2010 FIFA World Cup South Africa™', fifa.com, 20 July 2011, www.fifa.com/worldcup/archive/southafrica2010/organisation/media/newsid=1473143/index.html.
2 D. Zirin, 'Let Them Play: Behind FIFA's Decision to Ban Iran's National Women's Team', *Nation*, 8 June 2011, www.thenation.com/blog/161228/let-them-play-behind-fifas-decision-ban-womens-team-iran (accessed 15 January 2012).
3 S. Perkins, 'Exploring Future Relationships between Football Clubs and Local Government', *Soccer & Society* 1, 1 (2000), 102–13.
4 T. Miller, G. Lawrence, J. McKay and D. Rowe, *Globalization and Sport: Playing the World* (London: Sage, 2001).
5 T. Miller, *Television Studies: The Basics* (London: Routledge, 2010).
6 Ibid.

7 R. Levermore, 'CSR for Development through Sport: Examining Its Potential and Limitations', *Third World Quarterly*, 31, 2 (2002), 223–24; M. Silk, D. Andrews and C. Cole (eds.), *Sport and Corporate Nationalisms* (Oxford: Berg, 2005).

8 K. Bandyopadhyay, 'Uncovering the Sleeping Giant Syndrome: India in Olympic Football', *Sport in Society*, 12, 6 (2009), 792–810; Mohun Bagal v East Bengal: India's all-consuming rivalry, www.fifa.com/classicfootball/stories/classicderby/news/newsid=1414458.html (accessed 15 January 2012).

9 'IMF cuts 2012 GDP growth forecast to 4.9%', *Business Standard*, 10 October 2012, http://www.business-standard.com/india/news/imf-cuts-2012-gdp-growth-forecast-to-49/489121/

10 R. Bali, 'Football Is the Highest Played Sport in India–Atul Pande, Ten Action+ CEO', Goal.com, 22 October 2011, www.goal.com/en-india/news/1116/interviews/2011/10/22/2722565/football-is-the-highest-played-sport-in-india-atul-pande-ten (accessed 15 January 2012).

11 A. Nandy, *The Tao of Cricket: On Games of Destiny and the Destiny of Games* (New Delhi: Oxford University Press, 2000); N. Mehta, 'Batting for the Flag: Cricket, Television and Globalization in India', *Sport in Society*, 12:4–5 (2009), 579–99.

12 IMF World Economic Outlook 2012, http://www.imf.org/external/pubs/ft/weo/2012/02/pdf/text.pdf

13 W. Manzenreiter and J. Horne, 'Playing the Post-Fordist Game in/to the Far East: The Footballisation of China, Japan and South Korea', *Soccer & Society* 8, 4 (2007), 561–77.

14 'China Talks of Bid for World Cup in 2026', asiancorrespondent.com, http://asiancorrespondent.com/37946/china-talks-of-bid-for-world-cup-in-2026 (accessed 15 January 2012).

15 FIFA, *2010 FIFA World Cup South Africa™ Television Audience Report*, www.fifa.com/mm/document/affederation/tv/01/47/31/30/keymarketsummaries.pdf.

16 G. Dyer, 'China cracks down on football match-fixing', *Financial Times*, 22 June 2010, www.ft.com/intl/cms/s/0/b4a8272c-0753-11df-a9b7-00144feabdc0.html (accessed 15 January 2012).

17 J. Frank, 'Missing from the World Cup? China', *Los Angeles Times*, 19 June 2010, http://articles.latimes.com/2010/jun/19/world/la-fg-china-soccer-20100619 (accessed 15 January 2012).

18 X. Li, 'Chinese Youth Losing Interest in Football', *Times of India*, 22 October 2011, http://m.timesofindia.com/PDATOI/articleshow/10452359.cms (accessed 15 January 2012); T. Zhe and Y. Yu, 'Wanda's 500m Yuan to Boost Chinese Soccer', *China Daily*, 4 July 2011, www.chinadaily.com.cn/business/2011–07/04/content_12830765.htm (accessed 15 January 2012); M. Bristow, 'Sponsors desert Chinese football', BBC.co.uk, 1 April 2011, www.bbc.co.uk/news/world-asia-pacific-12936084 (accessed 15 January 2012).

19 T. Miller, 'Soccer Conquers the World', *Chronicle of Higher Education*, B6–B9 (4 June 2010).

20 S. Brown, 'Exceptionalist America: American Sports Fans' Reaction to Internationalization', *International Journal of the History of Sport* 22, 6 (2005), 1106–35.

21 Lexington, 'The Odd Man Out', *Economist*, 8 June 2006.

22 A. Barra, 'Nil and Void', *Village Voice*, 9 July 2002, www.villagevoice.com/2002–07–02/news/nil-and-void/1 (accessed 15 January 2012).

23 'As the World Cup Starts, Conservative Media Declare War on Soccer', *Media Matters for America*, 11 June 2010, http://mediamatters.org/research/201006110040 (accessed 15 January 2012).

24 'Latin@' refers to U.S.-based people of Latin American descent. The old, conservative term was 'Hispanic', which most now reject in favour of 'Latino/a' – to get around the gendered or inelegant nature of the term, progressives in Latin America now write 'Latin@'.

25 Miller, 'Soccer Conquers the World'; M. Garrahan, 'Beckham's mission to convert US nears end', *Financial Times*, 3 November 2011, p. 4.

26 A. Melville, 'USA vs. Mexico: A Conflict of Interest?', *Forbes*, 10 August 2011, www.forbes.com/sites/sportsmoney/2011/08/10/usa-vs-mexico-a-conflict-of-int erest (accessed 15 January 2012).

27 Ibid.

28 Garrahan, 'Beckham's mission to convert US nears end'.

29 www.youtube.com/watch?v=ZxHzLF2qqnE (accessed 15 January 2012).

30 www.youtube.com/watch?v=bpvWrwsyCGk (accessed 15 January 2012).

31 www.youtube.com/watch?v=DtKuw7gdIRk (accessed 15 January 2012).

32 J. Longman, '$1 Billion World Cup TV Deal Reflects Soccer's Rise in U.S.', *New York Times*, 22 October 2011; K. Baxter, 'It's Easy to Flag Down American Fans at this World Cup', *Los Angeles Times*, 21 June 2010,http://articles.latimes.com/2010/jun/21/sports/la-sp-world-cup-usa-fans-20100622 (accessed 15 January 2012).

33 Longman, '$1 Billion World Cup TV Deal Reflects Soccer's Rise in U.S.'; Garrahan, 'Beckham's mission to convert US nears end'; Miller, 'Soccer Conquers the World'.

34 J. Williams, 'FOX to Offer NFL and English Premier League Double Header', *Washington Examiner*, 17 September 2011, http://washingtonexaminer.com/blogs/watch/2011/09/fox-offer-nfl-and-english-premier-league-double-header (accessed 15 January 2012); 'Fox soccer channel sets new record for Chelsea v Liverpool telecast', epltalk.com, www.epltalk.com/fox-soccer-channel-sets-new-record-for-chelsea-vs-liverpool-telecast-29232 (accessed 15 January 2012).

35 J. Ourand, 'Fox Soccer's Nathanson Discusses Net's Commitment to Sport', *SportsBusiness Daily*, 1 September 2011,www.sportsbusinessdaily.com/Daily/Issues/2011/09/01/Media/Fox-Soccer.aspx (accessed 15 January 2012); Williams, 'FOX to Offer NFL and English Premier League Double Header'.

36 T. Miller, *Television Studies: The Basics*.

37 Ibid.

38 Ibid.

39 FIFA, 'FIFA and the Environment',www.fifa.com/aboutfifa/socialresponsibility/environmental.html (accessed 15 January 2012).

40 J. Mitchell, 'Sustainable Soccer: How Green Projects at International Sporting Events Benefit the Fans, the Global Climate, and Local Populations', *Sustainable Development Law & Policy* 7, 2 (2007), 52, 84.

41 A. Collins, C. Jones and M. Munday, 'Assessing the Environmental Impacts of Mega Sporting Events: Two Options?', *Tourism Management* 30, 6 (2009), 828–37.

42 Climate Neutral Network, 'Greening 2010 FIFA World Cup', http://unep.org/climateneutral/Default.aspx?tabid=496 (accessed 15 January 2012).

43 D. Estrada, 'World Cup 2010: Climate change fouls and goals', *Guardian*, 3 June 2010, www.guardian.co.uk/environment/2010/jun/03/climate-change-world-cup (accessed 15 January 2012).

44 C. Death, '"Greening" the 2010 FIFA World Cup: Environmental Sustainability and the Mega-Event in South Africa', *Journal of Environmental Policy & Planning* 13, 2 (2011), 99–117; S. Cornelissen, B. Urmilla and K. Swart, 'Towards Redefining the Concept of Legacy in Relation to Sport Mega-Events: Insights from the 2010 FIFA World Cup', *Development Southern Africa*, 28, 3 (2011), 307–18.

45 'SA Unveils Plans for Green World Cup', iol.co.za, 16 September 2008, www.iol.co.za/news/south-africa/sa-unveils-plans-for-green-world-cup-1.416554 (accessed 15 January 2012); Climate Neutral Network, 'Greening 2010 FIFA World Cup'.

46 N. Shachtman, 'Green Monster', *Foreign Policy*, May/June 2010, www.foreignpolicy.com/articles/2010/04/26/green_monster?page=full (accessed 15 January 2012); P. Bond, 'What South Africa Really Lost at the World Cup', *Transnational Institute*, June 2010, www.tni.org/article/what-south-africa-really-lost-world-cup-0 (accessed 15 January 2012).

47 A. Cartwright, 'Green Own Goal? The World Cup's Carbon Footprint and What Can and Can't Be Done about It', *Perspectives* 2 (2010), 20–22.

48 G. Agamben, *What Is an Apparatus?*, trans. D. Kishik and S. Pedatella (Stanford, CA: Stanford University Press, 2009).

49 Zirin, 'Let Them Play'.

50 M. Scott, 'European clubs' desire for greater autonomy could wreck World Cup', *Guardian*, 28 July 2011, www.guardian.co.uk/football/2011/jul/28/fifa-uefa-clubs-world-cup (accessed 15 January 2012).

51 D. Conn, '"I am afraid of what has happened to football"', *Guardian*, 28 November 2007, www.guardian.co.uk/sport/blog/2007/nov/28/iamafraidofwhathashappen (accessed 15 January 2012).

52 O. Gibson, 'Uefa president, Michel Platini, worries game is going pear-shaped', *Guardian*, 26 August 2011, www.guardian.co.uk/football/2011/aug/26/michel-platini-uefa (accessed 15 January 2012).

53 K. Marx, *Capital: Vol. 1: A Critical Analysis of Capitalist Production*, 3rd edn., trans. S. Moore and E. Aveling, ed. Frederick Engels (New York: International Publishers, 1987).

Figure 15.1. Lionel Messi of Barcelona celebrates scoring their third goal at the Camp Nou, Barcelona. UEFA Champions League – Barcelona v Arsenal, 8/3/2011. Credit: Colorsport/Dan Rowley.

JED NOVICK

The Game-Changers: Lionel Messi and Cristiano Ronaldo

Cristiano Ronaldo and Lionel Messi. The two best footballers in the world playing for the two best teams. On the face of it, they're yin and yang. Ronaldo is Real Madrid personified: arrogant, muscular, proud, strong. Messi (Figure 15.1) is his mirror image at Barcelona: stylish, dignified, gracious, principled. Madrid bought Ronaldo for a world-record fee from the next biggest financial beast in the football jungle. Messi was taken on by Barça when he was 13. He was small and delicate and had to be treated for growth hormone deficiency. (His treatment cost £500 a month, a bill Barcelona were prepared to pick up and River Plate, his local team in Argentina, were not. It wasn't a bad investment.)

Ronaldo/Messi. Madrid/Barcelona. The king's team and the people's team. These are the great rivalries of our times, thrown up almost too perfectly, reflecting, if not exactly the struggle between good and evil, then something not far off. Maybe we'll characterise it as the battle between muscle and romance. Of course it's romantic fiction, but without that, what is football?

Enter 'Cristiano Ronaldo arrogant quotes' into Google and you won't be short of reading matter. At the time of writing (Christmas Eve 2012) the search engine came up with 2,510,000 results in 0.38 seconds.

'It's surely because I'm good looking, rich and a great footballer. They're jealous of me. I don't have any other explanation,' said Ronaldo after receiving jeers and chants in Croatia when Real Madrid played Dinamo Zagreb in September 2011.[1] 'I am the first, second and third,' he said in November 2008 when asked to name the three best players in the world. He conceded that Messi, Kaká and Fernando Torres were 'good candidates', but believed he had surpassed all of his rivals for the FIFA World Footballer of the Year and Ballon d'Or awards. Later in the same interview he said: 'Oh, I'm ready for harassment (from women). I'm used to that.'[2]

We could go on, but the point is made. The problem is this: he's right. He is good-looking and rich. He is a wonderful footballer. In January 2009, before the awards merged, he was crowned FIFA World Footballer of the Year for 2008 to go with the Ballon d'Or he had won a month earlier.

In July 2009, Real Madrid paid Manchester United £80 million for his services, nearly £30 million more than the game's next highest transfer fee – also paid by Real Madrid, when they signed the Brazilian Káka from AC Milan for £56 million weeks earlier. In the 2010–11 season, he scored 53 goals.

The question is not whether Ronaldo is arrogant but why he isn't more arrogant. And the answer to that question is the same as the answer to why, at the time of writing, he hadn't won either the Ballon d'Or or the FIFA Footballer of the Year award since 2008. The answer is Lionel Messi.

'He Makes the Incredible Routine'

Born in Rosario, Santa Fe, Argentina, in 1987, Messi is, by any measure, the player of the moment. There isn't a superlative that hasn't been attached to him. Forget for a minute journalists and commentators. Sir Alex Ferguson: 'Messi is amongst the best ever.' Pep Guardiola: 'Messi could be the best player of all time.' Xavi: '[Messi is] the player that will be the best in history. Leo will break all the records. I don't even want to compare Messi to anyone else – it just isn't fair. On them.'[3]

In January 2012, he became only the fourth player to win the Ballon d'Or three times (joining Johan Cruyff, Marco Van Basten and Michel Platini). He received more than twice as many votes as the runner-up – Ronaldo. He was also named FIFA World Player of the Year for the third successive time – and no one, not one of the illustrious names you can read about in the pages of this book, has achieved that. He's been top scorer in the Champions League for the past three seasons. In 2010–11 he scored 53 goals in 55 games.

The numbers, though, tell only one side of the story. There is, as Sid Lowe wrote, 'the intangible sensation: the control at speed, the softness of touch, the variety in his play, the vision, the simplicity, the mastery of the tempo, where stopping is as important as starting, the sheer, jaw-dropping ridiculousness of it. The relentlessness of his brilliance; he has made the incredible routine.'[4]

As with all the great players, one of the keys is balance. Only 5 feet 7 inches, he has a low centre of gravity and covers the ground quickly. There's a sense that even when he's standing still, he's leaning forward. The ball seems tied to his feet and he has, as Richard Williams put it, 'a similar gift for what Argentinians called the *gambeta*: that sinuous high-speed dribble that carried Maradona to his famous second goal against England in Mexico in 1986.'[5]

He's nominally a centre-forward but plays more as a 'false nine'– or, as an earlier generation would have it, a deep-lying centre-forward à la Nandor Hidegkuti. The acid test for Messi will be on the international stage with Argentina. He probably has two World Cups left and what happens there will determine his place in football history.

The stats are off the scale. Real won La Liga in 2011–12 and beat Barcelona at Camp Nou for the first time in over a decade. In the same season, Messi hit 73 goals, the most yet in a single European domestic campaign. Meanwhile, Ronaldo took his total to an astonishing 160 goals in 155 games. Possibly tongue-in-cheek, he later claimed he was 'better than Messi and Real Madrid is better than Barcelona', though he added: 'You can't compare a Ferrari and a Porsche, because they have different engines.'[6] The Clásico on 7 October 2012 ended in a 2–2 draw. Each scored twice. On 9 December 2012, Messi broke Gerd Muller's record for the most goals scored in a calendar year, with his 86th, and ultimately tallied 91. The following month, he won the Ballon d'Or for a record fourth time. At the age of 25, he was at his peak. That he also came out in defence of teaching Catalan in schools did nothing to dim that halo. 'Put in the superlatives yourselves,' Guardiola said of Messi, 'I'm running out.' It's true, but it's equally applicable to both players.

'They are very different footballers and very different characters,' said the former Barcelona striker Eidur Gudjohnsen. 'It is incredible the standard that they are setting. They have taken the game to a different level, reaching standards that very few of us have seen anyone reach. It is so hard to say one is better than the other, but Messi narrowly has the edge. I have never seen anything like him. We'd be lucky to be watching one of them. To be entertained by both is a blessing.'[7] The rivalry between the two is like nothing seen before in football, more akin to a rivalry between two heavyweights. The biggest names, the most potent brands. (As a curious aside, figures published in 2012 show Messi and Ronaldo as only the ninth- and tenth-best-paid players in the world, on 10.5 million and 10 million Euros a year respectively.)[8]

It's entirely fitting that a book such as this should end with Messi and Ronaldo – the two best players of their day. They're why we love the game and tolerate its ills – their skill, their talent, their beauty, their strength. Some we love, some we don't, but the soap opera is part of the appeal, too. And countless millions of us get to watch. We're fans. So before you put the book down and go to bed, let's just remind ourselves of the words of Danny Blanchflower, the former Spurs and Northern Ireland captain: 'The great fallacy is that the game is first and last about winning. It's nothing of the kind. The game is about glory. It's about doing things in style, with a flourish, about going out to beat the other lot, not waiting for them to die of boredom.'[9]

NOTES

1 N. McLeman, 'Fans booed me because I'm "good-looking, rich and a great foot-baller"', *Mirror*, 15 September 2011, www.mirrorfootball.co.uk/news/Real-Madrid-star-Cristiano-Ronaldo-Fans-booed-me-because-I-m-good-looking-rich-and-a-great-footballer-article799459.html (accessed 15 January 2012).

2 O. Clive, 'Manchester United's Cristiano Ronaldo boasts he is the best footballer on the planet', *Daily Telegraph*, 17 November 2008, www.telegraph.co.uk/sport/football/players/cristiano-ronaldo/3474585/Manchester-Uniteds-Cristiano-Ronaldo-boasts-he-is-the-best-footballer-on-the-planet-Football.html (accessed 15 January 2012).

3 S. Lowe, 'To compare Lionel Messi to anybody else is unfair – on them', *Guardian*, 9 January 2012, www.guardian.co.uk/football/blog/2012/jan/09/lionel-messi-ballon-dor (accessed 15 January 2012).

4 Ibid.

5 R. Williams, 'Messi has all the qualities to take world by storm', *Guardian*, 24 February 2006, www.guardian.co.uk/football/2006/feb/24/championsleague1 (accessed 15 January 2012).

6 'Lionel Messi is the best player ever, claims Barcelona president', *Guardian*, 22 March 2010, www.guardian.co.uk/football/2010/mar/22/lionel-messi-barcelona (accessed 25 October 2012).

7 B. Smith, 'Barcelona's Messi v Real Madrid's Ronaldo', bbc.co.uk, 20 April 2012, www.bbc.co.uk/sport/0/football/17786045.

8 H. Jimenez, 'Nine players earn more than Cristiano Ronaldo', 4 September 2012, http://www.marca.com/2012/09/04/en/football/real_madrid/1346777676.html

9 Quoted, according to Google (12 January 2012), in more than 7 million web links, including www.fifa.com/classicfootball/stories/classicderby/news/newsid=107971.html.

FURTHER READING

The following list, compiled from selections by this volume's contributors, encompasses titles recommended for their insight and sheer enjoyment but not previously referenced.

Adamson, R., *Bogota Bandit: The Outlaw Life of Charlie Mitten*. Edinburgh: Mainstream, 1996.

Allison, M., *Soccer for Thinkers*. London: Pelham, 1967.

Appleton A., *Hotbed of Soccer: The Story of Football in the North-East*. London: Rupert Hart-Davies, 1960.

Armstrong, G., and Guilianotti, R., *Entering the Field: New Perspectives on World Football*. Oxford: Berg, 1997.

Armstrong, G., and Giulianotti, R., eds., *Football in Africa: Conflict, Conciliation and Community*. Basingstoke: Palgrave Macmillan, 2004.

Arnold, A.J., *A Game That Would Pay: A Business History of Professional Football in Bradford*. London: Duckworth, 1988.

Auclair, P., *Cantona: The Rebel Who Would Be King*. London: Macmillan, 2009.

Auf Der Heyde, P., *Has Anybody Got a Whistle: A Football Reporter in Africa*. Manchester: Parrs Woods Press, 2002.

Beck, P., *Scoring for Britain. International Football and International Politics, 1900–1939*. London: Frank Cass, 1999.

Bloomfield, S., *Africa United: How Football Explains Africa*. Edinburgh: Canongate Books, 2010.

Bower, T., *Broken Dreams: Vanity, Greed and the Souring of British Football*. London: Simon & Schuster, 2003.

Burke, G., *Parma: Notes from a Year in Serie A*. London: Gollancz, 1998.

Calzia, F., and Castellani, M., *Pallaavvelenata*. Torino: Bradipolibri 2003.

Catton, James A.H., *Wickets and Goals*, London: Chapman and Hall, 1926.

Chapman, P., *The Goalkeeper's History of Britain*. London: Fourth Estate, 2000.

Chastain, B., *It's Not About the Bra: Play Hard, Play Fair, and Put the Fun Back into Competitive Sports*. New York: HarperCollins, 2004.

Cosgrove, S., *Hampden Babylon: Sex and Scandal in Scottish Football*. Edinburgh: Canongate, 1991.

Cowley, J., *The Last Game: Love, Death and Football*. London: Simon & Schuster, 2009.

Davies, P., *I Lost My Heart to the Belles*. London: Mandarin, 1996.

Dunphy, E., *A Strange Kind of Glory: Sir Matt Busby and Manchester United*. London: Heinemann, 1991.

Eisenberg, C., Lanfranchi, P., Mason, T. and Wahl, A., *100 Years of Football: The FIFA Centennial Book*. London: Weidenfeld and Nicholson, 2004.

Ferguson, R., *Black Diamonds and the Blue Brazil: A Chronicle of Coal, Cowdenbeath and Football*. Aberdeenshire: Northern Books, 1993.

Fishwick, N., *English Football and Society 1910–1950*. Manchester University Press, 1989.

Foer, F., *How Soccer Explains the World: An Unlikely Theory of Globalization*. New York: Harper, 2004.

Gibson, A., and Pickford, W., *Association Football and the Men Who Made It*. London: Caxton, 1905–06.

Gill, J., et al., *Offside! Contemporary Artists and Football*. Manchester: Manchester City Art Galleries, 1996.

Giulianotti, R., and Robertson, R., *Globalization and Football*. London: Sage, 2009.

Green, C., *Every Boy's Dream*. London: A and C Black, 2009.

Green, G., *Soccer: The World Game – A Popular History*. London: Phoenix House, 1953.

Gregg, L., *The Champion Within: Training for Excellence*. Graham, NC: JTC Sports, 1999.

Hamilton, I., 'Gazza Agonistes', from *Granta 45*. London: Granta Books, 1993.

Hamm, M., *Go for the Goal: A Champion's Guide to Winning in Soccer and Life*. New York: Harper, 1999.

Holden, J., *Stan Cullis: The Iron Manager*. Derby: Breedon, 2000.

Inglis, S., *The Football Grounds of England and Wales*. London: Willow Books, 1983.

James, B., *England v Scotland*. London, Pelham 1969.

Johnes M., *Soccer and Society: South Wales 1900–1939*. Cardiff: University of Wales Press, 2002.

Kelly, S., *The Boot Room Boys: Inside the Anfield Boot Room*. London: Collins Willow, 1999.

King, A., *The End of the Terrace: The Transformation of English Football*. Leicester: Leicester University Press, 1998.

Kuper, S., *Football Against The Enemy*. London: Orion, 1994.

Lawton, J., *James Lawton: On Football*. Stockport: Dewi Lewis Media, 2007.

Leogrande, A., (ed.), *Il pallone é tondo*. Napoli: L'Ancora, 2005.

Longman, J., *The Girls of Summer: The U.S. Women's Soccer Team and How It Changed the World*. New York: Harper Paperbacks, 2001.

McGinniss, J., *The Miracle of Castel di Sangro*. London: Little, Brown, 1999.

Midwinter, E., *Parish to Planet: How Football Came to Rule the World*. Worthing: Know the Score, 2007.

Miller, D., *England's Last Glory: The Boys of 66*. London: Pavilion, 1986.

Napolitano, S., and Liguori, M., *Il pallonenel burrone*. Rome: Riuniti, 2004.

Nelson, G., *Left Foot Forward: A Year in the Life of a Journeyman Footballer*. London: Headline, 1996.

Nelson, M. B., *The Stronger Women Get, the More Men Love Football: Sexism and the Culture of Sport*. London: Women's Press, 1996.

Newsham, G., *In a League of Their Own*. London: Scarlet, 1998.

Novick, J., *In a League of Their Own – Football's Maverick Managers*. Edinburgh: Mainstream, 1995.

Pannick, D., *Sex Discrimination in Sport*. London: Equal Opportunities, 1983.

Parks, T., *A Season with Verona*. London: Secker and Warburg, 2002.

Pennacchia, M., *Il Generale Vaccaro*. Rome: Nuove Idee, 2008.

Quirke, P. A., *The Major: The Life and Times of Frank Buckley*. Stroud: Tempus Publishing, 2006.

Reng, R., *The Keeper of Dreams*. London: Yellow Jersey, 2004.

   A Life Too Short: The Tragedy of Robert Enke. London: Yellow Jersey, 2011.

Richards, H., *The Swansea City Alphabet*. Cardiff: St David's Press, 2009.

Seddon, P., *A Football Companion*. London: British Library, 1999.

Signy, D., and Giller, N., *Golden Heroes: Fifty Seasons of Footballer of the Year*. London: Chameleon, 1997.

Stead, P., and Richards, H., *For Club and Country: Welsh Football Greats*. University of Wales Press, 1999.

Steen, R., *The Mavericks: English Football When Flair Wore Flares*. Edinburgh: Mainstream, 1994.

Stelling, J., *Jelleyman's Thrown a Wobbler: Saturday Afternoons in Front of the Telly*. London: HarperSport, 2009.

Studd, S., *Herbert Chapman: Football Emperor*. London: Souvenir, 1998.

Tabner, B., *Through the Turnstiles*. Harefield: Yore Publications, 1992.

Ticher, M., (ed.), *Foul: The Best of Football's Alternative Paper*. London: Simon & Schuster, 1988.

Tischler, S., *Footballers and Businessmen: The Origins of Professional Football in England*. New York: Homes Meyer, 1981.

Vialli, G., and Marcotti, G., *The Italian Job*. London: Bantam Press, 2006.

Wagg, S., *The Football World*. Brighton: Harvester Press, 1984.

   Giving the Game Away: Football, Politics and Culture on Five Continents. Leicester: Leicester University Press, 1995.

Wahl, A., and Lanfranchi, P., *Les footballeurs professionnels des annees trente a nos jours*. Paris: Hachette, 1995.

Walvin, J., *The People's Game. The History of Football Revisited*. Edinburgh: Mainstream, 1994.

Whannel, G., *Blowing the Whistle: The Politics of Sport*. London: Pluto Press, 1983.

Williams, J., Dunning E., and Murphy P., *Hooligans Abroad: Behaviour and Control of British Fans in Continental Europe*. London: Routledge and Kegan Paul, 1984.

Williamson, D., *The Belles of the Ball*. Devon: R & D Associates, 1991.

Winner, D., *Brilliant Orange: The Neurotic Genius of Dutch Football*. London: Bloomsbury, 2000.

Yallop, David, *How They Stole the Game*. London: Poetic Publishing, 1999.

Young, P., *A History of British Football*. London: Stanley Paul, 1968.

   Football Year. London: Sportsman's Book Club, 1958.

INDEX